MAKERS OF THE MODERN MIND
A GUIDE TO THE THINKERS WHO FORMED THE MODERN LEFT

JORDAN B. COOPER

WEIDNER
INSTITUTE

Makers of the Modern Mind: A Guide to the Thinkers Who Formed the Modern Left
Copyright 2025 by Jordan B. Cooper
Published by The Weidner Institute
A Division of Just & Sinner

Just & Sinner, Ithaca, NY 14850
JustandSinner.org

ISBN (Paperback): 978-1-952295-82-9
ISBN (Hardcover): 978-1-952295-83-6

CONTENTS

INTRODUCTION

Writing a book on intellectuals who formed the modern left is not something that I would have envisioned myself engaging in when I began my academic writing career. I am trained as a Lutheran dogmatic theologian, not a political theorist or cultural commentator (though theology has much to say about both of those areas when done rightly). The direction of my work that ultimately led to the construction of this book arose more from personal circumstance and a sense of necessity than from academic interest. I do not particularly enjoy reading Marxist or post-Marxist theory and would not have chosen such a thing as a field of study. However, like many of my intellectual endeavors, it feels like this topic chose me, more than my seeking it out.

Much of my time is spent engaging with the world of Lutheranism in the nineteenth century. During this period, historical critical methodologies had become prominent in the study of both the Old and New Testaments, which led to various challenges to the veracity of the biblical narrative and of core doctrinal commitments. Friedrich Schleiermacher's *On Religion: Speeches to Its Cultured Despisers* (1799) had proposed a response to these challenges through a Christianity that was not so dogmatically committed, leading toward the construction of Protestant liberalism. Those who were committed to more traditional Christian beliefs then had to face a twofold challenge to their faith: the strengthening forces of rationalist secularism, and the Protestant liberals within the church who had begun to challenge the most fundamental dogmatic teachings of the Christian faith. The best theologians of this time did not resort to mere insularity, ignoring the intellectual developments within the broader academy and only reading and engaging with others in their segments of the church. American Lutheran theologian Revere Franklin Weidner, for example, engaged deeply in European philosophical literature (Kant, Hegel, and Schelling, among others), read widely in textual and historical criticism, and still maintained a strong traditional theological commitment to classical Lutheranism as outlined in the Lutheran Confessions of 1580. A read of Weidner's work confirms that he did not merely *dismiss* academics who presented challenges to classical Christian thought, but that he read them thoroughly and carefully while also offering significant and substantive critiques of their positions. Further, he was able to recognize when an opponent had a valid point or when a development in modern philosophy was a positive one, rather than simply dismissing everything new out of hand.

It is my commitment to engage with trends in the modern academy as Weidner did which led me to the subject at hand. This shift toward broader philosophical issues in my own study began with an interest I had in one particular Christian doctrine: union with Christ. In attempting to discover why this teaching—which was prominent in earlier Lutheran sources—had been neglected in recent years, I found that the reasons for this shift were not strictly theological at all, but philosophical. Some Protestant liberals had adopted certain assumptions about the world that were core elements of Kant's philosophy, and these assumptions led them toward different theological conclusions than those held by earlier authors. Throughout my study, I began to realize just how central philosophical commitments are to conclusions made about issues that are not "philosophy" in the proper sense. This is not just true of academics—philosophical ideas are an essential element of how *anyone* views themselves and the world around them. Even if you are unaware of what your philosophy is, or what long-dead academic helped to form that philosophy, you still *have* one (or, more likely, a confluence of several) and operate within that philosophy. It is only through the study of these ideas that these assumptions can be recognized and challenged.

THE MODERN LEFT

With all of that said regarding the importance of understanding the ideas at work in academia, the subtitle of this book is not "a guide to the thinkers that formed the modern academy," but "a guide to the thinkers that formed the modern left." In some ways, the two phrases are nearly synonymous, as the most prominent universities in the Western world are dominated by left-leaning professors and use curricula that not only *teach* ideas that conform to a progressive view of the world, but often *assume* that such a perspective is the only one any thinking person could have. At some of the top universities in the United States, a student can graduate with a degree in political science having never read more than a few small selections of the writings of the founding fathers of the United States, Edmund Burke, or any of the influential conservative intellectuals in the mid- to late-twentieth century. Those same students *are* required to read significant portions of the writings of Karl Marx, Michel Foucault, and other theorists on the far left end of the political spectrum. Many students—especially in the humanities—will graduate from an academic program (even at the doctoral level) without having *ever* encountered serious academic pushback to the hegemonic progressive ideology that has surrounded them throughout their entire academic career.

Because of this ideological skew, many conservatives have chosen to simply forsake the academy altogether. Many parents conclude that these institutions exist for the sole purpose of tearing down the moral, cultural, and religious teachings that the parents have imparted to their children throughout their eighteen years at home. This retreat from universities is certainly understandable, but there *are* alternatives to progressive education. Religious colleges seek to answer this liberal dominance in our educational system by providing academic programs that align with the religious traditions to which those schools belong. The mistake, I think, is to forsake academic work altogether and adopt some kind of retreat from the life of the mind, as if such a pursuit is only for those who have a progressive view of culture and politics.

Those people and institutions that are considered "conservative" today, at least in the United States, are not particularly well known for intellectual rigor or academic credibility. There are multiple reasons for this. One is that the dominance of left-leaning voices within the academic world has largely overshadowed the voices of dissenting opinions, such that conservative academics remain unknown precisely *because* they are conservative. Such academics who speak openly about their views on issues of public life find it difficult to get faculty positions at well-known universities, where discrimination is seen as unacceptable in all forms—other than in the marginalization of dissenting opinions. Another reason is that conservatism is often defined in the public eye, not by its philosophers, theologians, and poets, but by its loudest personalities on social media. This leads to the perception that conservatives are simply contrarians who produce click-bait content, whose philosophy is defined by its opposition to prevailing ideas rather than by a credible positive vision of the good life.

Despite this perception, there are a significant number of great thinkers, writers, and professors who have either identified themselves or have been identified as conservatives. When I use the term "conservative" here, I am not speaking about politics, and I am certainly not using it as a synonym for the Republican Party in the United States. I am speaking about something far more fundamental to our lives and the way in which we perceive the world around us. The English conservative philosopher Sir Roger Scruton once defined conservatism as "the instinct to hold onto what we love, to protect it from degradation and violence, and to build our lives around it."[1] Conservatism is a disposition toward the past that receives the inheritance (religious, cultural, political, and otherwise) that has been given with gratitude rather than resentment. Conservatism is not a naïve idealizing of the past, nor is it a mere refusal to change, nor an attitude of indifference to injustice. It is a recognition that it is far easier to destroy than to create, and that it is far more valuable to protect and preserve that which is good than to approach the world around us with disdain. It is a recognition that the idea of human progress is a mythology like any other and that history, despite its many evils, is a gift to be received rather than an obstacle to be overcome.

Just as conservatism is more than a political party, modern progressive ideology is not synonymous with a singular set of political policies. If it were, I would leave such questions to the actual experts in the field of politics. The leftist ideology, as explained in this book, speaks about far more than policy. As many Marxists contend, this ideology is totalizing—it addresses *everything*. As totalizing systems, ideological movements on the left often propose their own answers to the most basic questions of human existence: Who am I? Is there a god? Do I have a soul? Can I know anything about the world? How do I relate to other people? What is right and what is wrong? Because the implications are so far-reaching, these ideas deserve an examination from those engaged in various fields—not just politics.

WHAT TO EXPECT IN THIS BOOK

This book began not as a book at all, but as a series of lectures on Marxist thought. It was my hope that these talks would provide some background on key Marxist thinkers for students I had been speaking with who wanted a better grasp of the ideological

---

[1] "Douglas Murray And Roger Scruton On The Future Of Conservatism & Debate| The Spectator," YouTube, June 17, 2019, https://youtu.be/uu5T3sWAgow?si=WZZGvHDs3ZG3CZMt

influences on their professors. My initial idea was to present four lectures that would cover Marx, the birth of Western Marxism, Critical Theory, and post-Marxism. As I prepared this series of talks, I began to realize that if I were to do this well, it would have to become something significantly bigger than that. It was clear that I could not adequately explain Marx's ideas or context without giving some background on Hegel's philosophy. I then realized that Hegel himself, who is notoriously difficult to understand, could not be properly understood without a grasp of some of the philosophical questions and problems that he addressed. This then led to a discussion of Kant, and then eventually back to the beginning of modern philosophy with René Descartes. It was Descartes who first raised the major questions that have been driving much of the academy for the last four hundred years.

This is the reason this book starts so far back in history with a figure whose life begins just after the end of the Middle Ages. While it would not be fair to categorize Descartes as part of the "modern left," he did begin a major shift away from inherited philosophical traditions that had their roots in the Greek thought of Plato and Aristotle. Through this shift, Descartes created a set of questions that have dominated philosophical discourse in the following centuries. The overview of Descartes presented in the next chapter is followed by an examination of two of the other most important philosophers in the early modern era: David Hume and Immanuel Kant. Though Hume is sometimes considered a conservative regarding his views on politics, his skepticism was quite radical, and his ideas laid the groundwork for Immanuel Kant's philosophy. Like Descartes, Kant is a thinker who looms large over the academy today, as many philosophies developed since his day are either responses to or built upon elements of his system. By the end of this chapter, the reader should have some basic groundwork to understand the essential elements of modern philosophy and the questions that guide it.

The next chapter moves away from the highly theoretical ideas of the early modern philosophers toward the emergence of the political ideology of liberalism. This section explores three thinkers: Thomas Hobbes, John Locke, and Thomas Paine. With the publication of his influential book *Leviathan*, Hobbes proposed a new theory of government based upon abstract reasoning about what humanity would be like in a non-governmental state of nature. This brought about the view that government is primarily concerned with the protection of rights, and that the state arises from a social contract based on the consent of citizens. Locke builds on Hobbes's theory by expanding upon the nature of rights, giving more precise definitions of the purpose and limits of government, and giving guidelines for the justification of revolutionary political action. Paine is not an academic like the other two theorists, but a popular author. His approach to the consensual nature of the social contract throughout generations and the disconnectedness he proposes between the past, present, and future exemplify the values of left-liberalism that stand in contrast to the conservative approach to the state as taught by Edmund Burke. Paine presents one way liberal commitments can translate on a popular level.

The third chapter explores the rise of historicism with the philosophy of G. W. F. Hegel and the transformation of Hegelian philosophy into historical materialism through Karl Marx. Hegel, sometimes considered a conservative thinker, moved philosophy away from considerations of timeless abstract principles and into the realm of history. For him, ultimate reality is to be found in the unfolding of the world spirit as seen through the life of nations and the rise and fall of great figures in history. Following Hegel's death, students of his philosophy divided into conservative and liberal schools. Karl Marx, part of the latter, applied Hegel's historicism to economic class relations. Marx rejected the existence of any immaterial spirit and contended that history is determined by physical processes—particularly those economic processes of production and consumption. In his conception of European history, capitalism had created vast inequalities between those who controlled the means of production (the bourgeoisie) and those who were involved in the process of production (the proletariat). This exploitation of the working class must inevitably lead to revolutionary action and the rise of a communist state, bringing economic equality to all classes in society.

The fourth chapter explores the ideas and figures associated with the beginning of Western Marxism, following the death of Karl Marx and other first-generation Marxists. Marx had predicted that a socialist revolution was inevitable, but by the early twentieth century, it became apparent that such an occurrence would not happen naturally in the way that Marx had foreseen. Marxists began to think about ways that theorists could mobilize the masses to force revolutionary action. This culminated in the Bolshevik Revolution in 1917, when the government of Czar Nicholas II was overthrown and Vladimir Lenin's Communist Party formed the Soviet Union. The first figure overviewed in this chapter, Georg (György) Lukács, was a Hungarian Marxist who briefly held a position in the short-lived Republic of Councils in Hungary. Lukács influenced later Marxist thinkers in two primary ways. First, he moved away from Marx's scientific socialism, which believed that revolution was an inevitable part of the historical process, toward one that believed that the masses must achieve class consciousness through the concerted effort of Marxist theorists. Second, Lukács moved Marx's categories into academic subjects well beyond economics, such that the ideology became more totalizing in its scope. The second thinker addressed here, Antonio Gramsci, began to use Marxism as a means of cultural critique through his idea of cultural hegemony, which contends that the bourgeoisie do not control the proletariat purely by economic exploitation, but also through the spread of cultural ideas and products that serve the interests of the upper class. It is through these thinkers that Marxism becomes all-encompassing.

Building on this move toward Marxism in cultural analysis and critique, the fifth chapter discusses the school of thought known as "Critical Theory." Following the First World War, a group of progressive theorists began an organization known as the Institute for Social Research in Frankfurt, Germany. Diverging from the Russian Marxists who desired continued violent revolutions to expand the communist cause, the Critical Theorists attempted to construct alternative visions of Marxism that focused on culture, analysis, philosophy, art, and critique. In this project, they formed what was considered a "theory of everything." The first figure discussed in this chapter is Theodor Adorno, who argues against the privileging of reason both in modernity and in classical thought, arguing that oppositions should be left in tension, rather than resolved. Adorno applies dynamics of power and oppression to the examination of societal structure. He argues that one of the ways in which the upper class remains in power is through the commodification of art by means of the "culture industry," which pacifies citizens and influences them to accept the status quo. The second thinker examined is Herbert Marcuse, who attempts to use the tools of Freudian psychology to answer the question of why the proletariat did not naturally revolt against their own exploitation. Marcuse pushes even further with his argument that a true revolution would necessitate a complete destruction of Western civilization and a total restructuring of human life.

The sixth chapter moves into the subject of linguistics and the rise of structuralism. The twentieth century experienced what has been called the "linguistic turn" in philosophy. Rather than focus on the nature of human knowledge, many scholars shifted their studies toward the structure and use of language. Among these linguistic movements was Ferdinand de Saussure's structuralism, which examines linguistic signs and their meaning. Saussure argues that language systems are holistic systems of meaning that are self-contained. These systems are made up of signs, which are composed of signifiers (words) and the signified (that to which a word points). The chapter then moves to a figure who uses structuralism for political purposes: Roland Barthes. An influential thinker in the field of literary theory, Barthes contends that linguistic systems are constructed in such a way that they privilege the powerful and disempower the proletariat. Through his use of structuralism and neo-Marxism, Barthes constructs a method of interpretation whereby elements of culture can be examined in order to discern the underlying ideas and biases (what he calls "myth") that underlie them. Barthes also challenges the notion that authors determine the meaning of the texts that they write, arguing that texts bear meaning in themselves.

Following this discussion of structuralism is a chapter on the movement that grew out of it, known as post-structuralism. Often tied together with the term "postmodernism," post-structuralism emphasizes the arbitrary nature of language and the lack of objectivity in human perceptions of the world. This section overviews the ideas of Jacques Derrida, the French intellectual who formulated the idea known as deconstruction, wherein texts are taken apart through the reversing of binary oppositions within them. For Derrida, words do not point to anything external to themselves but instead are to be understood only with reference to other words. He also challenges the Western world's centralizing of reason and argues that reason must be balanced with unreason. Next, this section discusses Michel Foucault. Foucault argues that power is ubiquitous in human society, such that power dynamics are at work in nearly everything that human beings do. One of these types of power is called "biopower," which refers to the control of bodies through the leaders of society. Foucault argues for resistance against oppressive power structures through subversive bodily acts and for the uncovering of dynamics of power through historical analysis.

In the final chapter, the discussion turns toward gender and sexuality. The revolutionary ideologies discussed throughout this book are often applied today to sexual and gender differentiation, in which context it is argued that patriarchal systems are continual means of oppression throughout society. First, the chapter summarizes the rise of feminism and the connections between feminist ideas and other modern movements. Second follows a discussion of the thought of Simone de Beauvoir, whose book *The*

Second Sex lays the groundwork for second- and third-wave feminism. According to Beauvoir, Western society has often viewed women as the "other" and has centralized males, leading to vast inequalities between the sexes. Third, the chapter explores Judith Butler's idea of gender performativity. Gender, for Butler, is not biological but societal. To be a male, a female, or to identify with an alternate gender identity is to portray a particular role in society by taking upon oneself a certain identification, way of dress, and behaviors. In this way, gender is not given, rather it is performed through repeated ritual actions. The final part of the chapter offers an overview of the idea of intersectionality, wherein dynamics of power and oppression are extended beyond the narrow focus on economics in earlier Marxism or on sex differences in feminism to include a breadth of different intersecting elements of one's identity that are tied to various forms of oppression.

This book does not cover everything. There are several thinkers and movements that are influential for the development of progressive ideology in the academy yet are absent here. There is not, for example, an extensive discussion of Critical Race Theory and other academic movements that are centered on racial dynamics. There are two reasons for the omission of this and several other influential thinkers and movements. First, there are not enough pages to cover everything. Significant omissions were necessary to prevent this book from being an inaccessible length. Second, my editorial decisions were driven by my desire to maintain focus on the deeper metaphysical conceptions that lie behind modern ideologies, rather than addressing specific current issues. There are plenty of contemporary treatments of Critical Race Theory, for example. My hope is that by the end of this book, you will have a general understanding of, not just current debates, but the ideas, thinkers, and movements that stand at the root of so many current discussions in the public sphere and have shaped the academy into the present day. Too often, our discussions fail to get at issues of first principles, which is where disagreement often lies.

RENÉ DESCARTES AND THE BIRTH OF MODERN PHILOSOPHY

Though one might assume that "modern philosophy" is simply shorthand for speaking of philosophy in the recent past, this term is used by philosophers and historians more precisely with reference to a specific era of philosophical inquiry. The term "modern philosophy" refers to philosophical shifts in the seventeenth and eighteenth centuries that challenged many of the most foundational assumptions of the ancient Greek, Roman, and Christian consensus. It is this era—in which the West moved away from its prior medieval forms of thought and life—that is termed "modernity." Like any significant historical change, the development of modern thought includes several thinkers and movements, along with various social, technological, and political factors. Here, I am limiting myself to a discussion of a select few key philosophers who formed modern philosophy. While many thinkers comprise the first wave of modern thinkers, it is René Descartes who has most often been identified as early modern philosophy's *central* figure. He is regularly referred to as "the father of modern philosophy."[2] With Descartes, a new problematic was developed which would become the groundwork for most philosophical inquiry since his time. The word "problematic" as used here refers to the set of questions and ideas that guide one's research, thought, and writing. In order to understand this shift from medieval philosophy to modern philosophy, we first need to explain the problematic that guided ancient and medieval thought.

---

[2] Skirry, "Rene Descartes (1596-1650)."

THE BASICS OF CLASSICAL PHILOSOPHY

While there are significant ideological differences between figures as diverse as Plato, Aristotle, Heraclitus, Augustine, and Aquinas, these core thinkers in the Western world seek to answer many of the same basic questions (and also work with some of the same assumptions about the world and man's ability to know it).[3] It is these shared questions that drive their philosophical systems and serve as the basis by which they interact with other philosophers—both previous ones and their own contemporaries. Although these thinkers address numerous questions, I have broken down the problematic of classical philosophy into four of the most central guiding questions.

The first of these questions is: How do the one and the many relate? The world appears to be made up of many disparate things, and yet there is unity in this same world. Think, for example, about sheep. A shepherd cares for multitudinous sheep, which can be spoken of both individually and collectively. Each sheep has its own body, will, and actions. And yet despite their individuality, there is unity among these individual animals. This is why the shepherd can use the broad category of "sheep" to refer to a collection of these individual animals. This uniform attribution of these animals as "sheep" is not specific to a particular collection of specific individuals. It is not the combination of these *specific* sheep that makes the broader category a useful one. Think, for example, about a shepherd's flock over time. At the very beginning of his life of shepherding, the shepherd refers to his animals as a "flock of sheep." Consider that this shepherd continues to shepherd for another fifty years of his life. After these five decades, this shepherd's flock is still properly referred to as "sheep," just as they were in the beginning of his work, even though every individual sheep that was there in the first place had died by this time. In fact, even if sheep as a species went extinct, the idea or concept of "sheep" would remain unchanged. In other words,

---

[3] For more on the primary assertions and questions of the classical philosophers, see my book *The True, The Good, and the Beautiful*. See also Copleston, *Greece and Rome*.

the *idea* of sheep is something universal, not dependent upon any individual particular object or collection of objects. Plato referred to these universal ideas as "forms," which he argued were more "real" in some sense than individual objects that are subject to change and decay. Philosophers since Plato's time have expanded upon this idea of forms or universals in a variety of directions.[4] Though not always agreed on exactly how these forms relate to material objects, all those who affirm the general existence of universals are referred to as "realists."

The second question is: How do change and constancy coexist? In many ways, our experience of the world is defined by the changes that we encounter within it. We see infants brought into the world, feel the pains of aging, and watch loved ones die. People grow, seasons shift, and political regimes rise and fall. Yet in spite of this, other aspects of the world remain the same. Even though the seasons change during a year, for example, we still experience those same four seasons each year. The process of birth, life, growth, sickness, and death is a universal one. The relationship between change and constancy is not simply that some objects change and others do not, as often change and constancy are found within the same object. Consider the example of a river. The ancient philosopher Heraclitus, in defense of his view that the universe is in a constant state of flux, contends that a person cannot step in the same river twice, as the water will never be exactly the same from one moment to the next due to its constant movement.[5] However, even while Heraclitus's point that rivers constantly change is undoubtedly correct, we still refer to ever-changing rivers with the same name from one moment to the next. The Nile River remains the Nile River despite its many alterations throughout many centuries. We recognize that objects change, but that there is an underlying consistency underneath that change. From the time of Plato onward, many philosophers

---

[4] For a good brief overview, see: Frost, *Basic Teachings of the Great Philosophers*, 10-20.
[5] Feser, *Last Superstition*, 29-30.

contended that there is some kind of unchanging reality which stands behind the changing world around us, providing stability and constancy.[6]

The third primary question discussed here is: What is the connection between things and ideas? If I decide to take a hike in the forest, as an illustration, there will be several individual physical objects all around me that we generally refer to as "trees." I have an idea of what a tree is in my head, as does the reader of this book (most likely). Along with this idea of a tree exists the actual sound of the word "tree" when spoken out loud. What exactly is the connection between the *objects* I encounter on my hike, the *idea* of a tree that exists in my head, and the verbal *sounds* that come out of my mouth when I say the word "tree?"[7] The idea of "tree" seems to be connected to the actual trees that I see or touch, but those trees are not exactly identical to the concept of "tree," as the category of "tree" includes many kinds of trees that are not represented in this hypothetical forest. The difference between the actual trees and the broader idea used to categorize them is seen in that the idea of a tree does not exist in my head only when I am near one. It might be present in my thoughts when I am on a boat in the ocean with no trees in sight, or alternatively, I might be physically next to a tree without thinking about trees at all. In light of all of this, the philosophers ask: What exactly is the relation between this idea that forms itself in my head and the actual things that I encounter? For Plato, Aristotle, and most of the medieval Western philosophers (nominalists excluded), the connection between ideas and objects is not imagined, but real. There is a sense in which the individual tree shares in the idea of what a tree is. In other words, the idea in my mind and the object I

---

[6] Nahm, *Early Greek Philosophy*, 62-67. This, for Plato, is the realm of the forms. In Christian thought, this unchanging reality is the heavenly realms, and the Platonic forms are often identified with ideas in the divine mind.

[7] The connection between ideas and words is explored in the chapter on structuralism in this book.

encounter are intimately connected. This means that my ideas impart real knowledge about the world around me.[8]

The fourth classical question mentioned here is: How should human persons live in the world? This is also referred to as the study of ethics. The classical thinkers believed in an objective moral order in the world that can be discovered through reason. Some ways of life are right, and other ways of life are not.[9] Generally, they viewed ethics through the lens of virtue. Virtues are elements of one's character that can be developed through habituation, which allow one to make ethical and right choices in one's daily life. The field of ethics is further divided into that of individual ethics and of social ethics. The former deals with the development of personal character, and the latter addresses the function of social institutions such as the state, family, or church. Virtue ethics is teleologically driven, meaning that this approach to ethics is goal-oriented. There is an overall purpose or higher good toward which people are called to orient their lives, and ethical actions are those that move toward that goal (*telos*).[10]

To be clear, modern philosophers as a whole do not ignore all of these questions or simply dismiss all of Plato, Aristotle, or Aquinas as useless (though some do). They do, however, begin to answer these questions in radically different ways than earlier thinkers. Further, these authors begin to introduce new questions in philosophy, which often supersede these central four and other older ones that dominated the medieval era. This shift occurs largely through a move away from the field of metaphysics. One of the primary divisions of philosophy, metaphysics refers to the study of reality or being (ontology). Modern philosophers introduce skepticism about the world, which makes many of the concerns of metaphysical inquiry far less certain. Because of this, modern philosophers begin to focus

---

[8] Freeman, *Great Ideas of Plato*, 129-142.

[9] By "classical" here I am referring to the Platonic and Christian traditions. There were skeptical schools of thought in ancient Greece and Rome that did not hold to such an objective standard of ethics.

[10] For an overview of virtue ethics, see: Crisp, *Virtue Ethics*.

more intently on the field of epistemology—the study of knowledge. In the seventeenth century, questions began to arise as to whether human minds really have access to the world as it is or if knowledge is reliable at all. Thus, the primary question to be addressed in the early modern era was: How do we know anything?[11]

SETTING THE STAGE FOR DESCARTES

Such radical moves in the history of thought never occur through one isolated thinker. Rather, they arise from philosophical, theological, cultural, and political circumstances across many decades—often centuries. Thus, in order to understand why Descartes makes the moves he does, some context must be set forth regarding the intellectual and religious climate of late-medieval Europe and why this shift away from metaphysics toward epistemology occurred.

The first factor to be mentioned is the rise of nominalism. The classical philosophers were metaphysical realists, meaning that they believed that universals are (as the name implies) real. To use the prior example, the metaphysical realist contends that the concept of "tree" is an objectively existent category, so that when someone encounters individual trees, they understand by those particular trees something more universal than those specific objects. This is because each individual tree shares in that universal form or essence of "tree." The controversial French scholastic philosopher Peter Abelard (1079-1142) argued against this consensus, proposing that the universal concepts that we use to speak about individual things are only linguistic constructs.[12] In this nominalist view, humans use words like "tree," not because the idea itself is real or universal, but merely to have a common linguistic way to categorize individual objects that share common characteristics. Many scholastics in this period rejected Abelard's position, and for a time Aristotelian metaphysical realism predominated among scholastic theologians

---

[11] Israel, *Modern Enlightenment.*
[12] Brower, *Cambridge Companion to Abelard.*

and philosophers through the writings of Albertus Magnus (c. 1200-1280) and St. Thomas Aquinas (1225-1274).[13] The later Middle Ages, however, saw a revitalization and growth of nominalism (and the related idea known as conceptualism) with William of Ockham (1288-1348) and Jean Buridan (c. 1300-1358).[14] Nominalist convictions remained among some thinkers in France into the post-Reformation era in which Descartes lived.[15]

The second intellectual movement that strongly influenced the birth and growth of modern philosophy was the Renaissance.[16] Though dated differently in divergent parts of Europe (Italy, France, and Germany each had their own Renaissances), by the mid-fifteenth century, it had begun to change the entire European academy. This movement constituted a rebirth in learning and the arts, largely through a rereading of the classical works of the Greeks and Romans. It also included the move toward a more realistic approach to painting that sought to portray depth and movement, as was common among the ancient Greeks. The rebirth of learning in the Renaissance also included the birth of textual studies, in which scholars developed criteria to determine the genuineness of historical documents. Renaissance scholars also began to move away from the church's reliance on St. Jerome's Latin translation of the Bible, called the Vulgate, toward the Hebrew Old Testament and the Greek New Testament, resulting in the growth of language studies. This rebirth in learning began to move authority into the hands of scholars and away from traditional church authorities. Textual studies, for example, raised significant questions about the veracity

---

[13] Aristotle's writings were brought back into the Western world largely through the Islamic philosophers Averroes and Avicenna.

[14] Conceptualism is the view that universals exist, but only as concepts within the human mind.

[15] Heiko Oberman's classic study *A Harvest of Medieval Theology* remains an invaluable summary and examination of late-medieval nominalist philosophy and theology.

[16] For a good but brief summary, see: Brotton, *The Renaissance*.

of some supposed-historical texts that were used to defend the existing European order under the papacy.[17]

The third significant event that drastically changed European society prior to the life of Descartes was the Protestant Reformation.[18] Growing out of the rebirth of learning in the Renaissance, theologians used these new resources of learning to challenge some of the historical and theological claims made by the medieval papacy. The reformers argued that there is no biblical or historical support for the idea that Jesus granted the successors of St. Peter sole and perpetual authority over the church. Further, the reformers criticized various church practices that arose in the late Middle Ages that are not rooted in Scripture or the testimonies of the early church (the granting of indulgences, the cult of the saints, the treasury of merit, Marian devotion, purgatory, and the withholding of the blood of Christ from the laity, among others). One of the results of the Reformation was a religiously divided Europe, along with a new series of political, cultural, and intellectual challenges to be faced by those on both sides of the Reformation divide. While some historians want to place the blame almost entirely on Martin Luther and the Reformation for the birth of the negative elements of modernity, the reality is far more complicated. Descartes's own philosophical ideas were impacted quite significantly by French Jesuits who were self-conscious nominalists in contrast to Lutheran and Reformed orthodox scholars of the time who were often unapologetically realist.[19]

---

[17] A text called *The Donation of Constantine* had been used to argue that the Emperor Constantine had delivered authority in his kingdom to the Bishop of Rome. This document, now recognized universally as fraudulent, was central for medieval papal claims.

[18] The most often used recent historical overview of the Reformation is MacCulloch, *The Reformation*.

[19] See: Cooper, *Prolegomena: A Defense of the Scholastic Method*. Elements of nominalist thought began to enter into Lutheran discourse with the rise of German rationalism under the influence of Gottfried Wilhelm Leibniz, Samuel Pufendorf, and Christian

Fourth, and finally, the scientific revolution had begun. As the nominalists challenged the consensus of the classical philosophers with regard to metaphysics, so did scientists begin challenging the predominance of ancient Greek science in the Western world. In the Middle Ages, many of the conclusions of Aristotle had been accepted as reliable accounts of scientific phenomena in astronomy, physics, biology, and other fields. This is not to say that there were no scientific developments at all during the supposed "dark ages," but those developments generally worked on the basis of earlier Greek models. The beginning of the move away from the older consensus is often dated 1543, when Copernicus published his argument for heliocentrism. The medieval consensus held that the heavenly bodies (the sun, stars, and other planets) revolve around an immovable earth, which was viewed as the central point of the universe. In a radical departure from what was taken for granted by the world for many centuries, Copernicus contended that the sun held the central position in our galaxy, rather than the earth. This shift in astronomy led to changes in the understanding of a variety of scientific phenomena through scientists like Galileo and Kepler.

Seventeenth-century Europe was in crisis, as religious wars raged between Protestants and Roman Catholics. Challenges to the accepted ideological consensus were being raised in nearly every field of research: Historians put papal claims into question; the reformers demonstrated that many accepted truths of the medieval church were neither biblical nor historic; scientists contended that the world had mostly been misunderstood; and the discovery of the Americas demonstrated the limited nature of European knowledge of the world. In view of this, Descartes sought to provide a new foundation for knowledge within the academy.

Wolff. These ideas were opposed by the Lutheran orthodox, who retained scholastic realism in one form or another.

RENÉ DESCARTES

René Descartes was born in 1596 in La Haye, Touraine, France, to a modest noble family. His mother died not long after René's birth, after which his father remarried and moved to Rennes. Descartes was left in the care of his maternal grandmother, and then, following her death, lived with his great-uncle in Châtellerault. Much of young René's education was in a Jesuit context, as he began his education at the Jesuit school Royal Henry-Le-Grande at La Fleche in 1606, where he would complete his studies in 1614. Unlike his own later-developed philosophical system, his teachers at this time were heavily influenced by Aristotle, and his education was classical. Amid the traditional environment of his early education, Descartes also encountered the new and controversial theories of Galileo, as well as the writings of several esoteric mystics who were fundamental to the development of Descartes's own thought.[20]

Following his early education, Descartes's family insisted that he study law. Descartes went to Poitiers from 1615 to 1616, where he studied both civil and canon law. After graduation, Descartes was committed to a life of study, rather than the stable career in the legal profession which his family had hoped for. He moved to Paris and joined the Dutch army, where he served for four years before resigning and traveling through Europe. In Paris, Descartes sold off land that he had inherited and was consequently able to live a relatively comfortable life off of those profits. With this financial independence, Descartes had the ability to devote himself to his studies and writings.

Throughout his life, Descartes spent significant time among both Roman Catholics and Protestants. A Protestant influence is evident in the fact that he studied at the Protestant Leiden University and then served the Protestant Dutch army. Roman Catholic

---

[20] This biographical information comes from Dicker, "Descartes," in *Blackwell Companion to the Philosophers*, 209-210, and Enrique Chavez-Arvizo's introduction to: Descartes, *Key Philosophical Writings*, vii-xxii.

institutions and thinkers, however, were equally essential to his formation. In addition to receiving a Jesuit education, Descartes was influenced heavily by a number of counter-Reformation figures— though not primarily on theological matters, which it does not appear were pressing to him. According to Descartes's own testimony, he considered himself a Roman Catholic while spending his last years in Protestant Sweden. However one places Descartes within the religious conflicts of his day, it seems to be the case that Descartes was not particularly concerned with either Catholic or Protestant theological distinctives. On a philosophical level, his views diverged significantly from the convictions of both the Aristotelian Jesuit education he received at a young age and the then-predominant Lutheran and Reformed scholasticism of his day, which was also generally committed to a strong metaphysical realism. This divergence from the philosophical commitments of religious orthodoxy led to an unfavorable reception of Descartes's work from many traditionalists. In 1663, the Roman Catholic authorities placed Descartes's works on the Index of Banned Books.[21]

DESCARTES'S METHOD

As trust in older methods of doing both philosophy and science started to wane, Descartes began to create what he believed to be a superior model of intellectual inquiry, which he thought would guide man in the post-medieval world. He set forth this method primarily in three works during his career: *Rules for the Direction of the Mind* (1628), *The World* (1633), and *Discourse on Method* (1637). Though not as widely read as his *Meditations on First Philosophy*, these works present the methodological considerations that are essential to understand if one is to properly grasp the reasons why Descartes thinks and reasons as he does throughout the latter work.

---

[21] The most comprehensive set of Descartes's writings in English is Cottingham's three-volume *Philosophical Writings of Descartes*.

In his earliest book on method, *Rules for the Direction of the Mind*, Descartes sets forth four basic principles of intellectual inquiry. The first of these is perhaps the most significant in differentiating his own work from that of others in earlier ages: Accept nothing as true that is not self-evident.[22] For Descartes, absolutely nothing could be taken for granted. Classical philosophy approached the world with many unproven assumptions, such as the general reliability of the intellect in understanding the world around it. Christian philosophy had proceeded with even more unproven assumptions than these earlier Greek thinkers. Descartes attempts here to get rid of as many biases as possible to allow for pure, objective rationality in coming to conclusions in philosophy and science.

The second of these rules set forth in Descartes's text is: Divide problems into their simplest parts. Rather than deal with broad claims, Descartes urges, scholars should break research questions down as simply as they possibly can.[23] This allows the inquirer to address each individual problem without assuming answers to other related questions. Third, and related to this, Descartes argues that one should then proceed from simple to complex problem solving.[24] This means that each individual element of a given topic of research is addressed on its own terms, and questions related to that specific thing are answered, prior to the making of any broader conclusions and claims regarding the subject at hand. Fourth and finally, Descartes tells researchers to carefully recheck each element of their work to be sure that no mistake has been made.

Descartes used this methodology not only in his famous philosophical arguments, but also in his scientific research. Descartes began to create his own scientific system guided by these

---

[22] Descartes, "Rules for the Direction of the Mind," in *Key Philosophical Writings*, 362.
[23] Ibid., 380.
[24] Ibid., 381.

four rules. In his book *The World*, Descartes set forth a new model for science which he believed would create a comprehensive replacement of the old Aristotelian consensus.[25] In this work, Descartes moves away from Aristotle's teleological view of nature—the idea that natural phenomena are to be explained through categories of purpose or meaning in nature—to a mechanistic one. The world, for Descartes, is like a well-run machine. It contains a combination of different physical parts that each have a unique role to play within the world. This machine (nature) essentially runs on its own through a series of scientific laws and determinate physical processes. Like the other mechanistic scientists of the early modern era, Descartes believed that all physical reality could be broken down into small elements called "corpuscles." The motion in nature, such as the movement of planets or the rotation of the earth (Descartes promoted the heliocentric model of the universe), was grounded in the motion of these tiny corpuscles. This mechanistic corpuscularian view of the universe was used by Descartes to explain temperature, density, weight, the nature of light, the motion of heavenly bodies, the forms of matter, and many other phenomena.

One of the distinctive features of this broader shift to mechanistic material explanations of all scientific phenomena is that it divorced theological claims from scientific ones. As discussed in the summary of Descartes's *Meditations* below, he contends that each person has a soul that is distinct from the body and that God ultimately stands behind the material universe. This spiritual realm, however, is essentially cut off from significant interaction with the natural world for Descartes. Faith, morality, and purpose simply do not have a part to play within scientific observation and thereby must be relegated to the private sphere of heart and mind. This isolation of science from theology is not original with Descartes; it was popularly adopted earlier by a thinker who influenced Descartes in significant ways but is relatively unknown today: Pierre Charron.

---

[25] See Ariew's translation of Descartes, *The World and Man*.

The Importance of Charron

The first principle Descartes outlines—accept nothing as true that is not self-evident—is perhaps the most important for both Descartes's philosophical and scientific systems. Descartes begins methodologically by doubting premises that were taken for granted in classical thought. This approach of methodological doubt was already prominent among a number of French skeptics, such as Pierre Charron.[26]

Though not often discussed in the present age, Charron had a notable influence in the seventeenth-century French academy. Most well-known as a philosopher, Charron was ordained as a priest in the Roman Catholic Church and received an influential position in Cahors as grand vicar and theological canon, and later as chief secretary to the general assembly of the clergy. As surprising as it may sound to the contemporary reader, it was a Roman Catholic priest who was the most influential academic skeptic of his day. During his own lifetime, he was more popular than his acquaintance Michel de Montaigne, though the latter would have a longer-lasting impact. Charron's ideas were set forth in two works: *Les Trois Vérités* (1593) and *De la Sagesse* (1601). The latter of these is most relevant to the development of Descartes's thought and to the general philosophical milieu of seventeenth-century France.

In *De la Sagesse*, Charron makes a strong distinction between natural and supernatural theology. The latter is concerned with issues of metaphysics, divine providence, and other traditionally theological subjects. In contrast to both the Thomistic Roman Catholic philosophical tradition and the then-current Protestant scholastic tradition, Charron denies that natural theology can provide any definitive knowledge of God at all. Theology, for Charron, is sequestered to a totally differentiated sphere from other forms of knowledge, such that rational contemplation and scientific investigation cannot deliver theological conclusions. Charron's work

---

[26] This discussion of Charron is largely based upon Neto, *Academic Skepticism*, 1-44.

is an exposition of this non-theological way of knowing that he calls *"la sagesse"*—wisdom.

Charron relies on the famous Socratic contention that the man who is wise is one who acknowledges that he does *not* know as he ought. This idea has often been interpreted as an encouragement to epistemic humility on the way toward gaining wisdom—a recognition that knowledge is always something to be sought after, rather than simply assumed. Charron contends instead that this Socratic approach presents the wise man as one who *never* commits definitively to anything. According to Charron, human beings accept all sorts of things to be true simply because they *seem* to be true (what we might call "common sense"). This acceptance of things as true based on verisimilitude (the appearance of truth) is a hindrance to wisdom, as it accepts unexamined ideas based on nothing more than custom or assumption. This common phenomenon is, for Charron, a form of dogmatism. The wise man is called to make an effort by means of his will to refuse to acknowledge such things as true at all. Charron introduces systemic methodological doubt here, directing the theoretician to begin his intellectual enterprise with the dismissal of accepted first principles. The conclusions that the wise man *does* come to should be held with relative detachment and non-commitment, as reason is only capable of producing probable and practical conclusions rather than definitive metaphysical ones. Wisdom is, therefore, found in the suspension of judgment (*epoche*). Methodological doubt, suspension of judgment, and the claim that reason cannot arrive at metaphysical truths as found in Charron are all influential ideas that Descartes responds to in his *Meditations*.

MEDITATIONS ON FIRST PHILOSOPHY

While Descartes's scientific writing was significant in both its scope and initial influence (he is the namesake of the Cartesian plane, for instance), his longest-lasting contributions to academic discourse are in the field of philosophy. In his *Meditations on First Philosophy*, Descartes sought to provide a philosophy that is both indebted to

Charronian skepticism and is also a positive alternative to that same Charronian skepticism. While Charron contended that doubt itself is to some degree the essence of true wisdom, Descartes believed that, although one could *begin* philosophical inquiry with doubt, the quest for knowledge could lead beyond doubt to a certain attainment of knowledge. Steering philosophy away from a skeptical approach in which one is only able to deal in probabilities, Descartes sought to find an indisputable ground of knowledge out of which a new rational philosophy could be built. Descartes believed that if he could answer Charron's dilemma with some kind of logically provable starting point, he could build from that certain truth a knowledge of other indisputable facts. If this is the case, then one need not live in Charron's prized constant state of uncertainty and ideological non-commitment.

Descartes begins his thought experiment by asking whether sense experience actually corresponds to reality. On any given day, a person has experiences of many different kinds which are assumed to be real. Imagine some of these events which you might encounter in an ordinary day. You sense the cold floor on your feet as you walk onto a wooden floor in the early morning. You smell the coffee brew as you await your first sip, and then you taste that delicious freshly ground single-origin medium roast from Ethiopia. You experience frustration in your inner emotional life as you drive out to work in the morning and are delayed by construction. You hear from and learn about your coworkers at your place of employment during the day. You experience a sense of accomplishment as a project you had been working on is successful. You feel tired in the afternoon and relieved when the workday is done. You feel the texture of the pages of a book about modern philosophy as you read at home. You enjoy the taste of your dinner as you chew and swallow it. You go outside later in the evening where you feel the breeze and watch the sunset, delighting in the beauty of it all. But how do you know that any of these experiences are actually *real?*[27]

As Descartes recognizes, there are times when we experience something that *seems* real, but we later find out is not. There are dreams that are nearly indistinguishable from reality. There are psychological disorders that lead to hallucinations of sight, sound, or both. In our lifetime, research has confirmed that people are capable of creating all sorts of false memories that feel just as real as true ones, even to the point of having immense emotional trauma associated with events that never happened.[28] Perhaps all of our daily experiences, such as those mentioned earlier, are just like those false memories? In order to explore this possibility, Descartes posits the theoretical existence of some kind of evil genie who enjoys deceiving people. What if there is a powerful, malicious being who creates an illusion of all of your experiences, just to mess with you? Perhaps your closest friends and loved ones do not actually exist but are mere hallucinations placed into your mind by this creature. Maybe the entire history of your life has been made up.[29]

Through this thought experiment, Descartes believes that he has found one thing that is essentially indisputable: his own existence. It is in this context that Descartes utters what is likely the most well-known statement ever uttered by a philosopher: *"Cogito ergo sum"* (I think, therefore I am).[30] Even if it were the case that you could not prove that any of your experiences were real, or that your family and friends exist outside of your own mind, you could still acquire definitive knowledge of something: your *own* existence. Descartes believes that this entire thought experiment necessitates the existence of some person or mind who is engaged in these thoughts, as thoughts must necessarily be connected to a thinker. As much as one might doubt about the universe, the doubts one has

---

[27] Descartes, *Meditations*, in *Key Philosophical Writings*, 17-19.
[28] Rubin, *Remembering Our Past.*
[29] Ibid., 19-23.
[30] Ibid., 25.

must exist within a doubter. Therefore, the existence of such an individual is *beyond* doubt, and further, it serves as an indisputable foundation of truth. For Descartes, self-knowledge is a definitive ground of knowledge from which other truths about reality can and must be determined. In this way, Descartes believes that he has discovered an element of reality which is more than mere probability, and thus he escapes Charron's dilemma of probabilistic reasoning and non-commitment to propositional truths.

Descartes's *cogito* contains within it two definite truths: First, he thinks, and second, he exists. From these two first principles, Descartes derives several other conclusions about reality. The first of these is the nature of what constitutes a "person." In short, a person is defined by Descartes as a "thinking thing."[31] This definition arises from Descartes's mode of reasoning. If thinking is the first definite and provable reality, and if the existence of the self arises from this act of thinking, then thinking itself is the most certain thing that can be said about human nature: A person is one who has the experience of thinking. Thinking, in this context, does not identify complex logical reasoning or deep intellectual inquiry, but the act of having subjective mental impressions. It is this conscious experience of having a thought that differentiates a human from something like a robot or a zombie (or, Descartes argues, from animals, who he does not believe have conscious experience or souls).[32] This means that man is not identified primarily by his local extension (i.e. the physical body). Descartes's approach is referred to as an "idealist" one, meaning that reality is to be found in the realm of ideas and that truths about the universe are to be arrived at through a process of

---

[31] Ibid., 29.

[32] In the philosophy of mind, people use the word "zombie" to speak about theoretical people who act like humans but have no inward conscious experience whatsoever. It is not used to refer to the undead flesh-eating creatures of George Romero films. Philosophical zombies are, on a popular level, what people refer to as an "NPC."

logical deduction and rational contemplation.[33] This differs from the empiricist view, which contends that experience, rather than rational contemplation, is the primary source of knowledge.[34]

From here, Descartes challenges his evil-genie hypothesis by asking whether there is a way to prove that a good God exists, rather than this ultimate malicious being. In response to this question, Descartes formulates a variation of St. Anselm's ontological argument for the existence of God, which proceeds from the idea of a perfect being.[35] Descartes notes that along with his conception of the self, he has an idea in his mind that God is a perfect being. Descartes asks where this idea of a perfect being came from. He reasons that the concept of perfection could not possibly have its origin in his own mind, since he is certain of his own imperfection. The reality of Descartes's imperfection is apparent in the very nature of this whole thought experiment: The experiment is based on the recognition of the limits of his own knowledge; it attempts to arrive at knowledge he does not already have, hence admitting that something is lacking within Descartes's being. In short, Descartes *cannot* be a perfect being if he does not even have an absolute idea of what is real and what is not. Since imperfection is unlike perfection, the idea of perfection could not arise from imperfection. Therefore,

---

[33] In this way, Descartes aligns with Plato, as both thinkers argue for the superiority of the immaterial over the material—at least in terms of the identity of the self and in the existence of an immaterial source of material things (God).

[34] Usually, empiricism is contrasted with rationalism rather than idealism. Idealism contends that ideas are the ultimate reality, while rationalism is the belief that logical processes are the best way to arrive at truth. While the two ideas are not precisely synonymous, they do generally coincide with one another.

[35] Anselm's argument begins with the premise that God is that than which nothing greater can be conceived. To be great, one must exist, as existence is greater than non-existence. With this being the case, God must, by definition, exist. This argument appears in the eleventh century monk's work the *Proslogion*, which can be found in Anselm, *Major Works*, 82-104. It has been debated consistently since Anselm's own time and has more recently seen something of a renaissance with a revised argument known as the "modal ontological argument." Kane, "Modal Ontological Argument," 336-350.

the idea of a perfect being that exists in Descartes's mind must have come from somewhere outside of his own intellect. Not only could it not have arisen from Descartes's mind, but it could not have arisen from *anything* imperfect. He concludes that the only possible originator of the concept of a perfect being is one who *is* a perfect being. This is the very definition of God.[36] Therefore, God must exist.

This conviction of divine existence leads Descartes to reason that one's mental life and experiences cannot be categorized as mere deception from some evil genie. He has demonstrated that God exists and that God is defined by his perfection. Perfection necessitates goodness, as evil is opposed to perfection. Therefore, the theoretical deceptive genie is not perfect and could not be the source of the concept of a perfect being. A perfect, and thereby morally good, God would not deceive his creation by making all sense experience and reasoning totally unreliable. Therefore, Descartes argues, we can justifiably and reliably trust our own experiences of the world to correspond to what is actually real. We are not being perpetually deceived by a malicious spirit. Descartes believed that his attempt to begin the rational process by finding and proving an indisputable foundation for knowledge was successful. Reasoning can reasonably arrive at the conclusion that the self exists, that God exists, that the material world exists, and that human experience and logic are generally reliable. In this way, Descartes believed that he had provided a means of avoiding the Charronian skeptical approach to the world in which nothing is definitively known or committed to. Not all philosophers, however, find Descartes's argumentation so compelling.

SUBSTANCE DUALISM

Another distinctive of Descartes's philosophy is his approach to substance dualism. This phrase refers to the belief that human beings are composed of two distinct things: the mental and the physical. The

---

[36] Ibid., 34-52.

roots of dualism are quite ancient, as dualism often serves as shorthand to identify the belief in a distinction between body and soul. Among the ancient Greek philosophers, Plato and Aristotle were both dualists (though the Platonic and Aristotelian conceptions of soul and body are distinct from one another).[37] Aside from more recent attempts to formulate a Christian physicalism, nearly the entire Christian tradition is similarly committed to a strong ontological distinction between body and soul. For both the ancient Greek philosophies of Plato and Aristotle and the Christian tradition, there is a connection between the physical and the transcendental immaterial that exceeds the narrow nature of the relation between the two realities that is found in Descartes. The ancient Greeks, for example, contend that souls are not unique to humans, as there are souls in both plants and animals. This is not to say that plants have a conscious internal thought life (the *rational* soul marks subjects as distinctively human), but that there is an immaterial and transcendent element that permeates all of life. This belief engenders a teleological approach to the world, in which there is a *telos*, or goal, of every natural life form and physical process. The entire material world is imbued with meaning, as it is not only designed but guided and continually sustained in its being. If there is inherently a tie between the material and immaterial that is pervasive in nature, then the question of the relationship between body and soul is not difficult, as it is simply one instantiation of a broader phenomenon that constitutes reality. For Descartes, however, the material and

---

[37] Plato views human beings primarily as souls, rather than bodies. Aristotle provides a stronger connection between body and soul within the categories of his hylomorphic view of ontology. Hylomorphism is the idea that all things are composed of both form and matter. Aristotle argues that, in terms of philosophical anthropology, the soul is the form of the body (which is matter).

ideal are not so intricately linked, as he views nature more as a machine than as a cohesive, purposive series of ordered processes.[38]

Recall that Descartes defines man by thought; a human person is a "thinking thing." This conception of a person affirms the notion of self as inherently mental rather than physical. For Descartes, mental properties are absolutely distinct from physical properties. To illustrate this distinction, think about the kinds of words we use to speak about thoughts compared to physical objects. We regularly categorize ideas or thoughts as either true or false, while we do not judge physical things with those same identifiers. If I were to point to someone's head and declare that individual's brain to be true or false, such an action would (rightly) be deemed nonsensical. Even though the brain is the place where thoughts—which may be true or false—happen, the brain itself cannot be true or false. This type of judgment is a categorically wrong one to use regarding an object.[39] If, however, I referred to a thought going on inside of that same head as true or false, such a statement would be perfectly understandable. Just as mental properties cannot be applied to physical objects, so are physical properties impossible to apply to mental ones. Thoughts, for example, do not have weight, mass, or texture. It is just as nonsensical to ask about the density or height of a thought as it is to declare a physical object true or false. Descartes reasons that because the mind and the body have totally different properties, they must be fundamentally distinct things.

For Descartes, then, the body and the soul are separate substances.[40] The body is a physical substance, and the soul is a mental substance. One must define exactly what Descartes means by

---

[38] Moreland and Rae provide some helpful differentiations between the Platonic and Cartesian notions of the soul in *Body & Soul*, as does Feser in *Philosophy of Mind*. For a modern defense of Cartesian dualism, see: Swinburne, *Mind, Brain, and Free Will*.

[39] To refer to my belief about or experience with a physical object as true or false would be sensible, but that is a judgment on the veracity of my belief or experience rather than on the physical thing itself.

[40] Descartes, *Meditations*, 72-90.

"substance" here to rightly grasp his meaning. In his use of the word, a substance must be able to exist on its own; this differentiates a substance from a property. This means that the body and the mind, in Descartes's rendering, are essentially independent things. Neither is the property of the other, nor do they form some third thing when conjoined. However, he continues to contend that they do somehow interrelate. This leads to a serious dilemma. If the body and soul are independent, and if they are fundamentally different kinds of things without common properties, how can they possibly relate to one another as elements of the same person? If the soul or mind is only mental and thereby has exclusively mental properties, how can its mental acts affect the actions of a physical thing (the body)? Descartes attempts to resolve this problem by proposing that there is a place in the brain, the pineal gland, where mental properties and the physical body converge. Descartes's proposal here is quite tenuous and does not satisfactorily resolve the dilemma. Since Descartes's time, philosophers have written extensively about the "mind-body problem" Descartes introduced, as is evident in the pages of this book.

While Descartes did not intend to introduce a totalizing secularization of the physical sciences, or to isolate all questions of purpose to the internal life of isolated individuals, his philosophy is an important step on a path toward these moves in Western philosophy. Descartes's approach to the physical world as a mechanical reality made up of small physical self-moving pieces leaves no clear place for the presence of transcendent guidance or sustenance within natural phenomena. In the Cartesian method, ideas of purpose, consciousness, the soul, and God are not relevant to the natural operations of the universe. Because Descartes locates considerations about transcendence within the internal life of a soul, which is not present in animal or plant life, he has essentially interiorized all considerations of identity, purpose, sin, redemption, freedom, God, and the soul, such that they do not play a significant role in one's understanding of the external operations of the physical world. As a result, nature became desacralized, and religion became privatized.[41] While his work is an attempt to provide a robust answer to Charronian skepticism and to defend the existence of both God and the soul, Descartes fails to do so in a manner that accounts for the relationship between the physical and the transcendent beyond the interior life. Rather than providing a definitive solution to the philosophical dilemmas of his day, Descartes's work led to a series of new challenges and problems to be addressed by philosophers in the following centuries. Among those who rejected Descartes's answers to the questions he posed was David Hume.

DAVID HUME

Often viewed as the arch-skeptic among the Enlightenment philosophers, David Hume countered Cartesian idealism with an empiricism that was critical of any and all claims of indisputable knowledge. Though it would not be fair to say that David Hume was *only* a critic, much of his influence lies in his critiques. From arguments against the miraculous, to the questioning of Descartes's *cogito*, to his denial that there is any coherent human subject, to his reformulation of the idea of causation, to the existence of the external world at all, there was nothing that was beyond Hume's critical pen. Whatever one thinks of Hume's conclusions on these issues, there is no doubt about the clarity of his intellect or the rhetorical force of his writings. At the very least, one can praise Hume for causing his interlocutors to sharpen the arguments for their positions in response to his critiques.

David Hume was born in Edinburgh, Scotland, on April 26, 1711, to a well-off family. His father, a lawyer by profession, died when David was only two years old. As his mother never remarried, David was raised without a father or stepfather. He studied at Edinburgh University beginning at the age of twelve, though after some time, he

---

[41] See Taylor's *Secular Age* for a full account of the desacralizing of the world in the modern era.

got sick and took a break from his personal studies to recover from what seems to have been a nervous breakdown. Eventually, Hume recovered and moved to France, where he would write his most important work, *A Treatise of Human Nature* (though it was not successful at the time of its release). He soon moved back to Scotland with the hope of receiving a professorship, but Hume was denied teaching positions on multiple occasions due to his critical writing on religion. After facing continued rejection in his home country, Hume moved back to France, where his views were welcomed amidst the increasingly secular French academy. Hume's major critique of traditional religion, *The Dialogues Concerning Natural Religion*, was published posthumously and became a cornerstone of Enlightenment secularism.[42]

EMPIRICISM

As discussed in relation to Descartes, European philosophers during the Enlightenment period can be roughly divided into two philosophical schools: rationalism and empiricism.[43] The rationalists (Descartes, Spinoza, Leibniz) believed that rational inquiry is the best way to arrive at knowledge. Rationalists often argue that the physical world is full of change and difference, such that while one can gain *particular* knowledge through the senses, it is difficult to find *universal* truths through the observation of the natural world. Experience might tell you, for example, that the act of lying often leads to bad outcomes, but only through reason would one come to the ethical conclusion that lying is universally a moral breach. The rationalists were generally optimistic about what knowledge was attainable by means of reason alone. The empiricists (Hume, Locke, Berkeley), in contrast, contended that knowledge is to be gained primarily

---

[42] The biographical information here mostly comes from Harris, *Hume*.

[43] I say "roughly" here because these two modes of inquiry are not mutually exclusive, and there are rationalist elements in the empiricists along with empiricist impulses among the rationalists. One might identify these more as tendencies than as strict, unbridgeable categories.

through observation. John Locke, for example, refers to the mind as a *tabula rasa* (blank slate), which gains ideas only as a person experiences the world through the senses. The empiricists prioritized observational reason and repeated scientific experimentation. They tended to be far less optimistic about the results of logical deduction.[44]

Hume is the most anti-rationalist of the empiricists. In his view, reason is not nearly as important in daily life as most philosophers assume.[45] This leads Hume, at times, to blatantly denigrate reason (largely for rhetorical effect). For example, in a reversal of a classic philosophical principle, Hume states that reason is a mere "handmaiden" to the passions.[46] For both the Greeks and the Christian tradition, the passions should be subservient to reason in the virtuous person. Individuals have various desires (passions), whether bodily or intellectual, that they have impulses to fulfill. In the most base bodily sense, this includes things like food, money, and sex. The man who is ruled by his passions engages in each of these pleasures whenever he feels the need—and is consequently a gluttonous, greedy whoremonger. Reason, according to the classical traditions, is superior to the passions because it *guides* the passions and puts them in proper moral boundaries. Through reason, the

---

[44] For an overview of each of these schools of thought into the twentieth century, see: Aune, *Rationalism, Empiricism, and Pragmatism.*

[45] Hume's critique of the liberal optimism about unaided reason has led to the categorization of Hume as a conservative. Rationalists believed that history and experience were less important to the values and laws of a nation than rational deduction. This led to the discarding of inherited traditions and laws in favor of semi-utopian visions of an imagined state formed on the basis of abstract principles. While it is true that Hume is a conservative in the sense that he believed in the importance of heritage, culture, and tradition, he is not conservative in an ideological sense, as he radically reforms the entire basis of human knowledge through the same kind of thoroughgoing skepticism that would later characterize much of the post-Marxist left. As is shown in later chapters, some Western Marxists combine the denial of historical inheritance and tradition of the Enlightenment liberals with the Humean rejection of the unified self.

[46] Hume, *Treatise on Human Nature*, Book II, Part III, Section III.

virtuous person learns moderation. For Hume, however, one *should* be ruled by one's passions and pleasures, and reason should *not* help one to moderate such desires.

Hume's skepticism of rationalism is clear in his rejection of Descartes's *cogito ergo sum*. Hume questions whether Descartes is rationally justified in affirming his own existence on the basis of internal impressions of doubt. For Hume, there is no indisputable argument that the existence of impressions of doubting necessitates an individual to whom those impressions are inherently attached. How does one know that thoughts arise from a thinker? Perhaps the connection made between thought and thinker is mere prejudice or assumption. In questioning the veracity of the Cartesian argument, Hume seeks to demonstrate the insufficiency of reason and the weaknesses of the rationalist methodology. Philosophy cannot base itself on supposed indisputable claims and the deductions that supposedly arise from them.[47] It is important to note here that there are divergent interpretations of Hume's intention in making these skeptical arguments. Some contend that Hume's goal is not the creation of a purely skeptical philosophy, but the provision of a rhetorical challenge to the prevailing rationalist views of the mind, which would lead toward a more positive non-rationalist approach. Others argue that Hume's philosophy is inherently skeptical, rather than constructive. While that particular debate will not be resolved here, it is worth noting that, regardless of Hume's intentions, his philosophy did provide the basis of a thoroughly skeptical epistemology for some later thinkers.

In explaining his evaluation of Descartes's *cogito*, Hume refers to the thoughts or doubts described by Descartes as "impressions."[48] Hume uses this term consistently throughout his writing to refer to immediate, direct thoughts. They are the

---

[47] Ibid., Book I, Part IV, Section VI.

[48] "All the perceptions of the human mind resolve themselves into two distinct kinds, which I shall call *impressions* and *ideas*." Hume, *Human Nature*, Book I, Part I, Section I.

conscious, unreflected experiences of the mind. Some examples include: getting upset as someone insults you, enjoying a bite of an apple, seeing a friend across the street, or hearing a song come on the radio. These experiences are direct feelings and sensations. Impressions are distinct from what Hume calls "ideas." Ideas are later reflections upon and reasoning about impressions. One might, for example, think back to a time when they were insulted and analyze why someone would say such things. Hume's ideas are not directly derived from experiences, but are the result of impressions. This is an element of Hume's rejection of abstract reasoning as understood by the rationalists. Along with this, Hume also challenges the belief in innate ideas.

For many rationalists, as for the classical Greek philosophers, some ideas are innate, while others are derived.[49] Innate ideas are those things that are known by the intellect inherently, or intuitively, rather than derivatively through experience. These innate ideas (or combinations of innate ideas) are what philosophers refer to as *a priori* truths. For Hume, there are no *a priori* truths. All human knowledge derives from impressions. This means that human theorizing, the making of new ideas, stories, or pieces of art, are all reducible to practices of combining impressions into different patterns. These human endeavors contain nothing truly *new* (and nothing derived from innate knowledge). If all reasoning is just reflection upon impressions, this means that the human intellect is simply not capable of extrapolating the meaning of things. Ideas like God's existence or the soul are not directly revealed through impressions, as claims about their veracity merit more than a combination of sensory experiences. For Hume, only natural

---

[49] In his dialogue the *Meno*, Plato famously contends that all learning in life is really recollection, rather than the adding of new information. He argues that all people preexisted their bodily form, and that in this non-bodily life we had access to the world of the forms. As we learn in this life, we are simply being brought back to knowledge that is already inherent within us. For a summary of this, see Freeman, *Great Ideas of Plato*, 49-60.

phenomena can be subjected to rational deduction. Even then, however, Hume challenges received wisdom regarding the natural world in significant ways.

HUME ON CAUSATION

Before explaining Hume's influential ideas surrounding causality, it is important to outline the classical approach to causes to which he is responding. In the medieval and early modern academy, much of the discussion of causes followed the Aristotelian mode—though Descartes and others began to shift this significantly. Roman Catholics, Lutherans, and Calvinists all relied on the Aristotelian causes in their systematic theological writings, their philosophical work, and their educational systems for the young.[50]

Aristotle outlines four different types of causes.[51] The first of these is an *efficient cause*. This aligns most closely with how the term is generally used today. An efficient cause is that which actualizes the potency in another object and thus enacts change. For example, a ball has the potential to be thrown, but it cannot throw itself. This potentiality to be thrown is actualized when a child picks up a ball, moves his arm, and throws the ball. The child's action here is the efficient cause of the ball being thrown. Second, the *material cause* refers to the matter that makes up a thing. In this case, the rubber that makes up the ball would be its material cause.[52] The *formal cause* refers to the form or shape that matter takes to make an object. In this case, it is the round shape that makes the rubber a ball rather than some nonspecific rubber blob. Last is the *final cause*, which is about teleology, or a thing's purpose. The final cause of a kid's ball is to be thrown around. There are plenty of further distinctions made

---

[50] For a thorough description of how Aristotelian causality is used in scholastic philosophy (and the subsequent problems with Hume's critique), see: Feser, *Scholastic Metaphysics*, 38-63.

[51] Aristotle, *Metaphysics*, Delta: II., 115.

[52] Material causes do not have to be literal physical matter. For example, the material cause of words is syllables, and the material cause of a sentence is words.

here, such as primary and secondary causes, instrumental causes, ministerial causes, etc.[53] The point is that in earlier forms of thought, the human mind is assumed to be capable of surmising the connection between things and the purpose of things. Hume's empiricism does not allow for this.

Hume asks whether there is anything that can be proven regarding causes using his empirical approach to philosophy. In particular, he is concerned with the question of causal necessity. By "causal necessity" Hume means a necessary connection between a cause and its effect, such that a certain cause will always have the same resultant effect under the same conditions. Take the example that Hume himself uses, of fire and its seemingly resultant heat. Our recollections of encounters with the element tell us that when we approach a fire, we experience a sensation of heat. We thus assume that the heat is caused by the fire, rather than this being the result of some bizarre coincidence in which every time we are near fire, we also encounter heat. But, Hume asks, are we really rationally justified in that assumption? If all thoughts are based directly on sense impressions, and sense impressions do not tell us about the inner nature of the things we encounter, then we cannot say with any certitude that there is causal necessity in anything.[54]

Fire certainly *seems* to cause heat, but my conclusion regarding this causal connection is based solely upon my own particular experiences with fire. Perhaps other people have had experiences with fire where there was no heat given off. Or, even if it could be definitively proven that there has never been a case of a fire existing without heat being felt (something that would be impossible to do), there would still be no indisputable ground for assuming such a connection to be determinate. Even if something had been universally the case in the past, it may yet change in the future.

---

[53] These show up within theological works in the seventeenth century. As an example, see the discussion in Muller, *Post-Reformation Reformed Dogmatics*, Vol. I. 238-247.

[54] This discussion is found in Hume, *Human Nature*, Book I, Part III, Sections II-V, XII-XIV.

Perhaps the experience of heatless fire is one that simply has not been had yet. Here, Hume points out another assumption humans make that cannot be proven: The future is like the past. We make claims about the world based on the way things have been in the past, but there is no proof that such continuity is a universal, unchanging principle.

Hume tore down the artifice of Aristotle's causes in his rejection, not merely of final causality in the natural world (something that began with Descartes), but of causality *in toto*. In Hume's system, humans do not have any real access to the workings of the universe. We can never say with certitude that any event is caused by another event. We cannot reason toward truth; the human intellect is limited to the function of reflection and discovering patterns among impressions based upon experience. The intellect does not grasp truths beyond subjectivity, and is therefore incapable of grasping the transcendent. For Hume, we do not know the external world at all; we only know our impressions of it. There is a sense, then, in which all knowledge is reduced to self-knowledge, though even the idea of the continuous self is viewed with a skeptical eye.

THE HUMAN SUBJECT

With Hume, a pattern emerges among modern philosophers of questioning the existence of a real, self-consistent, persisting identity to which subjectivity is attached. As much as Descartes and other early rationalists departed from classical metaphysical convictions, they retained a commitment to the existence of a persisting self, which is often identified with the soul. For Descartes, thoughts require a subject who *has* those thoughts, and who is more fundamental than they are. In other words, the thinker is not *composed* of thoughts, but the thinker is an actual preexisting entity from whom individual thoughts flow. What constitutes the individual subject, for both the classical tradition and the rationalist, is something fundamentally immaterial and unchanging. Because it is immaterial and unchanging, changes to the body, growth in intellect, the shifting of ideologies, and other fluctuations that occur throughout life, do not alter the fundamental "I" that stands underneath them. You are a singular person who remains "you" in all circumstances, because you are prior to, or more ontologically basic than, your experiences. For Hume, this is not the case.[55]

As mentioned above, Hume is unconvinced of Descartes's argument for the existence of the subject, as Hume denies that the causal move from thought to thinker is rationally justified. Hume's critique of Descartes is connected to the empiricist's similar rejection of metaphysical causality. If, as Hume contends, thoughts are mere impressions, and if causal relations can never be proven, then it is impossible to move from impressions to a subject who has those impressions. At one point, Hume does consider whether there could theoretically be some singular impression that *could* definitively demonstrate the existence of a continuous self, but is unable to come up with one. One might, as a rebuttal to Hume, contend that successive patterns of thought accomplish this, as impressions do not arise as separable, disconnected events, but as interrelated moments which can form complex causal chains. In other words, there *must* be a singular thinking subject who can put thoughts or experiences together in a continuous, sequential, interrelated thought life. Hume rejects this argument, contending that it is yet another example of assuming causal relations where none can be indisputably affirmed. While we might *think* that continuous logical thought processes are the result of a singular personal subject thinking through ideas, this is no more assuredly true than the connection between fire and heat.

Hume himself writes that he is unsatisfied with his own treatment of this issue at the end of his *Treatise on Human Nature*, but fails to provide any further explanation of why that is the case, and similarly fails to offer any corrective or alternative view. While some

---

[55] This is laid out in Hume, *Human Nature*, Book I, Part IV.

scholars disagree, I am convinced that Hume's system as a whole is more destructive than it is constructive. He offers serious and well-argued critiques of inherited assumptions, but does not provide a coherent positive way forward for philosophy.[56] Further, regardless of the logic of his arguments, they are intuitively false. One need not provide a logically coherent proof to affirm that continuous subjects exist. You could not possibly function in the way that you do if this were not true. For example, the only reason you can pick up a book like this one and read through it (with the assumption that it bears some kind of coherent meaning) is that you continuously exist to perform the action of reading throughout the whole process of reading the text. Your experience with this book is not reducible to separable, disconnected impressions of reading. Reading necessitates a reader, just as thinking necessitates a thinker. Similarly, a book necessitates an author. If this book were a combination of simple impressions of writing that were attached to no continuous authorial identity, it would be far less coherent than it is. The irony in this denial of a persistent self by Hume is that he spent his life writing books about ideas to convince readers of the veracity of his positions, even though his own position denies that there is any certainty of the existence of either the writer or the reader, or of a singular subject who has coherent, connected, rational thoughts. Nonetheless, regardless of how nonsensical some of these conclusions seemingly are, Hume did provide a serious challenge to philosophers that would be addressed most thoroughly by Immanuel Kant.

---

[56] Scholars of Hume are divided here, with some taking a more positive view of Hume's work. The evaluation given here arises from my own reading of Hume's treatises.

IMMANUEL KANT

A giant in the field of philosophy, Immanuel Kant has shaped the development of Western thought on almost every issue that he wrote on. Even in the present day, philosophers continue to wrestle with Kant's ideas, questions, and critiques, and how they speak to present contexts. Despite his physical death over two centuries ago, Kant's voice still speaks. From his ethical theory to his proposal for what later became the United Nations, Kant's fingerprints can be seen throughout the twenty-first-century world. He has shaped philosophy, theology, and politics in significant ways, and this influence is felt across political and ideological lines.

KANT'S LIFE

Immanuel Kant was born in 1724 in Eastern Prussia to a devout Lutheran family.[57] His religious upbringing was decidedly Pietistic. Pietism began as a religious revival movement at the end of the seventeenth century in Germany and then spread throughout northern Europe. Pietists believed that some in the Lutheran church had neglected to emphasize the importance of conversion through religious experience and of holy living. They contended that concern for orthodox doctrine had relegated these issues to a place of relative unimportance, as long as proper dogmatic standards were upheld.[58] In response to these problems, Pietists began Bible study groups called conventicles and emphasized the need for personal conversion. By the time of Kant's birth, this movement had grown significantly, which led to an increasing emphasis on both internal spiritual experience and the importance of moral living. It is likely that these ideas shaped some of Kant's later considerations, as he wrote extensively about personal sense-experience and moral duty. He would eventually relegate all religion to those categories alone.

---

[57] A good and brief biographical account of Kant's life can be found in Scruton, *Kant*.
[58] On Pietism see: Shantz, *Introduction to German Pietism*.

Kant attended the University at Konigsberg beginning in 1740 at the age of 16.[59] While there, he encountered the philosophy of a growing rationalism, which significantly challenged his theological beliefs. Kant studied under Martin Knutzen, a professor of metaphysics and logic, who caused the young student to question the existence of the supernatural, leading to a personal crisis of faith. Early in his studies, Kant was also committed to the same kind of mechanistic approach to nature that was present in Descartes, among other early modern philosophers, through his study of Newtonian physics. Along with growing doubt about the theological teachings of his upbringing, Kant also began to question the validity of the idealism of Descartes and his followers on the continent. At this time, Kant was exposed to the debates between the empiricists and rationalists in European philosophy. Ultimately, Kant would formulate a philosophical system that he believed would bridge this divide.

The influences on Kant's thought were diverse. Initially, he read broadly in rationalist texts, which convinced Kant that he could not remain within the strict theological commitments of his father's Lutheran faith. This rationalist turn in his thought shifted, however, when Kant encountered the writings of David Hume. Through a reading of Hume's *Treatise of Human Nature*, Kant writes that he was awakened from his "dogmatic slumber" and began to rethink nearly all of his philosophical commitments. [60] It was this encounter with Hume that would shape the questions he asked—and the consequent philosophy that arose as he answered them. Kant believed that while many of Hume's critiques were fair, his skeptical stance toward any universal claim was not a necessary outcome of them. Kant contended that both a commitment to reason as a tool for discovering universal and objective claims and experience as a means

---

[59] Kant would remain at Konigsburg as a lecturer after graduation until his death in 1804. He was not a man who desired change, as is also evidenced by his taking the same walk every single day at exactly the same time.

[60] Kant, *Prolegomena to Metaphysics*, 4:260.

of understanding phenomena could be synthesized into one coherent system.

THE RELATIONSHIP BETWEEN REASON AND EXPERIENCE

The synthesis of idealism and empiricism that Kant formulated is exposited in his most well-known work, *Critique of Pure Reason*, first published in 1781. One of the most important philosophical texts ever written, this book expands upon the interrelation between reason and experience, arguing that both methods of gaining knowledge can be synthesized into one coherent framework, in which reason grasps universal facts while experience teaches the individual about the particulars of history. To best understand Kant's argument, two distinctions within the philosopher's writing must be noted.

The first distinction to be made is between *a priori* knowledge and *a posteriori* knowledge. Knowledge that is *a priori* is not dependent upon one's experience of particular events. If, for example, I were to ask you to describe my sweater, you could not do so without a direct experience of seeing that piece of clothing. Logic alone could not derive the answer to such a question since there is nothing logically necessary about either my own or the sweater's nature which would dictate that it had a certain hue. You could, however, make the statement, "Your sweater is some kind of knit material that is meant to cover the upper part of a body," since such a statement makes a universal claim regarding the *definition* of a sweater. This definition is not dependent upon sense experience, nor is it a judgment about one particular sweater. The assertion is universal because there is no sweater that is not some kind of knit material that is meant to be placed over the top part of the body; if it did not have those features, it would not be a sweater at all.[61]

Two important characteristics of *a priori* statements, for Kant, are that they are both *universal* and *necessary*. The color of my

---

[61] A helpful summary of Kant's use of language and basic argument can be found in Gardner, *Kant and the Critique of Pure Reason*, 52-58

sweater is neither of those things, and thus is not *a priori* knowledge. A judgment about the color of my specific sweater is not a universal statement about sweaters. Regarding the second characteristic, it is also not logically necessary, since I could have chosen to wear a sweater of a different color. Even if, say, I had a strange phobia of non-white sweaters, "Jordan always wears only white sweaters" would still not qualify as an absolutely necessary statement, since there are theoretical instances in which the judgment might be wrong. Perhaps someone kidnapped me and forced me to wear a red sweater, or played a trick on me while I was sleeping and snuck a different sweater on me. Or maybe I'm colorblind and don't realize that the sweater I put on is not white. The earlier statement, however, that a sweater is a knit material that covers the top part of the body, is universal, as it applies to all sweaters. Further, it is also *necessary* in that these stated qualities *must* be the case, or else the object is not a sweater at all. The statement is, therefore, an *a priori* judgment. The classic example that Kant gives of an *a priori* statement is: All bachelors are unmarried men. Like the prior example, this truth is both universal and necessary. There is no possibility of the existence of a bachelor who is also married.[62]

Knowledge that is not *a priori* is *a posteriori*. As the opposite of *a priori* knowledge, *a posteriori* judgments are contingent and particular.[63] *A posteriori* statements arise from judgments based upon specific experiences. If my wife were to walk into my office and look at me while I am writing this chapter, she would see that I am wearing a white cricket sweater. She would have arrived at that knowledge, not through the abstract rules of logic, but through her sense of sight by seeing me wearing this specific article of clothing while in my office. This truth (that I have a white cricket sweater on) is contingent, as I could have easily worn my green cable-knit sweater today, or no sweater at all, depending on several unique factors.

---

[62] Kant, *Critique of Pure Reason*, 103-104.
[63] Ibid., 79-84.

Along with this judgment being contingent rather than necessary, it is also particular rather than universal, as it is a claim about *one* object (my sweater), rather than a universal declaration about nature.

One might object to this that it seems possible for a statement to be both universal *and* contingent. Perhaps in the future, all world governments will mandate that every book be produced in a hardbound volume only, and every paperback book will be burned. It might be universally true, in that circumstance, that every book is a hardback rather than a paperback, while such a statement is also contingent upon a specific set of historical circumstances. What Kant means by *a priori* judgments, however, is more than making claims that might be *incidentally* universal. While it might be true that there are no paperback books in this theoretical world due to specific events in history, those events might later develop such that paperback books are printed once again. For something to be true based on an *a priori* judgment, that thing must be true, not just in a point in history, but in all possible worlds. There are possible worlds in which paperback books do or do not exist, but there is no possible world in which a bachelor is a married man.

Kant agrees with idealism in his belief that there are many truths that can be known through reason. These rationally determined elements of reality are those things which are known *a priori*. In identifying these *a priori* truths, Kant refers to some universals as preconditions of experience. These are things that are known, or assumed, by the human intellect in order to comprehend one's experiences of the world. Kant includes both space and time in this category. In his view, the concept of space is not derived through an observation that objects appear to be related in a spatial manner. Instead, a preconception of the existence of physical space and of the fact that physical objects are contained within space renders objects comprehensible to the intellect. Similarly, the concept of time is a precondition for experience. The idea of time is not derived from the contemplation of how historical events appear to relate to one another. Instead, time is an innate idea; it is the lens by which the intellect categorizes events. These categories of precognition are described by Kant as *transcendental*. Consequently, Kant's system of thought is sometimes referred to as "transcendental idealism." It must be noted that Kant does not appear to believe that space and time are necessarily objectively real external truths. They are simply preconceptions of the human intellect, or modes by which the brain is able to categorize experiences.[64]

This leads to a second distinction that Kant makes, between *analytic* judgments and *synthetic* judgments. An analytic judgment is one that is made based upon the nature of a thing or idea. For example, the statement, "All bachelors are unmarried men," is an analytic judgment. As a bachelor is both unmarried and male by definition, such a conclusion that all bachelors are unmarried men is inherent in the idea of "bachelor" by itself. One does not need any additional information in order to arrive at this conclusion, since the conclusion is directly derived from the concept being analyzed. Another example is the statement, "All triangles have three sides," since it is definitional to triangularity that any triangular object has three sides. Both of these statements are examples of analytic *a priori* judgments. They are analytic in that they are conclusions made from the nature of the concepts alone, not derived from the combination of multiple concepts. They are *a priori* in that their conclusions are not derived through sense experience but through reasoning based upon ideas. One does not, for example, need to meet a certain number of bachelors in order to arrive at the conclusion that bachelors are unmarried, because the definition of bachelor in no way depends upon specific historical factors.

While Kant's conclusions here regarding analytic *a priori* judgments do not provide anything decisively new in Western philosophical discourse, his contention that there are also synthetic *a priori* judgments is an innovative, and influential, proposal. Synthetic judgments are those which combine two or more ideas to

---

[64] Ibid., 64-65.

arrive at a conclusion. Many truths of logic and mathematics are synthetic judgments. As an example, take the basic math problem 5 x 3. One arrives at a conclusion to this problem through the synthesis of three concepts: the number 5, the number 3, and multiplication. Not only is this multiplication problem synthetic, according to Kant, but it is also an example of *a priori* reasoning. The numbers 3 and 5, as well as the concept of multiplication, are not dependent upon one's experience of any single event or series of events. One will never be able to perform some experiment that disproves the number 3. Numbers are not derived from experience but are general categories through which one evaluates or judges that which is experienced by means of the senses. If, as Kant argues, synthetic *a priori* judgments are possible, this means that one does not need to adopt the kind of skepticism toward logical reasoning as capable of discovering truth that is present in the writings of David Hume. For Kant, because *a priori* judgments are possible, there is a standard for the evaluation and discovery of transcendent truths.[65] It is here that Kant affirms the conviction of the rationalists, that the intellect is capable of deriving certain conclusions from a combination of premises.

THE THING-IN-ITSELF

While the synthetic *a priori* gives priority to mathematical and other transcendental truths, Kant remains committed to the importance of personal sense experience. He makes some clarifications about the kind of knowledge which can be gained by experience, which he differentiates from knowledge gained through reason. He does this through a distinction between the *noumenal* and the *phenomenal*.

The noumenal realm is often described as the "thing-in-itself." These are things as they actually are, apart from our experience of them. In some ways, this is similar to Plato's forms, where there is a difference between the transcendent realm of ideas and the particular thing that one encounters in ordinary life. These

---

[65] Ibid., 128-137.

two thinkers differ, however, in that while Plato's forms set the groundwork for genuine understanding of the world, Kant denies that we have any understanding of this transcendent realm at all. For Kant, we do not actually have access to the world as it is. Instead, we only know what he refers to as the phenomenal realm. The phenomenal is the world of experience. It is here that Kant affirms the ideas of the empiricists, that there is much knowledge that is to be gained purely by experience rather than abstract reason. This knowledge, however, differs significantly from that which is knowable by reason.[66]

In order to better understand what the phenomenal is, let us look at an example: the cup of Earl Gray tea that I have in front of me. If someone were to ask me to define Earl Gray tea, I could explain all sorts of things about the tea, such as what it tastes like, what it smells like, how it looks in the mug, or the feel of the heat in my mouth. None of these things, however, actually explains what the tea *is*. Instead, these statements explain the *experience* that I have when encountering the cup of tea. These empirical descriptions are all explanations of phenomena, giving more information about myself and my experience with the drink than saying anything about the drink itself. For Kant, this is all I can know by means of experience. There is, for Kant, a strict barrier between the experience of a thing and the actual nature of the thing-in-itself. While Kant attempts to counter the absolute skepticism of Hume through this system, it is difficult to see how he escapes the trap of skepticism himself. While he does provide for some notion of the transcendental through his construction of the *a priori*, he still leaves people in a place where experience cannot clearly reveal anything about the external, objective world as it actually is. Further, if the thing-in-itself is so inaccessible to us, we might ask: How do you know that the noumenal realm exists at all? Perhaps there are mere phenomena,

---

[66] Allen, *Philosophy for Theology*, 210-213.

and that's all there is to it.[67] Kant does not develop a significant answer to this.

Kant's attempt to shift the relationship between the human subject and the world leads to what he refers to as the "Copernican revolution" in philosophy.[68] When Copernicus first presented his evidence that the earth revolved around the sun, his radical idea about the universe was rejected by many. If Copernicus was correct, this would mean that scientists had wrongly centered the earth in their cosmology for centuries. Since that time, however, rejection has turned into acceptance, so that hardly any try to refute his basic claim today. Kant believed that, like Copernicus, he was making a radical shift in the field of philosophy. While classical philosophy revolved around the external world into which one is placed, Kant instead argues that the center is the subject himself or herself.

This shift is centered on the relationship between subject and object.[69] For the classical philosopher, the human person as a subject is placed into an objective world that exists both in the particular things of creation and in the ideas that relate to those things. Human persons, as subjects, encounter objects, and those objects imprint themselves upon the minds of subjects. For Kant, this is backwards. Instead of the belief that subjects change in their encounters with objects, he contends that objects are affected by human cognition. We, as subjects, change objects. So, how exactly does this happen? In answering this, Kant goes back to his discussion of the categories of precognition (time, space, other *a priori* knowledge). He argues that we bring these *a priori* ideas about universality and necessity into our experience, so that those things form our understanding of objects. Remember that the objects here are not the things in themselves (the noumenal), but their reality as it appears to us (the phenomenal). Thus, Kant is not saying that the things in themselves are changed by

---

[67] Some later phenomenologists do take this extra step and deny the existence of the noumena.

[68] Kant, *Critique of Pure Reason*, 29.

[69] Meerbote, "Kant," in Arrington, *Companion to the Philosophers*, 342.

the subject. In fact, according to Kant, we cannot even speak of *ourselves* in a real, objective, and transcendent way. All we know of ourselves is, similarly, mere appearance.

With Kant, we find nominalism in its most sophisticated and long-lasting form. Like the earlier medieval nominalists, Kant argues that people do not actually have access to an objective and universal world of ideas. Instead, we bring categories and ideas into our subjective encounters with the things outside of us. In some sense, for Kant, our minds create the world, rather than receiving it. To be fair to Kant here, he certainly attempts to retain some type of transcendence in his thought, along with a universal grounding for science, mathematics, and morality. However, in doing so, he still retains Hume's skepticism in some fundamental ways, and consequently divorces humanity from transcendent meaning, value, and understanding in a real and objective sense, replacing these with experience and appearance.

Moral Philosophy

Along with contributing to the realm of metaphysics and epistemology, Kant is also among the most influential thinkers in the field of ethics. As a follow-up to the earlier book *A Critique of Pure Reason*, Kant wrote a text titled *A Critique of Practical Reason* in 1788 to address how moral philosophy fits into his system of thought. With continuing influence upon ethical theory, Kant's work outlines a deontological ethic that is consistent with his emphasis on necessity and universality.

As in his earlier writing, Kant is concerned with the dangers of absolute skeptical and relativistic accounts of philosophy as is seen in Hume and other empiricists. A pure moral relativism which relies on personal preference or desire is not capable of governing a society or even an individual human life. On the other hand, Kant also rejects classical approaches to ethics that dominate Christian theology or classical philosophy. These models are reliant on the concept of a natural law, which can be grasped and understood by the human intellect and then exercised through the practice of virtue.[70] For Kant, however, this relies on natural theology and the conviction that the thing-in-itself can actually be known, including the divine cause of the universe. As Kant denies such knowledge, he therefore cannot affirm the natural law tradition–at least in a classical sense.[71] As a path between the certainty of classical views and the skepticism of the empiricists, Kant offers a new way forward. He argues that the principles of philosophy that he outlined in his earlier work can be applied to ethics in order to make a coherent, logical system of morality.[72]

Just as all knowledge can be divided into the categories of *a priori* and *a posteriori*, so can ethical truths.[73] This leads to the question: Should a moral system be determined *a priori* or *a posteriori*? Kant argues for the former. There are good reasons for this. Think about a system in which morality is purely determined by *a posteriori* reasoning through personal experiences. There are plenty of instances in which something might seem ethical based upon its personal benefit to one person, while simultaneously harming someone else. Say, for example, that a man recently fell into financial misfortune and cannot feed his family. Perhaps he makes the decision to steal from someone else's business in order to pay his bills and financially provide for his family. This might seem, to this man, to be a good decision (especially if he isn't caught), as it helped him and his family. Further, he might never see the negative impact that his actions had upon anyone else, as he had no personal relationship with the business owner that he stole from, which reinforces for him that this is an ethical choice. The problem here is that if people totally

---

[70] Haines and Fulford, *Natural Law.*
[71] There is a kind of natural-law tradition in John Locke and other Enlightenment philosophers, but it differs significantly from the Aristotelian–Thomistic tradition.
[72] Much of this is not new with Kant. A move away from classical natural law theories toward a strong division between positive law and divine law began with the writings of Samuel von Pufendorf in the late seventeenth century.
[73] Kant, *Critique of Practical Reason*, 132-147.

personalize ethics, they can always come up with a reason as to why various ethical rules do not apply to them, particularly in situations when they happen to benefit by not obeying such rules. There must be a standard for universal ethical rules if the world is not to fall into pure subjective ethical chaos.

For Kant, morality is to be determined *a priori* just like mathematics. Experience cannot create or determine a moral rule, as this leads to the kind of subjectivism just described. In order for an act to be properly moral, in Kant's system, it must be both universal and timeless. Those things which are morally good according to Kant's system are called categorical imperatives. An ethical decision is one that is right at all times, in all places, and in all circumstances. If, for example, stealing is wrong, it is universally so. Therefore, the man described above cannot ethically justify a breach of that law based upon personal circumstances. If theft is wrong, there is no time or place, according to Kant, in which theft can be ethically justifiable. This still leaves the question as to why one should obey moral laws.

In classical thought, there is an end, or goal, to all good actions. Ethical acts help to both form the character of the virtuous person and contribute to the greater good of society. For Kant, ethics are not so much about character, but duty.[74] A man or woman should do a good thing simply because it is their duty to do so. This duty-oriented ethic is referred to as *deontology*. Right actions are also connected, for Kant, to both rationality and freedom. It is always the rational decision that is the good decision, and, for Kant, being more rational also means being more free. This means that the one who obeys moral duties is the one who truly experiences freedom. In response to the mechanistic determinism of much Enlightenment thought, Kant emphasizes the importance of the subject's will in decision making. In his view, all ethical actions ultimately flow from a good will. Further, good actions do not treat other people as means,

---

[74] Ibid., 171.

but instead as ends in themselves. Thus, there is a kind of teleology here in Kant's ethics in which other persons become the end of ethical actions.[75]

Kant's moral theory remains a choice that some ethicists opt for today, as it provides an objective and logical measure of ethical norms. There are, however, some significant shortcomings. Most obviously (and discussed often), the absolute universalizing of moral imperatives is difficult to reconcile with some situations that appear to be obvious exceptions. For example, in a general sense, lying is wrong. Most people agree on this point. However, one could imagine scenarios in which deception might be morally justified. For example, if someone was in my home hiding from a stalker, and that stalker came to my door and asked if their victim was in my home, most people would agree that it would be ethically justified for me to lie since this action was taken to protect the other person. Despite its challenges, however, Kant's deontological ethic retains a significant influence in philosophical ethics.

RELIGION

A final area of Kant's thought to be explored here is his approach to religion. Kant has alternately been described as a harsh critic of Christianity and as a great defender of religion in an age of secular rationality. Reflecting on his own religious upbringing, Kant believed that he could retain the most beneficial and significant elements of his childhood faith while simultaneously fitting religion into his rational system. His most famous work on the subject is titled *Religion within the Bounds of Reason Alone* (1792).

Much of Kant's approach to religion can be gathered from his other basic premises. Kant rejects any traditional arguments for the existence of God as inadequate to definitively prove God's existence. There are two reasons for this. First, God is in the realm of the

---

[75] Though most of what is discussed here is from his *Critique of Practical Reason*, Kant's *Introduction to the Metaphysics of Morals* is another influential ethical text which should be read by anyone seeking to understand Kant's ethical system.

noumenal, or the thing-in-itself. As established, Kant does not believe that such a thing is in any way accessible to the human intellect. It is true that the *effects* of belief can be experienced as phenomena (such as a religious conversion), but for Kant, this does not prove anything about the actual cause of such phenomena. Second, Kant adopts Hume's critique of Aristotelian causality and, in doing so, negates Aquinas's causal arguments, which are dependent on an intimate connection between cause and effect.[76] The field of natural theology, for Kant, is irrelevant and unprovable.

Kant does believe that religion has a place in an Enlightenment society, but primarily because it is useful, rather than being literally true. He contends, for example, that the existence of God serves as a basis for morality. It strengthens the idea of duty to have a lawgiver to whom one owes such duty. Further, the idea of punishments and rewards in an afterlife gives helpful motivation for obedience to one's duties. Kant also writes against traditional religious ritual and hierarchy, as the purpose of religion is internal rather than external. Several of these themes are picked up by the Protestant liberals of the following century, who attempt to merge the new rationalism with religion.

In all of the areas discussed here (and some others that are absent in this survey)—metaphysics, epistemology, ethics, and religion—Kant shaped nearly all major thinkers who would arise following his death. It is Kant's system that first attempts to take the challenges, questions, and divergent ideas of the academy during the modern era and answer them with one singular, cohesive ideological system. In Kant's view, he did so by preserving some sense of transcendent objectivity with the realists, while also affirming the importance and uniqueness of sense experience. Whatever one thinks of the viability of Kant's solutions to the questions he sought to answer, Kant's brilliance and ingenuity are undeniable.

---

[76] Aquinas, *Summa Theologica*, First Part, Q. 2.

CONCLUSION

Though almost four hundred years have passed since the beginnings of modern philosophy with the publication of Descartes's *Meditations on First Philosophy*, the problems addressed by modernity have yet to be definitively answered. Descartes, Hume, and Kant continue to shape current discourse both in the academy and on a popular level, even if their influence is unrecognized. In my own view, this influence has not been entirely positive. While some of the methodological approaches of the moderns are to be credited for the explosion of scientific discoveries, medical breakthroughs, and advancing technologies of the last few centuries, modern philosophers also introduced a methodology that begins with skepticism toward knowledge of the objective world, and consequently displaced theology from its nascent academic position as chief of the sciences. The ripples from this shift become evident as they flow through the thoughts presented in the rest of this book.

THE BEGINNINGS OF LIBERALISM: HOBBES, LOCKE, AND PAINE

Along with the changes that occurred within the fields of metaphysics and epistemology in early modern philosophy emerged new models of political life. Many factors played into this, such as the loss of influence of the traditional church authorities, growth in literacy rates, scientific and philosophical developments that opened up new ways of thinking, and increased skepticism toward established norms and authority structures. Amid such changes, seventeenth century philosophers began to apply the same principles of reason that they had applied to other philosophical and religious concerns to the realm of politics in order to deal with the new social dynamics of a post-Reformation West. As religious wars raged between Roman Catholics and Protestants, a united Europe under one branch of Christianity was recognized to be an unachievable reality. While Roman Catholics, Lutherans, and Anglicans contended for political systems in their own territories that retained their Christian theological and philosophical foundations—along with a strong alliance between church and state—other thinkers offered secular alternatives for a view of government based upon social consensus rather than divine right.

This resulted in the formation of what is broadly known as liberalism. In contrast to the common American use of "liberal" as an alternative to "conservative," the political ideology of liberalism as discussed here is neither left nor right, but includes both left and right political approaches within it.[77] Though an exact definition of liberalism is difficult to construct, there are some general principles

---

[77] There has been a recent pushback against liberalism as a whole by some political philosophers with the rise of postliberalism. See: Deneen, *Why Liberalism Failed.*

that characterize the liberal order in opposition to other political systems, such as: the protection of individual rights as the foundational purpose of government, the idea that the power of the state arises from the consensus of citizens, the privileging of personal freedom in social order, the priority of reason in the establishment of law, and a belief in religious pluralism in social life. These ideas, often unchallenged in the modern West, are the result of the developments of a number of thinkers, but three in particular are addressed here: Thomas Hobbes, John Locke, and Thomas Paine. The first two are undoubtedly the most influential figures in the construction of liberal political thought, while the third serves as an example of the application of liberal ideas to actual popular political contexts.

THOMAS HOBBES

Born on April 5, 1588, in Westport, England, Thomas Hobbes was the son of a vicar of minimal education and means. After his father was involved in a physical altercation with other clergy, Thomas and his family were forced out of London and moved in with Thomas's uncle, who had made a modest fortune as a glove manufacturer. First attending Malmesbury school for his primary education, Thomas later studied at Oxford and then St. John's College, Cambridge. At both universities, Hobbes learned the scholastic method of doing theology and philosophy, which he would later depart from significantly. While serving as a secretary and tutor for William Cavendish, the third Earl of Devonshire, Hobbes was exposed to the new scientific learning, which departed from the classically accepted models, meeting figures such as Francis Bacon and Galileo. This turned Hobbes's attention away from older metaphysical approaches to science and philosophy and toward the formation of a modern approach to philosophy, physics, and politics. While he wrote extensively on all three subjects, along with much translation work, it is his political writing that is most influential. This political writing was a response to, and a development of, popular works of his time—especially that of Hugo Grotius.[78]

THE INFLUENCE OF GROTIUS

Though Hobbes's work on politics is often cited as the first foundational work for the liberal tradition, he draws heavily from another writer five years his senior: the Dutch thinker Hugo Grotius. It is in Grotius's 1625 book *The Laws of War and Peace* that some of the driving questions of liberal theory are first posed. In this work, Grotius follows Descartes's model of skeptical inquiry, beginning with the tearing down of accepted ethical theories, after which he then seeks to construct his own theory out of unaided reason. In his examination of various ethical theories, Grotius believed that he had found a point of broad agreement: the right of self-preservation. If any social life is to be possible (whatever form it may take), there must be laws and regulations that preserve the lives of citizens. For Grotius, this serves as the single most important role of the state. All law, therefore, must follow this core principle.[79]

While one might view Grotius's approach to law here as one of pure skepticism, he himself did not see it that way. His approach was an attempt to give a rational response to those skeptics who argue that moral law is nothing more than an arbitrary imposition on citizens by civic authorities. At the same time, like Descartes, Grotius rejected the strongly Aristotelian view of the state which prevailed in both Roman Catholic and Protestant Europe. In this view, there is a natural law which is a transcendent source that stands behind the creation of positive law (that which is created and imposed by the state). Through natural revelation, the ethicist is able to discover both the common good (that which is good for society as

---

[78] These brief autobiographical comments come from the information in Tuck, *Hobbes*.

[79] A good summary of the basic argument of Grotius's *Laws of War and Peace* can be found in Tuck, *Hobbes*, 39-42. For an in-depth treatment of Grotius's thought, see: Lesaffer, *Cambridge Companion to Hugo Grotius*.

a whole) and personal virtue (that which should be practiced by the individual). It is the role of the state to enforce laws which coincide with this common good and to provide societal conditions that encourage the development of personal virtue. For Grotius, such virtues and values are not so rationally demonstrable. This is shown by the fact that so many states and cultures cannot come to consensus about these matters, and all are just as adamant that they are correct in their particularities. This principle of right, for Grotius, resolves this issue by providing an indisputable foundation for the state.

Grotius is certainly not the first to speak of the importance of self-preservation, or of the role of the state in making the conditions for that possible. From a secular perspective, Montaigne had made the same basic argument.[80] The uniqueness of Grotius's formulation of preservation is in his positive construction of the preservation of life as found in his use of the language of rights. The idea of "rights" provides a moral and ontological groundwork for the state, which is absent in Montaigne. The identification of rights and persons here is a novel development; prior to Grotius, rights were attached primarily to things rather than to persons (i.e., someone is said to have a right to property). Though he himself was an Arminian Christian, Grotius contended that even if the claims of Christianity were not true, his claim about rights would still stand as an indisputable truth of reason. This provides the basis for secular society based on reason as an alternative to the prior Christian West guided by revelation.

HOBBES ON THE STATE OF NATURE

From Grotius, Hobbes gets the idea of natural rights which govern civil society. In his development of the idea of right, Hobbes provides a unique contribution in political discourse that would guide later

---

[80] Montaigne does not have any singular works on political theory, so his ideas on the subject have to be extracted from essays on other topics. For an overview of Montaigne's political thought, see: Schaefer, *The Political Philosophy of Montaigne*.

political theory: the idea of the state of nature. Rather than open with a discussion of the state in its present condition, the nature of the good or virtue, or divine revelation, Hobbes begins with a consideration of man as he exists in a state of nature. This theoretical state of nature describes the way in which men and women live in the world apart from the existence of political order. The government is established to keep this natural state within boundaries, and thus the duties and purpose of political powers flow forth from the problems of humans in this state. For that reason, the state of nature takes a central place within Western political theory in the liberal tradition, from the writings of Hobbes into the present day.

The question then is precisely what this state of nature is. How exactly do men and women function within this non-political order? This natural state, for Hobbes, is essentially one of war. Without government, men see themselves as having a right to anything that they desire. This becomes a problem when multiple people claim the right to the same object or territory. Conflict arises between parties with no one to arbitrate such disputes. Out of this grows a life of violence, fear, and death, which Hobbes refers to as "poor, nasty, brutish, and short."[81] This state of constant conflict means that there can be no civil society. Industry, arts, education, and religion cannot exist in such a state. As Hobbes contends, the state of nature is a war of "all against all."[82]

It is important to note here that Hobbes views human society as an amalgamation of individuals, rather than as a cooperative community.[83] For Hobbes, people have isolated personal wills and rights which they use to get whatever they desire from others in the state of nature. Everyone can decide for him or herself what is good, true, right, and just. Without the imposition of an external order through the state, there simply will not be any grounds of agreement

---

[81] Hobbes, *Leviathan*, 62.
[82] Ibid., 85.
[83] Ibid., 60-64.

between people on these matters. The role of the state, built from these presuppositions, is not simply the establishment of a unified civic and social life for a community of people, but to guard the individuals in a society from one another.[84] Common beliefs, morals, and practices are enforced in a society, not for the sake of conforming to an actual moral goodness that exists outside of the social order, but so that people are less inclined to harm one another due to differing beliefs.

Hobbes's approach to human nature is in some sense both more pessimistic and more optimistic than the traditional Augustinian one that reigned previously in the Christian West. On the one hand, he portrays men and women in a state of nature as purely selfish beings, ready to enact any kind of evil deed for the sake of their own preservation. In this way, humans are inherently self-interested and are not naturally oriented toward communal life directed at a singular good. On the other hand, Hobbes argues for the essential goodness of natural human desire and emotions. The Greeks argued that the affections are often oriented toward those things which please the bodily appetites (hunger, thirst, lust), and that reason had to guide and direct those affections. There is, in classical thought, therefore a superiority of the intellect over the passions, with the understanding that the human emotional life is often disordered, and that proper moral reasoning is needed to reorient such desires. For Hobbes, however, the emotional life of men and women is generally a useful guide to human action in the world.[85] The selfishness of people in the state of nature is only the result of threats to self-preservation. In other words, if people's bodily lives are protected, there is no longer any reason for people to harm others, and thus people generally will not do so.

---

[84] To be clear, Hobbes does believe in some kind of unity in common life, as is evident from the earlier chapters of the *Leviathan* in which he discusses social custom, religion, and communal roles. This common life, however, is imposed from the sovereign, rather than arising from man's created nature.

[85] Ibid., 23-30.

In looking at the wars of religion that devastated seventeenth-century Europe, Hobbes makes the observation that conflict arises (both interpersonally and globally) when there are competing conceptions of the good, or that which is worthy of praise.[86] Because of this, Hobbes argues that there must be some common moral language which is shared among citizens that mitigates such conflict. Unlike the theological polemicists of his day, Hobbes was skeptical about the possibility of achieving moral consensus merely through academic disputation. Instead of rational discourse, then, Hobbes believed that such moral language and consensus was to be imposed by the political order. This then places the duty of right and wrong within the hands of the sovereign, as it is only through the external imposition of order that consensus is possible and that constant conflict will cease.

WHAT ARE RIGHTS?

Though Hobbes founds his idea of the social order on rights, he does not have a fully developed conception of multiple rights, nor of a general category of right in which self-preservation is only a part. Instead, for Hobbes, the preservation of life is really the only right. As the singular right, this also serves as a groundwork for a kind of ethical good. For Hobbes, there is no inherent right to do things which go against this central need for self-preservation. This is not, therefore, the kind of right to do whatever one pleases that becomes common in some later liberal thinkers. For Hobbes, there would be no human right to partake of harmful drugs or to engage in senseless risky behavior, as they are not conducive to personal preservation.[87]

It is this right to preserve life that also provides a kind of psychological pushback against false ideas and moral conceptions in society. As Hobbes argues, people are easily manipulated, as

---

[86] See Hobbes's work *De Cive* (On the Citizen) for a more detailed treatment of this issue.

[87] Hobbes, *Leviathan*, 64-71.

persuasion works not merely on the basis of rational argumentation but also of emotional appeal. For this reason, the religious conflicts of his day could not be resolved solely through debate. Further, Hobbes observes (and Grotius before him) that people often hold views that fluctuate over time, or views that are inherently at odds with one another. Underneath all such malleability of ideas remains this one central internal desire for self-preservation, which is a guard against ideological manipulation. No matter how much ideas may change, there lies within man this consistent internal desire to preserve life.

The desire for the existence of an authoritative state is ultimately, then, a self-interested one. While this desire for, and right to, self-preservation exists in a state of nature, it is far more likely that one will face death in such a state. It is therefore advantageous to the individual that some kind of state is enacted to promote societal order. This conviction of Hobbes (with precursors in Montaigne and Lipsius) constitutes a massive change in Western political discourse.[88] For classical Christian political theory, the human order exists for the good of individuals as a reflection of transcendent divine law. It is not imposed by individuals, and it is not valued for purely self-interested reasons.[89] In Hobbes's view, the state exists for the good of the self-interested individual, rather than for a singular communal good that unites humanity with the divine order. All of this together leads to a divergent view of where exactly the state comes from.

---

[88] Lipsius was a French philosopher who wrote an influential political text titled *Politicorum sive Civilis Doctrinae Libri Sex* (Six Books on Politics or Civil Doctrine). Through the use of Stoic philosophy, Lipsius provided a defense for a relatively absolutist monarchical position that he hoped would bring an end to religious wars following the Reformation.

[89] See the contrast in Luthardt, *Moral Truths of Christianity*, 173-201.

THE SOCIAL CONTRACT

For Hobbes, the state of nature comes to an end when people discover that the giving up of certain actions and desires for the sake of a common authority that will bring about an end to the war against all is worth the sacrifice. Some kind of compromise must be made among individuals in a society in order to create a situation of social stability and the preservation of life. This means that people cease to be their own judges of justice and injustice and grant that authority to another. Private judgment inevitably leads to conflict and thus must be discarded.

This giving up of private judgment and delegating it to another creates two new social realities. The first of these is the commonwealth, which is now a unified citizenship and nation that agrees to live together in mutual harmony.[90] The second is the sovereign.[91] The authority of the sovereign is a delegated authority. The creation of this new state and the power of the sovereign are both granted by the people. This idea, that the creation of governmental authority is from the ground up, is what is later usually referred to as the social contract. Citizens of a nation agree to give up certain things in order to live in a mutually beneficial state in which political authority is delegated, which preserves their right to life. With the creation of this new state, there is an assured survival of both the weak and the strong, rather than a constant battle for authority and power among the strong. The benefits delivered in this society are thus universally advantageous.

A problem arises here for Hobbes, and for social-contract approaches to the state more generally, regarding the keeping of this social contract among citizens to submit to a particular sovereign. In the state of nature, people have no problem with lying if such a thing is advantageous for their own survival. If this is true, and the contract is essentially a promise between multiple parties, is one not able to

---

[90] Hobbes, *Leviathan*, 85-88
[91] Ibid., 88-94.

simply break the contract if it is advantageous to do so? One could certainly imagine an instance within this immediate post-social-contract proto-state in which this might occur. Locke would later answer this problem with his contention that a theistic conviction is necessary for the social order, as citizens then fear some kind of divine punishment if the contract is broken. Hobbes, however, does not evoke divine authority here (or anywhere, really). Instead, he makes the simple claim that if one party making a contract keeps a promise, the other party will most likely do the same, so long as that contract does not threaten the right to life.[92] This does not exactly answer the problem, however, as it simply pushes it back a step. Hobbes does not have a clear answer as to why the first party would be motivated to keep such a promise within this state of nature. Nonetheless, in Hobbes's view, the social contract simply *has* been upheld around the world, and because it has, a sovereign has been granted authority over the commonwealth.

THE SOVEREIGN

As the name "Leviathan" suggests, the sovereign as described by Hobbes is not a moderated, non-invasive power. Like the monster described in the Bible, the sovereign wields significant power, and he does so in order to restrain men and women from re-entering that savage state of nature, thus preserving the lives of citizens. Hobbes does not envision a careful system of checks and balances with a strongly democratic process in which the common citizens use their rights or intellect to determine the direction of the leaders of the state. The sovereign's power, for Hobbes, is nearly absolute.[93]

There is a sense in which Hobbes's sovereign serves a representative function. As a human person, he has the same vested interest in preserving the fundamental right to life as do those of the commonwealth. The sovereign is not, however, so concerned with

---

[92] On things that result in the dissolution of the commonwealth, see Hobbes, *Leviathan*, 167-175.
[93] Ibid., 123-126.

the good of his citizens that he chooses to lead in a selfless act of benevolence. He, like everyone else, serves in his own best interest— he wants his life to be preserved. There is ultimately an alignment between the keeping of peace for the well-being of the populace and this drive for self-preservation on the part of the monarch. If the sovereign rules unjustly, there is a higher risk of an unhappy citizenship, and thereby a higher risk of assassination. Therefore, although the drive is ultimately selfish, the sovereign does make decisions which benefit the commonwealth. In this way, the contracting of a sovereign is in the best interest of a populace, even if he may himself serve out of purely selfish motives.

Among the decisions of the sovereign is the giving of property to citizens.[94] For Hobbes, even in a state of nature, there is some private property. Self-preservation necessitates at least some ownership, but the duty of the sovereign to secure the self-preservation of multitudinous individuals means that there should not be an exorbitant amount of property accumulated by any singular person, such that some do not have enough for their preservation of life. Therefore, one should not retain more property than is necessary, at least not if there is a scarcity of resources. In times of economic endangerment, Hobbes grants the sovereign the ability to redistribute wealth such that everyone has the basic necessities for survival. The political authorities should not get involved in economic policy unless it is concerned directly with this primary objective of the preservation of life. When material inequalities are dealt with by the sovereign, this is done not for the purpose of achieving equity in the civic sphere, but in order to stop what might become a life-threatening conflict between parties in the commonwealth. Here Hobbes sets forth a foundational liberal principle: The decisions of the state should be determined by the preservation of right.

---

[94] Ibid., 128-131.

The absolute power of the state in Hobbes's system is most apparent in the areas of theology and other ideological issues. It is here that the later liberal tradition would depart from Hobbes significantly. As was apparent in the wars of religion following the Protestant Reformation, differences in doctrinal commitments could, and would continue to, lead to bloodshed. Being an adherent to some of the more skeptical philosophies of his time, Hobbes was convinced that intellectual inquiry alone would not lead to doctrinal agreement among divergent groups. For this reason Hobbes contends that doctrinal disputes are to be decided by the sovereign.[95] While this may appear to contradict his focus on the preservation of rights, it is, in his view, necessary to preserve the right to life. Only if the sovereign determines doctrine would conflict among the populace on such matters cease. Though we would (rightly) view such a declaration from the sovereign as a tyrannical overreach, Hobbes viewed this as necessary to preserve the primary individual right.

Regarding the question of resistance toward tyrannical governments, Hobbes again bases his answer on the fundamental right of self-preservation.[96] Resistance toward the sovereign over theological or philosophical matters is never justified. If this were allowable, society would quickly devolve again into inter-religious war. This does not mean that resistance is never justified, however. If government rests on a social contract between citizens and the sovereign, that arrangement ceases to be valid once the contract is broken. For the sovereign, this would occur if he negated his primary responsibility to protect the lives of citizens. When self-preservation is challenged, citizens are within their rights to protect themselves by whatever means necessary. This right to self-preservation is more fundamental than the state, and thus the state cannot infringe upon it. When the state attempts to do so, resistance is necessary.

---

[95] Ibid., 186-193.
[96] Ibid., 112-113.

CONCLUSION

While Hobbes's system of government that he sets forth in *Leviathan* (and his other writing) is not liberal in the sense that the term is understood today, it does include several of the most important elements of later liberal thought. These include: beginning political discussion with a theoretical state of nature, the speculative consideration of the purpose of government toward a universal form, the idea of the social contract, the view of humans primarily as individuals who are by nature self-interested, the preservation of rights as the central role of government, and the unity of a social group as being founded in government. Locke would expand upon each of these points to create the basic ideological framework of the modern liberal political order.

JOHN LOCKE

John Locke is, in the fullest sense, the father of modern liberalism. While Grotius and Hobbes set the groundwork for the philosophy of Locke, neither system can be called properly "liberal" in the sense in which the term is most often used. Locke draws upon their idea of rights and places it within a coherent social and moral framework which would lay the groundwork for the American political system— among many others. Locke was not only a political philosopher, but he also wrote one of the most important texts in the field of epistemology with his work *An Essay Concerning Human Understanding*, in which the British philosopher sets forth a robust empiricist system without the thoroughgoing skepticism of Hume. While Locke's empiricism is touched on here, the focus of this section is on Locke's political theory.

LOCKE'S LIFE

John Locke was born in Somerset village in England in 1632 to devout Puritan parents of modest means.[97] John's father, though not himself directly involved in politics, was friends with a number of influential political figures—most notably, the parliamentarian Alexander Popham. These friendships provided some funding for young John's schooling, which would likely have been beyond his grasp without aid. John Locke studied in Westminster and then later attended Christ Church at Oxford. Initially most interested in studying medicine, Locke received the position of medical advisor under the Earl of Shaftsbury, which led to involvement in governmental affairs.

During this time, Locke studied extensively and wrote in the areas of theology, epistemology, education, and politics. After a succession crisis caused the Earl of Shaftsbury to leave England, Locke fled to the Netherlands to find safety, where he would live for six years. After his return to his home country, Locke became something of a celebrity, as his writings were broadly circulated during his own lifetime. In his later years, Locke served in public office but spent most of his time writing. In the midst of religious debate between Anglicans and Puritans, Locke pled for toleration toward the non-Anglican branches of Christianity in England. He also consistently fought for the freedom of the press, where ideas of various sorts were to be discussed and debated without strict censorship. It was during this late period of Locke's life that he wrote his most influential books, such as his *Essay Concerning Human Understanding* and his *Two Treatises of Government* (both published in 1689). Unlike for Hobbes and Grotius, there remains a school of thought today which proudly proclaims itself to be the heirs of Lockean political philosophy.

---

[97] This biographical information comes from Dunn, *Locke* and Lowe, "Locke" in Arrington, *Companion to the Philosophers*, 369-377. For a full biography, see: Woolhouse, *Locke: A Biography.*

RELIGIOUS TOLERANCE

The religious landscape of post-Reformation England was tumultuous. With the Pope disallowing Henry VIII's desired annulment, sixteenth-century theologians like Thomas Cranmer pushed both for separation of the Church of England from Rome and for the adoption of Martin Luther's reforms. This led to the creation of the Anglican church which, like much of the rest of Europe, contended with the strong political allegiances to the Roman papacy through warfare.[98] After a period of conformity with the Reformation under both Henry VIII and his successor Edward VI, Mary Tudor ascended to the throne and under the advisement of her cousin Charles V and husband Philip II reinstituted heresy laws against Protestants and demanded submission to the Roman Church. It was through her actions here that she received the famous title "Bloody Mary," as at least 300 Protestants were burned at the stake (with many others being killed by other means) during her reign.

The religious and political tensions in England did not end after Protestantism was officially restored by the Elizabethan Religious Settlement of 1559. Tensions remained in the church between those who desired to retain the traditional forms of worship and piety and those who desired far more significant reforms to the church. This was paralleled by growing tensions between parliament and the English monarchy. The Puritans argued that the church of England had retained far too many of the historical trappings of Rome and that more radical reforms were needed. Initially these pushes for reform surrounded two primary issues: requirements for clergy to dress in historic vestments rather than in the Puritans' preferred black academic gown, and the structure of church government.[99] The Puritans sought to use parliament to further these reforms, while the monarchy continued to push back and reinforce

---

[98] Rex, *Henry VIII and the English Reformation*.

[99] The best comprehensive overview of Puritan belief can be found in Beeke and Jones, *Puritan Theology*.

the episcopal structure and historic worship of the state church. This culminated in the Second English Civil War in 1648, in which King Charles I was publicly executed, and the Commonwealth of England was established in 1649 under the leadership of Oliver Cromwell. This new establishment, which lasted for eleven years, created religious toleration through the abolition of the Religious Settlement of 1559. In 1660, Charles II came out of exile and retook his throne, bringing an end to Cromwell's Commonwealth and restoring the monarchy and the historic episcopacy.[100]

Locke's political writing must be understood in the context of these struggles of post-Reformation England. His parents were devout Puritans, and despite the theological concerns one might justly have about Locke's own writings, he considered himself a devoted Christian and tended to favor the Presbyterian and congregational church over the Anglican episcopacy. Keep in mind that in Locke's time, England was distinctively and explicitly Christian. No rival groups were contending for the freedom to worship as Zoroastrians or Buddhists. Ideas of tolerance, therefore, are of inter-Christian tolerance rather than total religious pluralism. Locke's first major political writing, his *Two Tracts on Government* (which remained unpublished during his own lifetime), addresses this question in 1660 after the Restoration.

Within the political order and its relationship to religion, there are two concerns that must be taken seriously for any proposal to provide lasting peace. The first is the allowance for the freedom of conscience. If people are forced by law to attend a church, or send children to a school, that promotes a particular doctrinal commitment or religious practice that offends the conscience, this puts citizens in the position of having to choose civil disobedience to protect their religion. This is what led to the Second English Civil War. The second concern is for social order. If there is absolutely no

---

[100] For a compilation of the important political writings of seventeenth-century England, see Malcom, *Struggle for Sovereignty*.

civic religion, and all people are encouraged simply to act according to the dictates of their own consciences, then people can use conscience as an excuse to simply do whatever they like. Locke recognized that much rebellion fomented under the pretense of religious conscience.

Locke's argument in these early tracts is a response to another author, Edmund Bagshaw, who wrote a book titled *The Great Question Concerning Things Indifferent in Religious Worship.*[101] In this treatise, Bagshaw argues for the supremacy of conscience, in opposition to the reinstitution of classical forms of worship being enforced throughout England. For Locke, Bagshaw's proposal would lead, once again, to complete disorder. At this point in his career, Locke is an immovable defender of political authority and tradition. He contends that the majority of people are simply not capable of arriving at clearly formulated and articulated views on ecclesiastical and political matters. Further, to leave everything up to the conscience is to make room for rebellion and anarchy. If the state requires the wearing of the surplice in worship, this is an adiaphora (something indifferent, i.e. it is neither divinely commanded nor forbidden), and the church should obey. It is part of the magistrate's duty to override personal judgment for the sake of civil order. In some sense, Locke follows Hobbes here in viewing the political order as having precedence over the religious one in order to create unity and disallow anarchy under the magistrate.

By 1667, Locke had changed his mind significantly on these matters toward a more liberal view of religion and the state. In his *Essay on Toleration* (which is not the same as the more well-known *Letter on Toleration*), Locke argues that the state should allow for a diversity of beliefs.[102] This is not because Locke no longer cares about

---

[101] Maclear, "Restoration Puritanism and the Idea of Liberty."

[102] A critical edition of Locke's essay can be found in Locke, *Essay Concerning Toleration* edited by J. R. Milton. This volume contains other writings of Locke which are often not included in volumes of his compiled political works.

civic order, but because Locke now believes that toleration of many religious commitments would aid civic order. If the state allows for a broad tent (all still within the bounds of Christendom), then these divergent groups do not need to constantly fight with one another for control—as had been the history of English national life since the Reformation. The magistrate must not dictate doctrine, nor should he force all citizens to conform to his own beliefs. However, he is not to be unconcerned with matters of religion. As the magistrate's role concerns the safety and bodily life of the commonwealth, he is to regulate religious observance only insofar as it serves those ends. In theological matters, the king is no more qualified to dictate theological commitments than any other lay member of the church, and therefore these things are to be given to the individual conscience.

THE SOCIAL CONTRACT

While Locke's ideas surrounding religious toleration were certainly influential, his most important contributions to political philosophy are found in his concept of the social contract as outlined in his *Two Treatises on Government*. The purpose of this treatise is to argue for justified resistance to tyrannical authority. This question had been raised continually since the time of the Reformation. In his early writings, Martin Luther was adamantly opposed to active resistance against any magistrate, whether just or unjust.[103] As Luther saw it, God had installed them in that position himself, and therefore to resist earthly authorities is to resist God. This position became more difficult for Lutherans to defend when Emperor Charles V was increasingly hostile toward the Lutheran princes in Germany, and just resistance by the princes was viewed by some as the only possible way in which the Reformation would ultimately succeed. Out of this grew the doctrine of the lesser magistrate, wherein it was argued that there were times of justified resistance where a lesser magistrate

---

[103] Wright, *Martin Luther's Understanding of God's Two Kingdoms*.

(also acting in his God-given sphere of authority) could make active moves to overtake an unjust tyrant.[104] This was set forth in the Magdeburg Confession of 1550, which laid the grounding for Locke's arguments here. Locke goes much farther in these treatises than simply asking the usual question, "What circumstances make one a tyrant and make resistance justified?" Instead, Locke sets forth a treatment of the nature of the state itself.

Locke's discussion of the nature of political authority is mostly in the context of critique. His *Two Treatises* was a response to the political theorist Robert Filmer who opposed all forms of revolution and resistance to authority, arguing that to engage in such actions was to overthrow the divine order.[105] Authority, for Filmer, originates from God who granted dominion to Adam on the seventh day of creation. This authority was absolute, giving Adam a kind of ownership over all of his descendants until their death. This absolute power was eventually granted to Noah and then passed on from him to his descendants and then to the patriarchs. All political power, for Filmer, is granted from this absolute power. With no notion that authority is shared or delegated, in this view, anyone who has authority has it absolutely and is bound by no one within his domain. This applies to fathers in households and to kings in their territories. If this authority is given directly by God, it cannot be taken away, and any attempt to remove someone from authority is an act of sin. Filmer opposed democracy and prized social order through the exercise of absolute authority by the monarch.

In response to Filmer's doctrine, Locke argues that this view essentially severs man's relationship to God, instead placing him in direct service to the king.[106] Filmer argued that the magistrate not only had authority over his subjects, but that in some real way he

---

[104] See Whitford, *Tyranny and Resistance* for an overview of the confession and the historical circumstances surrounding it.

[105] Cuttica, *Sir Robert Filmer (1588–1653) and the Patriotic Monarch*.

[106] Locke, *Two Treatises*, 55.

owned them along with all other possessions in his territory. Locke argues that this would make murder more of a crime against the king as an owner than against God who gave dignity and a right to life to individual men. Further, it means that nearly everyone on earth is a mere slave with no autonomy, subject to the decisions of kings. Locke argues that there is a fundamental equality of all human beings which stands behind the social order—and this includes magistrates.

It is here that Locke lays out his own concept of the state of nature, which differs in important ways from Hobbes's view.[107] For Hobbes, human life is essentially isolated. There is no natural cooperation within humanity that is not voluntary association after the creation of the state through the social contract. Locke can speak about both man's sinful and unsociable nature as well as a natural sociability that exists apart from the social contract. Locke, however, is not all that concerned about the moral elements of human nature in this theoretical state like Hobbes is. Instead, Locke talks about the state of nature as a way to identify the natural rights of man which exist apart from state power. In other words, Hobbes discusses the state of nature asking the question, How did the state come to be? While Locke does so asking, What are man's natural rights?

Within this theoretical state, Locke argues that human beings are all equal. This conclusion is not merely theoretical, as men who are not under the same political authority still occasionally meet each other. When this occurs, they can interact simply as human beings who share a nature despite not sharing a common civic authority. Locke is more concerned with who men are as divinely created than he is about the history of the state.[108] Hobbes's view was attacked by Filmer and others because it did not align with the biblical narrative. Hobbes was viewed as a critic of historical Christianity who desired to create his own history of world events to replace the one revealed in sacred Scripture, which is why Hobbes

---

[107] Ibid., 101-106.
[108] Ibid., 106.

could not accept the divine right of kings. There is truth to this accusation, but it need not be pointed at Locke (at least not in the same way). Locke's political system is not dependent upon any historical claim at all; it is instead dependent upon the fact that human beings are still human beings apart from the political order. Human persons have an equality which is inherent *a priori*, rather than having a personality, rights, and duties that are grounded solely in the political order.

If all people are equal, as Locke contends, and authority is not inherent to certain people in an absolute sense (the Filmerian view), then where does proper political authority actually come from? In a historical sense, people often come to power through violence, deceit, and corruption. Though such things occur, this does not mean that power as such is the justification for its own authority. Conquest serves as no grounding for the state's authority, and it only creates a state of more violence rather than an actual civil society. Instead, Locke argues, the state's legitimacy arises through consent—the social contract.[109] Citizens of the commonwealth consent to submit to various authorities and laws in order to promote the kind of society in which they, and other citizens, can flourish. Locke follows Hobbes in arguing for the basis of government in a consented-to social contract, but he does not do so solely based upon the principle of self-interested bodily protection.

The difficulty with Locke's view, and with all social contract theories, is that while it sounds sensible to claim that states arise through consent, this is simply not the reality of how states come to be. Nearly any government, if traced back far enough, has its beginnings in conquest or revolt. Even when the founding of a nation is done in some kind of consensual way (like in the United States), this never includes all citizens, and it does not include future generations. If all people are truly free to join a society via social contract or to reject that contract and do something else, how can any

---

[109] Ibid., 133.

government truly have generational stability? What exactly is it that binds each generation to an old contract in which they had no part? Locke never answers these questions, and following generations of political theorists have proposed a variety of answers to them. Regarding the nature of consent, some have argued that what Locke is talking about here is *tacit* consent, rather than active, purposeful consent.[110] In other words, if you use government services, pay taxes, and do other things that a citizen does, you are by doing such things giving your consent to live within that social contract. In free societies, people are free to leave their place of living if they no longer consent to such an arrangement. The latter question about future generations has led to a division between conservatives, who believe in inherited social bonds through generations, and liberals, who argue for constant generational change within the social contract.[111] With this groundwork for Locke's idea of the social contract now laid, we move on to explore what rights and duties look like within a civil society that lives under this contract.

DUTIES AND RIGHTS

As a Christian, Locke contends that the grounding for the moral order of the world is in natural law. Natural law refers to God-given laws in the world which exist apart from, and are foundational for, social systems. These laws are inherently right or wrong in an objective sense. Further, this natural law is universal, rather than particular. These natural laws differ, for example, from some of the laws given to Old-Covenant Israel which were the property uniquely of the Jewish people and, in Christian understanding, are no longer applicable in the New Covenant. This natural law differs from revealed law in that it can be known by means of reason and conscience, rather than being solely known through Scripture. For Christian theologians like Thomas Aquinas and Martin Luther, this

---

[110] Bennet, "Locke's Theory of Tacit Consent."
[111] On the necessity of social bonds and community in a conservative perspective, see: Nisbet, *Quest for Community.*

natural law is quite broad in its scope, as it includes the Ten Commandments and many other moral imperatives.[112] This includes addressing open sacrilege, which both Aquinas and Luther argue should be suppressed by the state for the good of the commonwealth. In liberal political theory, the scope of natural law is significantly narrowed, often becoming synonymous merely with respecting the consenting will of others and ceasing from restricting someone else's liberty. Locke begins the move toward this latter view, though he himself is not as restrictive in his definition as many who come after him.

For Locke, God has granted man both rights and duties which are to be protected and enforced in the political social order.[113] This already demonstrates a significant departure from Hobbes's perspective, wherein it is right alone which creates the basis of civil society, rather than duties. For Locke then, both natural rights and natural laws serve as the basis for society. There is significant debate as to how these two pieces fit together. One interpretation contends for significant continuity between Locke and Hobbes, arguing that though he argues for the necessity of duties, Locke prioritizes rights as the primary ground for any political system. Other interpretations argue instead that there is significant continuity between Locke and the earlier Christian tradition which relies heavily on natural law as the basis for the state, with rights being a secondary consideration. Part of the problem here is that Locke himself never gives a clear explanation of exactly how rights and duties cohere, nor does he give a precise definition of natural law. This seeming tension in Locke's thought reflects the two major strains of political thought in the Western world: liberalism and conservatism. Liberals argue that the primary function of the state is the maximization of freedom through the protection of individual rights. The state is not to impose significant moral restraints upon citizens but exists merely to stop

---

[112] Baker, *Natural Law.*
[113] Locke, *Two Treatises,* 58-59.

citizens from infringing upon one another's rights. Conservatives, in contrast, believe in the importance of moral order and argue that, though the state should protect liberty, it also must place restraints around citizens in order to point them toward the moral life and assure the survival of a unified national culture.

It is important to identify which rights Locke refers to when he argues for the preservation of rights within the state. Already by using "rights" in plural form, Locke has moved beyond Grotius and Hobbes, who speak only of one central right to self-preservation. Locke's treatises do not contain extensive discussions about what constitutes a right or how many there are, but he does clearly identify at least three: life, liberty, and property. With regard to the first, Locke affirms that there is a right for people to preserve and protect their own lives, and a civil society must protect the lives of its citizens. The only difference on this point between Locke and Hobbes is that Locke is clearer that this is a divinely given right and is therefore inalienable. Liberty is a bit more difficult to define in Locke, as sometimes he appears to use the term as mere freedom from political constraint, while at other times it is apparent that Locke does not believe that humans should be free to commit any act of evil that they like as long as it does not infringe upon another's rights. There are rules of behavior that are proper, for Locke, which are found in the law of nature.[114] Government should respect its citizens' right to act freely, while also disallowing actions that will disrupt the social order. The third Lockean right is that of property. Here, Locke directly criticizes Filmer's view that all property belongs to kings, and that these kings merely allow their citizens to make use of them. Locke contends, instead, that when someone purchases a good, receives it as a gift, or inherits it, that good truly belongs to the human person who owns it. Therefore, everyone is entitled to their own property, and no one may take from that which belongs to someone else. It is

---

[114] Devine, "John Locke: The Harmony of Liberty & Virtue."

therefore the duty of the state to ensure that such property rights are respected.

WHEN RESISTANCE IS JUSTIFIED

This finally now brings us to the point where we can answer the question that led Locke to his *Two Treatises*: Can resistance to a political order be justified?[115] In order to understand Locke's response to this, we first need to grasp how important trust is for the political order. Any contract is based, to some degree, on trust. There must be some reason to think that the signing or making of a contract will actually result in the other party consistently following whatever duty this has bound them to. As mentioned earlier, Hobbes faced a problem here when he argued that society begins with a contract, but that people are inherently selfish. If this is so, why should it be the case that such selfish people would keep their end of a contract?

Locke is able to provide an answer to this question where Hobbes could not. The theme of trust is one of the most central in Locke's philosophical thought more generally—not just in relation to the social contract. While Hobbes views humans as primarily self-isolated creatures, Locke argues that trust is foundational to human existence. Without trusting other people, our lives would be impossible. Promises and bonds are made even within a state of nature, so they are more basic to human interaction and discourse than is the state. Here, Locke invokes a belief in God as a necessary underpinning for relationships built on trust. Atheism, he argues, provides no moral framework at all and thus would lead to the kind of dilemma posed above: Why would fundamentally self-interested individuals not simply break contracts if it is in their self-interest? With a belief in a transcendent God who has a moral order, there is reason for subjects to keep their word, because those promises are bound up in a transcendent order. For this reason, John Locke believed that civil society should not tolerate atheism.

---

[115] Locke, *Two Treatises*, 188-193.

A contractual social situation can only remain functional as long as trust is present. The moment that the civil magistrate begins to foment distrust by breaking the terms of the contract, there is no longer civil order.[116] The proper functioning of the magistrate is his keeping civil order between citizens and stopping war among the populace. When the magistrate begins to use his office merely to exercise power in his own self-interest, he creates a situation of war between him and the commonwealth. When this occurs, resistance to tyranny is justified, and its cause is not the populace, but the king who has created such a situation. Locke clarifies here that he is not speaking about any and every injustice of a ruler. To some degree, every ruler is unjust, and yet that does not validate rebellion in any and all situations. Locke refers to actions of the magistrate that would actively threaten the lives and liberty of the majority of the populace. For Locke, the initiation of the state of war is never justified, and thus citizens should never take the first step in doing so. This is why in a scenario where resistance is justified, it is the magistrate, not the people, who has created a state of war. In doing so, he has now given up his status as ruler and has in turn become a tyrant. The tyrant is not a real leader but a usurper, and it is just to resist him for that reason.

CONCLUSION

John Locke is the most important political philosopher to the formation of the liberal order which now shapes most Western democracies. Locke provides a political framework which protects the rights and freedoms of individuals, preserves the Christian undercurrent of civilization while providing a way out of inter-Christian war, and defends the necessity of natural law as grounding for the moral order of the state. Locke, however, leaves a lot of underlying tensions unresolved. What exactly is the natural law? How many moral duties are bound up in it, and how does this moral

---

[116] Ibid., 193-209.

law relate to God's nature? How many rights are there? How far does human freedom in the state go? How exactly is it determined that a ruler has become a tyrant? What does consent mean, and how do future generations relate to a contract their ancestors put together? Why is it that Christians have the freedom of toleration but other religions do not? Conservatives who follow in Locke's tradition (to some extent) like Edmund Burke and Friederick Julius Stahl argue for continuity with prior social structures and customs, as well as significant moral limitations on the kind of freedom that the state promotes and protects. Others, like Thomas Paine, take Locke's ideas in far more extreme directions.

THOMAS PAINE

Perhaps it seems odd to include a figure who was a politician and pamphleteer, rather than a scholar, in a work like this; he is the only figure included in this volume who is not an academic in the proper sense. The fact is that political movements do not rely only on the work of scholars (nor should they) but are often also driven by those writing popular works and engaging in activism. Thomas Paine certainly did both of those things—and more successfully than most. Even so, Paine was quite well-read and adept on his own, regardless of his lack of an academic position. We have here before us a figure who was quite prolific in his writings, most famously penning a book called *Common Sense*, and had a significant impact upon the American Revolution. What concerns us in this chapter is not so much that direct involvement in American politics, however, but Paine's conception of rights. In Paine we see the most extreme end of the liberal philosophy that relies on the foundational ideas of Grotius, Hobbes, and Locke. In Paine, tradition, social order, and custom are viewed with suspicion, and society is conceived of, not as an organic whole, but as a voluntary collection of autonomous beings. These things are not unique to Paine by any means, but he serves in this volume as representative of these broader conceptions that remain influential among many.

PAINE'S LIFE

Thomas Paine was born on February 9, 1737, in Norfolk, England.[117] His father was a corset maker and a farmer, having no noble title or significant wealth. Following his education at the Thetford Grammar School and a brief time as a privateer, Paine undertook an apprenticeship under his father and eventually opened his own shop where he made and sold corsets. He married Mary Lambert in 1759, who died in childbirth not long after. On top of the death of his wife and unborn child, Paine's business also fell apart. After this, Paine took other jobs, first as a supernumerary officer and then as an excise officer. It was in this second role that Paine's activism began. Paine was appointed to a position in Lewes, Sussex, where he joined the town's governing board; married his second wife, Elizabeth; and made connections with anti-monarchist activists. In 1772, Paine published his first political writing, which was a small pamphlet asking for better treatment for excise officers. This led to Paine losing his job and consequently separating from his wife. Paine then moved to London, where he would meet Benjamin Franklin and accept his offer to move to Pennsylvania.

After arriving in the New World, Thomas Paine became general editor of *Pennsylvania Magazine,* a widely read and highly influential publication that reached the working class and academics alike. Paine's most influential political work was his 1776 book *Common Sense,* which was widely circulated during the American Revolution as it provided extensive justification for the war by outlining the tyrannical actions of George III and calling for America to be a bastion of liberty in the world. The work is not particularly interesting as a text of political philosophy, but it is a masterpiece of persuasive rhetoric. Paine helped to gather funding for the

---

[117] Unger, *Thomas Paine and the Clarion Call for American Independence.*

Revolution and may have had a hand in writing the Declaration of Independence. His popular reputation among early American leaders took a significant hit when he wrote a pamphlet called *Public Good* in 1780, where he argued that the western lands of North America belonged to the US government rather than to individuals who laid claim to them (including Washington, Jefferson, and Madison). Paine's tarnished reputation led him to move to France, where he would eventually aid their revolutionary efforts.

Paine arrived in France with Col. John Laurens in March of 1781, where they would meet with the French king Louis XVI. During his time in France, Paine made connections with several influential people who would become leaders in the 1789 Revolution. After his brief tenure in Paris, Paine spent time back in his home in New Jersey, but he had lost most of his closest American friends and allies. For that reason, he traveled back and forth to both London and France, eventually deciding to devote himself to the French Revolution. For this cause, Paine took up his pen and offered a pointed critique of British parliamentarian Edmund Burke's 1790 book *Reflections on the Revolution in France*.[118] Burke's book has often been considered the foundational text for modern conservatism; Burke fights vehemently against revolution, prizing custom and social order. This was not because Burke believed that there were never justified circumstances for political resistance, as Burke was sympathetic to the American cause. The French Revolution, however, carried an important difference from the American Revolution (which Burke referred to as an English civil war rather than a revolution). The French revolutionaries did not desire continuity but believed in a complete overthrow of the current powers and a replacement of them to create a top-down utopia based on liberal principles. Burke predicted that this would create tyranny (and he was vindicated in this). Paine's response to Burke is found in his book

---

[118] Levin, *The Great Debate*.

Rights of Man, where Paine systematically lays out his view of rights and the authority of the state.

RIGHTS OF MAN

Edmund Burke argues that social bonds are multigenerational. Each person is born into a particular family and culture, which brings along with it unique social circles, bonds, and obligations. Therefore, something like a Lockean social contract is passed on from generation to generation. You are bound to the conditions of the state into which you are born and consequently are part of the continuance and further formation of that state. The social order is a kind of inheritance that each person receives by nature of their granted citizenship, and thus it should be treated with gratefulness and respect. For Burke, people are not to be defined merely as free agents (though they are free) who are self-determinate. Much of what we are is given to us, rather than self-made. This does not mean that the social order is static. It does and should change at times, especially when there are injustices—such as in the transatlantic slave trade. Changes that do occur should grow out of the culture, history, and heritage of a people, rather than through some top-down imposition of an ideal order as the French Revolution desired.

For Paine, Burke's ideas here are completely wrong. In Paine's view, there are no obligations that can be given or demanded from one generation to the next. He contends rather bluntly that "Every age and generation must be as free to act for itself, *in all cases*, as the ages and generations which preceded it."[119] The idea set forth by Burke, that continuity must be maintained from generation to generation, is dismissed by Paine as a kind of tyranny from the grave. There are two important assumptions here that undergird Paine's conviction. First, Paine views the past as a kind of straightjacket, holding us back from moving and acting freely. Like many in the Enlightenment era, Paine believes that humanity is increasingly

---

[119] Paine, *Rights of Man*, 17.

moving toward a free and rational existence; this requires a break from the Christian past, which is seen as a hindrance to progress, an era when superstition reigned supreme over reason. For the laws of a nation to be determined by prior generations is to be tied to backward social views. No longer are the older generations to be respected as purveyors of wisdom gained through their many life experiences, but rather they are to be dismissed as dying or dead generations whose backward ideals need not be carried forth into the future. The second assumption here is that people are purely autonomous and self-determinate. If people are by nature perfectly free, they cannot have any obligation or commitment which they did not explicitly choose. Consent becomes a moral norm—and to some degree the only moral norm.

Paine views the idea of inherited obligation as a kind of slavery. To say that a generation can determine laws or customs for a later generation is to claim ownership over others—to treat people as property. Paine's account of the social order is quite simplistic, as he categorizes everything either as an autonomous, freely acting agent or as property. To be a free agent, for Paine, is to have no obligations other than those which are self-chosen. A free agent is able to obtain, create, and sell property freely because property is not personal. To demand loyalty from future generations is to take away free agency and thereby to deny personhood and categorize people as property.

The dead, for Paine, have no rights, nor any claim to the world which comes after them. They should therefore be of no concern regarding the way any current generation chooses to live. Paine refers to the idea of generational obligations as the creation of a "political Adam," whereby through the creation of any new form of governance, all generations are necessarily bound to a contractual arrangement in which they never had any involvement.[120] This is a reference to the Christian doctrine of original sin, particularly in its Reformed variation within federal theology. In Reformed federal

---

[120] Ibid., 19.

theology (which was prominent among the Puritans) it is taught that God made a covenant with Adam, the first man.[121] He served as a federal head, representing the entire human race. Whatever Adam chose to do, whether keeping God's covenantal obligations through obedience or disobeying those obligations and being severed from covenantal blessings, would impact not only him but also his posterity. All future generations are bound by the decisions of Adam in Eden. Paine's reference to this is significant because it identifies something that is essential to the Christian view of human generations. There is a universal human bond among all people, and this bond can and does lead to blessings, curses, or obligations from generation to generation. Though people are, to some degree, free agents, they are also bound by innumerable factors, such as their social roles, family line, and political context. As is made clearer in Paine's later writing against the Christian religion, his form of liberalism cannot coexist with traditional Christian doctrine.

With this dismissal of inherited custom and law, the question now arises as to exactly how the nature of governments is to be determined for Paine. In response to Burke's critiques of the revolutionaries in France, Paine argues that they followed something far better than mere reforms for gradual improvements to a preexisting system set up by the dead: reason. Government in civil society arises, for Paine, through the "contemplation of the rights of man" using unaided human reason.[122] Rather than the state arising through the culture of a people, the state is instead the creation of political theorists who then impose these ideals onto the populace. There is a strong trust here of the power of human reason. This view believes that rational thought experiments and theorizing are capable of determining the ideals, function, and structure of the state better than the inherited practical wisdom and forms of political order which developed through centuries. Politics is at its core a

---

[121] Hildebrand, *Reformed Covenant Theology*.
[122] Paine, *Rights of Man*, 23.

rational, theoretical enterprise that is then implemented through political activism.

Paine, like other liberals who share his ideals, follows the rationalist strain of modern philosophy. Just as Descartes believed that he could come to an indisputable ground of knowledge through reason alone, the French revolutionaries believed that they could create a just and flourishing state through the rational contemplation of rights and principles. The ideal state was then to be imposed by means of revolution and the imposition of power against anything that threatened this ideal order. Conservatives like Edmund Burke were skeptical about the abilities of human reason. They tended to be empiricists, believing that the political order was never as simple as the imposition of principles onto a nation through power. Instead, governments develop and change through the many experiences of a nation, its people, and its politicians. Governments are simply never going to conform to some absolute ideal, and attempts to make them do that inevitably lead to tyranny. Instead, the Burkean contends, it is prudence that guides the shape of the political order. This does not mean that there are no ideals of course, but it acknowledges that they will never be fully realized in human society.[123] Paine's dependence on reason raises the question of what exactly these rational ideals are which society must implement.

The fundamental element of civic society, for Paine, is the equality of humankind. All rational formation of the ideal state must arise out of this singular conviction. What he means by equality is more than equality of value or dignity, but absolute social egalitarianism. Paine is adamant that any hierarchical form of social order (such as an aristocracy) is an affront to this principle of equality. Further, it is this principle which stands behind Paine's

---

[123] This depends on the Christian conviction that the human world is one of sin and that only at the eschaton will evil be finally and fully defeated. Until that time, humans must do the best they can with a world that is an amalgamation of both good and evil.

rejection of generational obligation.[124] Equality must be applicable, not only to contemporaries across a society, but also to different generations. This means, in a contemporary application, that Thomas Jefferson or George Washington should have no more say about the shape of the United States government than those living today. In fact, their views should have far *less* influence as a dead generation. Paine does attempt to root his view of equality theologically, arguing that there is a fundamental unity of the human race which arises through the direct granting of life and freedoms by God at the moment of an individual's birth.[125] Though it is clear that Paine is no orthodox Christian, he attempts to show his point through the creation account of Genesis 1-3, which makes no mention of differences among men. This proves, in his view, that rights are to be applied equally to all. But what exactly are those rights?

Paine divides rights into two categories: natural rights and civil rights. The first category identifies those rights which man has related to his own independent existence. These are those that are necessary for self-determination. This includes rights of mind, body, and the pursuit of personal happiness. Essentially, this is the right of someone to do as he pleases so long as he does not infringe upon this principle of self-determination for another person. Civil rights, in contrast, refer to those rights than each man has in relation to broader society. These civil rights are all rooted in the more fundamental natural rights. When people come together to form a society, some of these natural rights are granted to the state and become civil rights. Paine gives the example of judgment. While an individual has the natural right to make a judgment about another person's actions, he or she has no ability to carry out that judgment. When each person takes their own natural right of judgment and places it into the common realm of civil society, the natural right is

---

[124] Paine, *Rights of Man*, 38.
[125] Paine, *Rights of Man*, 38.

replaced by a civil right in which judgments are not only made but are also enacted. In other words, for Paine, there is no giving up of rights in society at all, but instead, civil society under the social contract makes man and woman even more free.[126]

Paine draws the roots of this civil society out of the actual historical existence of a state of nature. As he sees this state, each man was sovereign, autonomous, and self-determined. Human life was, by nature, independent rather than communal. As this self-determined autonomy is the very essence of human life, it is also the only principle by which any government is legitimate. Proper governmental authority, for Paine, always arises from a constitution. A constitution is not a government document but is an agreement of individuals which creates the only legitimate basis for state power.[127] In this constituted state, Paine argues, there should be no promotion of religion by state power. In addressing the perpetual problem of religious war in post-Reformation Europe, Paine contends that all religions are basically the same, as the essence of religion is the adoration of the divine.[128] If that is the case, there is no need to squabble about theological debates. The heart of this is in Paine's unwavering commitment to reason alone. If religious commitments cannot be determined by reason (in the sense that Paine is defining it), then they have no place within the civil order—which is purely a rational enterprise.

CONCLUSION

Thomas Paine shows many of the weaknesses, and unresolved tensions, within the liberal project as a whole. This is not to say that there is nothing positive to be gained from Hobbes or Locke (albeit far more from the latter), but that, like the development of nearly any idea in human history, there are some paths it can take that are more

---

[126] Ibid., 40.
[127] Ibid., 42.
[128] Ibid., 55.

societally destructive than politically beneficial. The first of these is the nature of liberty. A recognition of self-determination is necessary within any state system if it is to avoid tyranny. However, Enlightenment thinkers generally overestimate how much of life is really freely chosen. Many factors in human life which might be considered (by us at least) to be the result of autonomous choice are simply not so. There are limiting factors to our choices that cannot be eliminated, such as our upbringing, genetic limitations, dispositions, opportunity, familial and social connections, financial status, etc. While liberal societies have generally created better social mobility where such factors do not determine one's life in an absolute sense, they simply cannot be entirely erased.

A further problem is the move toward viewing freedom as not simply freedom from tyranny, but freedom to do whatever one pleases.[129] Locke does not do this, but the French revolutionaries clearly do. This coincides with the loss of the view of liberty found in classical Greek and Christian sources, in which true liberty is found in the life of virtue. The passions (i.e. base desires) enslave us, as they stop us from acting in accord with reason, and tie us to patterns of behavior that we often do not actually want to engage in (addiction, for example). True freedom is having control over these desires and living in such a way that we are formed as virtuous citizens. The loss of this classical understanding among many liberals also leads to either the neglect of the duties which must accompany rights or the flattening out of duties into a singular category: the duty to preserve the rights of others (which is what Paine does).

The concept of rights itself continues to grow among liberals. With Grotius and Hobbes, there was one singular right to self-preservation. This right to life was expanded by Locke into further rights of property and liberty. With the *Declaration of the Rights of Man*,

---

[129] Patrick Deneen's argument contends that there was a move from a classical approach to liberty which is based on self-restraint and virtue to a modern liberal one which is based on nothing more than freedom from constraints (moral or otherwise).

the French revolutionaries argued for a more absolute definition of rights, such that natural rights included nearly every free action of man which did not directly infringe upon the rights of others. This continual expansion of rights poses two significant problems. First, rights have become entitlements. To say that I have a right to something is often synonymous with "I am entitled to" whatever that thing might be, with no corresponding duty to accompany these rights. Second, rights are often not argued for but merely asserted. The language of rights being grounded in facts that are self-evident has been used as an excuse to declare some kind of right as a basis for law and morality without any further moral, legal, or rational justification for doing so.

Finally, liberal political philosophy tends to praise resistance and rebellion and view the past with resentment. The problems here are, I think, in Locke's inability to make a clear case as to when political leaders are in breach of a social contract and enact a state of war in which rebellion is justified. Earlier Protestant writing on political resistance, such as in the Magdeburg Confession, is quite narrow in its view of situations in which such resistance is justified. Further, these older ideas of resistance do not grant ordinary citizenry the freedom to act on their own to bring about a new order whenever they determine that a breach of contract has occurred. (The orthodox Lutheran and Reformed theologians had no notion of a social contract at all and rejected such an idea when it was proposed.[130]) They argued instead that active resistance is the duty of lesser magistrates, who had established, called positions of authority by which they could resist tyranny for the wellbeing of their people. In the liberal tradition, there is an almost constant skepticism toward authority, such that power can be viewed as an evil in itself, rather

---

[130] Luthardt, for example, says that "No state was ever produced by the mere resolve of the will and by compact. And we may thank God that compact is not a foundation of the State, for we know well what compacts are worth. The State has a firmer basis. It was not created by the free resolves of the will, for a people living in a lawless and irregular manner has no inclination for order." Luthardt, *Moral Truths*, 177.

than only the abuse of power being evil. In some cases, this leads to a push against any and all hierarchical societal structures, with the goal of creating an absolutely egalitarian form of life.

My purpose here is not to say that everything about the liberal political order should be rejected. Plenty of conservative voices within the liberal tradition pushed back against each of these tendencies while retaining the best of Locke's ideas. Edmund Burke defended hierarchies, tradition, and custom, while also affirming man as a free being and pushing for limitations upon government overreach. James Fennimore Cooper praised the opportunities and social mobility brought about by the constitutional order of the United States, while also promoting a kind of neo-aristocracy through his idea of the gentleman. The German theorist Friedrich Julius Stahl put together the most comprehensive and consistent political philosophy among conservatives, which defends constitutional limited government and the protection of rights within a social order that is bound together by a common good bound up in God's world order. More recent thinkers like Russell Kirk and Roger Scruton did the same in the twentieth century. The point I want to get across here is that many of the ideologies discussed throughout this book are rooted in some of these unresolved tensions within political liberalism itself rather than being total departures from classical liberal thought, as if Karl Marx's revolutionary ideas arose from nowhere.

HISTORICISM IN GERMANY: G. W. F. HEGEL AND KARL MARX

arl Marx is among the most influential—and most criticized—political philosophers in history. Unlike the majority of the intellects in this field of study, Marx's name is known far outside of the bounds of the academy. Among both non-scholars and academics, alternate perspectives on Marx present contradictory pictures of the man and his system. For some he is a hero, for others, a villain. His system is viewed by many on the left as a devastating critique of the capitalist systems which developed in the early modern West.[131] Alternatively, on the right, Marxist regimes are often seen as instruments of suffering and oppression, being the cause of more deaths than any other political system in human history.[132] However one evaluates the arguments that he makes or the governments that have arisen as a result of his ideas, Marx's importance is undeniable, as is his centrality to any study of contemporary political thought.

Like any thinker, Marx must be viewed in the context of his own social, economic, and intellectual environment—in his case, nineteenth-century Europe. At that time, there were growing ideas of utopian social progress, as well as an increased belief that modern economic systems had, to some extent, resulted in social inequalities that harmed those in the lower class.[133] Further, the kind of

---

[131] Such as: Eagleton, *Why Marx Was Right*.

[132] As an example, see: Kengor, *The Devil and Karl Marx*.

[133] Manuel, *Utopian Thought in the Western World*. This book shows the importance and prominence of utopian themes in the modern world well before the rise of their Marxist proponents. To be fair, Marx and Engels themselves never considered their ideas explicitly utopian, though critics of their system remain convinced that, at least to some extent, it is.

revolutionary fervor that drove the American and French revolutions still remained throughout much of Europe, as was evident in the German revolutions in 1848.[134] Amid these political conditions, Marx was highly influenced by the philosophical move toward the study of history. These ideas are set forth most clearly in G. W. F. Hegel. This German philosopher proposed a philosophical system that contained a thorough explanation of nature, art, ethics, knowledge, and nearly every other basic aspect of human thought. Kant is the only true rival to Hegel in the modern world in the creation of such a comprehensive intellectual system. Unlike Marx, Hegel is not a self-identified leftist thinker, and he is often viewed as a conservative in some important ways. Following Hegel's death, his students divided into right-wing and left-wing groups dependent upon their interpretation and application of the ideas of their teacher. For conservatives, Hegel had reintroduced metaphysics and religion into philosophy in a serious way, thus leading to a rejection of some fundamental principles of the Enlightenment project. Further, Hegel understood that governments are the products of history and culture, rather than rationally constituted thought experiments to be imposed upon a populace. Leftist thinkers, like Marx, saw in Hegel's idea of historical development a basis for human progress and revolution.

This chapter begins with a discussion of Hegel's ideas as set forth in his monumental work *The Phenomenology of Spirit* and then consequently explores Karl Marx's revolutionary ideas in light of his Hegelian commitments.

G. W. F. HEGEL

Georg Wilhelm Friedrich Hegel was born in 1770 in Stuttgart, Württemberg, in southwestern Germany, to a middle-class Lutheran family.[135] He faced a number of difficulties in his early life, including the death of his mother when Hegel was only thirteen through a

---

[134] German Bundestag, "Revolution and the National Assembly."
[135] Pinkard, *Hegel: A Biography.*

sudden illness—which he also contracted and barely survived. Hegel's education included both classics (with an intensive study of Latin) and the great works of the Enlightenment thinkers who retained a stronghold in the academy in his day. In his teenage years, Hegel desired to join the Lutheran clergy, and in pursuit of ordination he attended the University of Tübingen to study theology. At this time, Tübingen had moved away from traditional Lutheran orthodoxy and had become a center for Enlightenment rationalism.[136] During this period at the university, Hegel encountered the writings of the French author Jean-Jacques Rousseau and the popular critic of traditional religion, Gotthold Ephraim Lessing.

Through his reading and conversations with fellow students—including the well-known German idealist Friedrich Schelling—Hegel's interests shifted from the discipline of theology to that of philosophy. Though he completed a theological degree and published some theological writings early in his career, he moved gradually into the field of philosophy in both his writing and lectures.[137] After graduation, Hegel worked for a time as a tutor and was eventually offered a position as a lecturer at the University of Jena, where he would lecture on metaphysics and other related topics.

Hegel released his magnum opus, *The Phenomenology of Spirit*, in 1807. The attention received from this work led to a number of offers to teach from other schools. In 1816 Hegel accepted a teaching

---

[136] The German theological academy was more clearly divided a few decades following Hegel's education into those who followed the critical approaches of Protestant liberalism (Tübingen being the center of much of it) and those who were called neo-Lutherans—including Hegel's successor at the University of Berlin, Friedrich Julius Stahl. These neo-Lutherans were committed to the theological claims of older Lutheran orthodoxy and to the divine inspiration of the texts of the Old and New Testaments. Many of these orthodox theologians taught at the University of Erlangen.

[137] Hegel, *Early Theological Writings*.

position as professor of philosophy at the University of Berlin, filling the previous position of Johan Gottlieb Fichte (another well-known German idealist philosopher). He remained in his position there as chair of philosophy until his death from cholera in 1831. Along with pursuing his philosophical career, Hegel married in 1811. He had two sons with his wife, Marie Helena Susanna, as well as an older third son from a prior relationship.

INFLUENCES ON HEGEL'S THOUGHT

Though Hegel would depart significantly from earlier Enlightenment philosophers (particularly with his reinvigoration of metaphysics), his formative influences were largely Enlightenment thinkers. The most significant of those was Immanuel Kant. It was Kant who had set forth the problems and questions that Hegel's system attempted to answer, as was the case for most philosophers (and theologians) of Hegel's time. The points of overlap between Kant and Hegel, both in their ideological conclusions and their methodologies, are numerous enough to be the subject of many dissertations and articles, so they cannot possibly all be covered here. I have limited myself to three of the most significant points in which Kant's writings impact the Hegelian project.

The first area of Kant's influence upon Hegel is in the emphasis on and interconnectivity between freedom and reason. In the earliest modern thinkers, such as Descartes and Charron, the universe was seen as a mere machine with a set of fixed laws that functioned like a physical mechanism one might use in a factory. This approach to the universe, if applied to humanity, left little to no room for freedom of action or will. While Descartes saw freedom in the internal life of the mind or soul, he was never able to compellingly demonstrate a connection between the thoughts of the mind and the actions of the body. Many scientists simply had no place for the freedom of the will at all, believing instead that humans were mechanistically determined like all other physical objects in the universe.[138] In response to these challenges, Kant, the early liberal philosophers, and the romantics all sought various ways to reemploy concepts of freedom that were consistent with the beliefs of modernity. Hegel continued this trajectory toward an emphasis on freedom. Unlike some of the liberals, Hegel did not conceptualize liberty in an individualistic sense, but instead grounded freedom in the underlying World Spirit. Further, this freedom, for Hegel like for Kant, is intimately related to rationality. There is an interconnectedness between freedom and reason such that, for both Kant and Hegel, to be more free is to be more rational. Similarly, to be more rational is to be more free.

The second major point of contact between Kant and Hegel is in their theorizing about the relationship between subject and object. The question "How does the individual subject relate to the world of objects?" is, in some ways, the one that drives Kantian philosophy more than any other. These questions arise in modern philosophy as a result of Descartes's isolation of the subject as an internal soul, distinct from the materiality of the world of objects which are determined by mechanical laws. As discussed earlier, David Hume questioned the reality of both subjects and objects by placing everything under the category of "impressions." Kant acknowledged the reality of both subject and object, but doubted whether subjects have access to objects as they are in themselves apart from their impact upon sensory experience. In response to these challenges, Hegel denied that there was such a strong divide between subject and object as these earlier thinkers believed, arguing instead that all things are united by one singular spirit.

The final point to mention here regarding Kant's impact upon Hegel's thought is in Kant's political philosophy (an idea not covered in the overview of Kant above). Kant has a universalized

---

[138] This approach that sees the mind as reducible to physical properties alone remains a popular one among some philosophers of mind in more recent years. Paul and Patricia Churchland along with Daniel Dennett are prominent examples.

notion of national interaction that sets the groundwork for an understanding of *nations* as subjects, rather than only seeing *individuals* as subjects.[139] While social contract theorists argued that each given society is a collective of individual subjects who come together with a set of agreed upon restrictions and rules for the sake of peace, Kant contended that the same could be done among nations. He proposed that nations themselves could be viewed as subjects that then make contracts with each other for the sake of global peace. This concept, which laid the groundwork for the United Nations, led to a conception of the subject as a collective, which was more fully realized in Hegel than in Kant's own thought.

Another philosopher who influenced the ideas of Hegel was his predecessor at Berlin, Johann Fichte (1762-1814).[140] While Kant distinguished between the phenomena and noumena with the assumption that the noumenal actually existed, even if inaccessible to human subjects, Fichte questioned whether there really was a "thing-in-itself" at all. If Kant was right that the human subject was unable to learn anything definitive about the noumena, why must we confess that it exists? Convinced that Kant's reasons for belief in the noumena were insufficient, Fichte discarded the notion altogether. Following this conviction that there is no thing-in-itself, Fichte concludes that there is also no subject-in-itself. Like Hume, Fichte argues that the idea of the self is mere phenomena. Fichte does not, however, revert to pure Humean skepticism, but instead argues for a kind of objectivity and universality in phenomena. While he rejects the notion of an individual, atomized self, Fichte contends that there is an "absolute ego," which is universal and thus underlies all reality. Reality is, therefore, to be sought in the universal rather than in the particular. This idea of an absolute ego is one of the primary influences upon Hegel's conception of the World Spirit.

---

[139] Kant, "Perpetual Peace," in *Political Writings*, 93-130.
[140] Fichte, *Foundation of the Wissenschaftlehre*.

A final influence to mention here is Hegel's friend Friedrich Schelling (1775-1854).[141] Though not nearly as well-known as Hegel, Schelling's philosophical innovations were essential for the development of the German idealism of *The Phenomenology of Spirit.* Like Fichte, Schelling addresses the subject-object divide that dominated Kantian thought. In his attempt to bridge the gap between the human subject and the noumena, Schelling argues that there is no individual subject who is totally cut off from the real objects that exist outside of him. He proposes, therefore, that there is an "absolute identity" which includes both subjects and objects. Thus man is not isolated from the world, but rather both man and world are part of the same underlying fundamental reality. History, however, does not appear as some undifferentiated, singular monad, and thus Schelling has to account for the existence of difference and change in the world from within this unifying reality. In doing so, Schelling proposes what is now often known as the Hegelian dialectic. This unified reality of absolute identity contains both affirmation and negation within itself, and it is moving continually toward a process of synthesis. This idea is often summarized by the popular distinction between thesis, antithesis, and synthesis (though popularly attributed to him, that language is never used in Hegel).

Before exploring Hegel's ideas, let me define the term "German idealism" (which has already appeared in this chapter). Idealists, in short, are those who believe that ideas are the ultimate reality, rather than the physical world. Plato, for example, is an idealist in a classical sense, since he believes that all particular material things in the world are only reflections of the greater and more universal ideas in which they participate. The phrase "German idealist" refers to the newer form of idealism that arose in Germany during the late Enlightenment era from Kant through Hegel. Kant was an idealist for his belief in the supremacy of *a priori* judgments and universal principles over against sense experience. Hegel and

---

[141] See: Bowie, *Schelling and Modern European Philosophy.*

Schelling were idealists in their belief in the universal progress of ideas through the development of the World Spirit.

HEGEL'S METAPHYSICS

With this historical and ideological background in view, we can examine Hegel's own ideas. Though his contributions to philosophy are many, one of the most important is his reintegration of the discipline of metaphysics into philosophical discourse. Within the skeptical rationalism that drove early modernity, ideas of being were considered relatively unimportant compared to the discipline of epistemology. Hegel sought to end the constant doubt about the nature of reality that had reigned since Pierre Charron by proposing a new form of ontological realism. This was done, not through a reintegration of Platonic or Aristotelian ideals, but through the creation of a metaphysical system in which becoming has a primacy over being.

There are two necessary distinctions to be made in order to explain Hegel's system. The first is between the natural world and the Geist.[142] The natural world is, as one might guess, the sphere of natural physical objects and processes. This natural world is governed by scientific laws and is therefore subject to experimentation and study. Like the Enlightenment thinkers who preceded him, Hegel was a proponent of Newtonian physics and the various new scientific developments of his day. Hegel recognized the philosophical problems that these new sciences raised—especially the issue of human freedom. Human decisions are not truly free if they are mechanistically governed by material processes and scientific laws alone. This not only impacts questions of purpose, or teleology, in one's personal life, but also has significant implications

---

[142] The relationship between spirit and nature is developed in Hegel's *Encyclopaedia of the Philosophical Sciences*. For Hegel, these two elements are not bifurcated, as he rejects all forms of dualism, but do remain conceptually distinct. The spirit, for Hegel, both precedes nature and completes nature, such that the natural world is not a mere self-existent, non-purposive machine.

for history as a whole. A pure material scientism has no understanding of purpose in history (a point in which some modernist scientists diverged far from the Christian conception of history as the outworking of divine purpose). Hegel sought to address these issues with a contention that there is both freedom and purpose in the workings of the universe. It is with this in view that he explains his idea of the Geist.[143]

The German word *Geist* is, unfortunately for English readers, not easily translated. In English editions of Hegel's works, it is most often rendered either as "World Spirit" or as "World Soul." These terms attempt to communicate the primary idea Hegel is promoting—that there is a unifying reality underneath nature that is not exclusively physical. This Geist is different from the Cartesian isolated, individual soul; Hegel is speaking about something far more universal. Because of his theological training, Hegel does use Christian theological language to speak about this Geist as Spirit, but the way in which dogmatic terms are used is generally not in the same sense that classical Christian orthodoxy uses them. Nonetheless, Hegel retains several distinctively Christian convictions, such as his insistence that ultimate reality is not merely physical and that there is purpose in historical events, both individually and collectively. It is for this reason that Hegel's influence on German theology is quite significant.[144]

Traditional Christian theology contends that God is immutable, meaning that he is, in both his essence and his purpose, unchanging. History, in contrast to the divine nature, is in a constant process of change. In biblical history, there is a temporal movement from creation to the Fall to redemption, and finally to the consummation of all things at the eschaton. God does not stand

---

[143] "It is this final goal—freedom—toward which all the world's history has been working." Hegel, *Philosophy of History*, 22.

[144] For an overview of this Hegelian turn in theology, see: Livingston, *Modern Christian Thought*, 143-171.

totally apart from history but is intimately involved in it providentially. Nevertheless, God and world history remain distinct. For Hegel, there is no unchanging God as a being who stands outside of history; there is instead Geist that *is* history.[145] For Hegel, this World Spirit is in a continual process of becoming, which occurs through its own self-realization.

This is where the second important philosophical distinction for Hegel must be mentioned: the difference between being and becoming. The classical realist tradition, best exemplified by the Platonists, privileges being over becoming. For Platonists, that which is unchanging and universal is superior to that which is changing and particular, as demonstrated through the concept of the forms. Early and medieval Christian theologians adopted these Platonic contentions and similarly affirmed the superiority of the changeless by arguing that God is distinct from the changing world.[146] Though deeply involved in the world, God remains a transcendent being who stands above the world, unaffected by the changes that occur within it. Hegel challenges this Platonic-Christian consensus.

It is to be noted that Hegel is far from the first person to privilege becoming over being. Such views existed among some ancient Greek philosophers—though not in the Platonic traditions. Most well-known, as discussed in the first chapter, is Heraclitus who made the argument that the universe is more change than it is constancy with the example of the ever-flowing river. Permanence, for Heraclitus, is an illusion; reality is change. The views of Heraclitus share another point of contact with Hegel: monism. For Heraclitus, though individual things change, there is a constant reality that underlies and unites the changing world. He believed this to be the element of fire. This element is constantly changing its structure and shape, though still remaining in some sense the same fire. Heraclitus does not only mean the physical element of fire here, as he also

---

[145] For more on this see my book: Cooper, *The Doctrine of God*.
[146] Markos, *From Plato to Christ*.

identifies this fire with Zeus. In other words, God is a singular reality that unites all things, and though he remains constant, he also changes as the world does. Hegel (as Heraclitus certainly would) denies the Kantian view that reality is made up of concrete particulars. Instead, all is one in the *Geist*.

Despite these similarities between Heraclitus and Hegel, they differ on the issue of teleology. The ancient Greeks generally believed history to be eternal and cyclical, rather than progressive. It is Christianity (along with Judaism) that introduced the idea of history as moving ahead toward some kind of end goal. For Hegel, history does not change arbitrarily in the way that a fire or a river changes from moment to moment, but rather it develops through a series of historical epochs that build upon one another. This progressive view of history is often referred to as historicism. History is the unfolding of the Geist in its own self-development. Hegel believed that various historical periods could be examined from this perspective, and that through such an examination one would be able to determine the place and ideas of the Geist in any given age. As an example of this, Hegel was preparing to publish his *Phenomenology of Spirit* as Napoleon and his army entered the city of Jena where Hegel was teaching. Writing of this event later, Hegel referenced Napoleon as the personal embodiment of the Geist.[147] In other words, the World Spirit was showing itself at that moment through this particular individual's political campaign.

This historicist view of idealism contends that one should not try to construct abstract, isolated truths apart from historical events. There is no eternal law of morality, for example, that one can speak of apart from the development of historical ages in which moral norms are constructed and developed. This view strongly distinguishes itself from the kind of Enlightenment liberalism, which contends that there are a number of objective, unchanging

---

[147] From Hegel's Letter to Neithammer (October 13, 1806), in *Hegel: The Letters*.

truths that can be determined by means of reason alone.[148] Moral truths must be understood in light of their epoch—Hegel uses this term to describe various ages within the historical process.[149] If, for example, the historian is to study the morals in ancient Greece, that work must be done through the examination of the culture and context of Greece, rather than through an abstract rational evaluation of whether or not those ethical norms are correct according to some universal, unchanging standard of moral obligation.

THE DIALECTIC

As mentioned above, the historicist dialectic is not unique to Hegel's philosophy, as it was first proposed by Schelling. Nonetheless, it is Hegel, rather than Schelling, who is most commonly associated with dialectical thought—following generations never took up the title "Schellingians" to describe their philosophical systems but instead called themselves "Hegelians." It was Hegel who argued for the approach in its most compelling form. Despite the centrality of dialectical thinking in Hegel, and in the traditions that follow him, there remains significant debate surrounding Hegel's use of the dialectical method. This is why there are a variety of contradictory approaches that fall under the broader Hegelian label. The overview here does not delve deeply into divergences in interpretation of Hegel which arose soon after Hegel's writing was published—and still remain in scholarly discourse—but covers the more undisputed aspects of Hegel's dialectical method.

Hegel's dialectic addresses the issue of relationality. Like many earlier philosophers, Hegel asks the questions, "How is it that

---

[148] Hegel interacts with Lessing here who famously created what is known as "Lessing's ditch." Essentially, Lessing argues that all historical claims are uncertain, and that it is therefore only the abstract truths of reason which can be relied upon as measures of objective fact.

[149] Hegel speaks of "epochs" in multiple works, such as his *Philosophy of History* and *Philosophy of Right* (though abbreviated here).

individual particular objects that are fundamentally different in essence and function relate to one another and share within the same basic reality?" and "Do relations between things change the constitution or essence of things?"[150] Attempts to answer these questions have been part of philosophical discourse from its Greek inceptions. Aristotle, for example, argued that relations between things of different essences are accidental properties rather than essential ones.[151] This means that a thing is what it is (its essence) independent of its relation to something else. Nonetheless, relations are not merely incidental or unimportant, as two distinct things being in relation to one another can often change those things (though these changes are accidental rather than substantial). As an example, think of the relationship between iron and a fire that heats it. These two objects have completely different essences. Nonetheless, when they are in relation to one another, they affect one another. When iron gets hot enough through its exposure to fire, the iron's properties change. It takes on qualities of fire, like heat and light. The iron does not *become* fire, however, but retains its essence as iron.

Aristotle furthers this explanation of accidental relations by contending that relations can actualize potentialities within persons or things.[152] Iron, as a material, has the potentiality to become hot and malleable. Fire actualizes this potentiality by causing the iron to become hot and malleable. This is true of people as well. I, for example, have all sorts of potentialities which would never have been actualized if I had not gotten married. My potentiality to be a father has, for instance, been actualized through my wife's giving birth to our children. In Aristotle's model, a person or object can experience genuine and consistent change through relationships. Hume's denial

---

[150] "The relation between subject and object, inner and outer, self and world, is, [Hegel] believes, entirely mysterious, unless we recognize that we are dealing with a division within thought (or spirit) itself." Scruton, *Modern Philosophy*, 153.

[151] Aristotle, *Metaphysics* V.15, 1021a29–1022a14.

[152] Aristotle, *Metaphysics* IX.1–9, 1045b35–1051b24

of Aristotle's distinction between act and potency made it difficult for philosophers to explain how objects are capable of changing one another.

Hegel responds to this consistent problem in post-Humean philosophy by arguing that relations are not merely external to objects. Instead, for Hegel, relations are essential to a thing's identity.[153] Hegel goes beyond Aristotle here with his contention that relations actually constitute reality. Relations are essential properties rather than accidental ones. Hegel's argument arises from his monistic metaphysic in which all things are one within the World Spirit. If all things exist within the World Spirit, then relations are internal to this World Spirit. Relations are not merely separable, distinct, atomized objects bumping into one another. This all fits consistently when one is speaking about objects that are aligned with one another, one might contend, but this does not seem to explain tensions or oppositions between things. Can reality be constituted by relations of contradiction? Hegel answers in the affirmative—this is essential to the nature of the dialectical process.[154]

---

[153] "This self-equal essence relates itself only to itself. It relates itself *to itself* so that there is an other essence to which the relation directs itself, and the relating *to itself* is in fact [the act of] *estranging*, or it is that very self-equality which is inner difference." Hegel, *Phenomenology of Spirit*, 98 (par. 162/100).

[154] There is a paradoxical relation here for Hegel between contrast and unity. He says, for example, that "this coming-to-be-equal is likewise immediately an estrangement, for it is only as a result of that estrangement that the understanding sublates the differences and posits the One of force by means of making a new difference between force and law, but which is at the same time no difference at all." Ibid., 99 (par. 101/163). It is precisely within self-differentiation that unity is found. As an example of this, Hegel speaks of self-consciousness, whereby the thinker differentiates between himself as subject (the one who is thinking) and object (one who is being thought about). Yet, amid this self-differentiation, there is undoubtedly a single self that is forming such a differentiation only as part of the pattern of thought, though no distinction exists in reality. For Hegel, this is true not only of *self-consciousness*, but also of the consciousness of *any* object whatsoever, since all are one.

There are many tensions within the world for Hegel. And yet, Hegel believes that these tensions are inevitably to be overcome through the self-realization of the Absolute. Hegel's dialectic is often presented—on a popular level—in the following way: In history, some kind of *thesis* is presented. There is, after this, some kind of inevitable pushback against this, which is called the *antithesis*. These opposite ideas then come together to form some kind of *synthesis*. Some have summarized this by claiming that for Hegel, the truth is always somewhere in the middle. Though this reflects elements of Hegel's ideas, it is, as a whole, an insufficient explanation of Hegel's dialectical process. For Hegel, the thesis and the antithesis are not totally separate ideas that exist externally to one another that are then merged into some third reality. Instead, for Hegel, there is the one Geist that contains the tensions of thesis and antithesis within itself. Out of these tensions flows a process of synthesis or resolution in history as the visible self-actualization of Spirit.[155]

The Spirit, for Hegel, comes to know itself through growth in both rationality and freedom. The emphasis on these two elements of the Spirit reflects Kant here. For Hegel, the world is in the process of becoming more rational and more free through continued societal progress. As part of this process of development, Hegel viewed his own writing as the culmination of all philosophical thinking up to his own time. In his estimation, Hegel had proposed the most rational system yet written that, he believed, sufficiently answered the most essential questions about the nature of the universe. It is important to place Hegel in the context of an age in which Europeans were highly optimistic about the future of human civilization, and in which there were growing hopes about the possibility of an earthly

---

[155] Scruton provides a better summary of the trifold Hegelian dialectic than is popularly repeated, as three "moments" in the dialectic. In the first, a concept is applied abstractly. Second, that abstraction can only be understood as it is mediated by rival conceptions, and it is thus set in opposition to these. Third, this conflict is resolved by means of a transcendental synthesis through the intellect. Scruton, *Modern Philosophy*, 151.

utopia. Such optimism would last throughout the nineteenth century, only to be challenged after the outbreak of the First World War in the following century. Nonetheless, in Hegel's belief, the following years would continue in movement toward greater freedom and rationality.

DIALECTIC AND HISTORY

In his *Lectures on the Philosophy of History*, Hegel presents a history of civilization within his proposed dialectical framework.[156] Hegel divides history into clearly defined epochs which each have their own unique set of beliefs, morals, and events. While making clear divisions in historiography is necessarily an imprecise process and will generalize to some degree, nearly every historian does this to some extent. We refer to the eras of the Late Middle Ages, Renaissance, and Reformation, which are all, in reality, quite intertwined and nearly impossible to divide neatly. To provide any coherent picture of history at all, generalization is a necessity. Further, the availability of historical documents, and of historical research in general, was significantly different in the early nineteenth century than it is today. Hegel works within rather limited parameters in his portrayal of history.

So how exactly does Hegel approach the study of these various epochs? When providing a survey of history in any era, historians can choose from a variety of approaches. The focus could be on the great men and women who shaped those times, the development of ideas (like this book), the growth and spread of social movements, or war and territorial expansion. No historian can adequately address all of those areas in a single text. Hegel focuses

---

[156] Though not highly criticized at the time of its release, the portrayal of history Hegel presents has since been a magnet for critique from professional historians, as his overview is quite simplistic. Divisions between cultures and eras are not nearly as neatly separable as Hegel's treatment implies.

his history on what he calls "the State."[157] By "states," Hegel is not referring primarily to governments but to individual nations and cultures. This flows out of Hegel's convictions surrounding the interrelations among people, so that a nation is a kind of collective subject. This focus on states does not, however, mean that Hegel is unconcerned with individual great figures in history. Though states have a primacy in the narrative of history, there are occasional individuals who embody the Geist within themselves. Hegel mentions Julius Caesar, Alexander the Great, Martin Luther, and Napoleon as examples of this (and he appears, to some extent, to include himself).[158]

This historical development that Hegel describes is not exclusively consistent upward progress. The Geist, as a collective personality, experiences the same kinds of setbacks in its growth and development that any individual life does. This is evident through the mistakes that are made throughout the history of nations, which often lead to profound loss or great conflict. These mistakes are part of the negative aspect of the dialectical process and will eventually lead to a greater resolution.[159] It is important to recognize this, as it explains why Hegel's thesis is not negated by something like the outbreak of the First World War. Such a setback could be described by a Hegelian as a necessary element of the self-development of the Geist.

---

[157] "The State is the divine Idea, as it exists on earth. In this perspective, the State is the precise object of world history in general. It is in the State that freedom attains its objectivity, and lives in the enjoyment of this objectivity. For the law of the State is the objectification of the Spirit; it is will in its true form." Hegel, *Introduction to the Philosophy of History*, 42.

[158] "The great men in history are those whose own particular aims contain the substantial will that is the will of the World Spirit." Hegel, *Ibid.*, 32.

[159] Hegel speaks, for example, of the world as a "doubled world, which is divided and opposed within itself." *Phenomenology of Spirit*, 282 (par. 265/485).

HEGEL ON RELIGION

While Hegel is not known primarily as a theologian, it is that field of study which began his career. Many theologians were impacted by Hegel's move toward historicism, often incorporating his notion of a God who develops or changes with his creation, such as with Alfred North Whitehead's process theism. Hegel's own relationship to Christianity, especially later in his career, is debated. He uses theological terminology throughout his work, but it is often unclear how seriously or literally he uses those terms. Following Hegel's death, divergent strains of interpretation took his ideas in different directions depending on how those figures understood him to be using theological terminology. Some—the left Hegelians—took his ideas in a materialist direction, believing that there is no real underlying immaterial force involved in the development of world history. Others interpreted him in a more strongly idealist direction, while theologians like Hans Martensen incorporated some of his ideas into an orthodox Christian system.

There are some things about Hegel's view of religion that are straightforward in his writings and do not need much interpreting. He contends that the development of world religions throughout history is part of the world process of the self-development of the Geist. In his understanding, the earliest human beings were polytheistic, believing in and worshipping tribal deities. As the Geist developed, there was a move toward universalization. This appeared first within the Jewish faith, which eventually rejected earlier polytheism for a belief in a singular creator God. Christianity, for Hegel, is the absolute religion, as it is within Christianity that this process of universalization becomes complete.[160] Not only is there one singular divine being, but this God also welcomes all people from all nations and cultures. Nothing, for Hegel, surpasses the religion of Christianity within the development of the world.

---

[160] "The Idea can discover in Christianity no point in the aspirations of the Spirit that is not satisfied." Hegel, *Lectures on the Philosophy of History*, 342.

Despite his praises of Christianity, Hegel does not contend that the theological claims of Christianity—such as the veracity of the recorded events in Christ's life accounted for in the Gospels—are literally true in a historic sense. This is in contrast to the then-current neo-Lutherans at the University of Erlangen (where Hegel had been offered a teaching position) who contended for a strict orthodoxy.[161] For Hegel, the religious terminology in the Christian faith is used more in a symbolic sense than a literal one, and that symbolism reveals certain truths about the Geist. The story of Christ is not about a historic person in Israel in the first century but about the truths which underlie those stories. Take, for example, the doctrine of the Trinity. Hegel believes that the doctrine of the Trinity manifests truth about the dialectic. In this dialectic, the infinite God (Father) becomes finite (the incarnate Son) in order to reveal himself as Spirit.[162] The incarnation then has veracity as a kind of universal reality about the Geist—and consequently about all of humanity—but is not true in its particularity as a truth regarding the specific man named Jesus of Nazareth.

Unlike some of the rationalist thinkers who preceded him, Hegel does not view religion as a hindrance to be overcome, nor does he limit religious convictions to the category of superstition. His view of Christianity is largely positive. However, Hegel believes that the ideas of Christian orthodoxy will ultimately be superseded by a more universal form of Christianity that recognizes underlying universal truths of the Geist that were placed within symbolic language. Like Kant, Hegel contends that Christianity must arrive at totally

---

[161] Hegel, does, in some sense, view his own philosophy as consequentially related to Luther. As Lowith summarizes, "Hegel's Protestantism rests upon the fact that he understood thus the principle of freedom as the conceptual development and consummation of Luther's principle of assurance of justification by faith." Lowith, *Hegel to Nietzsche*, 18.

[162] A succinct explanation of Hegel's Trinitarian thought can be found in the article: Leithart, "Hegel's Trinity."

different theological conclusions in order to be part of a viable rational philosophical system.

CONCLUSION

Of all the thinkers addressed in this book, Hegel's ideas are probably the most complex. For this reason, the summarization of his ideas and of his contributions to the development of Western thought in the modern era is extremely difficult. Hegel wrote on nearly every major area of philosophy, and he also contributed to the fields of theology and history. To summarize just some of the major contributions he made to philosophy, here are five aspects of Hegel's thought that shaped academic discourse after him: First, Hegel believed that society was in a time of progress. For Hegel, the world is continually moving toward something greater. Though not always a direct upward process, in Hegel's dialectic, there is more wisdom in the present and the future than in the past, since human ideas are the product of the Geist's growth in freedom and rationality. Second, Hegel reincorporated metaphysics into philosophical discourse. It again became intellectually viable to discuss the nature of being. Third, Hegel led to the conception of reality as a totality, rather than as a series of disconnected particulars. Fourth, Hegel moved away from the Kantian view of truth as a set of timeless and eternal propositions and instead views truth as historically dependent. Fifth, and finally, this historicist view of truth led to a kind of moral relativism, where ethical concerns are not to be addressed through timeless rationality but through particular historical epochs (thus subject to change). Many of these ideas would shape the thought of a passionate German political philosopher named Karl Marx.

KARL MARX

Karl Heinrich Marx was born on May 5, 1818, in the town of Trier in western Germany.[163] Jewish by ancestry, Marx's parents had converted to Christianity just prior to his birth. Though Karl was baptized in a Lutheran church, his family does not appear to have been particularly devout. Karl's father, Heinrich, was seemingly more devoted to the principles of rationality as promoted in the Enlightenment than to religious faith of any sort. Heinrich was well-read in the areas of both philosophy and politics, leading to Karl having a similar interest in both fields. Philosophically, Heinrich was particularly interested in the writings of Immanuel Kant. Politically, Heinrich was a strong proponent of liberalism and argued against the monarchical system in Prussia at this time. The political activism of his father formed young Karl's values and life direction. Both of Karl's parents were from influential families that, while not among the highest financial class, had attained a modest amount of wealth.

At sixteen, Karl Marx began attending the University of Bonn in order to study literature. Marx did not devote himself seriously to those studies, which resulted in his father transferring him to the University of Berlin where he would receive a more rigorous education. While in Berlin, Marx became interested in both law and philosophy rather than his originally chosen field of study in literature. Through the Hegelian influence on some of his professors in Berlin, Marx became interested in G. W. F. Hegel's philosophy of history. While Marx was never particularly interested in the metaphysical elements of Hegel's system, Marx believed that some combination of Hegel's historicism and radical politics would pave the way for a more just future.

Marx's college experience formed him not only through the development of his academic interests but also in the personal

---

[163] The standard biography of Marx in English has, for many decades, been: McLellan, *Karl Marx: A Biography*, which was first published in 1972 and has received a number of editions since.

connections that he made there. The most important of those connections, in his own personal life, was his eventual wife, Jenny von Westphalen—a daughter of noble parentage. In terms of his political life, Marx became involved with a group of politically active and philosophically adept students who were known as the "Young Hegelians." This group was composed of left-wing radicals who desired to use Hegel's dialectics for revolutionary political purposes. At the head of this group were two well-known critics of Christianity: Bruno Bauer and Ludwig Feuerbach. While Bauer had some impact upon Marx, it was Feuerbach who was most influential in aiding the development of Marx's worldview. Feuerbach, in opposition to the German idealists like Hegel, was a strict materialist, believing that there is no transcendent, non-physical reality in the universe.[164] Feuerbach argued that human beliefs about God are merely projections of the self. Faith is nothing more than psychological phenomena, not a trust in some kind of spiritual reality outside of the self. Feuerbach developed "historical materialism,"—an atheistic approach to the Hegelian dialectic that Marx relied on throughout his writings.

Marx initially desired to work in academia, and as a part of working toward that goal, he completed his doctoral studies in 1841 with a thesis on the ancient atomists (a group of early materialists in Greece) in which Marx critiqued the discipline of theology.[165] The Young Hegelian leader and anti-Christian rationalist Bruno Bauer was Marx's advisor for this work.[166] At this time, the Prussian government was (understandably) suspicious of the Young Hegelians for their political radicalism. Because of this, Marx, like some of the other radicals, was unable to receive a teaching position at a state university. Having given up hope of receiving an academic position, Marx then became a journalist. Throughout his writing

---

[164] See: Newcomb's new translation of Feuerbach, *Essence of Christianity*.
[165] Nahm, *Early Greek Philosophy*, 148-207.
[166] Rosen, *Bruno Bauer and Karl Marx*.

career, Marx wrote for a variety of left-wing publications. First he wrote for *Rhineland News*, which was eventually censored, and then was an editor of the *German-French Annals*. After this publication was also censored, he wrote for another leftist newspaper, *Vorwart* (meaning "Forward").

In 1844, at a café in Paris, Marx met his co-laborer Friedrich Engels, with whom he would write the famous *Communist Manifesto* in 1848. It was Engels who convinced Marx that a socialist revolution would only be possible through a working-class uprising. At this time, Marx also moved in important ways away from his former teachers, both Bauer and Feuerbach, as he believed them to be too speculative. For Marx, what matters is political action–not philosophy. During his life Marx moved, with his family, throughout Europe (Brussels, Paris, Cologne, London) working with revolutionary groups and publishing occasional articles. Marx never worked a regular job and was thus unable to financially support his family. Instead of taking up regular work, Marx relied on inheritance, the generosity of Engels, and especially the wealth of his father-in-law to provide for his family. Even with this unearned income, Marx spent significantly beyond his means, continuing to beg others for money when he spent what he had been gifted. After struggling with a variety of health issues throughout his life, Marx died in 1883 of pleurisy. Though his writings did have an impact in his lifetime, it was only after Marx's death that Marxism became a prominent political ideology.

DIALECTICAL MATERIALISM

At the core of Marx's view of history is his commitment to what he calls "dialectical materialism."[167] By speaking of his method as

---

[167] Engels defines the socialism he and Marx promoted as a move away from the older Hegelian idealist variety to a time in which "socialism was no longer an accidental discovery of this or that ingenious brain, but the necessary outcome of the struggle between two historically developed classes—the proletariat and the bourgeoisie." Engels, *Socialism: Utopian and Scientific*, 91.

dialectical, Marx identifies his belief in a process of affirmation and negation throughout history as is found in the writings of Hegel and Schelling.[168] In Marx's form of dialecticism, history is viewed as essentially progressive. Like Hegel, Marx contends that historians are able to examine human societies through time and trace process of negation and synthesis which moves the world from one epoch to another. Similarly, like Hegel, Marx privileges becoming over being. For Marx, however, there is no underlying World Spirit that is identified with this growth. As mentioned already, Marx has no concern for metaphysics. This dialectical process, for Marx, is mostly discussed within the context of economic systems and law, rather than the kind of broader philosophical, religious, or moral ideology that was essential to Hegel's thought.[169]

Marx's use of the term "materialism" clearly distinguishes his view of history and philosophy from that of Hegel. In his idealist metaphysic, Hegel believed in the reality of both ideas and consciousness—identified with the Geist. In contrast to this, Marx adopted the materialist views of Feuerbach and the other Young Hegelians—for Marx, there is no reality beyond the material.[170] In this way, Marx's ideas are inherently atheistic. For Marx, there is no underlying World Spirit, God, or anything else that is guiding history; all is the result of natural physical processes. Because of this commitment to physicalism, Marx is not as concerned with ideas, as Hegel was, but with action. For Marx, social change occurs, not in the minds of philosophers and theologians, but through political activism. This is because, for Marx, real history is found in physical

---

[168] Engels says, "Dialectics ... comprehends things and their representations, ideas, in their essential connection, concatenation, motion, origin, and ending." Engels, *Socialism: Utopian and Scientific*, 82-83.

[169] These things are not simply unimportant for Marx, but they are positively discounted as part of a mistaken idealist form of historiography that is dependent upon "religious illusion" as the driving force of history. Marx and Engels, *German Ideology*, 43.

[170] Though Marx and Engels both criticize Feuerbach for being inconsistent in his materialism. *German Ideology*, 43-47.

events—particularly in social relations—whereas for Hegel, it is grounded in the realm of Spirit. Therefore, when Marx evaluates history, he looks at the development and shape of economic systems rather than the genealogy of ideas.

Marx's belief that social progress is a necessary aspect of the historical growth of human societies arises from his materialist commitments. In his discussion of nations, Marx (like Hegel) uses Kant's language that societies can be spoken of as subjects that mirror the life cycles of individual people. As a human gets older, there are inevitable changes that occur in their body and mind. As long as they do not face death from an accident or disease, every person grows from childhood to adulthood and then eventually into old age. This process remains essentially the same in all material beings, because the stages of human life are the result of an inevitable and unchangeable biological process. Societies, for Marx, can be viewed in the same manner. There are, he believed, inevitable stages of growth and development in nations just as there are with individual people. Just as there is no providential divine hand behind the process of human development in Marx's materialist view, so there is also no God or Spirit behind societal change. Marx and Engels refer to their view of national development as "scientific socialism," contending that the inevitability of socialist societies is as much a law of nature as are the biological changes that occur in human development.[171] In a truly scientific sense, there is nothing about this proposal that merits the use of the term, as though there were any experimental studies or observations that would identify the move toward socialism as some kind of social inevitability. Nonetheless, it presents Marxian socialism with the veneer of being a science, rather than the theoretical political framework of a philosopher.

---

[171] Marx writes that in his view, "the evolution of the economic formation of society is viewed as a process of natural history." *Capital*, 15.

HUMANS AS SOCIAL RELATIONS

While Marx's philosophical anthropology is certainly not among the most-discussed topics in treatments of his thought (or one of the most central to his own writing), it is an essential element of the system that arose through his influence. Despite the relatively little attention Marx pays to these questions within his vast corpus, there are echoes of his conceptions of the individual throughout his work. Since Marx's writing expounds upon the nature of human society, and society is a collection of individuals, there is an inherent connection between the two. While Marx does not write extensively on his view of human identity, or of the mind-body problem, what he does say is significant. Further, it is essential to discuss his perception of the self because the ideas expressed by Marx about human identity are formative for several later neo-Marxist and post-Marxist systems and philosophies.[172]

Among the clearest expressions of Marx's view of humanity is in his 1845 work *Theses on Feuerbach*, in which Marx discusses the ideas of his former teacher. While Feuerbach initially formed Marx's materialist commitments, these theses display significant points of departure from the older thinker. After his graduation, Marx began a gradual process of de-abstractifying his ideas. While philosophers such as Feuerbach were rightly materialist (in Marx's view), they did not apply that framework consistently, as they sought to make change in culture through the theoretical world of academic writing and teaching. If reality is inherently biological and physical, as both Feuerbach and Marx believed, then change is also most effective through physical means. As part of his critique of the abstraction of Feuerbach and many of his fellow Hegelians, Marx sets forth his own view of the human person which, he believed, would correct the abstractions of Feuerbach. He writes, "The human essence is no

---

[172] Judith Butler, for example, is heavily influenced by Marx's earlier work— particularly his Theses on Feuerbach.

abstraction inherent in each single individual. In its reality it is the ensemble of the social relations."[173]

This stands in stark contrast to the classical traditions, in which humans are understood to be beings who have both body and soul and who have an essential and consistent identity within themselves. It is this continuity of subject that stands behind the Christian view that there is inherent value within each individual person—dignity is inherent to the self as divinely given. In order for the individual to have value, there must first *be* an individual. Descartes understood this, but he isolated that individual by identifying it solely within the inner self, neglecting the broader purposes and communities into which people are placed. Liberals like Thomas Paine or John Stuart Mill similarly grasped the essence of the self as something inherent with innate dignity, but they overestimated the role of freedom in defining the self, to the detriment of the social nature of men and women. Marx moves away from this individualistic tendency by moving toward a view that identifies human beings with their social relations. In other words, there is no human essence inherent to each person. There is only society, which defines people in relation to each other.

Marx and Engels do speak about the existence of individuals in their work *The German Ideology* (1846), which was written around the same time as the prior theses. The introductory section of the book states, "The first premise of all human history is, of course, the existence of living human individuals."[174] Despite how it might initially sound, this is not an affirmation of a classical conception of the individual. In the text, Marx and Engels denote ways in which other thinkers have often distinguished humans from animals, such as their use of religion or human consciousness, and they contend that—at least in a historical sense—humans only began to understand themselves as distinct from animals when they began to

---

[173] Marx, "Theses on Feuerbach," Thesis VI in *Marx and Engels Selected Works*. Vol. I:14.
[174] Marx and Engels, *German Ideology*, 20.

produce. Production, therefore, is foundational to the human essence. Consequently, human identity is, at its core, material. They write:

> This mode of production must not be considered simply as being the reproduction of the physical existence of the individuals. Rather it is a definite form of activity of these individuals, a definite form of expressing their life, a definite mode of life on their part. As individuals express their life, so they are. What they are, therefore, coincides with their production, both with what they produce and with how they produce. The nature of individuals thus depends on the material conditions determining their production.[175]

Material conditions are not only formative for human beings as they live among one another but are actually constitutive of their nature.[176]

This idea that human beings *are* their social relations, and that these relations are primarily economic in nature, leads to a perception of individuals in society in which one's value is limited to one's place within the economic system. Those, therefore, who exist in society as exploitive controllers of production are defined by such exploitation, as there is no dignified nature which lies underneath such economic actions. In this view, acts of revolutionary violence

---

[175] Marx and Engels, *German Ideology*, 20.

[176] For Marx, the material is always primary, and any conception of consciousness or thought is only born out of material circumstances. "The phantoms formed in the human brain are also, necessarily, sublimates of the material life-process, which is empirically verifiable and bound to material premises. Morality, religion, metaphysics, all the rest of ideology and their corresponding forms of consciousness, thus no longer retain the semblance of independence. They have no history, no development; but men, developing their material production and their material intercourse, alter, along with this their real existence, their thinking and the products of their thinking. Life is not determined by consciousness, but consciousness by life. In the first method of approach the starting-point is consciousness taken as the living individual; in the second method, which conforms to real life, it is the real living individuals themselves, and consciousness is considered solely as their consciousness." *German Ideology*, 25.

toward oppressors who are inherently exploitive is not difficult to justify.

This materialist economic anthropological turn is what leads later Marxist revolutionaries to prioritize the collective political community at the expense of the dignity of individuals. Communist regimes around the world have often implemented mass violence toward citizens without regret, as long as such actions serve the good of the nation. Marx was not himself engaged with these later revolutionary movements, as he led more of a theoretical life of activism through writing, and thus one might question whether Marx would have supported the specific actions which were taken in the Bolshevik or Chinese Revolutions in the early twentieth century. Regardless of whether the connection between Marx and these specific acts of violence is direct, the fact that there is a connection is undeniable. Ideas have consequences.

Marx's Economic System

The preceding discussion of the philosophical background of Marx's ideas lays the groundwork for what Marx believed to be the most important topic in historical analysis: economics. In the minds of some, Marxism is solely an economic system that presents an alternative to the capitalism of the mid-nineteenth century. If the question that Communism addresses is *only* one of economics, then Marx's system is ideologically neutral, subject to implementation within a variety of religious or other ideological contexts. I contend, however, that this is not the case. Marx's philosophical materialism and his dialectical approach to history developed first in his study and writing. Only as he moves away from the abstractions of philosophy does Marx become more committed to exclusively political concerns. One cannot divorce his economic system from those earlier philosophical components of his thought. Attempts to hybridize Marxism, such as efforts toward "Christian Marxism," inevitably fail to remain consistent with the principles of either system.[177]

Marx, like Hegel, explores history through various epochs by looking at specific states and cultures.[178] In doing so, Marx challenges some of Hegel's ideas about what exactly defines a given society. As an idealist, Hegel emphasizes the *ideas* of various cultures as a primary moving force in history. This, for Hegel, is sometimes exemplified in the actions of select great men who embody the Geist of their particular epoch. Marx rejects this notion that history is defined chiefly by ideas, or that it is primarily great men or women who change society. In Marx's view, society is essentially constituted by labor, and thus a proper study of history is a study of labor relations.

This centralizing of labor in Marx's thought is likely due, in significant measure, to the birth of the Industrial Revolution.[179] Western societies, during Marx's life, were moving away from their agrarian economies toward industrial ones. The development of modern technologies and the increased use of iron and steel led to the building of factories throughout Europe and the United States. Factory work significantly changed the shape of the family, work, and towns. Laborers were more clearly divided in terms of both their income and their roles in their vocations. While in a traditional society work varies from day to day as one is responsible for a number of different tasks, factory work assigns each person one particular task within a machine-based environment. It is not difficult to see how this led to depersonalization and a sense of meaninglessness and monotony for many workers. Further, early factories were quite

---

[177] There are and have been Christian socialists who are explicitly non-Marxist. See Hans Martensen's *Christian Ethics Vol. II: Social Ethics*, for example. Christian socialism predates Marxism and rejects most of Marxism's premises.

[178] A brief overview of these historical periods and the development of capitalism can be found in Section VIII of *Capital*.

[179] Though it centers on England, Allen, *The Industrial Revolution*, is a good, concise historical overview.

dangerous, and in their early days, factories were not bound by labor laws that assured some kind of just treatment and pay. Growth in production also led to an increased wealth gap, such as in the Gilded Age (1877-1896) in the United States, which began at the end of Marx's life.

For Marx, capitalist societies could essentially be divided into two distinct groups: the ruling class and the workers.[180] More popularly, this is expressed in the difference between the bourgeoisie and the proletariat. The distinction between these two classes is not simply the difference between having more and less wealth (though that is part of the equation). Rather, for Marx, the bourgeoisie are those who control the means of production, and the proletariat are those who actually produce at the behest of the bourgeoisie. For Marx, this leads to exploitation of the workers by those who are in charge of the workforce. The proletariat become mere tools or machines to produce products, bringing wealth to the bourgeoisie while the workers who are actually producing things are paid little.

This system also leads to a state of alienation, wherein the workers are alienated from the actual things that they produce.[181] This kind of alienation is new within the capitalist system and differs from the way that work has functioned in classical societies. Think, for example, of the difference between the blacksmith and the person working in a factory that produces books. If the blacksmith is making, for example, a horseshoe, he is involved in the entire process

---

[180] This manifestation of class struggle in capitalism is part of a broader historical dynamic of oppression. "The history of all hitherto existing society is the history of class struggles. Freeman and slave, patrician and plebeian, lord and serf, guildmaster and journeyman, in a word, oppressor and oppressed, stood in constant opposition to one another, carried on an uninterrupted, now hidden, now open fight, a fight that each time ended, either in a revolutionary re-constitution of society at large, or in the common ruin of the contending classes." *Manifesto of the Communist Party*, in *Works of Marx and Engels*, I:108.

[181] Marx treats this subject of alienation in his posthumously published *Economic and Philosophical Manuscripts of 1984*. What is mentioned above is only one of multitudinous kinds of alienation discussed by Marx.

of creation from beginning to end. He takes the material, heats it up, forms it into its proper shape, and then sells it. There is a direct connection between the one who creates the object and the profit received by it. Furthermore, the blacksmith has the pleasure of seeing both the beginning and the completion of the created object, and thus he can delight in the work as it progresses. The individual working in a book factory might work on one machine all day, such as one that puts glue on the interiors of textbooks to attach their covers. The worker, in this second example, is not involved in the printing or binding of the pages together, nor does she see the results of the process afterward. Certainly, the process is efficient, and the worker is able to put covers on hundreds of books per day, but she is simply treated as another machine involved in the process of production.

Connected to this is Marx's theory of value.[182] Often referred to as the "labor theory of value,"—though the term is not used by Marx himself—this idea equates the value of an object directly with the labor that is required to produce it.[183] The basic question here is this: What exactly determines the value of any given commodity? There are three different ways in which one can speak of the value of an object according to Marx.[184] First is the *use* value. This is to say that to be valuable at all, a commodity must have some kind of use (whether practical, aesthetic, or otherwise). Someone could work hard and long hours to create an ugly and completely useless object; the time and effort it took to make such an object does not automatically make the object valuable. Second is *exchange* value. This is simply the amount of money (or other resource) that one will give

---

[182] Pradella speaks of Marx's two most important contributions as the "materialist conception of history and the theory of surplus value." Pradella, "Karl Marx," in *Routledge Handbook of Marxism and Post-Marxism*, 26.

[183] This idea is not unique to Marx, as a form of it was already used by the famous economist Adam Smith. However, this idea today is nearly exclusively tied to Marxist economics.

[184] Marx explains this theory of value in *Capital*, Book I, Part I, Chapter 1.

in order to own an object. Someone might scribble on a piece of paper and then put it up for sale for $500 on eBay, but that piece of paper is not actually worth so much unless someone is willing to pay such a price. The third aspect of value for Marx is its *labor* value. This is the necessary labor time generally needed to produce a given commodity. This third aspect of a thing's value is what Marx most often identifies when speaking of value; it is this which leads to exploitation in a capitalist system.

In Marx's view, when someone pays for an object, that person is really paying for the labor that is necessary to create that object (along with the cost of the materials used). This does not mean that the value of a product differs depending on the speed at which any single worker creates it. For example, if one worker creates a shoe and is extremely slow, and another worker makes the same shoe but works quickly and efficiently, the first shoe is not worth more than the latter shoe even though it took longer to create. What matters is the average labor time. If the first person takes five hours to make the product, and the second person takes three hours to make the same product, the value is the average of four hours of labor time. For Marx, this four-hour labor time constitutes the actual value. In a just society, the worker would be paid what those four hours of labor are worth.

Capitalism, however, does not result in workers actually being paid what their labor is worth. Let us illustrate with the shoes again. Let's say that a man owns a shoe company and hires these two workers to make the shoes for him. In an average of four hours, these two workers each make a pair of shoes. Let us say that the materials used cost a total of $10 per pair of shoes, and each of the workers is given $30 for their work. The shoes then sell for a total of $80 a pair. The materials and the labor only account for half of the price paid for the shoe. What is the extra $40 for? Who gets it? This is what Marx calls *surplus value*. In short, the owner of the shoe company has exploited his workers by paying them less than half of what their labor is actually worth and taking this surplus income for himself. In a fair system, the entirety of the value of the shoe (apart from the cost of the materials used) would go to the laborers.

Marx's contention here is based on the assumption that the owner of the company provides nothing of value to the process of production; he merely takes money from those who have actually earned it. This idea, which stands at the center of Marx's theory, was challenged by a number of economists and political theorists following the publication of the *Communist Manifesto*.[185] Marx's critics pointed out that the person in a managerial position provides a significant value to workers in assuring stable paychecks. In a capitalist system, workers are paid regularly and in advance of actual sales made, so that workers do not have to wait for the created product to sell in order to receive payment for their labor. In capitalism, the burden of a business that suffers financially is not placed directly on workers but on the company itself. In modern capitalist systems, there are several other benefits to workers that are provided by the company directly. Along with ensuring regular payment, businesses also provide healthcare, severance packages if a job is lost, unemployment fees, and retirement funding. All of this is not to say, of course, that there aren't plenty of greedy CEOs who underpay their employees or exploit them in a variety of ways. Nonetheless, Marx's assumption that the bourgeoisie add nothing of value and only exploit the working class is simply unfounded.

Another influential idea present in Marx's economic theory is his idea of *commodity fetishism*.[186] This concept would become central for some later neo-Marxist thinkers and other social theorists, as is discussed in following chapters. Commodity fetishism contends that in a capitalist system, commodities are divorced from the labor that creates them. As an example, consider how modern people in the Western world consume meat. Someone who wants to

---

[185] See, for example, the Austrian economist Böhm-Bawerk's many critiques of Marx's theory of value, such as in his *Capital and Interest*, 315-327.
[186] Marx, *Capital*, Book I, Chapter I, Section 4.

eat meat can simply go to a grocery store and pick up a frozen, pre-packaged box that says "chicken patties" on it without thinking any further about how the product got there or what the product actually is. Modern meat consumers have often never hunted game, and perhaps have never even been in the presence of a dead animal apart from its being pre-cut and prepared in a package. The product in the grocery store is totally divorced from the process by which an animal is killed, butchered, processed, and packaged. The result of this, for Marx, is that the people involved in the production of a product are depersonalized and treated as commodities. Being divorced from the labor that created it, the product is treated as if it were a person itself.

This depersonalization gives buyers the impression that commodities have a kind of inherent value in themselves, rather than buyers recognizing that the value of a commodity arises from the labor of people who have made the product. This "fetishizes" commodities, meaning that commodities are treated as people. Out of this comes the false impression that the market is some kind of truly existent thing between commodities that controls itself. Relationships between products then hide the real social realities underneath them. Not only does this divorce the purchaser of a product from any social relation to the producer, but it also divorces the laborer from his own work. One who creates a product ends up seeing himself as an object and is alienated from the work of his own hands.

THE SOCIALIST REVOLUTION

Despite its inherent exploitation, alienation, and other failings, capitalism has one redeeming value for Marx: Capitalism is a brief but necessary stage in the development of the human economy. It sets forth an antithesis which is to be overcome through the greater synthesis to be achieved with revolutionary socialism. According to Marx's so-called scientific socialism, it was inevitable that capitalism would end with revolutions breaking out throughout Europe as the proletariat would rise up against the bourgeoisie and create a new and more just society. The question for Marx and his followers becomes, How exactly will this revolution occur?

In the beginning of Marx's intellectual development, he seemed to think, like his colleagues, that radical politics would arise from the academy and that revolutionary thought would create revolutionary action. Through both a growing general dissatisfaction with the academy and his growing friendship with Engels (who was not as optimistic about academic work), Marx began to shift his focus. Rather than lean on leftist intellectuals writing and teaching at universities, Marx moved toward a view in which the proletarian class would become an instrument of political change. For Marx, the working class has a nearly messianic role in bringing about the inevitable communist revolution.[187] This, he believed, would occur through a growth in what he calls "class consciousness," which refers to the proletariat's awareness of their own exploitation and alienation. Marx believed that this growing awareness would occur naturally and inevitably, so that revolution would arise from the bottom. Eventually, when revolution did not happen, later Marxists would argue that intellectuals were needed to enlighten the proletarian class of their exploited status in order to move the revolution forward.

As described in the *Communist Manifesto*, this Marxist vision of proletarian revolution would radically transform nearly every element of Western society. Communist governments would aid the plight of the masses, rather than only helping the few privileged individuals who benefit from capitalism. It is important to note here that Marx and Engels argue not simply for a significant change in the structure of European societies but for a complete overthrow of capitalist societies. It is not the reform of a flawed system that the communists sought, but the total destruction of Western civilization

---

[187] "The proletariat will use its political supremacy to wrest, by degrees, all capital from the bourgeoisie, to centralise all instruments of production in the hands of the State, i.e., of the proletariat organised as the ruling class; and to increase the total of productive forces as rapidly as possible." *Manifesto of the Communist Party*, 126.

in its capitalist form and the building of a new society in the model proposed by Marx and Engels.

The reason this shift must be radical, for Marx, is because every single element of Western society has been driven by the exploitation of the lower class. In response to concerns about departing from all traditional forms of family, education, and religion, Marx and Engels write that "the social consciousness of past ages, despite all the multiplicity and variety it displays, moves within certain common forms, or general ideas, which cannot completely vanish except with the total disappearance of class antagonisms."[188] They admit that this will also result in "the most radical rupture with traditional ideas" of any shift from one political form to another in world history.[189] The mode of examination here, and thus the mode of political action, is absolute.

The kind of absoluteness one finds here in Marx and Engels, of a world that is completely wicked and must be rebuilt from the ground up, is something of a secularized version of Christian eschatology. They await a clear rupture from this world of exploitation to one of justice enacted by a centralized state. Rather than the return of the Messiah, which brings about the death of sin and the making of a new creation, the Marxian vision sees proletarian revolutionaries rise up to destroy the system of capitalism and reform society without class and greed.

Though some Marxists have attempted to walk back Marx's own extreme statements, it seems that Marx desired the total eradication of private property. He says, for example: "In this sense, the theory of the Communists may be summed up in the single sentence: Abolition of private property."[190] The desired future of the communist is one in which all things are shared in common. The

---

[188] Marx and Engels, *Manifesto of the Communist Party*, 126.
[189] Ibid.
[190] Marx and Engels, *Manifesto of the Communist Party*, 120. The document does clarify that it is explicitly speaking about the dissolution of *bourgeoisie* private property.

inevitable result of this is the dissolution of freedom. As Edmund Burke and other classical conservatives recognized, property rights are essential if a society is to retain individual liberty. If all must be shared, then someone must be put in a position to determine how everything is to be distributed. There is no realistic scenario in which human beings rise to such positions out of pure benevolence, nor in which the members of a society will freely offer up their property for the good of society. In order for a communist society to arise, such a reality must be created by coercion. For Marx, this is accomplished through the "dictatorship of the proletariat," in which someone rises from the proletarian class into a position of power and then uses that power to serve the good of the proletarian class.[191] Such a proposal presumes an optimistic anthropology, believing that power could be delegated to a select few who would genuinely use that power for the good of citizens rather than for personal gain. Even a cursory study of Marxist societies should quell such optimism.

The revolutionary utopian socialism that Marx and Engels desire relies on a denial of, or indeed a replacement of, the Christian doctrine of original sin. As a holistic system, Marxism presents itself as an alternative worldview to both the Christian and rationalist ones which predominated the West before it. Marxists often display a kind of religious fervor in the defense and imposition of their ideology, and when communist governments arise, traditional religion is suppressed. Marxism presents a metanarrative of history and of society in which the basic elements of the Christian system are replaced with alternatives. The universality of corruption in the Christian doctrine of sin is replaced by the universality of economic exploitation by the select few who control the means of production. The proletariat then takes on a kind of messianic, redemptive position regarding that plight. For Marx and Engels, intellectuals

---

[191] The ten proposals offered at the end of the *Communist Manifesto* all center on the giving up of power, property, and liberty to the state, in order that the state might ensure the equality of persons within it.

take on a kind of priestly role in pointing society to this messianic act. There is a hoped-for eschatology, or end to history, in which a classless society brings an end to exploitation. And, without a clear system of ethical norms, many Marxists believe that the achievement of such ends is to be accomplished at any cost.

MARX AND ENGELS ON RELIGION

Although this totalizing economic worldview developed by Marx and Engels definitively sidelines the importance of traditional religion, both thinkers make claims regarding religion specifically. While Marx does speak negatively about Christianity, Engels is far more vocally opposed to traditional religion than his compatriot. The thoughts of both figures on the subject set the groundwork for far more detailed negative responses to traditional religious belief among later Marxists, neo-Marxists, and post-Marxists.

Marx's approach to religion is often viewed through the lens of his famous statement that religion is the "opiate of the masses."[192] This phrase is often taken as an insult toward Christians, observant Jews, and other people of faith, as a claim that religion is like a mindless drug that stupefies its adherents. This is not exactly what Marx means. The "masses" are, after all, the very proletariat that Marx is fighting for. Marx believed that religion has often served as a comfort to those who are exploited by the ruling classes, delivering something positive to the marginalized. In his day, however, Marx believed that these religious hopes were no longer needed. In fact, in a time of immanent revolution, religion becomes a distraction from the problems faced by the oppressed in the world. If people are pointed to an eternal hope in a future life, then they are demotivated from trying to improve their living situation in their present one. To further the class consciousness of the proletariat, the coming socialist revolution would need to shed its past theological

---

[192] This quote originally appears in the introduction to Marx's work *A Contribution to the Critique of Hegel's Philosophy of Right*.

allegiances in order to unite the proletariat under their concern for things of this earth. Ultimately, the society Marx desired was one in which religion would have no place.[193] The complete destruction of religious faith has been attempted in communist governments throughout the world since.

Remember, again, that the foundation of Marx's philosophy is in Feuerbach's materialism. His most basic metaphysical starting point is in a denial of the supernatural and a commitment to eliminativist physicalism. When Marx declared his departure from Feuerbach in the theses discussed earlier, his departure did not include any real metaphysical shifts away from this approach toward anything more idealist or theological. To the contrary, Marx continued to claim his materialist worldview throughout his life. Even more blunt than Marx on theological issues is Engels, who unambiguously denounces religion. In his book *Ludwig Feuerbach and the End of Classical German Philosophy* (1886), Engels summarizes his view on the subject with the following words:

> Thus the question of the relation of thinking to being, the relation of the spirit to nature—the paramount question of the whole of philosophy—has, no less than all religion, its roots in the narrow-minded and ignorant notions of savagery. But this question could for the first time be put forward in its whole acuteness, could achieve its full significance, only after humanity in Europe had awakened from the long hibernation of the Christian Middle Ages. The question of the position of thinking in relation to being, a question which, by the way, had played a great part also in the scholasticism of the Middle Ages, the question: which is primary, spirit or nature—that question, in relation to the church, was sharpened into this: Did God create the world or has the world been

---

[193] "The religious reflex of the real world can, in any case, only then finally vanish, when the practical relations of everyday life offer to man none but perfectly intelligible and reasonable relations with regard to his fellowmen and to nature." Marx and Engels, *Capital*, 92.

in existence eternally?[194]

For Engels, the Christian view of the world—and the views of idealist philosophies more generally—is simply the remnants of "ignorant notions of savagery." He opts for the materialist solution, in which there is no God or divine plan behind the world at all. In Engels's view, religion would pass away as societies progressed toward socialism. Again, this rejection of traditional religion would become clearer in the implementation of communist regimes around the world throughout the twentieth century.

COMMUNISM AND THE FAMILY

Both Marx and Engels viewed the family, like religion, as a good and necessary element of past societies at a certain stage of social progress. Both authors also acknowledge that there are a number of social benefits to familial life in certain cultural systems. The family offers companionship to individuals, along with some kind of protection and assurance of provision. Like religion, family is viewed as something that was provisionally good for a time, but is no longer so in the coming socialist era. Further, despite its benefits, the familial structure has also been the grounds for immense corruption.

Unsurprisingly, the concern that Marx and Engels have about families is an economic one. Dividing people in a society along family lines often leads to the hoarding of wealth among a select few circles of people. It is no secret that familial lines protect wealth; they have done so as long as society has existed. The children of wealthy parents are likely to also become wealthy through inheritance. In aristocratic societies such inheritance is built into the system itself. In democratic capitalist societies, greater social mobility allows for a larger transfer of wealth between families rather than only within them, but even in such democratic societies there are lineages of wealth that span multiple generations, such as in those families who

---

[194] Engels, *Feuerbach: The Roots of Socialist Philosophy*, 57-58.

are today considered "old money." [195]   Engels argues that capitalist systems preserve money in the hands of a select few families, which results in unbridgeable and vast wealth inequality in society. This monopolizing of financial assets is further secured by the fact that wealthy families usually encourage their children to marry within other wealthy families. This intermarriage between individuals of the upper classes serves to keep that money within a small circle of individuals and therefore cuts off the working classes from any chance of sharing in it. For Marx and Engels, such a thing would not occur in a communist society where there is no private property.

Engels also questions whether the accepted Christian idea of perpetual monogamy between a husband and wife is really a necessity.[196] In his historical analysis, Engels argues that primitive societies did not have families at all in the modern sense and that polygamy and other forms of sexual promiscuity were perfectly acceptable in many earlier cultures. Having rejected objective moral values, Engels contends that there is nothing inherently morally superior about a monogamous marital relationship compared to other forms of sexual and social relations. In his view, the Christian ideal should not be viewed as normative, and it was only viewed as such because of the imposition of that ideal by the upper classes. Further, as one might expect in a collectivist approach, Engels believes that childrearing is not only the responsibility of the parents

---

[195] "Abolition of the family! Even the most radical flare up at this infamous proposal of the Communists.

On what foundation is the present family, the bourgeois family, based? On capital, on private gain. In its completely developed form this family exists only among the bourgeoisie. But this state of things finds its complement in the practical absence of the family among the proletarians, and in public prostitution.

The bourgeois family will vanish as a matter of course when its complement vanishes, and both will vanish with the vanishing of capital." Marx and Engels, *Manifesto of the Communist Party*, 123.

[196] This argument is in Engels's 1884 work *The Origin of the Family, Private Property and the State*.

at their home but is also a duty of the state, which should be intimately involved in the instruction and training of the youth.

MISES'S CRITIQUE: POLYLOGISM

One final idea belongs here in this discussion of Marx and Engels: the nature of truth and knowledge. As a man of action, Marx was not particularly interested in questions of epistemology, just as he largely dismissed the discipline of metaphysics. It is rather difficult for any thinker, however, to simply avoid epistemology altogether, especially when constructing something as totalizing as a model for an entirely new social system.

The fact that Marx himself did not deal in-depth with the nature of truth does not mean that other Marxists remain similarly silent here. One example of a thinker who did broach this subject more extensively was the contemporary and colleague of Karl Marx, Joseph Dietzgen (1828-1888).[197] In his writing, Dietzgen does not generally use the language of truth when discussing ideas, but rather its related term, *ideology*. Dietzgen refers to ideologies as sets of basic ideas that exist within a particular people group. The roots of this approach to ideology can be seen in Hegel's epochal approach to history in which Hegel speaks about the change and growth in ideas of morality, religion, and other subjects without making claims about the superiority of any one moral system over another. While this process of epochal change is not purely subjective for Hegel—since it is rooted in the development of the World Spirit—there is no objective basis for morality at all in the materialist left-wing Hegelians like Engels, Marx, or Dietzgen. Truth and morality are simply reflections of the beliefs of various cultural epochs and people groups.

With Marx's emphasis on class differentiation going beyond Hegel's divisions between epochs, it was now possible for Dietzgen to speak about different systems of morality and truth existing

---

[197] Dietzgen, *Some of the Philosophical Essays.*

within the same epoch between different classes. In other words, for Dietzgen, the bourgeoisie and proletariat have completely different ideas of what is true and ethical. These systems of beliefs are not referred to by Dietzgen as truths but instead as ideologies. In describing this element of Dietzgen's thought, the Austrian economist Ludwig von Mises uses the term "polylogism" to note that there is no universal logos, or reason, that Marxists can appeal to in order to have rational debate, since they do not believe in a universal principle of reason. Instead, for the Marxist, there are only ideologies, and these ideologies reflect the social classes of their adherents more than they do actual engagement with rational ideas. Mises summarizes the Marxist's perspective well:

> Ideologies do not need to be refuted by discursive reasoning; they must be unmasked by denouncing the class position, the social background, of their authors. Thus Marxians do not discuss the merits of physical theories; they merely uncover the "bourgeois" origin of the physicists.[198]

For Marxism, the underlying reality of social discourse is not truth, but power and class. The classes, in this view, are so divided that there is no universal logic to which both can appeal. There is only opposition. This theme is a consistent one in both later Marxists and postmodernists.

Conclusion

Marx has been read and written about by multitudinous interpreters who disagree with one another on some fundamental aspects of Marxist thought. One of these areas of dispute is the relationship between the ideas of the early Marx and those of the late Marx. It is clear that his earlier writings are more Hegelian and consequently more philosophical in orientation, whereas his later writings are

---

[198] Mises, "What the Nazis Borrowed from Marx," *Mises Institute*.

more strictly economic and political. It is not as clear exactly how far late Marx departs from early Marx, or whether there really is such a clear ideological break at all but rather a shift in emphasis and subject matter. Another dispute exists as to how totalizing Marx is in his views of the abolition of class and private property. Some of Marx's statements appear to be quite all-encompassing in this regard, but some interpreters argue that Marx did not actually desire to get rid of all notions of property and any distinction between classes or roles in society; he merely opposed the strong proletariat/bourgeoisie divide. These different readings of Marx (and not just on these two issues) gave rise to the various schools of Marxist thought in the following century.

While, like Hegel, Marx's thought is difficult to summarize due to the breadth of his writing, I have broken it into five core elements that impact later thinkers addressed in this book. First, for Marx, there is no transcendence or immaterial reality. Following Feuerbach, Marx believes that there exists only the physical world, and all must be understood by means of material reality. Second, Marx believes that people are defined by their social relations, rather than as distinct persons or substances. For Marx, this relationality is economic, but later thinkers expand this socio-relational anthropology to gender, sexuality, and race. Third, for Marx, people can broadly be divided into exploiters (the bourgeoisie) and the exploited (the proletariat).[199] While, again, this is an economic issue for Marx, this division between classes later becomes the groundwork for broader oppressor and oppressed dichotomies used

---

[199] This principle of division between the oppressor and oppressed is not only a dynamic within capitalist society, for Marx, but forms all historic social systems. "The history of all hitherto existing society is the history of class struggles." *Manifesto of the Communist Party*, 108. It is therefore a lens through which all human history and social institutions are to be evaluated.

in feminism, critical race theory, and queer theory.[200] Fourth, Marx believes that society is progressing, and that improvement means destroying the past rather than preserving it. Real change in society is and must be revolutionary. Fifth, for Marx and Engels, this revolution ultimately means the loss of traditional structures in society, including organized religion and the traditional family structure.

Marx was certainly not wrong about the reality of exploitation within industrial society. As many recognized, during the rise of industrialization, there absolutely were abuses of workers in low-paying jobs, along with increasing wealth gaps between the rich and the poor. One does not have to be a communist to recognize these inequalities or to offer solutions. The difference between Marx and others of a more conservative tendency on these matters is that Marx believed the only solution to be a total destruction of the existing system, while others argued for the implementation of legal protections around workers and other economic reforms within the system. This reformatory approach led to child labor laws, mandated safety inspections, limitations on the number of hours one was required to work, etc. Marx and his contemporary disciples, however, believed that true justice only arises through a totalizing framework with political revolution.

---

[200] I have often been told by classical Marxists when critiquing Marxism that Marx does not speak so much of "oppression" and that these categories arise with later thinkers, and thus they depart from classical Marxism. Though Marx does speak about the concept in more economic terms, the terminology of oppression is ubiquitous throughout his writings.

MARXISM AND CULTURE: GEORG LUKÁCS AND ANTONIO GRAMSCI

Karl Marx's work led to the development of various schools of thought, each given the label "Marxism." There is no singular idea or set of ideas described by the Marxist designation, as thinkers took his ideas in a variety of directions. These divergent directions arose from three considerations. First, there were different readings of the ideas of Marx himself. As mentioned in the prior chapter, some authors viewed the earlier, more philosophical writings of Marx as vestiges of older views to be discarded for his later more political writings, while other interpreters believed that Marx's philosophical thought was an essential element of his ideological system. Second, there were divergent approaches to the implementation of Marx's thought. While some authors, with Marx, initially believed in the inevitability of socialist revolution, it eventually became clear that if communist regimes were going to be implemented, Marxist activists must take a more active role in bringing them about. Thinkers did not always agree about how to do this. Third, some thinkers who followed Marx began to expand the earlier author's economic concerns into the area of culture. This chapter explores two prominent Marxists who followed this route: Georg Lukács and Antonio Gramsci.

GEORG LUKÁCS

Though not nearly as well-known to the English-speaking world as Karl Marx, Friedrich Engels, or the later critical theorists, Georg Lukács is one of the most important political theorists of the twentieth century. His influence is felt both in the direction of Marxism beyond the time and ideas of its founder and in the development of a strongly critical approach to the humanities, in which literature and other art forms are viewed almost entirely through the lens of the class struggle, as if there is hardly anything else worth saying with regard to works of great beauty.[201] Known as the "father of Western Marxism," Lukács formulated what would become the most prominent Marxist philosophy in Europe following the First World War. Changing circumstances in the world, along with the lack of predicted socialist revolutions in the nineteenth century, meant that Marxism had to be reformulated in order to retain relevance in an early-twentieth-century context. Lukács did just that, and in doing so, led the way toward the later development of Critical Theory.

LUKÁCS'S LIFE

Georg Lukács was born in Budapest, Hungary, in 1885 to an upper-class family.[202] Like many other Marxist leaders, Lukács was not himself a member of the proletariat, though it was his consistent claim that he fought for the lower classes. Lukács's father was not only a successful investment banker but had also been knighted, making him a baron. According to custom, this meant that Georg was also a baron by inheritance. Like Marx, Lukács was of Jewish ancestry, but his family had converted to Lutheranism. Similar to Marx's family again, it does not appear that Lukács's parents were particularly devout in their Lutheran faith, and it is likely that this

---

[201] The reason for this is likely due to the fact that the majority of Lukács's writings (which tend to be quite long) have not been translated into the English language. For the English-speaking world, his ideas are more well-known through his influences, such as in the Frankfurt school, than through his own writing.

[202] See Lukacs's autobiography *Record of a Life*. For a treatment of Lukacs's intellectual biography, including the various changes that occurred within his thought, see Lowy's *Georg Lukacs: From Romanticism to Bolshevism*.

conversion was more for social reasons than genuinely theological ones.

Lukács attended both the University of Kolozsvar and the University of Budapest. At the former school he received a PhD in political science, and he was later awarded another doctorate in Budapest in the field of philosophy. At this early point in his career, Lukács was primarily interested in the arts (particularly in the philosophy of art). He was part of a drama troupe throughout college and wrote his second dissertation—for his degree in philosophy—on the history of modern drama. Soon after Lukács completed his second dissertation, he began writing books on the idea of the novel and on philosophical aesthetics. Though he moved away from his first area of study in politics in his primary writing commitments, Lukács nonetheless maintained his interest in the field. His political interests became more central to his life when Lukács married the political activist Jelena Grabenko in 1914. Following this marriage, Lukács became active in an influential group of intellectuals known as the "Sunday Circle" (1915-1918). In their regular gatherings, these intellectuals shared and debated ideas about art, culture, and philosophy.[203] As their conversations gradually moved farther into the realm of the political, the individuals involved diverged on a number of practical political questions, which eventually led to them disbanding. Following this split, Lukács's attention turned elsewhere.

In October of 1917, the Russian far-left Bolshevik party led by Vladimir Lenin led an insurrection against Russian leadership, leading to the overthrow of the then-provincial government in Petrograd. This event, known as the Bolshevik Revolution, caused Lukács to rethink his philosophical and political commitments. Though just prior to this revolution Lukács had published a critique of the Bolshevik party, he was soon devoted to the communist cause

---

[203] Interestingly, the figures involved in this circle were almost all idealists, in opposition to Marx's strong materialism.

and consequently joined the Communist Party of Hungary in 1918. This involvement in the Communist Party eventually led to Lukács holding multiple official positions in the briefly reigning Republic of Councils in Hungary in 1919. This communist-led government lasted just under six months before being overthrown. In his short tenure as People's Commissar of Education and Culture, Lukács sought to promote the communist revolution by firing all non-communist professors and appointing new Marxist intellectuals to academic positions who would promote the destruction of the ideals of the former ruling class. When the socialist revolution failed, and the state of Hungary was taken back from the Communist Party, Lukács went into hiding but was eventually caught and subsequently arrested. After a petition was written and widely circulated calling for his release, Lukács was set free.

Years later, Lukács would travel to the Soviet Union where he worked for a time at the Soviet library known as the "Marx-Engels Institute." Though there is debate surrounding the matter, Lukács seems to have initially been sympathetic to Stalin's regime, though it is clear that he departed from Stalin after leaving the Soviet Union. At one point, due to disagreements between his ideas of Marxism and those of the reigning regime under Stalin, Lukács was internally exiled within the USSR, being sent to Uzbekistan. After World War II, Lukács returned to Hungary where he again became involved in the Hungarian Communist Party. He was then involved in the Hungarian Revolution of 1956 where Lukács served as a minister of the Hungarian Communist Party. After this second revolution failed, Lukács voiced stronger opposition to Stalin's communism and accused Stalin of departing from true Marxism. Lukács died in 1971 in Budapest as a loyal member of the Hungarian Communist Party.

Lukács's expertise in such a variety of academic fields brought Marxist ideology into conversation with art, broader philosophical questions, literature, and sociology. While Karl Marx's most well-known writing was narrowly focused on economic exploitation, Lukács brought Marx's fervor for revolutionary politics into a variety of other academic disciplines. Part of the uniqueness of Lukács among Marxists in this regard is his continual interest in the early Marx over the late Marx (largely due to Lukács having access to a number of previously unpublished works of Marx in the 1930s). Because of the philosophical emphasis of these earlier writings of Marx, Lukács's approach to communism was more Hegelian than that of most of his peers, causing him to move beyond Marx's strict economic categories.[204] It is because of some of these differences with other Marxists that Lukács was viewed as unorthodox by many of the Soviets in Stalin's regime. This also demonstrates that many Marxists were united at this time only in their desire for revolution, rather than on strict ideology. For this reason, Marxist groups splintered quickly as several schools of thought were birthed out of varied interpretations of Marx. When such differences between Marxist groups were made clear, communist leaders tended to have no qualms about exiling or imprisoning their fellow communists as dissidents when they diverged from the party line.

Over Lukács's lifespan, he underwent ideological shifts that mirrored the tumultuous events of his biography. Scholars have generally divided Lukács's work into three separate periods. The first is Lukács's early writing, which extends from his first essays in 1909 to his committed conversion to the communist cause in 1918. The second period is that in which Lukács is most Hegelian, from 1918 through about 1925. It was during this period that Lukács wrote what might be his most influential book, *History and Class Consciousness*, which is cited throughout this chapter. Third and finally, Lukács's mature thought extends from the mid-1920s through his death in 1971. It was during this period that, according to Lukács's own account, he had adopted pure Marxism in its materialist form.[205] It is

---

[204] "HCC [History and Class Consciousness] is one of the first contributions in the Marxist tradition that recognizes Hegel as an inevitable source for understanding Marx." Bonente and Medeiros, "György Lukács," in *Routledge Handbook of Marxism and Post-Marxism*.

[205] Breines, "Young Lukács, Old Lukács, New Lukács."

notoriously difficult to discern neat and clear divisions in ideology as one reads Lukács's work, and there are differing approaches to the issue of how disconnected Lukács's mature thought is from his early thought. In an overview like this one, these divisions cannot be spelled out as clearly as one might desire. It may be helpful to look at the dates of the texts cited within this chapter to discern when in this threefold division of Lukács's work each theme or idea under discussion here was exposited.

HISTORICAL MATERIALISM

As did many Marxists in this era, Lukács rejected the earlier deterministic approach to materialism. Marx believed that socialist revolutions would occur soon after his own writing, as members of the proletariat would inevitably grow in their own class consciousness as part of the natural process of societal development. History shows, however, that such a thing simply did not happen. Contrary to Marx's and Engels's expectations, the working class did not rise up and fight against oppressive systems; the revolutions that did occur in the nineteenth century were driven not primarily by the proletariat but by socialist intellectuals. Lukács believed that this reality demonstrates that, contrary to Marx's scientific socialism, history is not a mere machine whose direction is determined by purely material processes. For Lukács, the transition from capitalism to Marxism would not be achieved by the mechanical forces of history but instead must be fought for.[206]

It is here that Lukács demonstrates his strong Hegelian leanings by bringing human subjectivity into view as an essential element of the historical process. For Hegel, the dialectical process is deeply (though not exclusively) subjective, as both objectivity and subjectivity are united in the World Spirit—which is reflected in consciousness. While Marx's material emphasis overshadowed any concern for conscious experience as relevant to his socialist project,

---

[206] Lukács, "Class Consciousness," in *Lukács Reader*, 222-245.

Lukács contended that both Hegel's subjectivism and Marx's material dialecticism were necessary elements of a successful socialist revolution.[207] To clarify, Lukács does not adopt Hegel's strong idealism. He does not write much about the Geist, nor does he echo Hegel's theological concerns. Lukács specifically draws the importance of subjectivity in world history from Hegel and then incorporates it into Marx's material framework.[208]

This subjectivity is clear in Lukács' rejection of a strongly contemplative historical materialism. In his view, many Marxian theorists engaged in political and philosophical discourse about the processes of history, economics, exploitation, and other ideas, but they did nothing to actually enact change. This, for Lukács, is the danger in Marx's deterministic approach—one might simply wait around for the revolution to occur. This increased emphasis on political action arises as the center of Lukács's thought, displacing philosophical discourse about the objective nature of the political situation, ethics, or other concerns. Further, Lukács makes the argument that whether one wants to be involved in the dialectical process or not, everything that the theorist does is connected to the historical development of human society. Thinking through social revolution is part of the revolutionary process itself, especially if individual conscious awareness is a manifestation of broader class consciousness. Because all are involved in the class struggle, there is no ability to stand outside of the revolution and examine it via dispassionate analysis. Lukács follows and develops Marx's emphasis

---

[207] There is an argument made by some that this subjective turn was not entirely a Hegelian one but arose instead through Lukács's study of Husserl's phenomenology. See: Westerman, "Reification of Consciousness."

[208] By "subjectivity" here I don't mean individual subjective perception. Individual subjectivity, for both Hegel and Lukács, is a manifestation of collective consciousness. For Hegel, this collective subjectivity is primarily that of the states as they develop throughout distinct historical epochs. For Lukács, this subjectivity manifests through classes in the economic order, and each epoch manifests distinct struggles of class consciousness—though Lukács contends that only since capitalism are classes now aware of that consciousness.

here with the centralizing of the political. Both thinkers subordinate metaphysics, theology, and ethics to the class struggle. Nearly every area of human endeavor is a mere reflection of the temporal political order. Revolutionary politics has a totalizing grasp over human life in this mode of thought, becoming the lens through which all else is to be viewed. For Lukács, *everything* is political. *Everything* relates to the fight for revolution. There is no neutral party, action, or idea.

In terms of the distinction between the proletariat and the bourgeoisie, Lukács reiterates Marx's views of exploitation, contending that the bourgeoisie control the means of production and that the proletariat are the producers.[209] The bourgeoisie exploit the proletariat by profiting off of their labor by taking the surplus value of their work. Where Lukács goes beyond Marx is in his contention that one must view reality through the eyes of the proletariat to have a true conception of the world as it is.[210] Because of this contention, Lukács falls under the polylogism critique that Mises applies to subjectivist Marxist thinkers. There is, for Lukács, no external, objective, real set of facts to which the members of both the bourgeoisie and the proletariat have access. What the two share is the class struggle, and within that class struggle are two distinct consciousnesses. These two distinct types of consciousness—that of the bourgeoisie and of the proletariat—are subjectively manifested by these respective groups as elements of dialectical contradiction to be overcome through the proletarian revolution. As such a dialectical contradiction, they cannot and will not be reconciled through any cooperative resolution or intellectual inquiry. The consequence of

---

[209] Though Lukács acknowledges the existence of other classes, he views them as mere remnants of feudal society who are not as deeply embedded within the real struggle of modern capitalism. "Bourgeoisie and proletariat are the only pure classes in bourgeois society." Lukács, *Class Consciousness*, 232.

[210] Lukács takes it for granted that class interests drive nearly all of one's perceptions of the world, such that, although in theory the bourgeoisie should be able to arrive at a correct knowledge of the situation of the world, its own class interests make that an impossibility. Lukács, *Class Consciousness*, 233.

Lukács's view is that there are two fundamentally different realities, and each side can only see their own. There is a sense, then, in which the perception of "truth" is solely a proletarian capacity.

The contention here, that political and ethical concerns can only be properly understood by a supposed oppressed party, has significant parallels to conversations on controversial subjects today. Think, for example, of the debates surrounding the legality or moral permissibility of abortion. Abortion advocates commonly contend that a man has no place to speak to a moral and ethical issue that involves the body of a woman, since he is not female and has no access to female subjectivity, thereby being bereft of the ability to make ethical judgments about such a matter. The assumption in this type of argumentation is that truth is only to be understood by the affected or oppressed group. This contrasts with the perspective that truth claims present a set of objective facts that can be rationally debated without regard for the subjective experience or identity of the interlocutors. This contemporary perception of truth as subjective is a manifestation of the Lukácsian turn.

CONSCIOUSNESS AND TOTALITY

The divergent subjective positions of the bourgeoisie and the proletarian classes do not lead Lukács to a position of absolute relativism, in which there remain two opposed but equally valid approaches to the world. Lukács unequivocally privileges the perspective of the proletariat, as theirs is referred as a "true consciousness," which is contrasted with the bourgeoisie "false consciousness." For Lukács, it is theoretically possible that the bourgeoisie could arrive at a scientific understanding of the necessity of revolutionary change, but the nature of the class struggle necessitates that the bourgeoisie could only do so if it were able to observe *society from a class standpoint other than that of the bourgeoisie.* Since the class struggle itself drives the thought processes of the bourgeoisie, this is a practical impossibility. For this reason, Lukács can speak of the rise of a false consciousness among the ruling classes as having a kind of "objective" necessity, since it "is in the class situation itself."[211] Therefore, only the proletarian class understands reality as it is.

Lukács refers to these ideological systems, both the false consciousness of the bourgeoisie and the true proletarian consciousness, as grasping the totality of life. Lukács uses the Hegelian conception of reality as monistic, meaning the world is a singular process of which all things are a part. Society is not a composite of disconnected ideas, institutions and personalities, but a singular, interdependent organism.[212] Because of this, compromise or rational integration of divergent perspectives is not possible in the quest for a just society. Lukács imagines two visions competing for the future of society, and one must win. He states that "only from the vantage point of these classes [the bourgeoisie or the proletariat] can a plan for a total organization of society *even be imagined.*"[213] There must be one singular vision which drives the entire organization of a society, and for Lukács, it must be that of the proletariat.

This perspective of totalization leads to a view of complete overthrow and restructuring as the sole means of liberation. If every element of a system is driven by the consciousness of its ruling class, and if the present ruling class is driven by a *false* consciousness, then there is nothing which must not be dismantled. This also means that, because only the proletariat has a proper understanding of reality, the proletarian consciousness must revise and restructure every element of the social order. There simply is no possibility of justice arising from anything other than the proletarian class as it manifests this true consciousness of the world. This leads Lukács toward a messianic view of the working class—much like Marx—in which this

---

[211] Lukács, *Class Consciousness*, 229.

[212] The totalizing nature of revolutionary action arises from Lukács's conviction that hegemonic bourgeois ideology already is total, as it "really does embrace the whole of society" and "does attempt to organize the whole of society in its own interests." Lukács, *Class Consciousness*, 236.

[213] Lukács, *Class Consciousness*, 232.

class is the bearer of both truth and the means of liberation to inaugurate a new age.[214]

This Lukácsian form of Marxist political theory (often simply referred to as Theory) has two primary areas of emphasis: the class consciousness of the proletariat and the totality of all things. While both of these concepts have their roots in Marx and Engels, Lukács frames them in a different manner. Regarding class consciousness, Marx believed that awareness of exploitation would arise naturally within the proletarian class simply from the nature of exploitation. This did not occur. For Lukács, the mistake made by Marx here was in his neglect of the subjective element of social development. The move from capitalism to socialism was to be achieved, not merely by biologically determined mechanisms, but through the subjective awakening of the lower class to their exploitation. If class consciousness had not arisen naturally and internally from within the proletariat, then someone must bring about a revelation of this consciousness to that class.

In Lukács's vision, Marxist intellectuals are to analyze the reasons for this lack of consciousness and then aid in its arising among the proletariat. As one of these intellectuals, Lukács provides some of the reasons he believes that this consciousness remains hidden. The most central, in his view, is the lack of integration between the immediate economic interests of workers and the long-term goals of political revolution.[215] Workers are not so concerned with the far future when they are in need of more immediate economic aid, so they do not share the same interest in the formation of a socialist state that drives figures like Lukács. As long as socialist theory and immediate economic justice remain distinct in the eyes of the proletariat, there will be no motivation to align with the leftist

---

[214] "[T]he proletariat has been entrusted by history with the task of *transforming society consciously*." Lukács, *Class Consciousness*, 239.

[215] "Here, in the centre of proletarian class consciousness we discover an antagonism between momentary interest and ultimate goal." Lukács, *Class Consciousness*, 240.

intellectuals in their quest for a just, communist society. For Lukács, this necessitates an intentional integration (synthesis) of theory and practice that brings the masses to a consciousness of the immediate, practical benefits of revolutionary politics.

This role of both analysis and synthetic integration of theory and practice in the dialectic provides a kind of prophetic role for the leftist intellectual. As discussed in more detail below, Lukács makes a strong differentiation between the underlying consciousness of the working class and the actual views of individual working-class people within capitalist societies. The contradictions inherent to the subjective self-understanding of the proletariat necessitate this prophetic type of revelatory activity among academics, since the issue of proletarian subjectivity must somehow be resolved in order that revolution might result from it. This leads to a view of academic work in which the goal of intellectual endeavors is a political one, centered in the mobilization of the proletariat to establish a communist state.

The second point to inform all Theory is its totalizing nature. Hegel created a system which addressed topics as broad as art, religion, ethics, history, and knowledge. He could do this because of his view of the integration of all reality within the self-development of the Geist. Lukács follows Hegel here, contending that his Marxist ideological system is similarly universal in scope. The unity of all things within the socio-historical economy, along with the conviction that true consciousness is grounded in an underlying proletarian conception of the world, provides a systemic worldview through which the theorist can perceive all things. This totalizing nature of Lukács's system is apparent in the vast scope of his own interests and areas of writing. As a comprehensive system, Lukács's ideas cannot be rightly understood as isolated claims of history, society, or economics that can be integrated into a variety of philosophical or theological systems. As Lukács contends, his Marxist system is a replacement of all prior Western metanarratives, including both the Christian and Enlightenment rationalist ones.

REIFICATION

The idea of reification likely is the most often cited contribution of Lukács to later Marxist discourse.[216] Reification is based upon Marx's idea of commodity fetishism, the idea that humans treat commodities as if they are persons, or objects of value in themselves. According to Marx, this notion is mistaken, as value is found in personal labor that is used to make objects, rather than in the materials themselves. True relationships are between multiple persons, not between persons and things. In a proper economic relationship, it is understood that the commodity is only a mediating factor between people. Capitalism reverses this, so that commodities take the place of people.

Along with this idea that objects are treated as subjects, Lukács says that subjects are in turn treated as objects. Rather than as ends in themselves (to use Kant's language), people become means to create commodities. Reification is the name for this process wherein people and commodities trade places in the capitalist system. As industrialization led to humans making machines, so did it also in some sense make people *into* machines. This mechanistic view of the worker means the loss of two elements that have been viewed as central to personhood since the Enlightenment: authenticity and freedom. The worker cannot be truly free, as he or she simply does whatever work is required in the process. When freedom is lost, there is no authenticity, as life is lived for the sake of the capitalist machine. This process impacts how those workers are viewed by the consumer and by the bourgeoisie, and also by the self. People begin to view themselves as mere machines, dehumanized by this process.

---

[216] For a modern interpretation and use of Lukács's concept of reification, see: Patnaik, "Emergence of Class Consciousness."

MARXISM AND THE WEST

As stated earlier, Lukács is often described as the father of *Western Marxism*. This title reflects Lukács's attempt to integrate Western art and literature with his Marxist-Hegelian framework. As Lukács shifts his ideological commitments (though remaining a Marxist) throughout his life, so does he change his attitude toward literature, and his approach to the arts more generally.

Lukács's earliest—and most extensive—work on the subject of literature is his 1915 book *Theory of the Novel*.[217] Though his Marxism was not yet fully formed, Lukács had already identified alienation as a central problem of the modern world. With this in mind, Lukács contends that the popularization of classical texts arises from the need people have, in a modernity categorized by atomization, for integrated community. Classical texts provide a vision of this to modern men and women who are unable to enact such social systems in their own time. The novel, therefore, arose as a bourgeoisie art form meant to fulfill this need amid continuing disintegration of society through bourgeoisie norms and institutions. Ultimately, these texts never succeeded (and could not do so) in reintegrating people with one another and with communal life. There is, then, a positive use in the novel as a form for Lukács, but it is only a transitional one. Lukács sees in Tolstoy and some other nineteenth-century novelists the beginning of a move away from this intermediary art form toward something more akin to the classic epic. It is important to note here that Lukács never sees in the novel—or in any other form of art—the inherent value of the aesthetic. The writing is viewed as an element of social development, with its political end being the most essential consideration.

---

[217] For a summary of Lukács's work here, see: Shaw, "Capitalism and the Novel," 555-557. Though Lukács shifts his approach to the arts throughout his life (in line with his broader ideological shifts), many of his contentions remain consistent. From his *Theory of the Novel* (1915) to *The Meaning of Contemporary Realism* (1963) he retains his emphasis on historico-political interpretation, alienation, and realism.

As Lukács developed his view of literature during his early connections with the Soviet Union, he moved toward a prioritization of realism in literature and a skepticism toward the avant-garde.[218] This realism, in Lukács's view, is most evident in early-nineteenth-century literary production, in which social awareness was brought to the problematic conditions in European society. This culminated in the revolutions of 1848. Realist literature, for Lukács, is valuable in that it encourages the reader to look with a wholistic view at the events, norms, and ideals of society from an external perspective. There is some connection here between Marx's materialist conception of reality and the arts. If existence is entirely material, and if the relations of production constitute the essence of social reality, then art must serve to bring awareness to such realities rather than pointing the viewer or reader to some non-empirical realm or feeling. Art's value, then, is in its ability to display these material conditions. It is for this reason that socialist realism was the only allowable art form in Bolshevik Russia.

For Lukács, the art that developed following those revolutions had moved away from the realistic portrayals of European life in the earlier period and thus initiated a process of degradation. This degradation occurs in two ways. First, many writers used their work to defend the bourgeoisie order, rather than to display reality according to the proletarian perspective. Bourgeoisie art would always, by nature, proclaim and defend their own interests as inherent to the nature of the world, since it arises out of their own false consciousness. Second, the abstract art which arose in the early twentieth century was, for Lukács, a distraction from the problems of material production in late capitalism. Rather than leading people toward a consciousness of the reality of their social situation, these works of art moved away from reality into the realm of the ethereal. This divorce between art and life was, then,

---

[218] Hohendahl, "Art Work and Modernity: The Legacy of Georg Lukács," in *Reappraisals*, 53-74.

further evidence of the alienation of men and women from their material environment. Much like Marx viewed religion as an other-worldly distraction from the problems of this life, Lukács fears that abstraction in art leads to a similar abstraction in thinking, resulting in alienation from true knowledge of class warfare.

While it would not be fair to say that Lukács despises the Western inheritance in the arts, it appears to be the case that he sees its value as narrowly limited to political expediency. There is not much discussion of the aesthetic value of either literary or visual arts in his writing, as his discussions center nearly in toto on the social and political dynamics that are displayed in the composition.[219] As a result, literary examination becomes almost entirely a critical enterprise. Works which promote bourgeoisie values are deconstructed as tools of hegemonic oppression through the suppression of class consciousness. Works that are received positively are praised because they deconstruct bourgeoisie values. The aesthetic has no independent value as it is, but only as it points toward a political agenda. Lukács has no conception of the true, the good, or the beautiful, as such considerations are not grounded in the socio-political, which, for Lukács, is all-encompassing.

Regarding his critique of bourgeoisie art, Lukács argues that one of the ways that the powerful have continued to exert their influence and perpetuate their own cultural norms is through what he calls "fetishization." He defines this idea as when

> a given historical phenomenon is detached from its real social and historical basis, that its abstract concept (in most cases only some aspects of this abstract concept) is fetishized into purportedly independent being, into its own peculiar entity.[220]

---

[219] Lukács has plenty to say about things like the form of the novel (in his 1915 work, but also in much of his later writing), but form is subordinate to the message of the text, which is construed as political and concrete.
[220] Lukács, "Responsibility of Intellectuals," 129.

In view of his Hegelian approach to history as process, Lukács contends that cultural products of each age are not purveyors of independent universal or timeless truths and values, but are instead mere reflections of a given culture within its socio-historical context. In their continued effort to exploit the working classes and perpetuate their hegemonic ideals, the bourgeoisie abstractify these time-bound texts and contend for their transcendent and unchanging value. They then argue that any progressive move in history away from these ideals is a move away from timeless truths, which then leads to the support of reactionary fascism.

It is this antipathy toward the reigning cultural paradigms in capitalist society that leads Lukács to prioritize the socio-political views of an author as an essential element in determining the value of a work. He contends that it "is the view of the world, the ideology of the *Weltanshauung* [philosophy of life or worldview] underlying a writers work, that counts."[221] One's underlying political allegiances will impact nearly everything that an author has to say. This includes both the content of a work and the form which that text takes. Perspectives on capitalism, war, revolution, the ruling class, and various other issues are so comprehensive that these ideas will inevitably be portrayed within artistic products.

What this all means for political revolution is that in the hoped-for new regime, there must not only be a total political restructuring of society, but also a cultural one. This synthetic integration of the political and cultural is unique to Lukács's Marxism. Prior to Lukács, Marxists certainly argued for significant cultural change with the supposedly inevitable rise of socialism. However, because of the centrality of economic exploitation in Marx, for many early Marxists, societal restructuring was viewed mostly (though not exclusively) as an economic restructuring. For Lukács, bourgeoisie culture has pacified the working class, and therefore it is

---

[221] As cited in Shaw, "Capitalism and the Novel," 562-563.

not only economics but also culture that is in need of revolution.[222] In Lukács's view, the battle between classes in Western societies is at times most evident within important cultural institutions, and in the art that is produced and promoted in a culture. There is then a battle to be fought in culture and art along with politics in a more proper sense. It is important to note here that one finds in Lukács (among other Marxists) language of *war* against bourgeoisie values as expressed in culture. There is a current perception that the language of the "culture war" is a novelty within reactionary conservative commentators who, like Joseph McCarthy, see some phantom threat of Marxist infiltration in every television series or movie. Figures like Lukács (and Gramsci) state their intention to tear down received culture quite openly, and it is unfair to accuse conservatives of battling a phantom enemy in a war that Marxists introduced in the first place.

Due to the importance of literature and art in his thought, Lukács described his form of Marxism as Marxist humanism. As one who had academic training in philosophy and literature, Lukács sought to use those tools to support and foment the revolution. The pivot to focusing on culture and media among Marxists (not only Lukács) was an effective one, as media could be used as a means of awakening class consciousness among the masses and might thereby align them with revolutionary movements.

Lukács's approach to this can be seen not only in his writings but in the actions he took in Hungary. Along with creating socialist propaganda in the guise of literature and art, Lukács also actively suppressed materials that departed from revolutionary ideals. When Lukács served in his brief role as Commissar of Education and Culture in Hungary, he fired all professors who disagreed with

---

[222] This is because, for Lukács, economics and culture are not only mutually influential upon one another, but cultural ideologies actually constitute the economic struggle. "Ideological factors do not merely 'mask' economic interests, they are not merely the banners and slogans: they are the parts, the components of which the real struggle is made." Lukács, *Class Consciousness*, 231.

revolutionary politics. When he later joined the second failed revolution in Hungary, Lukács planned to continue such work by banning books with dissident opinions and bourgeois values. Lukács understood that control of education and media meant control of the population.

LUKÁCS ON ETHICS

Since his philosophy is a totalizing one, Lukács's writing addresses ethics as intimately related to politics, economics, and culture. He therefore discusses issues of morality more than the first generation of Marxists. In his developed approach to ethics, Lukács (unsurprisingly) does not adopt any kind of transcendent or universalizing system of morality such as that found in the classical natural law tradition or in Kant's deontological ethics. Instead, Lukács views ethics, like everything else, through the lens of class struggle.

In his early studies, Lukács (like many) adopted Kant's notion of ethics as formal duties. Though there are likely multiple reasons for Lukács's move away from this approach, among the most important was Lukács's exposure to the ideas of the German sociologist Georg Simmel. Simmel was broadly considered a neo-Kantian, but he manifested the Hegelian tendency toward totalization in his approach to social relations. Simmel believed that facts and values were not to be divided from one another into distinct spheres of reality (as occurred during the Enlightenment) and that no object or area of study was to be examined in isolation. All reality is integrated and must be understood within the context of dialectical contrast and unity. By 1911, when Lukács wrote his essay "On Poverty of Spirit,"[223] this method of integration as taught by Simmel had caused Lukács to depart from Kant's perception of universal moral duties.

---

[223] *The Lukács Reader*, 42-56.

According to this early essay by Lukács, Kantian ethics privileges form over reality, such that ethical norms are perceived as timeless, isolated forms that are disconnected from the historical circumstances that gave rise to such ideals. Lukács contends that ethics, like other spheres of life, is historically dependent and conditioned, and that ethical systems can only be understood and evaluated within the context through which they arose. The approach to ethics as universal and context-independent fosters alienation, as it removes people from their real-life person-to-person interactions and instead binds them to the timeless norms of some other world or sphere.[224]

Lukács makes a distinction here between ethics and goodness. According to him, "Goodness is an abandonment of ethic."[225] This is because ethics involves the divorce between man and his "empirical condition," while goodness leads to "authenticity" in life.[226] Lukács does not provide a clear, succinct definition of goodness in this writing (some of that is due to the nature of the work, which is in the form of a dialogue), but he contends that this goodness is divine, authentic, historical, and concrete. Lukács's move here is consonant with many other writings of this time period, when philosophical discourse continued to move away from the abstractions of Kantianism toward the relations of ordinary life— such as in Heidegger's distinction between authentic and inauthentic existence. The question to be raised is whether authenticity in itself provides enough clarity for the composition of an entire moral system, or whether a move toward concretion without universality ends in mere subjectivism.

As Lukács's interests became increasingly political, his discussions about ethics centered on the duties of political resistance

---

[224] See: Tihanov's essay, "Ethics and Revolution," for an overview of the development of Lukács's ethical thought, particularly as it is evident in his treatments of Dostoyevsky.

[225] "On Poverty of Spirit," 46.

[226] Ibid.

and what actions were deemed acceptable in the struggle against bourgeoisie power. One of the clearest essays in this regard is his 1919 writing, "Tactics and Ethics." By use of the word "tactics," Lukács intends to identify the means by which one's political goals are achieved. In this work, Lukács argues that there are two elements to social goals of any political movement or order: the immanent and immediate, and the transcendent and ultimate. Marxism, for Lukács, has united the transcendent as present in Hegel with immediate political concerns. The class struggle of the proletariat is both the immediate historical reality and the hope for an ultimate fulfillment of history's goal. It is here that Lukács proposes a clearly identifiable ethical norm by which tactics are considered worthwhile: their ultimate end in achieving socialism.

Lukács is quite straightforward about this, as he contends that "[t]he *only* valid yardstick is whether the *manner* of the action in a given case serves to realize this goal, which is the essence of the socialist movement."[227] The goal he identifies here is the liberation of the proletariat, which is not merely an instance of political justice but is an eschatological beginning of a new human existence. This socialist revolution is "a means whereby humanity liberates itself, a means to the true beginning of human history."[228] It is precisely because the end of these political actions is so grand and world-changing that ethical decisions regarding one's place in this class struggle are such an essential element of Lukács's ethics.

As Lukács defines ethics in this context, he identifies two elements of ethics: the social action of a collective group and the decisions which arise in the individual will. Because classes manifest themselves in individuals and individuals manifest the consciousness of their class, these two elements are deeply intertwined. For Lukács, ethical decisions must be made through the individual will, and those decisions must be in favor of either the

---

[227] Lukács, "Tactics and Ethics," 5.
[228] Ibid., 6.

proletarian revolution or the existent regime. A lack of commitment to either group is itself an ethically committed action in favor of the current reign of bourgeoisie power. Since everyone bears responsibility for both action and inaction, ethical decisions are an absolute inevitability.[229]

The conclusion that Lukács has no moral compass other than support of the revolution has been challenged by many interpreters as an unfair reading.[230] In my own examination of these early texts, however, such a conclusion seems unavoidable. Lukács consistently speaks about the uniqueness of this particular socio-historical moment and the need for the destruction of the current world order for the sake of humanity itself. If the result of these actions is so significant, it appears that anything that achieves this goal would be deemed a good act. Lukács clearly makes the raising of class consciousness the primary *telos* of all moral decisions.[231] That which promotes or affirms the old order is unethical, and that which promotes the achievement of the proletarian revolution is ethically justifiable. Lukács certainly recognizes the seriousness of the impact of moral actions, such as the taking of life in order to achieve one's political goals, but other than emphasizing responsibility in such scenarios, one finds no ethical system of decision making in Lukács

---

[229] Ibid., 7-9.

[230] For example, "The notion that in the early 1920s Lukacs propounded a theoretical justification of terror and crime in the service of revolution does not seem well founded." Breines, "Young Lukács, Old Lukács, New Lukács," 540.

[231] "Even now, for every socialist, the actual historico-philosophical pressure of the social ideal of socialism determines both the content of the objective possibilities for realizing that ideal and also the very fact that the criterion of possibility should itself be possible. For every socialist, then, morally correct action is related fundamentally to the correct perception of the given historico-philosophical situation, which in turn is only feasible through the efforts of every individual to make this self-consciousness conscious for himself. The first unavoidable prerequisite for this is the formation of class consciousness." "Tactics and Ethics," 9.

which would provide any kind of guidelines as to whether such a thing is justifiable or not, other than the political end of such acts.[232]

In this period of Lukács's writing, it appears that nearly any action can be justified as long as it leads toward this ultimate goal. The committed socialist is likely to find himself in a position of having to act in ways that bother his conscience but are necessary for the sake of revolutionary success. At one point Lukács states rather boldly that "Communist ethics makes it the highest duty to accept the necessity to act wickedly."[233] This is demonstrated in Lukács's own life as a communist leader in Hungary, such as in an instance when he served as a commissar of the Fifth Division of the Hungarian Red Army and ordered eight of his own men to face execution. When the ultimate, and only objectively certain, moral end of an ethical system is the overthrow of capitalism, nearly any action can be justified, so long as it aids that greater cause.

A final point to make here is on Lukács's conception of bourgeoisie values within his ethical system. In these early communist-era writings, Lukács speaks in totalizing terms regarding the dissolution of past bourgeoisie moral and social norms. For example, he admits that "the ultimate goal of socialism is utopian in the sense that it transcends the economic, legal and social limits of contemporary society and can only be realized through the destruction of that society."[234] For Lukács, traditional Western moral norms and social institutions have been constructed and

---

[232] "Everyone who at the present time opts for communism is therefore obliged to bear the same individual responsibility for each and every human being who dies for him in the struggle, as if he himself had killed them all. But all those who ally themselves to the other side, the defence of capitalism, must bear the same individual responsibility for the destruction entailed in the new imperialist revanchist wars which are surely imminent, and for the future oppression of the nationalities and classes. From the ethical point of view, no one can escape responsibility with the excuse that he is only an individual, on whom the fate of the world does not depend." Ibid., 8.

[233] As cited in Scruton, *Fools, Frauds, and Firebrands*, 139.

[234] Lukács, *Tactics and Ethics*, 5.

perpetuated as instruments of oppression, and they must therefore be demolished. Lukács speaks about the dangers of any "gesture of solidarity with the existing order" whatsoever.[235]

For Lukács, moral and social systems promoted by or inherited from the bourgeoisie are to be deconstructed rather than rationally examined. The only examination that the intellectual should engage in with these older moral systems is to expose and critique the underlying exploitative power dynamics within them. There are some similarities here between Lukács's approach to bourgeoisie social institutions and Engels's writing on the traditional family, in which Engels contends that the family structure developed historically primarily as a tool of monetary retention and growth. Lukács reiterates Engels's ideas here and furthers them by making such valuations even more all-encompassing, so that every inherited social norm, institution, and moral claim is to be reevaluated in light of the class struggle.

THE CONTINUAL PROBLEM

All of this is rather difficult to accept coming from Lukács, who was both a baron and a well-educated intellectual. While Lukács claims to work for the proletariat, he himself did not have significant connections with the working class but instead spent his time with other intellectuals. His argument that only the working classes have a true understanding of the world seems to be self-defeating, as this would cut *him* off from such knowledge. This apparent dilemma could be resolved if Lukács's views were the result of him spending his time listening to and reading the words of the oppressed classes, but such is not the case. The authors that Lukács cites in his own writing are mostly, like him, upper-middle-class intellectuals. There is a strong divorce between Lukács and the actual lives and experiences of those for whom he is supposedly working. This problem is not unique to Lukács but is quite consistent among

---

[235] Ibid., 6.

Marxist intellectuals. Nearly every influential Marxist philosopher arises, not from the working class, but from the middle class or upper class. Antonio Gramsci is the most significant exception to this trend.

This division between the Marxist theorist and the proletariat is further complicated by the differentiation that Lukács makes between the actual views of people within the working class and what he refers to as their class consciousness. This class consciousness is a kind of universal subconsciousness that exists within the masses yet does not necessarily clearly manifest itself in the words of those who are part of those masses.[236] In other words, the class consciousness of the proletariat is not to be strictly identified with the actual views of the working class. Lukács criticizes those who point out this rather obvious inconsistency in his thought by dismissing such a critique as opportunism. The question is, if the class consciousness cannot be discovered by actually listening to people of that class—and those people are the only people who truly understand the world—how can anyone possibly figure out what this class consciousness actually is?

In the end, only Lukács (and the like-minded) knows what that class consciousness is. Despite ubiquitous claims about the necessity of the proletariat in understanding the world, it is really the Marxist intellectual that understands history, class, and government, according to Lukács's theory. In this system, everything is supposedly to be done for the good of the working class, but what is good for them is ultimately discovered (and thus determined) by Marxist intellectuals. Rather than truly working for the liberation of others, it appears in his writings as if Lukács desires to remake society in his own image, excusing such actions with the rather patronizing claim

---

[236] "This consciousness is, therefore, neither the sum nor the average of what is thought or felt by the single individuals who make up the class. And yet the historically significant actions of the class as a whole are determined in the last resort by this consciousness and not by the thought of the individual—and these actions can be understood only by reference to this consciousness." Lukacs, *Class Consciousness*, 227.

that he knows the consciousness of the working class better than the actual working class.

In Lukács's system, the intellectual inhabits a unique role in Marxist societies. This view—that progressive academics have privileged access to the needs of oppressed peoples and that their primary end is to provide theoretical solutions to those needs for others to implement by way of activism—remains prominent in the contemporary Western academy. Often these academics have no connection whatsoever to those lower classes whom they purport to fight for. And yet, they hold it as a kind of sacred duty for the intellectual to bring forth class consciousness among the masses.

This reinforces the conception of a priestly function for academics in Marxist societies discussed in the prior chapter. Regardless of whether one uses religious terminology to express it, every society has a need for guidance, help, and direction among despondent people. Any comprehensive ideological system will necessarily result in some person, group, or class to provide this function. In Lukácsian Marxism, the intellectual provides this service as one who stands outside of societal divides and both calls out sin (exploitation) and provides the means of redemption (revolution). This class of intellectuals is supposedly one that is not part of the bourgeoisie but instead either arises from or seeks the interests of the proletariat. It is difficult to see, however, how the overthrow of the bourgeoisie and the positioning of the intellectual in this sage-like role is not merely replacing one privileged class with another.

LUKÁCS'S INFLUENCE

In his book *Introduction to Critical Theory*, David Held cites five key points in Lukács's thought that influence later neo-Marxist movements—particularly Critical Theory.[237] Each of these points appears in the following chapters with later thinkers. The first of these is the interplay between history and Theory. Lukács moves

---

[237] Held, *Introduction to Critical Theory*, 20.

away from some of the earlier Marxists, bringing in more rigorous philosophical ideas by means of Theory. Rather than divorcing ideas and action, Lukács believes that Theory itself is a significant element of the fight for socialist revolution within history. History is not determinate and mechanical but must be moved by activists, and Theory is essential to this progressive historical movement. Second is Lukács's idea that the intellectual has a role in developing the class consciousness of the oppressed classes, which was referred to earlier as the priestly function of the academic. Third, and perhaps most important, is Lukács's move from the narrow economic concerns of Marx to an understanding of culture as a means of production. For Lukács, culture exploits, and therefore any revolution which is to successfully cease exploitation must engage in the overthrow of current cultural forms. Fourth is the concept of reification, or the making of working man into a machine. Fifth, and finally, is the idea of totality, that each society has within itself the possibility of being recreated in toto. Many of these concepts appear in a different form in a thinker with similar concerns to Lukács: Antonio Gramsci.

ANTONIO GRAMSCI

GRAMSCI'S LIFE

Antonio Gramsci is unique among Marxist theoreticians in that he arose from the poorer class and consequently experienced significant oppression—economic and otherwise—in his own life, in contrast to the highly intellectual, upper-class backgrounds of many Marxist theorists.[238] Because of the reality of the struggles he and his family faced, Gramsci's hope for social revolution was grounded, not in academic interest, but in practical experience. There is a sense therefore in which Gramsci is an embodiment of the proletarian consciousness Lukács hoped for but rarely encountered. In Gramsci,

---

[238] For a biographical account of Gramsci's life, see: Fiori, *Antonio Gramsci: Life of a Revolutionary*, and Fretigne, *To Live Is to Resist*.

a proletarian intellectual had come to a self-understanding of his own place in the class war and had grasped the depth of bourgeoisie abuse.

Just six years younger than Lukács, Antonio Gramsci was born in 1891 on the island of Sardinia to the west of the Italian Peninsula. His father's family had moved to Italy from Albania at some point in the nineteenth century (the exact date is unknown). In Italy both Antonio's paternal and maternal lines were, for a time, financially stable. During Antonio's young childhood, that stability collapsed, and his father was arrested and charged with embezzlement. He served a six-year imprisonment during Antonio's formative years, from 1898 to 1904. Due to the loss of his father's income, Antonio, then still a child, was forced to work to provide finances to his family throughout these years.

Despite all of the difficulties faced by the Gramsci family, Antonio excelled academically. During his teenage years, Antonio moved in with his brother Gennaro in Cagliari (the capital city of Sardinia) to attend secondary school. This time would be particularly formative for Antonio's intellectual development. Gennaro had previously served in the Italian army on the mainland, and his experiences there led him to recognize significant abuses and prejudices of the middle- and upper-class mainland Italians toward those who lived on the island. At this time, significant industrialization was occurring on the mainland (particularly in the north), which led to prosperity that further divided the already-separated economic classes between Sardinia and the rest of Italy. These tensions were heightened further by the fact that the Italian army was actively suppressing the nationalist sentiments of the Sardinians who were calling for independence from Italy. It was through these experiences that Gennaro became a convinced socialist. Antonio was not immediately committed to the cause in the way that his brother was, but their many conversations led Antonio to think deeply about the oppression of his people, and about how that oppression might be overcome.

Following his graduation from secondary school, Gramsci attended the University of Turin, made possible due to his winning a scholarship in 1911. In his time at the university, Gramsci studied varied subjects, such as literature, philosophy, history, and linguistics. Among the diverse thinkers he encountered at this time were several Marxist intellectuals, such as Antonio Labriola who would help Gramsci form his own unique approach to neo-Marxist ideology. Antonio's views were not only shaped by intellectual forces during this period; he was also deeply impacted by the effects of the Industrial Revolution that he encountered while in Turin.

Industrialization had led to the building of several factories in the city of Turin. Like most factories during this era, these institutions were run by the wealthy and primarily employed those in poor regions. These workers were treated unfairly, given dangerous working conditions, and paid very little. Through his examination of this industrial life in Turin, Gramsci now had firsthand knowledge of the harsh realities that his brother had spoken of. Antonio followed his brother's political trajectory, becoming a similarly convinced socialist. He officially joined the Italian Socialist Party in 1913. Despite his strong academic abilities, Antonio did not actually complete his studies. He dropped out of school due to financial difficulties and health problems; the latter would deeply affect Gramsci for his entire life.

Gramsci's writing career began while he was in college. Along with devoting time to his studies, Gramsci joined multiple socialist student groups and began writing articles for a variety of socialist newspapers. He wrote several articles for the revolutionary publication *Il Grido del Popolo* (The Cry of the People) and became co-editor of the official newspaper of the Italian Socialist Party, *Avanti!* (Forward!), at just 25 years old.[239] He wrote extensively on the politics, economics, and culture of Turin. Along with having relatively widely

---

[239] Gramsci's writing was particularly for the Piedmont edition of the publication, which focused on the political circumstances of northwestern Italy.

read writings, Gramsci also became a popular speaker, as he began to communicate his ideas through speaking directly to exploited workers rather than simply talking to other academics. At this time in Italy, exploited workers began to form worker groups, hoping to secure protections against the abuses of the bourgeoisie. Seeing this as an awakening in class consciousness, Gramsci became involved in the education and mobilization of such groups toward socialist ends. Eventually, Gramsci would be elected to the provincial committee of the Italian Socialist Party, and he moved from being a regular contributor to *Il Grido del Popolo* to serving as its editor. Gramsci furthered this work in journalism through creating another new socialist newspaper titled *L'Ordine Nuovo* (the New Order).

THE POLITICAL SITUATION IN ITALY

A proper comprehension of Gramsci's work necessitates a basic understanding of the political situation in Italy during this time. The early twentieth century was a turbulent era for Italy (as it was for much of Europe), when many Italians tended toward radical ideologies in divergent directions. On the one hand, there was a growing nationalist sentiment and general distrust of modern liberalism, which led to the rise and popularization of fascist ideology, eventually leading to the formation of the National Fascist Party in 1922. On the other hand, there were increased frustrations regarding both growing abuses by the wealthy toward the poor and an ever-growing wealth gap between the classes through the process of industrialization. Seeing the successful Bolshevik Revolution in Russia, some Italians believed that they too needed a socialist revolution that would put an end to this prevalent exploitation.

Much of this political turmoil throughout Europe was fallout from the First World War. After the end of the conflict, strong nationalist movements began to grow in nations like Germany and Italy. While communist leaders emphasized that the growing distance between the upper and lower classes was the result of economic exploitation and that socialism would resolve such divisions, fascist leaders like Mussolini argued that the conflict between classes could be overcome through a mutual recognition of a strong national identity—especially as enforced by a powerful centralized state. These nationalist sentiments were further enflamed by what were seen by many as unfair provisions in the Treaty of Versailles that formally ended World War I. Many Italians felt that Italy was not awarded the land that it deserved at the conclusion of the conflict. Amid this turmoil, Mussolini fought for a unified party that would unite like-minded Italians against the communist party in their nation. He formed a group known as "the Blackshirts" who fought for Mussolini's cause, implementing violence toward socialist leaders throughout the country.

It was soon clear that Mussolini would use whatever means necessary to come to power and stop the Socialist Party. In 1921, he won a seat in parliament and then expeditiously transformed the Blackshirts into an official political party, the National Fascist Party. With compelling rhetoric Mussolini soon convinced many of the Italian people of his views, and a significant portion of the population of northern Italy was converted to the fascist cause. In 1922, Mussolini and his supporters marched to Rome and effectively took over the state. With a platform promising to bring order to a country in a time of chaos, Mussolini became a heavy-handed dictator, gradually taking away liberties from the populace and subsequently increasing the scope of his own power.

Just as the rise of fascism was largely the result of the state of crisis Europe faced following the Great War, so too was the growth in socialist ideologies. For many socialists, the successful Russian Revolution in 1917 was proof that Marx's predictions were correct: The era of the domination of capitalism in Europe would soon come to an end. Like many attempts to unify Marxist movements, the Italian socialists were unable to put together a unified socialist program, as socialist groups continued to disagree on how to go about their revolutionary activities. These divisions among Italian Marxists were solidified when the farther left group, known as the

Italian Communist Party, divided itself from the Italian Socialist Party in 1921. Gramsci was central to the founding of this more radical group, which centered around *L'Ordine Nuovo*. Gramsci's movement aligned itself with Lenin's regime and was connected to the Third Communist International—a movement for international communism under Soviet leadership. Gramsci would spend two years in the Soviet Union as a representative of the Italian communists, before eventually being sent to prison by Mussolini's government.

THE EARLY AND LATE GRAMSCI

Gramsci scholars divide the author's writings and ideas into early and late periods.[240] This is not because there is a strong and clear ideological break in Gramsci, as if he moved from one philosophy to a completely different one at some point in his life (like the linguistic philosopher Ludwig Wittgenstein famously did). Rather, his focus and methods change later in his career, as the hopes Gramsci had for change in his early life quickly showed themselves to be naïve. Along with many other young radicals, the young Gramsci was convinced that the Bolshevik Revolution in Russia was the beginning of an inevitable mass movement of European revolutions that would lead to the construction of a number of socialist states.[241] This conviction arose from Marx's scientific socialism, in which the move from capitalism to this other form of government was a historical inevitability. Similar to Lukács's hopes for Hungary, Gramsci believed that just as Lenin led the Bolsheviks, he would soon lead the Italian people toward a communist revolution through the growth in class consciousness among the proletariat.

Gramsci did not merely rely on hope, however. He had concrete plans and ideas about how this revolution would ultimately

---

[240] For a treatment of the development of Gramsci's thought, see: Fresu, *Antonio Gramsci: An Intellectual Biography*.

[241] The ultimate goal was not even the existence of separate socialist states, but an international communism.

come about. In Gramsci's view, revolution would come through the actions of the growing workers' councils.[242] Not merely an Italian phenomenon, workers' councils appeared in several nations that were struggling with the difficulties of industrialization—including Italy, Poland, and Germany. These councils sought to establish structures of governance in which workers were governed by other workers, rather than by the bourgeoisie alone. In this structure, workers would choose delegates through a process of elections, and those delegates would make decisions about working conditions, pay, and other things relevant to those who were involved in the process of production. The hope was that these councils would take decision-making power away from the bourgeoisie and put it directly into the hands of the proletariat. In Italy, workers' councils had been formed during workers' strikes from 1919 to 1920. While these strikes initially appeared to be quite promising to socialists, the protests were ultimately ineffective, and after their failure most communists in Italy lost any hope that these councils would effect the necessary change that they had hoped for.

Though Gramsci was not as dismissive of these workers' councils as some others were at this point—he retained *some* hope that further workers' strikes could still be effective—he began to focus his energies on international connections with the Soviets, rather than working merely on the local level in Italy. Gramsci moved away from the idea that there would be a separate and localized socialist system that would govern the people of Italy, and instead he hoped to bring the Italian people under the leadership of the Soviet communists. Gramsci was an internationalist in this regard, contending for an international communist society governed by Lenin. In an attempt to bring this about, Gramsci spent two years in the Soviet Union making connections with the Communist Party,

---

[242] Gramsci was not alone in these hopes. The Dutch communist Anton Pannekoek similarly believed that communist revolution could be achieved through these workers' councils.

hoping that upon his return to Italy he could convince his countrymen to submit themselves to Soviet control. It was with his return to Italy and his imprisonment that the second, and most influential, part of Gramsci's writing career began.

GRAMSCI'S IMPRISONMENT

As the competing systems of fascism and Marxism are mutually totalizing ideologies, it was inevitable that whichever of these groups ultimately came to power in Italy would eliminate the other. Just as Lenin's Russia removed all dissidents, so did Mussolini imprison socialist leaders when coming to power. Mere months after Mussolini came to power, in late 1922, Mussolini called for the arrest of the leaders of the Italian Communist Party. Gramsci avoided this initial round of arrests, as he was still in Moscow. At the end of 1923, Gramsci returned to Italy and attempted to salvage the Marxist cause, gathering the remaining devotees and writings of the Communist Party. Now the recognized leader of the Communist Party in Italy, Gramsci began a new publication titled *L'Unita* (Unity), stressing the need for all leftists in Italy to unite in the fight against fascism.

With Gramsci's rather public revolutionary activities, it was inevitable that he would eventually be caught by the fascist state. The nationalist leadership did not look favorably upon a figure whose primary goal was to bring the Italian people under the control of a foreign empire. Though Gramsci technically had immunity at this point as a member of the parliament, emergency measures in 1926 temporarily removed those provisions, and Gramsci was arrested.

Antonio Gramsci was convicted and sentenced to twenty years in prison in the town of Turi in southern Italy. While imprisoned, Gramsci's health worsened at a rapid pace. He had issues with digestion, constant headaches, and vomiting. There were several attempts to get him released, but they all ultimately failed. Eventually his health was bad enough that it was agreed that he be moved to a medical clinic. The care there was inadequate, and

Gramsci would die at only 46 years old. During those eleven years of imprisonment, however, Gramsci was quite productive. It was during this time that his most influential writings, now known as the *Prison Notebooks*, were produced.

GRAMSCI'S IDEAS

STRUCTURE AND SUPERSTRUCTURE

Gramsci's work attempts to answer the central question that nearly every other Marxist of his generation asks: Why didn't the revolution happen? Marx's predictions of the supposedly inevitable and imminent revolutions that would overthrow capitalism were not being fulfilled. The proletariat did not achieve strong class consciousness, and the people of Europe were not generally enthusiastic about joining the Bolsheviks when they were the only European group that successfully revolted. Though Gramsci was initially hopeful about the possibility of revolution through workers' unions in Italy, Mussolini's rise to power and Gramsci's own subsequent imprisonment forced him to rethink the mechanisms of revolution. In his *Prison Notebooks*, Gramsci works out a possible explanation for why the bourgeoisie was so successful in maintaining power in spite of their continued excessive economic exploitation of the proletariat.

While Gramsci followed Marx in his belief that economic exploitation through material production was a central problem of the capitalist system, he began, like Lukács, to understand that the bourgeoisie's control of production was not only material, but also cultural. Economic exploitation is one part of a broader system of abuses of power that are systemic throughout western civilization. For Gramsci, this explained why revolutions did not arise spontaneously among workers. If economics were the only concern, they would have.[243] Gramsci believed that in addition to economics, the masses are controlled by the values and products created and passed on in broader culture by means of the bourgeoisie.[244] These cultural factors that Gramsci identifies are what he refers to as the superstructure of society.

For Gramsci, society can be divided into two basic elements: the superstructure and the base, or structure.[245] The base is that which is directly related to production. This includes everything that traditional Marxism includes under the umbrella of exploitation. This involves, most obviously, the means of production: tools, machines, factories, the materials needed to produce, etc. The base also includes the relations that are involved in production, such as that between the proletariat and bourgeoisie, the relationship between workers and their products, the relationship between ownership and property, etc. On these various points, Gramsci reaffirms all of the basic elements of Marx's and Engels's system.

It is in the superstructure that Gramsci contributes new concepts to Marxist ideology. The superstructure, as defined by Gramsci, is everything in society that does not directly involve production. These are the elements of society that are often placed under the broader label of "culture."[246] This includes art in its various

---

[243] Speaking of the revolutionary consciousness which led to the French Revolution, Gramsci writes that "this consciousness was formed not under the brutal good of physiological necessity, but as a result of intelligent reflection, at first by just a few people and later by a whole class, on why certain conditions exist and how best to convert the facts of vassalage into the signals of rebellion and social reconstruction." Gramsci, *The Antonio Gramsci Reader*, 58.

[244] In the past, revolutions were only successful when "cultural factors ... helped to create a state of mental preparedness for those explosions in the name of what was seen as a common cause." Ibid., 59.

[245] For an overview of Gramsci's ideas of structure and superstructure, see: Texier, "Gramsci, theoretician of the superstructures," in Mouffe, *Gramsci and Marxist Theory*.

[246] The institutions and products of society are the material in which culture exists, but underlying that is a kind of "higher awareness" that one has of the purpose of

forms, general societal philosophy, religion, and media. Gramsci also includes in the superstructure the nature of the family and its privileged construction in a given society, the form and content of educational institutions, and the nature of law and government. Along with these elements of society that are most commonly identified with the humanities, Gramsci also speaks of scientific institutions and medical practices as elements of the superstructure. At the center of these various aspects of the superstructure, Gramsci places *ideology*. Ideology, in his use of the term, refers to the beliefs and values of a society. All of the elements of the superstructure are put in place by the powerful in order to promote and shape ideology.

For Gramsci, every society has both a superstructure and a base. These two elements, though distinct, are intimately intertwined with one another. There is a kind of mutual maintenance between them, so that the base of society helps to maintain the superstructure, and in turn, the superstructure helps to maintain the base. At the bottom of this interrelationship lies ideology. The ideology of a culture is displayed and sold through the material products that society creates (the base) and is taught and reinforced through cultural institutions (superstructure).[247] These institutions of society then promote ideas and messages that enforce the need for specific material products, and thus the superstructure promotes the base. This mutual reinforcement is not a mere coincidence or happenstance but is due to the intentional planning and actions of the rulers of society.

---

life, along with the rights and obligations an individual has. Gramsci, *The Antonio Gramsci Reader*, 57.

[247] Gramsci speaks of two different kinds of ideologies. The first are "historically organic." These are ideologies which are tied to the structures of society and form the basic psychology and organization of a particular society. The second are those which are "rationalistic." These are ideas formed in the academy through theorizing. While these might be useful to a degree in creating social movements, the former are far more intertwined with basic human thought and action in a culture. Gramsci, *The Antonio Gramsci Reader*, 199.

It is worth noting here that there are numerous interpretations of Gramsci on these points. Some interpreters argue that, like Marx, Gramsci's primary concern here is the base, and that his intention in discussing the superstructure is merely to support his economic concerns. Others, however, view Gramsci's work as a shift in Marxist thought away from economics to culture, thus giving higher importance to the superstructure. I will not attempt to resolve these debates in the present discussion.[248] For the sake of this work, what is most essential to understand—regardless of the variances of interpretation here—is that Gramsci helped to propel questions of culture and intellectual formation to the forefront of later Marxist discourse. Further, whether or not interpreters like Laclau and Mouffe (who contend for the centrality of culture and resistance to it in Gramsci's writing) interpret Gramsci correctly, their view of his writings has undoubtedly shaped Marxist treatments of culture in the academy.

Before moving on, I want to discuss the term "cultural Marxism." This concept and label has often been derided through a variety of media outlets as a right-wing bogeyman.[249] This, I think, is mistaken. The label is, in fact, an appropriate one to place on Gramsci and his work. This is not to say that the term has not been misused on a popular level or been far too broadly applied (such a thing usually occurs when a label moves beyond the academy into popular discourse. How many progressive college students refer to anything mildly conservative that they don't like as fascism?). There is, however, an academic tradition of Marxist cultural study that sees

---

[248] Texier contends that Gramsci's thought is not grounded in an opposition between culture and politics, but that instead Gramsci's work is "an attempt to grasp the underlying unity of these two movements and thus to arrive at a new concept of politics." Texier, "Gramsci, theoretician of the superstructures," in Mouffe, *Gramsci and Marxist Theory*, 51. This, I think, provides the best explanatory framework for Gramsci, in which politics and culture serve as a unified whole and the enforcement of proletarian hegemony necessitates a culturally driven politic which transcends the base-superstructure divide.

[249] For example, Paul, "Cultural Marxism: The Mainstreaming of a Nazi Trope."

culture as an instrument of critique through a Marxist lens and also contends that a successful socialist revolution necessitates the creation of cultural products which awaken revolutionary consciousness through the revealing of the realities of current class warfare. It is not difficult to find in academic databases articles from past decades that use the phrase "cultural Marxism" simply as a descriptive label applied to figures like Gramsci.[250] There is, therefore, an accurate way to use the label which is not pure conspiracy.

Cultural Hegemony

The most commonly discussed element of Gramsci's thought is his notion of *cultural hegemony*. The term *hegemony* is not unique to Gramsci, as this word had been used occasionally by prior revolutionary thinkers—including Lukács. Lenin, for example, uses the word hegemony in a positive sense to identify the unity of thought and action of the working class that leads to revolution. The term is hardly ever used in this positive sense today, as most authors follow Gramsci's more common use of the concept of hegemony as a reference to the hierarchically enforced unity of values and beliefs that the bourgeoisie use to maintain and perpetuate their power (though Gramsci does at times use it in the Leninist sense).

Regardless of whether it is used in a positive or negative sense, this term references that which is identified with power or with a ruling class. Gramsci argues that the bourgeoisie maintain their power through the promulgation of a particular ideology that serves their interests. This hegemonic ideology is dispensed through the superstructure of society, so that consumers of cultural products retain such ideas in their psyche. This ideological rule through culture is, in many ways, more powerful and effective than the use of

---

[250] As just a few examples to illustrate the point: Davies, "British Cultural Marxism"; Brenkman, "Theses on Cultural Marxism"; Dworking, *Cultural Marxism in Postwar Britain*. Many more articles and books using the phrase "cultural Marxism" to identify Marxist cultural critique from the 1970s onward could be listed.

the economic power that these upper classes maintain.[251] In Gramsci's view, it was because of the enforcement of cultural hegemony that exploited workers were pacified and had not yet engaged in a revolt against the exploitative class. Marx's predictions were flawed because he failed to understand how all-encompassing the power of the bourgeoisie actually is within culture. Through this cultural hegemony the rulers of society had been able to keep workers ignorant about the reality of their own exploitation.

For Gramsci, this hegemonic ideology includes those ideas, values, structures, and morals that keep the upper class in power. Through the superstructure of society, these things are all reinforced to the general populace with the goal that those lifestyles, actions, and values that are beneficial to the interests of the bourgeoisie are deemed "normal," and those things which diverge from this are considered "abnormal."[252] This Gramscian critique of normalization through cultural hegemony stands behind the development of common terms in leftist discourse that emphasize the centering or privileging of specific people or lifestyles over others such as heteronormativity, phallocentrism, or white privilege. In this conception of culture, norms are perpetuated solely for the purpose of exercising and retaining power, and thus norms should be challenged if power is to be challenged. Gramsci refers to the combination of all of the institutions, structures, and cultural forces

---

[251] As Im summarizes, "According to Gramsci, the supremacy of a class or a social group manifests itself in two ways: domination and hegemony ... The former is the rule by force and the latter is the rule by consent. For Gramsci, the maintenance of power by the dominant bourgeoisie in capitalist societies normally takes the form of the organization of consent rather than the naked use of force." Im, "Hegemony and Counter-Hegemony in Gramsci," 127.

[252] As Grell writes, "Through its occupation of positions of intellectual and moral leadership within the institutions of civil society, the dominant group's (or coalition's) 'view of reality' informs all tastes, morality, customs, religious, political and legal principles, and all social relations particularly in their intellectual and moral connotations ... It comes to constitute the 'common sense' of the majority of the population." Grell, "Hegemony and the 'Universalization' of Moral Ideas," 523.

that are used to reinforce hegemonic ideology as a *historic bloc*.[253] Within this historic bloc, the values and ideals of the upper classes are simply taken for granted. Consequently, the ideology promoted by this historic bloc then deems those things which would benefit the proletariat to be abnormal. This dynamic creates social pressure on a populace to retain the values of those with power, thereby causing the working class to neglect that which would benefit themselves.

Think about how this works regarding two particular areas of the superstructure. Examine, for example, how one could make such an argument concerning religion. The German philosopher Friedrich Nietzsche (who was certainly no Marxist) argues that Christianity promotes "slave morality" that was promoted by leaders in Western society to keep citizens docile amid poor living conditions so that they would be stopped from revolting.[254] Christianity, in Nietzsche's understanding, teaches that there is a divine source for governmental authority and a consequent divine mandate of obedience to those authorities, even to the point of valuing suffering under those powers. By teaching the value of love, rather than justice, Christianity disincentivizes people from improving their living situations. As a historical example of this supposed abuse of power, it was common for European monarchs following the Reformation to speak about the "divine right of kings" in which they contended that because their authority came from God, their word had to be obeyed at all costs. If God gave the magistrate authority, then to disobey the law of the magistrate is also to disobey God.[255] Through rulers making these claims, religion became an instrument of domination—a means by which the bourgeoisie reinforced its own power while silencing dissent from the masses. This religious hegemony is then disseminated through the superstructure of

---

[253] Gramsci, *The Antonio Gramsci Reader*, 193-194.
[254] This is explained in the first essay of of Nietzsche's *Genealogy of Morals* as part of his discussion of the distinction between the contrasts "good and bad" and "good and evil."
[255] Locke's opponent Robert Filmer is an exemplar of this view.

culture through the church, art, media, and education, which continue to reinforce the power of the magistrate.

Consider a very different example, from the sciences, to see how this dynamic works. While many contend that the sciences are disciplines of pure objectivity in a way that religion, art, and ethics are not, many leftist thinkers object to this characterization (such as Foucault, examined later). For Gramsci, the sciences stand with the humanities as parts of the superstructure of society; both are used as tools of hegemonic oppression. A modern Gramscian might use this argument to argue against a binary understanding of gender. The argument proceeds as follows: In Western society, it is taught from a variety of sources of cultural importance that there are only two genders into which every human being fits, namely, the dual biological sexes of male and female. This binary view is reinforced through the identification of maleness or femaleness with the possession of particular genitalia. This hegemonic ideology is enforced the moment a child is born, as a doctor makes a declarative determination of the gender of the child by identifying gender with genitalia. This social construct of the gender binary is then reinforced through social norms as shown in various cultural products, such as the use of the color pink for items made for girls and blue for similar ones made for boys. Educational institutions continue to reinforce this when they divide their classes for different activities between boys and girls, and movies and television shows also portray gender stereotypes in order to further reinforce these concepts.[256] The sex binary, rather than being a simple biological fact, is an arbitrary societal creation enforced in order to defend or promote the current order of those in power. Social institutions use

---

[256] Like Lukács, Gramsci emphasizes the centrality of educational institutions in forming the values of society. It is for this reason that the success of the proletariat depends upon "winning intellectual power." Gramsci, *The Antonio Gramsci Reader*, 70.

their influence to reinforce these things as normative when they are not inherently so.[257]

Like other Marxists, Gramsci does not believe that there is such a thing as transcendent good or evil that determines ethical norms that are right or wrong across time and culture. Instead, cultural norms are in a constant state of change, dependent solely upon what currently benefits the elite in a society. These elites use the idea that there is some kind of unchanging eternal order to make their values appear not only normative, but necessary. This, again, leads to the problem of polylogism, as Gramsci—like Lukács—does not believe that there is a set of clear ethical norms by which both the proletariat and bourgeoisie are to be governed. The various classes in a society simply do not and cannot understand the world in the same manner. This means that for Gramsci, there can be no reasoned, neutral debate about objective standards, only revolt by the masses against the oppressive class. Societal change will not happen through reasoned debate with an agreed upon set of values, but through immediate political action.

Within his discussion of the enforcement of cultural hegemony by the bourgeoisie, Gramsci makes a distinction between the state and civil society.[258] He contends that when people think about the use of force in society, it is generally attributed to the state. A government uses coercive power in order to punish crime and to reward what is viewed as good and proper behavior within a given

---

[257] To be clear, Gramsci does not discuss the issue of the gender binary. This is an illustration of how Gramsci's methodology is applied in relation to a current issue.

[258] Bates summarizes Gramsci's view: "Civil society is composed of all those 'private Organisms'—schools, churches, clubs, journals, and parties—which contribute in molecular fashion to the formation of social and political consciousness. ... Civil society is the marketplace of ideas, where intellectuals enter as 'salesmen' of contending cultures. The intellectuals succeed in creating hegemony to the extent that they extend the world view of the rulers to the ruled, and thereby secure the 'free' consent of the masses to the law and order of the land. To the extent that the intellectuals fail to create hegemony, the ruling class falls back on the state's coercive apparatus." Bates, "Gramsci and the Theory of Hegemony," 353.

society. It is easy to recognize the use of force when a government is enacting punishment through imprisonment, fines, or some other means. Gramsci contends, however, that this state power is not the only means of force or control in a nation. Coercion also happens through non-governmental forces in civil society through ritual, norms, and structures. Gramsci believes that in a well-functioning society, the state should ultimately be eliminated, though he contends that civil society must always remain. Since civil society is an inevitability, he believes that the structures and values of this society must be reformulated in order to defend and promote that which is beneficial to the proletariat, rather than the bourgeoisie.

Gramsci's approach to civil society as a tool of coercive force leads him to view every element of society through the lens of politics—particularly through the categories of exploitation and oppression. For Gramsci, the books that have been preserved in Western culture, the art that is traditionally seen as beautiful, the Christian religion, architecture, societal rituals, the family structure, and just about every other element of civilization is a means of exploitation, assembled and strengthened merely to serve the ruling class.[259] Gramsci's view of civil society reflects the same totalizing ideology found in the writings of Lukács. If everything in Western culture supports the bourgeoisie (as both Gramsci and Lukács claim), then everything must be overthrown if the abuses of the bourgeoisie are to be brought to an end. This attitude of resentment toward Western cultural inheritance leads to the discarding of the past with semi-utopian hopes of a future free from oppressive power.

---

[259] This is part of the final stage of a dialectical process in which divergent elements of society are synthesized together within a single hegemonic ideological system (the historic bloc). As Woolcock writes, "The last moment of the struggle occurs at the level of civil society when social integration is achieved. There the dominant class forges an ideological link between the economic, political, intellectual and moral aims." Woolcock, "Hegemony in Gramsci's Theory," 205.

REVOLUTION AND COUNTER HEGEMONY

One did not need to be a Marxist to see the problems with industrialization in the Western world. Plenty of conservative, center-left, and moderate voices spoke out against the growing obsession with wealth and production in the late-nineteenth and early-twentieth centuries and criticized both the abuse of workers and the ever-increasing wealth gap between the rich and the poor.[260] A significant number of non-Marxist answers to these societal issues sought to implement careful reforms and protections for workers in a variety of ways. The problem with these solutions, for Gramsci, is that they required compromise and slow, difficult change to the existing system. For Gramsci, total and immediate revolution is the only answer.

Rather than supporting the reformers who desired progress toward better conditions for exploited workers, Gramsci fights against the actions of these reformers by dismissing their activities as "passive revolution." Gramsci uses this term to refer to the idea that change to capitalist society must be done through a process of gradual reform. According to Gramsci, this kind of revolution is inauthentic. Rather than a true fight against exploitation, such reforms are simply an excuse for elites to take over the cause of radical movements in order to hamper and divert them so that such causes would preserve elite interests, rather than proletarian ones.[261] This kind of revolution is one "from above," where problems are addressed through historic social institutions, thus keeping the basic institutions of society intact. This passive revolution, in Gramsci's framework, is the appropriation of real proletarian reform by opportunistic politicians and academics. Because Gramsci harbored

---

[260] For an overview of some conservative responses to industrialization, see: Kolozi, *Conservatives Against Capitalism*.

[261] Forgacs defines this passive revolution as "a process whereby a social group comes to power without rupturing the social fabric (as in France) but rather by adapting to it and gradually modifying it." *The Antonio Gramsci Reader*, 247.

such an intense distrust of the upper classes (even those who claimed to support the Marxist cause), he believed that the bourgeoisie were simply unable to make real revolutionary change. Revolution, therefore, *must* come from the proletariat.

In rejecting the power of bourgeoisie voices altogether, Gramsci is left with a revolutionary movement cut off from most of those who are in power. Without the powerful on his side, how exactly is culture supposed to be changed in Gramsci's approach? Gramsci contends that this is to be done through the creation of a counterculture that arises from the proletariat. This new counterculture would largely be guided by intellectuals. This new class of intellectuals would not serve to justify the status quo under the existing ruling class—which Gramsci believed that many past academics did—but instead would arise largely from the working class.[262] Gramsci, after all, did this and was quite successful in coming to a position of prominence. With this proletarian background, this new group of intellectuals would put the interests of the proletariat into a central position and would then create just systems in order to ensure that they were treated rightly and exploitation was brought to an end.

What Gramsci fails to recognize here, as did the French Revolutionaries before him, is that, rather than simply being tools of oppression, tradition and established social institutions create boundaries that guard against quick moves to tyranny or mass violence. The creation of a completely new system entails the removal of any and all guardrails of an older set of established powers, and thus the new system is open to quick and easy manipulation dependent upon whoever happens to achieve power most

---

[262] Only the proletariat can provide intellectuals in the socialist system, since intellectuals are all driven by their own class interests. As King writes of Gramscian thought, "The intelligentsia, formed by the fusion of organic and traditional intellectuals within the dominant social group, defends that group's interest and expresses its world-view. Intellectuals organize and enforce the authority of the group they represent." King, "Social Role of Intellectuals," 26.

expeditiously. Gramsci also trusts that this new class of proletarian intellectuals would not again move toward the defense of ideology that serves their own self-interest. He fails to understand that the problem of self-interested work is not attributable to one particular class but is instead a problem inherent to each human heart. Those who enter into positions of power have a tendency to abuse that power and to manipulate elements of society in order to keep themselves in power. Revolutions tend to remove the guardrails that at least curb those tendencies, and they create vacuums of power where new individuals rise to influence without the necessary restraints of tradition.

The revolution that Gramsci hopes for is one that will be continual. It will require significant effort to bring about, and its continuation will also necessitate constant work. For this to be carried out, the proletariat must create its own *counter hegemony*. The term *counter hegemony* is used throughout Gramsci's writing with reference to his desire for the creation of a new superstructure that supports the socialist revolution, rather than bourgeois values. Gramsci's call for this new counter hegemony is a declaration of ideological war against inherited Western culture, as he seeks to replace the supposed bourgeois cultural values of European society with distinctly socialist ones. This fight for counter hegemony impacts all areas of society. As he writes in a 1920 article, "Questions of Culture," in *Avanti!*,

> The proletarian revolution cannot but be a total revolution. ...This revolution ... presupposes the formation of a new set of standards, a new psychology, new ways of feeling, thinking, and living that must be specific to the working class, that must be created by it, that will become "dominant" when the working class becomes the dominant class.[263]

---

[263] Gramsci, *The Antonio Gramsci Reader*, 70.

For Gramsci's project to work, there must be the creation of new social rituals, family structures, neighborhoods, literature, art, and media that tear down all previous beliefs and assumptions of Western civilization. Rather than passing down inherited wisdom, these new social rituals and pieces of media should be used to bring revolutionary ideas to the masses. Among all of these elements that constitute the superstructure of society, Gramsci is particularly interested in the media. He (rightly) understood the importance of popular media in impacting the mind and values of the average citizen who is not connected to the academy or to political power.[264] This impact has only increased since Gramsci's time through television and the internet. Since Gramsci has determined that all areas of life are political, every piece of media or art must therefore defend either upper-class interests or the socialist revolution. For Gramsci, the revolution must be at the forefront of the creation of any form of art or media.[265]

Left-leaning movements since Gramsci's time have often echoed this emphasis on ideological change through the arts and media. For example, the USSR outlawed all art that did not align with its values, embodied in the art form of so-called socialist realism, believing that all art must support the values of the Soviet state. Even outside Marxist states, throughout the latter part of the twentieth century much of Western art increasingly became politicized

---

[264] Gramsci often speaks of literature's role in portraying reality as it is, giving readers a view of the class struggle in a way that they may not recognize in their day-to-day life. Here, Gramsci holds to the same essential view as Lukács. "The artist necessarily and realistically depicts 'that which is,' at a given moment." Gramsci, *The Gramsci Reader*, 396.

[265] Gramsci does not himself speak of creating any specific school of art or particular art form (unlike Lukács's strong focus on realism, though it is difficult to see how Gramsci's views lead to any art form besides realism). He contends, however, that new values in this new culture will stir up the kinds of feelings and sentiments which will then lead to new socialist art forms. This begins with the creation of a "new culture," a "new moral life," and "a new intuition of life." Gramsci, *The Antonio Gramsci Reader*, 395.

through the growth of conceptual art, which often gives political messaging prominence over aesthetic value (and sometimes intentionally subverts aesthetic values). Beyond the fine arts, the twenty-first century has seen an increase in left-leaning social messaging in television and movies—particularly in that which is aimed at children. While Gramsci's influence is not solely responsible for these moves, his conception of counter hegemony and the role of the media and arts to bring such a thing about is a significant factor in the development of an increasingly politicized media.

GRAMSCI ON RELIGION

One final area of Gramsci's thought to be discussed here is his ideas surrounding religion and society. As mentioned above, Gramsci argues that religion is an element of the superstructure of society, alongside other cultural and educational values and institutions. This centrality of religion was particularly apparent to Gramsci due to the intimate relationship between Italian identity and the Roman Catholic Church. Throughout many centuries, the cultural values of Italy had been shaped by the leadership of the Roman Church, and the beliefs of that church formed the educational system of the Italian people. For Gramsci, this top-down imposition of the values and beliefs of the church was an integral element of the hegemonic culture supported by the bourgeoisie and forced upon the proletariat. The creation of a counter hegemony then required a change in the Italian people's theological views and commitments, just as it necessitated change in every other area of society.[266]

Like many Marxists, Gramsci sets Christianity—and to some extent religion as a whole—and Marxism in opposition to one

---

[266] Gramsci is far more critical of the Roman Catholic system than of either Protestantism or early Christianity. For Gramsci, there is something of a revolutionary spirit within the early pre-Constantinian church.

another.[267] This is due to Gramsci's commitment to seeing religion as a historical-materialist phenomenon, rather than as an expression of transcendent truth or the internal orientation of the soul. Fulton writes that Gramsci "took a major step forward in respect to Engels and the Marxist tradition as a whole by taking seriously, *as a source of power* the self-understandings of religious groups and the interpretations of the world in which those groups actualize their existence."[268] Religion is viewed, by Gramsci, solely in material terms as a manifestation of class disparities and power dynamics within a given age of a culture. Religion, then, must drive one to an analysis of its use in the support of hegemonic ideology. In view of Gramsci's consistent critique of religion throughout his life (and his adamant atheism), it seems that his desired socialist society cannot also be a religious one—at least in a traditional sense.[269] Both socialism and religion demand a totalizing grasp upon the individual and upon his or her views of reality, and contrasting totalizing value systems cannot easily coexist. Gramsci echoes Marx's concern that religious commitments are a distraction from the political concerns of life, as theology orients people toward a life beyond this one and thus disengages them from political battles in the present age. It was precisely this pushing off of hopes for liberation into the future which had served as a tool for continual domination by the ruling class. It is also worth noting that for Gramsci, every action taken by an

---

[267] Regarding religion as a whole, Fulton writes, "Gramsci ... seems to believe that religion in general always ends up losing sight of the social character of human actions by individualizing all moral responsibility and by pretending an equality between human individuals which religion has never actually achieved. ... He seems to imply that it can never achieve it either *because* of this general character." Fulton, "Religion as Politics in Gramsci," 214-215.

[268] Fulton, "Religion as Politics in Gramsci," 214.

[269] Regarding Gramsci's consistency in his opposition to Christianity, Fulton writes that "Gramsci viewed Roman Catholicism as socialism's greatest enemy insofar as Italy was concerned, and his detestation of the popes and Jesuits (with some exceptions) continued unabated throughout his life." Fulton, "Religion as Politics in Gramsci," 201.

individual is political in orientation; there cannot be, and is not, any area of life which does not exist under the broader umbrella of the political. For this reason, any theology or philosophy that is rooted in transcendence or theoretical formulations of truth is an inherent distraction from concrete existence. Like many other Marxists, Gramsci believes that philosophies of pure theory, transcendence, or abstraction have no value, as worthwhile philosophy is rooted in praxis.

While Gramsci clearly rejects traditional religion—especially the Roman Catholicism prevalent in his own national heritage—he recognizes that there is some deep human need for spirituality that religion fulfills.[270] There is a reason why people are drawn to spirituality, even if the particular form that spirituality takes is formed by hegemonic oppression. Gramsci, seeing the common religious devotion among the proletariat (which often sustained them with hope through exploitation), does not want to deny that aspect of the human experience. In light of this, Gramsci contends that it is communism that truly meets these needs of the people that they had previously sought to fulfill through religion. For Gramsci, Marxism is a form of secularized religion with its own art, literature, values, and rituals. This new secular religion was, in Gramsci's view, going to face a war with the Roman Catholic Church over the loyalties of the Italian people. And in this war, the church must face defeat if the people of Europe were to enter into a time of justice and peace.[271]

---

[270] Some authors, such as Bruce Grelle and Cornell West, have argued that religion as resistance can stand in coherence with Gramsci's system, such that the Italian Marxist does not condemn religion in toto, but its abuse by the ruling class. Grelle, "Hegemony and the 'Universalization' of Moral Ideas."

[271] Gramsci believed that the socialist revolution would "mark the end of the period of class-divided societies." This period of world history would still see humanity struggle with the forces of nature, but no longer would humanity be divided against itself. Gramsci, *The Antonio Gramsci Reader*, 71.

INFLUENCE

For such a significant figure, Gramsci himself lived a rather short life. Though his articles were once relatively widely read, and some of his speeches well-attended, he did not see significant political success in his own lifetime. Rather than his hoped-for Marxist Italy under the reign of the Soviets, his homeland had been taken over by a fascist dictator. It was in his time of imprisonment under the reign of Mussolini that Gramsci wrote his most enduring work, as he wrestled with how revolutionary Marxists could overtake the bourgeois oppression of Europe's past through the creation of this new counter hegemony by way of the media.

While Gramsci's works were read some following his death, he became a particularly significant voice in the 1970s when, through the growth of radical student movements, revolutionary ideas came to the forefront of much academic work in the Western world. A search for Gramsci's name in academic archives displays a significant increase in articles and dissertations written on the Sardinian Marxist in the 1970s and 1980s. Gramsci's enduring impact upon Marxism, and other related revolutionary movements, is due to his providing a compelling answer to the question of why revolutions often do not occur when populations are exploited or oppressed. This shifted the discourse among left-leaning academics away from a sole focus on economic factors and toward broader cultural ones. Through Gramsci, as well as Lukács, many leftist intellectuals began to view their fight against exploitative class privilege not merely as a fight for more just economic policies, but as a war against the West itself.

CRITICAL THEORY: HORKHEIMER, ADORNO, AND MARCUSE

While Georg Lukács was developing his form of Western neo-Marxism in Hungary, and Antonio Gramsci was attempting to bring Italy under the control of the Bolsheviks, another similar socialist movement began to grow in Germany. A group of intellectuals based in Frankfurt, often referred to as "the Frankfurt School," developed their own unique approach to Marxist cultural critique that they referred to as *Critical Theory*.[272] This totalizing ideology—or as they called it, "a theory of everything"— sought to address the dilemmas faced in the West following the First World War with a new model of Marxism. It is these thinkers who would bring neo-Marxism into a prominent position in the academy, not only in Europe, but also in the United States.

FOUNDATIONS

At the center of Critical Theory was an academic program called the Institute for Social Research, founded in 1923 by the German-Argentinian Marxist Felix José Weil. Weil completed his doctoral studies in political science at the University of Frankfurt, where he studied under the prominent Western Marxist Karl Korsch.[273] As an attempt to bring together Marxists who were not explicitly Leninists (as much of the Marxist academy was tied to Lenin during this period), Weil funded a conference in 1923 that brought together

---

[272] For overviews of Critical Theory, see: Rush, *Cambridge Companion to Critical Theory*; Bronner, *Critical Theory: A Very Short Introduction*; Felluga, *Critical Theory: The Key Concepts*.

[273] Korsch is sometimes considered the second founder of Western Marxism along with Lukács, though Korsch is not nearly as widely read today as is Lukács.

many of the most important Marxist thinkers of the time. The success of the conference encouraged Weil to establish a more permanent group to host similar discussions. With the financial help of his wealthy father, Weil founded the Institute of Social Research in that same year in Frankfurt.

The initially chosen director for this new institute was the professor of sociology Kurt Albert Gerlach, who unexpectedly died prior to the opening of the program. After this surprising loss, the Austro-Marxist Carl Grünberg was chosen as director of the Institute. The Austro-Marxists were a group of Marxists in Austria who rejected the Comintern.[274] Rather than aligning with the Soviets, or proposing another modern form of international Marxism, the Austro-Marxists sought the establishment of a nationalistic socialism that was not dependent upon the Bolsheviks. The ideology of the Austro-Marxists was far more moderate than that of thinkers like Lukács or Gramsci who hoped to destroy historic national identity through the radical, violent, and immediate overthrow of existing governments. The Austro-Marxists were instead interested in a gradual move toward socialist policies, often referring to their desired form of government as a democratic socialism, rather than the totalitarian socialism that overtook the Soviet Union. Grünberg served in this position as director for seven years before having a heart attack and consequently deciding to step down. He was succeeded by the more well-known author, Max Horkheimer.

It was under Horkheimer's leadership that the Institute attained its clear voice and (somewhat) unified message that would impact social thought in the Western world in a number of academic fields. This impact is strongly felt in the present day. At the time of Horkheimer's appointment, the Institute had been publishing an influential journal titled *Zeitschrift für Sozialforschung* (The Journal for Social Research) to disseminate the ideas being discussed by the

---

[274] *Comintern* is short for Communist International. This is the group of Marxists aligned with Lenin who sought to establish an international communist regime.

academics at the Institute. With essays from authors such as Theodor Adorno, Walter Benjamin, and Herbert Marcuse, this publication was at the forefront of academic Western Marxist theory. Just as Mussolini's fascist state sought punishment for Marxist dissidents, Hitler's rise to power in 1933 led to a similar attempt to silence ideas and institutions that were viewed as subversive to the Third Reich. It became clear rather quickly that organizations like the Institute for Social Research would come under intense scrutiny, and eventually prosecution, by the Nazis. For this particular institution, that scrutiny would be increased due to the presence of several Jewish scholars who were leading thinkers in the program. In order to escape persecution in Germany, in 1934 the Institute moved to New York City, where it affiliated itself with Columbia University (which had a significant number of professors who were sympathetic to Marxism). Because of the presence of this institute in the United States, and the quick translation of many of these theoreticians' works into English, Critical Theory has had a significant impact in the English-speaking world. Among the many influential critics at the Institute were Theodor Adorno and Herbert Marcuse, who are the focus of this chapter.

THEODOR ADORNO

Theodor Adorno was born to Maria Calvelli-Adorno della Piana and Alexander Wisegrund in Frankfurt, Germany, in 1903.[275] Like both Marx and Lukács, Theodor had a father who was ethnically Jewish but had converted to Protestantism, and Theodor's mother was Roman Catholic. Adorno's father ran a successful business exporting wine and had significant financial and educational resources at his disposal when raising Theodor. Many of these educational resources were used to train Theodor, among other members of the family, in music.

---

[275] For a biographical overview of Adorno's life, see Müller-Doohm, *Adorno: A Biography*.

Music played an important role in Adorno's life, both in his childhood and in his later career. Adorno's mother had been a professional singer, and his aunt—who lived with Adorno's immediate family—was an accomplished pianist. These family musical skills were also present in Adorno, who spent much time in his childhood playing piano. From his youth, he was particularly fond of the works of Beethoven. Adorno would later pursue a musical career, playing a variety of instruments, composing music, and also publishing a number of essays on the subject. While Adorno retained his love for Beethoven and Bach throughout his life (along with a strong distaste for jazz), his musical interests moved increasingly away from traditional musical forms and toward the experimental. He loved the avant-garde music of Arnold Schoenberg and those who followed his artistic methodology. Adorno studied for a time with one of Schoenberg's most successful students, Alan Berg, in Vienna.

Regarding his intellectual development, Adorno read extensively on a variety of topics throughout his younger years and devoted a significant amount of time to his studies, graduating at the top of his class. As a teenager, Adorno was already being drawn to revolutionary ideas, having encountered the works of both Lukács and Ernst Bloch. It was during these same years that the First World War broke out in Europe, and Adorno was increasingly disillusioned with the seemingly ubiquitous support among German leaders—including leading intellectuals—of German involvement in the war. Adorno ultimately concluded that if the Western intellectual tradition, as received in Germany, had led the German people to such conclusions, then the tradition itself must be wrong. This meant that there must be a change to the ideas and traditions of the German people if there were to be any hope for a better age for the people of Europe.

After graduating from high school, Adorno pursued both music and academic philosophy. He first studied music composition at the Hoch Conservatory in Frankfurt and then philosophy at Johann Wolfgang Goethe University (also in Frankfurt). Adorno's academic influences were varied and included figures as diverse as Kierkegaard, Freud, Lukács, and Tillich. Combining his love for the arts and philosophy, Adorno took it upon himself to formulate a philosophy of aesthetics. He displayed impressive academic and writing abilities in his work, and Adorno was offered a position at the Institute for Social Research, where he would lecture on philosophy. During his time at the Institute, Adorno secured his reputation as one of the most important leftist philosophers of the twentieth century and foundational to the ideas of Critical Theory.

When the Institute was forced to leave Germany and sought safe haven in the United States, Adorno moved to New York City to teach at Columbia University. After a short time on the East Coast, Adorno decided to travel to the West Coast, spending time in Los Angeles. While in the city, Adorno experienced the Hollywood movie industry in its formative years. This time that Adorno spent around Hollywood had a profound impact on him and his writings, as it shaped his later critique of Americans, movies, and pop culture. When the war ended, the Institute for Social Research moved back to Germany, where Adorno would once again live and teach. He became the director of the Institute in 1958 and is generally regarded as the most important thinker to come out of the school. In his later years, Adorno's popularity grew significantly through the student movements of the 1960s, when many young revolutionaries began to look to Adorno, along with other Western Marxists, for inspiration. Adorno passed away at the end of that decade, in 1969, and his popular work *Aesthetic Theory* was published posthumously.

RELATIONSHIP TO MARXISM

Scholarship on Theodor Adorno and on Critical Theory more generally is not always agreed regarding how accurate it is to refer to this stream of thought as explicitly Marxist. There are undoubtedly some clear distinctions between Marxism and Critical Theory, as Marx's ideas were far narrower in scope than those topics discussed and debated by the Frankfurt School. Many of Adorno's, and other

Critical Theorists', areas of study, teaching, and writing were simply ideas that Marx himself seemed to have no interest in and did not write about. Further, there are plenty of places in which each of the figures associated with the Frankfurt School would disagree with Marx or Engels. However, the same could be said for nearly *every* Marxist in the twentieth century, such as the two Marxists discussed in the prior chapter of this book. Hardly anyone writing in the twentieth century followed Marx on every particular. The question of whether Marx would have identified Adorno as one of his own ideological children may be uncertain, but it is clear that Adorno saw himself as such. Henry Pickford writes: "Adorno and other members of the Frankfurt School took themselves to belong to the Marxist tradition."[276] Consistent with all important Marxist thinkers, there are areas of both continuity and discontinuity between Critical Theory and Karl Marx.

If Marx's theory can be summarized by the distinction between the exploiting bourgeoisie and the exploited proletariat and the belief that control of production should be placed in the hands of workers rather than the ruling class, then Adorno is a Marxist. Throughout his writings, Adorno uses many of Marx's categories and affirms his primary ideas about economics and labor. While the scope of Adorno's thought is far broader than these, he retains that fundamental Marxist labor-centered framing when discussing various other issues about culture. While many post-Marxists would eventually shed the economic concerns of Marx almost entirely, this is not the case for Adorno.

Where Adorno most strongly differs from Marx is in his rejection of scientific socialism. Hardly any Marxist at this time was willing to say, with Marx, that class consciousness would arise naturally from the proletariat and that there would be a clear and inevitable transition from capitalism to socialism. While the Bolsheviks under Lenin took revolution into their own hands and

---

[276] *Routledge Handbook of Marxism and Post-Marxism*, 143.

forced a transition from their older system of government to a socialist one through tyrannical political rule, Adorno and the other Critical Theorists rejected this approach, instead arguing for other means to implement revolutionary change. The means to bring about these revolutionary changes, for Adorno, are cultural rather than violent and dictatorial. Adorno agrees with Lukács and Gramsci here that revolution is to occur through cultural means.[277] Attempting to address a variety of cultural issues, Adorno and others in the Frankfurt School began to apply some of Marx's categories to various academic disciplines, such as sociology, psychology, and art. Critical Theorists engaged in intellectual synthesis, bringing the thought of sociologist Max Weber and Freudian psychologists such as Erich Fromm and Wilhelm Reich into a Marxist framework.

A significant shift occurred in the relationship between classical Marxism and Critical Theory between the 1930s and 1960s—especially in the academic career of Adorno. When the Critical Theorists wrote in the 1920s and 1930s, Marxist strains of thinking were more clearly present. For example, in a 1937 essay, Horkheimer defines Critical Theory as a system which is,

> in its totality, the unfolding of a single existential judgement. Crudely formulated, it states that the fundamental form of the historically given commodity economy on which history rests contains in itself the internal and external contradictions of [its] epoch, which it generates in an increasingly intensified form.[278]

This is a rather traditional Marxist account, in which there is an assumption of historical progress in which economic forces lead to a series of contradictions in society that are eventually to be overcome

---

[277] Gramsci did not have a significant influence on the Frankfurt School, though there is much overlap between their ideas. Gramsci is far more pragmatic and activist in his work, whereas the Critical Theorists are more directly connected to the academy.

[278] As cited in Held, *Introduction to Critical Theory*, 40.

in a greater synthesis. From this would come socialist revolution and the establishment of Western societies governed by economic justice. All of this is consistent with the basic premises of Marx, Engels, Lukács, and Gramsci. This more direct Marxism was not long-lived, however.

While during the 1930s both Adorno and Horkheimer had held some hope for a possible proletarian revolution, these themes dissipated from these thinkers' writings into the 1940s. This move away from historical optimism was partly driven by their observations of the results of the Soviet revolution. The resulting government was not the socialist utopia some had naively hoped for; it became bureaucratic, technocratic, and authoritarian—many of the same points at issue with capitalist democracies.[279] The harshest critiques of the Bolshevik system would come from Herbert Marcuse's 1950 work *Soviet Marxism.* The Critical Theorists recognized that there was no quick solution to the growing disparities of capitalism and that no society had yet formed a government which was able to bring about the economic justice that socialist theorists had hoped for.

This is not to say that these thinkers suddenly became champions of capitalism. All of the Critical Theorists continue to speak critically of capitalist systems throughout their careers, focusing increasingly on the monopolization and consolidation of power by the wealthiest in society, which leads to a societal reshaping in the interests of the industrial leaders. The Critical Theorists' negative orientation toward capitalism is also evident in their consistent use of the phrase *late-stage capitalism* to define their historical epoch. A term commonly used by Marxists in the twentieth century (and still in use today), this phrase implies that the capitalist economic system is a temporary one that is soon to replaced by a future order (socialism, in the Marxist perspective).

---

[279] Held, *Introduction to Critical Theory*, 44.

This late-stage capitalism, as discussed by the Critical Theorists, exhibits notable differences from the capitalism of the nineteenth century that drove Marx's critiques. In the era immediately following the First World War, many people in the West (particularly in the United States) experienced a higher standard of living as the middle class expanded significantly—until the Great Depression in 1929.[280] In Europe and the United States, several labor laws to prevent abusive labor practices were implemented, such as bans on child labor, mandatory vacation time, hour limits for work weeks, and various other measures. While the specifics of these regulations varied from country to country, there was a general trend in the West toward instituting protections for workers. While these moves were positive, their implementation also coincided with increased monopolization by a select few large corporations and even greater wealth disparities during the Great Depression. With this monopolization, the powers of the state and private sector increasingly reinforced one another, developing into what Neuman called *state-capitalism*.[281] This occurred in its most dangerous form in Nazi Germany.

After 1940, Horkheimer and Adorno had all but given up hope for genuine socialist revolution, resigning themselves instead to a pessimistic outlook on Western political life. This resignation led many of the writers associated with Critical Theory to engage more thoroughly in critique of the cultural and political landscape of the West than in positive construction of a new or better order. In their critiques, these thinkers continue to employ many Marxist categories, themes, and arguments, and are for that reason still inheritors of the Marxian intellectual tradition.[282]

---

[280] This was not true in much of Europe. Germany's skyrocketing unemployment and rapid inflation is partially what led to the rise of the National Socialist Party.

[281] Held, *Introduction to Critical Theory*, 59.

[282] Aronowitz explains the relationship between Critical Theory and Marxism in the following way: "The task of Critical Theory was to 'extend' the Marxist analysis to

Critical Theory overlaps more with Lukács, perhaps, than with Marx himself. It was Lukács who first laid a solid foundation for understanding Marxism within the context of late-stage capitalism and its impact on artistic and cultural endeavors. Lukács's totalizing approach to ideology is similarly taken by the Critical Theorists, even if they do so without the same direct connection with activism as the Hungarian writer. Both Lukács and the Frankfurt School recognize the relationship between economic power and artistic power, believing that the powerful exert their dominance by means of the arts as they are given to the people in a given culture. Further, Adorno and Horkheimer draw upon Lukács's use of Marx's concept of commodity fetishism (applying it to media, not only physical products), as well as his notion of reification.

Another Lukácsian theme that appears in the writings of the Critical Theorists is the persistence of suffering in a technological society. Despite many rapid advancements in technology during the twentieth century—which greatly improved the overall quality of life for many—suffering has endured in several areas of society. Technology had undoubtedly alleviated some hardships in the early twentieth century, but it had also created many new ones. Theoretically, technological developments should make life easier, as people tend to innovate in order to create solutions to common problems. Despite the hope of these kinds of improvements, however, they did not make life for the average person all that much better. The explanation that Critical Theorists offer to this lack of life-improvement during such significant technological development is that the benefits of technological process have been hoarded and controlled through the concentration of wealth and resources by a wealthy few. These powerful people prevent the equitable

---

crucial spheres that arose in the twentieth century as a consequence of the passage of capitalism from its competitive phase to that of what he describes, following the denotation of his day, the 'monopoly' stage." Aronowitz, "The Unknown Herbert Marcuse," 144.

distribution of new technologies among the masses and thus create greater disparities between the upper class and the masses.

For the Critical Theorists the pervasive influence of capitalism in the areas of technology, culture, media, and the arts necessitates a comprehensive overhaul of each of these realms, as each has become a means of exploitation and commodification. If capitalism is truly to be replaced with a better system, one must challenge its totalizing control over the culture, structure, products, systems, and ideas in the modern Western world. It is due to this shared commitment to society as a totality that the Critical Theorists can speak of their model as a "theory of everything."[283] And while Adorno eventually comes to see the need for allowing the tensions in life to remain, Marcuse argues for society's complete transformation, even the creation of a "new humanity," due to this totality.

Anti-Modernism

Along with his more typical Marxist critiques of capitalism, Theodor Adorno also aims his critical pen toward many of the beliefs and values of modernity—especially as it arises from the philosophy of Immanuel Kant. Adorno set forth this criticism of modernity with Max Horkheimer in their 1947 book *Dialectic of Enlightenment*, in which both authors take Kantian German idealism to task. This book has sometimes been viewed as a precursor to postmodern philosophy, as Adorno and Horkheimer's critiques of modern thought provide some of the same arguments that would appear in postmodern literature in the following decades. The core thesis of this book is that Enlightenment thought, despite its rationalistic optimism, rather than freeing man from earlier supposedly

---

[283] As Held writes, the Critical Theorists "insisted on the inadmissibility of treating culture in the manner of conventional cultural criticism, in isolation from its position in the social totality. Any conception of culture which saw it as an independent realm apart from society was to be rejected." *Introduction to Critical Theory*, 76.

irrational mythologies, has subsumed everything under its own mythology of domination.[284]

As discussed earlier, the sixteenth and seventeenth centuries brought about significant changes in the Western world that included growth in scientific understanding, new technologies, and an increase in literary production. After the breakthroughs of learning that occurred through the Renaissance and the Reformation, literacy rates began to grow, and the newly created printing press allowed for the mass availability of books, which had not previously been possible. There were also a number of developments that made life more comfortable for men and women during and after this era, with medical breakthroughs and the creation of a rising middle class with the possibility of social mobility. These positive movements in so many areas of society led people to see themselves and their peers as more rational and moral than prior generations, leading them to look with skepticism toward things of the past, as modern thinkers were convinced that the world was gradually moving toward a peaceful future. Philosophers like Kant bound freedom and rationality together, believing that as modern people became more rational in their orientation toward the world, they also became more free.[285] For many modernists, this increase in

---

[284] Adorno summarizes Enlightenment with the following: "Enlightenment's program was the disenchantment of the world. It wanted to dispel myths, to overthrow fantasy with knowledge." In Horkheimer and Adorno's estimation, such an attempt was not achieved, as this quest for domination became its own mythological worldview. Horkheimer and Adorno, *Dialectic of Enlightenment*, 1.

[285] For Adorno, the kind of freedom prioritized with regard to man in the Enlightenment coexisted with a view of nature as mechanically determined, bound by the forces of necessity. While this reinforced the strong distinction between human beings and nature, this eventually led to the perception that men and women were also bound by the necessities of nature. This mechanistic approach, which sees human society as driven by the definite processes of history, was wrongly adopted by the early socialists. He writes that "socialism clung all too desperately to the heritage of bourgeois philosophy. The relationship of necessity to the realm of freedom was therefore treated as merely quantitative, mechanical, while nature,

human freedom would lead to growth in human understanding of, and commitment to, moral duty, and that ultimately would lead to a more just world. This historical optimism ended abruptly with the mass devastation caused by the two world wars in the early twentieth century.

Adorno's view of the world was shaped significantly by his experiences as an ethnic Jew during the rise of Nazism in Germany. Though Adorno escaped from the Nazis himself by immigrating to the United States along with the other Critical Theorists, the horrific acts of genocide toward his people in the Holocaust changed his thinking in profound ways. The Holocaust demonstrated to Adorno—and many others—that the modern world was one not only of technological progress, but also of mass violence. While many modern people believed that the world was moving toward a state of justice, the reality was that rationalism led to mass slaughter, totalitarianism, and the development of far more destructive instruments of war than previously imagined. There is a particular focus, in Adorno, on the development of technology. The rational man of the Enlightenment saw himself as a transcendent being, as a rational instrument who stood above nature and was able to manipulate nature toward whatever end he saw fit. Adorno rejects this idea of transcendent rational man, arguing that people are most-often led by other forces. The development of modern technologies, for Adorno, is led far more by a spirit of domination and destruction than by unaided enlightened reason.[286]

---

posited as wholly alien, as in the earliest mythology, became totalitarian, absorbing socialism along with freedom." Horkheimer and Adorno, *Dialectic of Enlightenment*, 32-33.

[286] "Enlightenment stands in the same relationship to things as a dictator to human beings. He knows them to the extent that he can manipulate them. The man of science knows things to the extent that he can make them. Their 'in-itself' becomes 'for him.' In their transformation the essence of things is revealed as always the same, a substrate of domination." Horkheimer and Adorno, *Dialectic of Enlightenment*, 7.

In discussing this idea of domination, Adorno formulates a series of distinctions of various types of domination that are strong forces in the modern world. The first kind of domination is the domination of nature by human beings. Modern thinkers tend to view themselves as singular subjects who stand outside of, and apart from, the natural world and are able to control and manipulate it.[287] This is exemplified in Descartes's view of the soul. In a Cartesian dualistic model, the natural world is governed by mechanical scientific laws of cause and effect, while the individual soul—which consists of a completely different substance than everything else around it—diverges from the natural world in nearly every way. This separated man of observation that Descartes proposes is, for Adorno, entirely mistaken. Like the other thinkers examined thus far who are influenced by Hegel's writings, Adorno rejects a strong subject/object divide, wherein the human being stands apart from nature as an individual subject to whom the natural world is a series of separable objects.[288] In Adorno's view, if humans began to understand their essential unity with the natural world, rather than pure separation and detachment, people would no longer feel the need to manipulate nature to create instruments of destruction as are present in modern warfare.

In addition to this ever-present battle between man and nature, a second kind of domination exists within individual persons. Regarding this domination of self, Adorno references the psychological idea of projection, where what is true about the self is attributed, by the psyche, to things other than the self, even when such things are not actually present. There is a kind of projection, according to Adorno, wherein the human mind often wrongly

---

[287] "Nature, stripped of its qualities, becomes the chaotic stuff of mere classification, and the all-powerful self becomes a mere having, an abstract entity." Horkheimer and Adorno, *Dialectic of Enlightenment*, 6.

[288] "The distance of subject from object, the presupposition of abstraction, is founded on the distance of things from which the ruler attained by means of the ruled." Horkheimer and Adorno, *Dialectic of Enlightenment*, 9.

projects things which are true about the internal self into the natural world.[289] This projection of the self is at the root of man's domination of nature. Adorno then speaks of a third kind of domination which flows out of these first two: the domination of others. The domination of others, for Adorno, arises from the domination of nature. Once people view themselves as manipulators of the natural world, then they are liable to view themselves in a similar way in relation to other people. For Adorno, this third kind of domination was manifest in the rise of the Third Reich.[290] There is then, in Adorno and Horkheimer's estimation, a connection between Enlightenment philosophy and the actions of the Nazis. Because modern thinkers emphasized human control of nature, people in positions of power began to display domination toward people groups who were deemed dangerous or inferior. For Adorno, this cycle of domination must stop.

Some of the critiques that Adorno makes here regarding the domination of nature and man's isolation from the natural in the modern world are similar, in significant ways, to critiques from conservative thinkers toward the Enlightenment project. Authors like Johann Georg Hamann, Edmund Burke, and Friedrich Julius Stahl criticized the reliance on unaided natural reason and its capabilities in modern philosophy. Similar moves away from rationalism are found in romantic artists like Caspar David Friedrich, who sought to display man in his essential unity with nature as that which reveals God, rather than as an object to conquer. Adorno does not, however, only critique Enlightenment rationality

---

[289] This projection is rather universal in the human experience. Adorno and Horkheimer write that "In a certain sense, all perception is projection." Horkheimer and Adorno, *Dialectic of Enlightenment*, 154.

[290] Adorno argues that it is in both the domination over nature—eventually transforming into domination over others—and the projection of the self onto a group deemed to be "other" (in this case, the Jews) that Nazism has its roots. This extended argument is in "Elements of Anti-Semitism" in *Dialectic of Enlightenment*, 137-172.

(as the aforementioned did), but criticizes the Western tradition in toto. Adorno believes that this flawed modernist view of natural reason arises from mistaken ideas in the classical Greek and Christian philosophical traditions.[291] In other words, the errors of Enlightenment thought were not departures *from*, but the consistent outgrowth *of* Western culture. Adorno and Horkheimer are explicit in their repudiation of the two pillars of Western thought: Platonic philosophy and the Hebrew Scriptures.

ADORNO'S APPROACH TO REASON

Despite these extensive critiques of Enlightenment rationality, Adorno and Horkheimer are not opposed to reason as such. They themselves wrote books and taught, after all, with the intent that their rhetorical and reasoned arguments would persuade others of the validity of their claims. Rather than simply dismissing reason, they are critical of a particular way in which reason has been used in the post-Enlightenment world. Adorno and Horkheimer define this wrong use of reason as *instrumental reason.*[292]

For reason to serve in an instrumental capacity is to say that it is merely a means to bring about some kind of end. While one might argue against what Adorno ultimately concludes on the basis of this, the reality of instrumental reason seems quite obvious, as such a thing manifests itself in ordinary human experience quite often. For example, when young children first begin to develop the capacity to reason, they tend to use that new ability as a means to get what they want. Perhaps a child wants a new toy. This child might

---

[291] In Adorno's view, there is no unchanging transcendental reality which lies beyond material human life. He does, however, allow for a *kind* of transcendence from within. His primary critique of classical and medieval thought is that its obsession with identification leads to domination of the objects or people being classified, thus disallowing dialectical tensions to stand. See Allison Stone's essay, "Adorno and Logic," in Cook, *Theodor Adorno: Key Concepts.*

[292] While this concept is evident throughout *Dialectic of Enlightenment*, it is explained more systematically in Horkheimer's 1957 book, *Eclipse of Reason.*

formulate a reason why their parents should buy them that particular toy. Perhaps that toy would help this child to learn, or to be more productive. These reasons are formulated solely in order to persuade their mother and father that this child should have that toy. The young boy or girl in this instance does not want the toy *because* of the use of reason but instead *uses* reason as a means to convince a parent to get what he or she wants. This instrumental use of reason, not unique to childhood, is common in every aspect of life. Recognizing this, Adorno criticizes Enlightenment optimism about humanity's capacity for thinking rationally through propositions in an unbiased manner. Instead of reasoning for its own sake, humans tend to use reason as a tool of power.

Adorno is largely dependent on Nietzsche here in his understanding of the relationship between reason and power.[293] While Kantians emphasize the interrelatedness of reason and freedom, Nietzsche contends that reason is inseparable, not from freedom, but from power. Nietzsche observes that reason is often used as a means to gain mastery over things. Humans, for example, do not learn about the scientific laws of the universe merely because they love knowledge for its own sake but in order to learn how to control the world around them. The person who gains knowledge also consequently gains power, or at least has more tools at his disposal that may aid in increasing power. This relationship between knowledge and power, for Nietzsche, also functions in the opposite order: having power also means having knowledge.[294] There is a drastic shift in Western philosophy here that goes far beyond Nietzsche. Through Nietzsche's influence, questions of power, rather than reasoned debate, become central for much of the academy—as

---

[293] "Nietzsche's liberating act, a true turning point of Western thought and merely usurped by others later, was to put such mysteries into words. A mind that discards rationalization—its own spell—ceases by its self-reflection to be the radical evil that irks it in another." Adorno, "Negative Dialectics," in *The Adorno Reader*, 72.
[294] Nietzsche's thoughts on the subject can be found in the posthumously published compilation of the philosopher's notes under the title *The Will to Power* (1891).

is evidenced in Adorno here, and even more comprehensively in Foucault. This focus on power leads to a general skepticism toward the assumptions and conclusions affirmed in traditional Western society. Perhaps these basic assumptions were handed down, not due their alignment with the principles of reason, but due to their ability to reinforce reigning power structures.

This conception of power taught in Adorno and Horkheimer, largely drawn from Nietzsche, underlies several of their criticisms of both classical and Enlightenment thought. This approach to power is, for example, an essential aspect of Adorno's rejection of the transcendental subject—i.e. a separable self that stands in a position apart from the world while also able to objectively observe it and understand it. These ideas of the self that dominate older thinking, for Adorno, arise out of human attempts at gaining power. If I set myself against the world as a distinctive subject, this gives me the ability to control nature.[295] In order, then, to stop this domination that is at work in instrumental reason, Adorno contends that we need to see ourselves as part of nature. This will also solve the problem of projection, which Adorno views as central in our misuse and abuse of nature. In Adorno's view, we project our own feelings of frustration, anger, disappointment, etc. onto the world around us, and then we use those feelings to exercise coercive control over nature, which we see as somehow at odds with us. If we cease viewing ourselves as distinct from nature, this projection of anger toward the "other" is no longer a significant problem.

It is essential to understand here that Adorno and Horkheimer are primarily, though not exclusively, responding to Kant. In criticizing the Enlightenment approach to a detached, rational self, they challenge Kant's popular noumenal/phenomenal divide, in which there is an objective noumenal world (the thing-in-itself) that exists apart from human perception and experience. Kant believed that even if humans have no direct access to things as they

---

[295] Adorno, "Negative Dialectics," 144-149.

are in themselves, the objective noumenal world still exists outside of human cognition. Adorno questions whether such an objective noumenal reality exists at all.[296] As a response to Kant's belief in the objectivity of the noumena, Adorno poses an alternative theory. Adorno contends that the idea of an objective external world that exists within the human mind is most likely the result of human evolution. From an evolutionary perspective, belief in the noumena is advantageous for survival.[297] When creatures view themselves as distinct from the world and believe that they are subjects who interact with an external objective reality, they are incentivized to conquer the world around them and then to protect themselves from the dangers of that world, which leads to higher chances of survival. In this view, belief in an objective world serves a utilitarian function, rather than being the logical conclusion to rational inquiries.

As much as Adorno portrays himself as a strong critic of Kantian philosophy, he himself continues to work within the framework of Kant's Copernican Revolution. Andrew Bowie summarizes Adorno's view well: "[Adorno] located objectivity in the subject's thinking, rather than seeing it as inherent in the world."[298] It is clear that Adorno sides with modern philosophy in one of the primary differentiations between classical thought and Enlightenment rationalism. Rather than departing from Kant and offering a true alternative, Adorno's approach here arises from some unresolved tensions within Kant's system. Adorno merely allows the subjectivity of the phenomena to overtake Kant's transcendental reason. For Adorno, then, there is no inherent and transcending meaning, purpose, and teleology in the world that is to be discovered

---

[296] "Once we concede the object's dialectical primacy, the hypothesis of an unreflected practical science of the object as residual after deducting the subject will collapse. The subject is then no longer a deductible addendum to objectivity." Adorno, "Negative Dialectics," 145-146.

[297] "For Adorno the very idea of an 'objective world' develops historically out of what is necessary for human survival." Bowie, *Theodor W. Adorno*, 36.

[298] Bowie, *Theodor W. Adorno*, 57.

by the human subject and then conformed to. Rather, the external world conforms to our own ideas and biases. This, again, is connected to the Hegelian rejection of a strong subject-object dichotomy. For Adorno, we are not transcendent subjects who have access to an objective world through our sense experience, but rather we are part of the totality that is the world.[299]

Adorno reflects the modern move away from a theologically oriented view of reality, in which a transcendent God underlies material reality, upholds the universe in its continued existence, and provides purposes in the world.[300] This is nothing new in his own thought, of course, but is a continuation of the post-theological worldview shared by many modern thinkers. Descartes isolated religion within the internal life of the soul while viewing the material world as a mere machine, devoid of final causality. Hume rejected all reasoning based on causes inherent to things and thus removed the necessity of an immovable divine cause. Kant believed that God was unknowable and that the purpose of religion was limited to practical moral action. Adorno, similarly, strongly rejects both the Jewish and Christian theological traditions. Unlike these other thinkers, however, Adorno has no desire to replace the older mythological conceptions of reality with a new, more rational one. The Enlightenment's narrative of a superstitious past now transcended through modern science and philosophy is, for Adorno, no less mythological than those worldviews which the Enlightenment claims to supersede.[301] While Adorno himself proposes no replacement of these mythological systems (as would a more utopian Marxist), what

---

[299] Adorno does acknowledge that there is a sense in which the distinction between subject and object is a valid one. This division is merely cognitive, however, rather than ontological. Adorno, "Subject and Object," in *The Adorno Reader*, 139.

[300] Adorno refers, for example, to the "devil myth" of the Middle Ages as an attempt to "imbue the world with an arbitrary meaning," which was also seen in the rise of new religious movements in the mid-twentieth century. Horkheimer and Adorno, *Dialectic of Enlightenment*, 162.

[301] This idea is the primary point of argument in chapter one of *Dialectic of Enlightenment*.

he does do is centralize examination of power relations within Theory. With no clear teleology and a distrust of reason, there is no transcendence or rational objectivity for Adorno.[302] This leads to a continual problem for leftist thinkers who follow in the Critical Theorists' footsteps. They promote a system which can only critique, since it is defined almost entirely by what it is against, rather than by a positive conception of the good toward which human beings are to strive.

While Adorno rejects the idea of the transcendent self and dismisses theological interpretations of reality, he does not deny the reality of subjective experience or of the universal human longing for meaning. Regarding subjectivity, Adorno argues that the fact that there are subjective experiences does not necessitate that there is a self-consistent subject that is having those experiences—similar to Hume's rejection of the Cartesian *cogito*. For Adorno, consciousness is not the result of Descartes's proposed inner mind, nor of an immaterial soul. Instead, Adorno believes that consciousness is created by social and economic factors.[303] Following Marx, Adorno continues the trend toward the totalizing of all things under the category of social relations, echoing and expanding upon Marx's centralizing of economic relations. Critical Theory places an increased emphasis on selfhood and identity as mere social

---

[302] Regarding the transcendent rational self, he writes, "What shows up faithfully in the doctrine of the transcendental subject is the priority of the relations—abstractly rational ones, detached from the human individuals and their relationships—they have their model in exchange." In other words, an emphasis on the transcendent subject as a rational being leads individuals to disconnect themselves from their relatedness to one another and to the broader world, which leads to domination. Adorno, "Subject and Object," 141.

[303] This theme appears in Adorno's early work *Kierkegaard's Thought: Construction of the Aesthetic* (1933), in which Adorno proposes a Marxist alternative to existentialism wherein existence is rooted in social relations, rather than in individual subjectivity. The theme is not as prominent in his later writing.

constructs, rather than inherent truths.[304] With Adorno, this is not just an explanation of *human* nature but of nature more broadly. He is critical of the idea that there are *any* objective and unchanging natures at all. For this reason, Adorno is critical of the search for universal scientific laws, which scholars attempt to remove from history and place in the realm of pure objectivity. Because Adorno adopts Hegel's conviction that nature and history constitute one unified whole, he contends that all things, scientific and otherwise, must be grasped in their historical context.

While historicism is, in some ways, commensurate with the Christian tradition's centralizing of historical events—most importantly, the resurrection of Jesus—Adorno's view is not one wherein the transcendent and universal overlaps with the historical and particular. Instead, Adorno's historicism is a rejection of the transcendent and universal altogether.[305] For him, there is nothing that can be understood outside of the historical epoch within which it exists. This is even true of the concepts of history and nature themselves, as Adorno believes that these ideas are in a constant state of flux along with everything else. All of this means that any concept of purpose must be founded in finite historical existence, rather than anything outside of the temporal order.[306] Morality, value, goodness, purpose, and beauty shift from one age to another due to the nature of the historical dialectical process. Conceptions of unchanging

---

[304] Regarding human nature, the denial that there is an unchanging essence of nature is widespread among the Critical Theorists. Horkheimer, for example, says that "the term 'human nature' here does not refer to an original or eternal or a uniform essence. Every philosophical doctrine which sees the movement of society or the life of the individual as emerging out of a fundamental, ahistorical unity is open to justified criticism." As cited in Held, *Introduction to Critical Theory*, 116.

[305] Adorno's view of history and truth can be found in his "Theses on the Language of the Philosopher" and in his paper "The Idea of Natural History." These are both texts from the 1930s, reiterating that these themes are more thoroughly present in that era than in his later work.

[306] To be clear, this does not only mean one's personal subjectivity, since human nature arises from social context and is not a self-subsistent identity.

norms are impositions of identitarian thinking that arise from a mistaken subject-object dichotomy and thus do not truly exist as non-contingent universals of logic or theology.

NEGATIVE DIALECTICS

As one would expect from a student of Hegel, Adorno believes that history is constituted by a dialectical process. In setting forth this dialectic, Adorno does not speak about tensions within the World Spirit that are overcome through a greater synthesis, as is the general Hegelian pattern. Instead of this positive drive toward synthesis, Adorno proposes what he refers to as a *negative dialectic*.[307] Older Hegelianism was teleological in orientation, believing that history is progressive by nature, leading toward the full self-realization of the Geist. Adorno's experiences in the world through the world wars led him to doubt whether such a progressive approach to historical process really reflected the nature of history. He concluded, therefore, that the teleological orientation of Hegel was mistaken.

What is this dialectical process if it does not achieve continual synthesis? Adorno affirms the reality of contradiction and tension between various people, nations, and ideas throughout history as a given. Where he departs from the typical Hegelian is that rather than arguing that these tensions must be reconciled, Adorno suggests that the contradictions in the world must be allowed to simply coexist with one another. There is no inevitability of, or need for, synthesis.[308] Not only does Adorno reject synthesis as an historical inevitability, but he also argues that the attempt to unify contradictions is actually an oppressive instinct of the human mind. Humans impose unity on systems, ideas, and people in the world in

---

[307] This phrase was first used in an essay of that title published in 1966. With this work, Adorno definitively broke with traditional Marxism with his denial that synthesis was a possibility.

[308] "Dialectics serves the end of reconcilement. It dismantles the coercive logical character of its own course; that is why it is denounced as 'panlogism.'" Adorno, "Negative Dialectics," 58.

order to suppress diversity. With this rejection of a synthesizing teleology, Adorno makes the allowance of diversity a moral end in itself. It is imperative upon society to reject the notion of any kind of universal human good toward which all people and institutions must point. Proposing that such a thing exists is, by nature, oppressive, as it stifles the values, actions, and beliefs of those who do not live in accord with it. It is because of his rejection of any transcendent purpose in history that Adorno praises the acceptance of diversity as the ultimate societal good.

This acceptance of diversity must, for Adorno, be accomplished through balancing reason and unreason. As much as Adorno criticizes the Enlightenment's ideal of rational inquiry, he does not argue that this use of reason is to be abolished; it instead must stand alongside those things that are defined as *unreason*, such as the needless human suffering caused by both world wars. In viewing these tensions between reason and unreason in the historical process, Adorno contends that the human subject must be subsumed under the reality of nature.[309] The human subject is not to be identified with an internal essence, but the subject is instead constituted by the total ordering of the world (particularly through the structures of society). Adorno believes that when society recognizes the priority of object over the individual subject, humans will eventually let go of the constant desire for domination over the natural world and simply allow the world to exist as it is, with its tensions intact.

As part of this proposal for unity in diversity, Adorno rejects what he refers to as *identitarian thinking*.[310] This term is used to identify the way in which people look at the external world by way of

---

[309] "Resolution of the tension between the individual and society is impossible. ... Negative dialectics affirms instead the non-identity between subject and object, the individual and society, as well as the particular and the universal." Bronner, *Critical Theory*, 111.

[310] Adorno, "Subject and Object," 145.

classification.[311] When a human encounters any given object, he tends to immediately place that object in some type of preconceived category.[312] This happens constantly. For example, if I see a tree while I am on a walk, that object is immediately placed into the category of "tree" before I think any further about it. And, if I *do* think any further about it, my idea of what a tree is will significantly form those reflections. Any time someone places objects or people into such categories, that person is imputing all sorts of assumptions to the individual object because of preconceptions that one has about the category to which it belongs. For Adorno, this identitarian thinking can lead us to deny the tensions or differences that exist in the world, because classification can cause us to try to force unity or uniformity where such a thing does not exist. Rather than attempting to manipulate things toward some predetermined end, Adorno argues that we should just leave things are they are.

Behind Adorno's views here is his belief in the necessity of contradiction. This negative dialectic that he sets forth can be summarized as the affirmation that things live in irreconcilable tension.[313] Even a cursory view of world history shows that the desire for uniformity in society—political, religious, cultural, ethnic, or otherwise—has been a cause of war and destruction. As humanity has not yet figured out any way to stop such conflicts, in fact they instead seem to heighten as technology further develops, Adorno contends that it is this desire for unity itself that is the problem. In the earlier part of his career, Adorno believed that if society was able to simply acknowledge contradictions without attempting to resolve them, peace would be achievable. Later, however, he became

---

[311] "Bourgeois society is ruled by equivalence. It makes dissimilar things comparable by reducing them to abstract quantities." Horkheimer and Adorno, *Dialectic of Enlightenment*, 4.

[312] "To think is to identify." Adorno, "Negative Dialectics," 57.

[313] "Dialectics is the consistent sense of nonidentity." Adorno, "Negative Dialectics," 57.

increasingly skeptical about such a possibility, doubting that this desired peace would ever become a reality.

ADORNO ON THE CULTURE INDUSTRY

Regardless of what changes Adorno may have undergone regarding his outlook toward the future, there are several points at which he remains consistent throughout his career. One of those consistent themes is his critique of pop culture—or what he calls the *culture industry*. Adorno is not alone among Critical Theorists in writing on high culture and its relation to pop culture. Walter Benjamin wrote extensively on the issue as well, though he arrived at quite different conclusions than Adorno did.[314] It is Adorno, nonetheless, who is most often cited on this topic, and his writings on culture, music, and aesthetics remain influential among both Marxist cultural critics and even among some conservatives who contrast the value of high art with the low-quality, mass-produced art of pop culture.

Adorno's views on culture are deeply intertwined with his own autobiography. As a musician, Adorno was always deeply aware of the connections between the values and thoughts of a society and the art that it produces. This became particularly apparent to Adorno when he observed the workings of Hollywood during his time in Los Angeles. He was disheartened by what he perceived as a disturbing resemblance to the authoritarianism of Nazi Germany in the mass media that was produced and consumed in the United States. Out of this came Adorno's concept of the culture industry, a term that highlights the existence of an industry, particularly prominent in North America, that engages in mass media production for the purpose of silencing and pacifying the populace. Adorno argued that the culture industry perpetuates mindless obedience through the use of this media.

---

[314] Benjamin believed, like many of the Soviets, that media could be used as an explicit tool of political messaging in order to change the beliefs of the masses, so that the populace might be used as a tool of revolutionary action.

I should note that Adorno and Horkheimer initially used the term "mass media" in their early drafts but later replaced it with "culture industry" when publishing their work. The reason for this change was to avoid implying that the media was created by the masses themselves. Art that is actually produced by average citizens is generally referred to as *folk culture*, which is quite distinct from the *pop culture* that Adorno criticizes here. In contrast to folk culture, the American culture industry was designed, not to share the ideas and values of the masses, but to control the masses through the imposition of the values and ideals of the powerful. As ardent Marxists, Adorno and Horkheimer sought to support artistic endeavors among the proletariat, believing that media that was created by the masses, rather than imposed on them, would be a positive good for society. The term *culture industry* underscores the fact that what is enforced from the outside is not actually culture in a true sense but a financial industry which abuses the masses through the sale of mindless entertainment.[315]

According to Adorno and Horkheimer, the culture industry, or mass media, establishes a mindless hegemony which serves to homogenize the perspectives of the masses, thus leading to media itself determining what is considered good or bad in society.[316] This faux-culture, through enforced homogeneity, suppresses creativity and consequently reduces individuals to a role of passive consumption. This, for these Marxists, arises out of the general values and abuses of capitalism. Just as the factory jobs criticized by Marx often consist of repetitive, mindless work that makes people

---

[315] "Culture is a paradoxical commodity. It is so completely subject to the law of exchange that it is no longer exchanged; it is so blindly equated with use that it can no longer be used. For this reason it merges with the advertisement." Horkheimer and Adorno, *Dialectic of Enlightenment*, 131.

[316] Media reinforces bourgeois hegemony by teaching that "everyone can be like the omnipotent society, everyone can be happy if only they hand themselves over to it body and soul and relinquish their claim to happiness." Horkheimer and Adorno, *Dialectic of Enlightenment*, 124.

into machines rather than free subjects, mass media serves as a form of thoughtless entertainment that stimulates the senses without offering substantial value or opportunities for critical engagement. [317] Just as happens with the processes of material production, there also is a process of reification with the media. Through this cultural reification, media is understood as that which has real value, and the viewer/listener is seen simply as a consumer whose value is found primarily in the money given to the corporation creating the media.

The culture industry increases its profits through the manipulation of the masses by convincing consumers of non-existent and artificial needs that can only be fulfilled through popular media. In order to sell any product, the maker of that product must demonstrate that this thing (whatever it might be) fulfills some need that the consumer has and that owning this product will bring some significant life improvement through the fulfillment of that need. [318] This is not only done for physical objects, according to Adorno, but is also at the heart of the advertising that occurs for movies and television shows. Hollywood's ultimate aim is the continued increase in profit, which occurs through the generation and promulgation of a sense of necessity in consuming their cultural products. Through Hollywood advertising, people feel that they *need* to see the next popular film or television series, whether that need is simply to be "in the know" for the purposes of socializing or to fulfill some internal desire to find out what will happen next in a multi-season series (hence the creation of the cliffhanger). There is no actual need that exists within the consumer that drives the media companies. The culture industry, particularly evident in mindless films and TV

---

[317] "Individuals are tolerated only as far as their wholehearted identity with the universal is beyond question." Horkheimer and Adorno, *Dialectic of Enlightenment*, 124.

[318] Since these supposed needs are artificially constructed, they are never actually fulfilled, leading consumers to continually come back with a sense that fulfillment will eventually come. "The culture industry endlessly cheats its consumers out of what it endlessly promises." Horkheimer and Adorno, *Dialectic of Enlightenment*, 111.

shows, prioritizes profit, rather than the fulfillment of actual needs or value.

The methods of media growth described by Adorno are quite apparent in the contemporary world, just as they were in his own time. There is no greater example of this principle than the movies in the Marvel Cinematic Universe (owned by the same Walt Disney corporation that was at the heart of Adorno's critique).[319] These movies began a trend, which has become normative in several other franchises, of including an after-credits scene following the ending of the film. These scenes show some event, a new hero or villain, or something else that is going to be present in the next film in the series. The story of a movie or movie series is never actually over but is just the beginning of some new story. This leads to a sense of need to see the next movie in the series, such that one will then pay for the next installment of the franchise in order to discover the meaning of what was revealed in the last one. And then, another mystery is set up for the following installment in a never-ending process of non-endings. This has all gotten to the point that movies, by themselves, often feel like advertisements for the next movie, rather than a self-contained coherent and cohesive story.[320]

The culture industry transforms individuals into passive recipients, diminishing their creativity and engagement with worthwhile endeavors. Instead of investing their time in meaningful activities, such as engaging in the production of real art, people become absorbed in consuming the products manufactured by the

---

[319] Adorno supposedly referred to Walt Disney as "the most dangerous American of all time," but I have been unable to track down this often-referenced quote in Adorno's writings.

[320] It is important to note here that one need not be a Marxist in order to be sympathetic to some of Adorno's criticism. Personally, while I do not believe Adorno's Marxism provides the solution to this issue, I find significant commonality with Adorno in his object of critique. Many conservatives, such as Roger Scruton, have voiced similar critiques of mass media, albeit from different perspectives (and with different proposed solutions based on radically divergent values between the two intellects).

culture industry. Consequently, the capacity for critical thinking and self-determination is stifled.[321] Consumers become captive to media corporations in a way that mirrors how citizens in a fascist civilization are captive to the state. Consider, as an example, the scenario where a man spends his entire day engaging in mindless work, only to return home and mindlessly consume television shows for hours on end. This man, even if he has a family at home, might eat dinner in front of the TV before eventually retiring to bed. In such a routine of consumption, life loses its meaning. Work lacks significance, and the media content consumed offers no genuine value. People become mere cogs in a machine, living out a meaningless, monotonous existence.[322] Through this captivity of the masses by media corporations, individuals no longer allocate time to reading books, nurturing their creativity, or producing art. They have become mere passive recipients of valueless entertainment that pretends to be art, leading to a kind of slavery to media empires.

HIGH ART

As one who had significant training in the arts, Adorno had an admiration for what is often considered "high art," such as the music of Beethoven and the operas of Wagner. While Adorno does not appeal to transcendent standards of beauty in his work, he is not a pure aesthetic relativist but operates with a real distinction between good and bad art. This affinity for the high arts by Adorno often leads to a prioritization of classical Western works over some which were

---

[321] "The spectator must need no thoughts of his own: the product prescribes each reaction, not through any actual coherence—which collapses once exposed to thought—but through signals. Any logical connection presupposing mental capacity is scrupulously avoided." Horkheimer and Adorno, *Dialectic of Enlightenment*, 109.

[322] "Only by subordinating all branches of intellectual production equally to the single purpose of imposing on the senses of human beings ... the imprint of the work routine that they must sustain throughout the day, does this culture mockingly fulfill the notion of a unified culture." Horkheimer and Adorno, *Dialectic of Enlightenment*, 104.

produced by the masses (such as jazz).[323] This has led to significant critique from some leftist thinkers. Many progressives have argued that the high arts have historically been privileged over others solely due to the preferences of the ruling class, rather than any clear standard of superiority. In contrast, with his disdain for pop culture and jazz, along with his own preferences for classical music and opera, Adorno often uplifts the aesthetic preferences of the elite rather than those of the working class.[324] This alignment with the high arts is more than simply subjective preference for Adorno; his theory of aesthetics drives these evaluations. For Adorno, valuable art has the ability to both challenge and transcend the limits of society.[325] It demonstrates that there is more to life than material production. While not identical to the Kantian perception of the sublime, there is some commonality with Kant's view of art here, where an encounter with beauty brings a person beyond their social context or other concerns as they come into contact with something more universal.

Unlike Kant, Adorno does not believe that an encounter with beauty in art is a transcendent experience (in the fullest sense at least), and he certainly does not align with the Christian perspective that an encounter with beauty is an encounter with God.[326] Rather than expounding upon these metaphysical connections between art and beauty, Adorno's focus remains political. Due to its independent nature, art challenges the status quo and thereby opens the mind of

---

[323] Adorno's criticisms of jazz are scathing and unrelenting. See his essay "The Perennial Fashion—Jazz" in *The Adorno Reader*, 267-279.

[324] This is not always the case. He is critical, for example, of Don Quixote as part of "art becoming bourgeoisified." Adorno, *Aesthetic Theory*, in *The Adorno Reader*, 241.

[325] Regarding the independence of art from society, Adorno writes that "art criticizes society just by being there. Pure and immanently elaborated art is a tacit critique of the debasement of man by a condition that is moving towards a total-exchange society where everything is for-other." Adorno, *The Adorno Reader*, 242.

[326] For a treatment of the classical and Christian approaches to beauty, see my work in Cooper, *In Defense of the True, the Good, and the Beautiful*, 135-161.

the viewer or listener to revolutionary ideas.[327] This does not mean, however, that art should be purely or directly political in its content or intent. Some critical theorists—most popularly Walter Benjamin—argue for the insertion of radical progressive propaganda into mass media as a tool to forcefully impose revolutionary views on the masses. In contrast to this approach, Adorno emphasizes the importance of *freely* engaging with revolutionary ideas through art that challenges the perspective of the viewer or listener.[328]

This divide between Adorno and Benjamin regarding the relationship between art and the political remains today both in the academy and in popular media. Some contemporary progressives advocate for the forceful embedding of their own cultural views and values into mass media, believing that by a kind of osmosis consumers of those media products will adopt such perspectives for themselves. Adorno cautions against such an approach, as it mirrors the coercive tactics used by the culture industry that he despises so strongly.[329] For Adorno, good art helps the revolutionary cause by revealing a higher purpose beyond the mundane aspects of capitalist society.[330] It serves as a catalyst for bringing people out of their slavery to economic principles of production and consumption, awakening them to fight for change. In summary, Adorno recognizes the political dimension of art but rejects the imposition of explicit

---

[327] "Art will live on only as long as it has the power to resist society." Adorno, *The Adorno Reader*, 243.

[328] As an example of art which encourages freedom, Adorno cites the works of Kafka, which portray the absurdities of modern capitalist bureaucracy while never making direct political commentary. He contrasts this with the realism favored by Soviet Marxists. Adorno, *The Adorno Reader*, 247.

[329] "If art works have any social influence at all, it is not by haranguing …. Any directly propagandistic effect evaporates quickly." Adorno, *The Adorno Reader*, 256.

[330] "Art's social impact, strictly understood, is very mediate. Its influence is due to the fact that art participates in spirit, which in turn congeals in art works, helping to determine changes in society, albeit in a subterranean, invisible fashion." Adorno, *The Adorno Reader*, 255.

political messaging in mass media. Mass media cannot be part of the solution to Western capitalism, since mass media *is* the problem.

As an anti-capitalist, Adorno contends that, while art is often driven by economic success, it should instead be driven by freedom and the pursuit of beauty. In light of this emphasis on artistic freedom, Adorno criticizes art that is supported by patronage or religious institutions, as ties to the specific artistic demands of patrons limit the creative freedom of artists. The Enlightenment began to free art from religious institutions, as creating and selling art was no longer possible only through these means. Men (and eventually women) could now pursue a career in the arts through increased economic prosperity, social mobility, and the creation of art museums and private galleries. This freedom to create whatever the artist desires to create had, in America, been stifled by the emergence of mass media and the culture industry.

A DEFINITION OF CRITICAL THEORY

It is only now, after some extensive discussion of the core ideas of the Frankfurt School, that this text attempts to define Critical Theory. This movement is far more difficult to identify with precision than is classical Marxism, as the multitudinous thinkers associated with Critical Theory have divergent fields of expertise—and often disagree with one another in areas where their writing does intersect. One cannot identify Critical Theory with any one thinker and thereby define the whole school with a singular individual's most prominent ideas. For this reason, David Held notes that many interpreters have concluded that "it is easier to say what critical theory is not rather than what it is."[331] Held cites a number of common lines of critique among the Critical Theorists, including: Kantian transcendentalism, Hegelian synthesis, philosophies of identity between subject and object, the inevitability of economic forces that necessarily end in socialist revolution, Marxist

---

[331] Held, *Introduction to Critical Theory*, 22.

humanism, Feuerbachian humanism, existentialism, phenomenology, and positivism.[332] This gives some guidance but has inadequate explanatory power. For a positive definition, an attempted construction can be drawn from one of the most prolific writers of the Frankfurt School—Herbert Marcuse.

This definition was first proposed by Douglas Kellner, who extracts a positive identification of the movement from Marcuse's writing.[333] This summary of Marcuse's vision is set forth in what Kellner calls the "three Cs" of Critical Theory. This definition remains incomplete and incomprehensive, but it does at least provide some of the basic principles used by these theorists. They are as follows.

1. Critical Theory attempts to *Comprehend* society. Critical theorists strive for a comprehensive understanding of how and why society operates as it does. They do so through an examination of the many facets of culture, including economics, art, anthropology, nature, science, media, and philosophy. Each of these areas is viewed through the lens of late-stage capitalism, as capitalism is believed to retain a pervasive influence in every aspect of society. Because the Critical Theorist approaches society as a totality, the neo-Marxist lens through which society is viewed must also be totalizing as the only valid means by which one can rightly understand anything about the modern world.

2. Critical Theory attempts to *Criticize* society. Critical Theory, as the name implies, is largely a critical enterprise, as it offers comprehensive and totalizing critiques of Western civilization. The goal, for Critical Theorists, is to scrutinize every societal structure and norm through the lens of exploitative power and oppression. This critical examination leads the theorist to find the ways in which power has been abused through hegemonic oppression, so that such unjust elements of society can be torn down. For Marcuse, even more

---

[332] Held, *Introduction to Critical Theory*, 22-24.
[333] This is drawn from Farr, "Herbert Marcuse," in *Routledge Handbook of Marxism and Post-Marxism*, 187.

than for the other Critical Theorists, this destructive enterprise is at the core of the discipline of Critical Theory.

3. Critical Theory attempts to *Construct* alternatives to capitalist society. Critical Theory, like other Marxist systems, has a utopian inclination, as these theorists seek to define and construct new social structures that are free from the oppressive dynamics that they have identified in capitalism. While different thinkers approach this task with varying methods and have diverse proposals, the overarching desire to dismantle the totality of the existing system of government, morality, and religion, and to usher in a new order to replace it, is pervasive throughout. Like Lukács and Gramsci, the Critical Theorists seek the construction of an alternative society from the ground up, rather than slow reforms within existing systems.

Critical Theory's three Cs include a totalizing comprehension of society, a critical examination and critique of its shortcomings, and the construction of alternative frameworks that challenge and transcend the existing order. In short, Critical Theorists attempt to tear down bourgeois society in the West and then reconstruct a new order in its place.

HERBERT MARCUSE

The definition above is drawn largely from the work of one of the most significant thinkers to arise out of the Frankfurt School: Herbert Marcuse. While all of the Critical Theorists are radicals to some degree, Marcuse's radicalism exceeds that of his peers. Born in 1898 and living until 1979, he had a long and prolific career, actively engaging in various intellectual pursuits—namely, writing and teaching—and making numerous public appearances.[334] Because of Marcuse's career as a "public intellectual," there are a vast number of interviews and discussions with him available in various media

---

[334] There is no single comprehensive biography of Marcuse in English. An account of his life can be found, along with those of other academics in the Frankfurt School, in Jeffries, *Grand Hotel Abyss*.

formats, which means that his views are easy to access for one who desires to look.

While many of the Frankfurt thinkers, such as Horkheimer and Adorno, grew increasingly pessimistic about the prospects of a genuine revolution as they aged, Marcuse remained firmly committed to the cause of revolution with a cautious optimism that transformative societal change would eventually arise within capitalist societies. Marcuse's optimism was echoed by (and was to some extent the result of) many of the student movements of the 1960s, in which young activists drew on the ideas of the Critical Theorists, among others, to fight for societal transformation. While Adorno's and Horkheimer's respective works were influential on the ideas of these young leftists (Adorno had something of a celebrity status among them), it was only Marcuse who shared their progressive hope for a just society free of exploitation.[335] It is not only this lingering optimism that sets Marcuse apart; while he shares many concerns and general ideas with Adorno and Horkheimer, he provides several unique contributions to the development of neo-Marxism and its integration within varied fields of study. One of these places of integration is in Marcuse's use of the ideas of Sigmund Freud.

FREUDIANISM

The influence of Freud is evident among all the Critical Theorists to some degree, just as it was among many academics in the early- to mid-twentieth century. Freud's theories did not only impact the field of psychology, but his work led to new questions, methods, and ideas that would be used in a multitude of academic disciplines—including those engaged in by the academics of the Frankfurt School. As the Critical Theorists were attempting to bring elements of Marxist theory beyond the fields of economics and politics, psychology was

---

[335] It is to be noted that optimism for revolution does not mean *immediate* revolution. Marcuse speaks at times about the move toward socialism and justice as a slow and long process not to be achieved amid the current conditions of the West.

recognized as a field ripe for fruitful examination within a critical framework. There were some proponents of Critical Theory (most notably Jacques Lacan) who were psychologists in the proper sense. Others, including both Adorno and Marcuse, merely dabbled in psychological literature as one element of their totalizing approach to ideology.

One element of the integration and use of psychological literature and methodology within the Frankfurt School was the conducting of psychological studies and experiments.[336] One of the most well-known was Theodor Adorno's attempt to define elements of an "authoritarian personality."[337] Adorno believed that if he could identify the specific traits and characteristics of authoritarians, these tendencies could be trained out of people's behavior at a young age. In Adorno's estimation, if these negative traits could be eradicated through training, the horrors present in the Second World War could be avoided in future conflicts. This study has been subjected to immense criticism from psychologists, as Adorno's criteria for authoritarian personalities are far from an objective set of agreed-upon measures. Further, it appears that the questionnaire used in this study identifies personality traits common among those with more conservative personalities and temperaments as inherently "authoritarian." This clear bias in Adorno's study leads him to see those who share his own temperamental orientations, and especially those who are self-proclaimed leftists, as the least prone to authoritarianism. Adorno appears to be blind to authoritarianism among those who are identified with the political left, assuming that fascist governments, like those of Nazi Germany, pose the sole threat to liberty and justice.

Following Adorno, Marcuse was similarly interested in the field of psychology—though his work in psychology centered on the

---

[336] For an overview of the Frankfurt School's work here, see Held, *Introduction to Critical Theory*, 136-143.
[337] Adorno, *The Authoritarian Personality*.

work of Freud, rather than the identification of authoritarian personalities. Marcuse believed that psychoanalysis could benefit the Critical Theorists' project by providing tools to examine the lack of revolutionary consciousness among the proletariat. With other twentieth-century Marxists, Marcuse was forced to reckon with the fact that Marx's predicted revolutions throughout Europe had not come to fruition. The driving question for him was the same that motivated Lukács, Gramsci, and others: *What is it about the proletariat that has stopped their revolutionary activity from materializing?* Several answers were given, proposing that the role of the media, the uniqueness of certain political situations, the divergence of various forms of power, or other factors were tools of pacification which demotivated the oppressed from engaging in revolutionary activity. While Marcuse did not deny that these factors played a role in the then-current political situation, he believed that a deeper answer for inaction could be found within the field of psychology. Through psychoanalysis, the revolutionary psychologist could probe far deeper into the consciousness of the masses, identifying the specific mental, emotional, and other psychological barriers to their mobilization. If these psychological barriers could be identified, they could then potentially be removed, which would then lead to genuine revolution.[338]

Marcuse's developed analysis of these psychological barriers in the proletarian psyche is found in his 1955 book, *Eros and Civilization*.[339] In this work, Marcuse identifies two principles at work

---

[338] It is a common critique of Marcuse that while he speaks so often of psychology, he was not actually engaged in clinical psychological trials or other more scientific forms of analysis. This means that his conclusions do not have verifiable data to support them. He writes more as a philosopher and social critic than a psychologist. As Kellner writes, "Marcuse's work lacked the sustained empirical analysis in some versions of Marxist theory and the detailed conceptual analysis found in many versions of political theory." Kellner, "Marcuse," in *A Companion to Continental Philosophy*, 394.

[339] A second, updated edition was released in 1966 and has been in print continually through the present day. Marcuse considered this his most important work.

within the internal life of each person: the *reality principle* and the *pleasure principle*. This distinction, drawn from Freud, identifies both an evolutionary and a developmental bifurcation of these elements of life.[340] The pleasure principle identifies the fact that human beings seek pleasure. We perform acts to bring us enjoyment in various forms through the senses (eating, drinking, sex, play, sleep, etc.). When a person seeks only pleasure, however, that individual is quickly confronted with a variety of negative consequences of pleasure seeking. For example, taking whatever one wants might lead to a conflict with another person who also desires that object, or eating too much might lead to sickness. Through these negative consequences of the unrestrained seeking of pleasure comes the reality principle. The reality principle refers to the internal recognition of the consequences of an unconstrained quest for pleasure. Out of the tension between these two principles of life arises *reason*, which functions as a balancing force between these competing principles of pleasure and reality. Through reason the mind learns to consider more than mere pleasure, as reason evaluates things with questions of use or benefit, judging the consequences of acting for self-fulfillment in one way or another. When someone seeks to do something pleasurable, reason assesses whether the consequences are positive or negative and determines action on that basis. In Marcuse's view, it is through this rational process of reason balancing these two principles that unified subjective experience arises, and the subject is formed.

The desire for pleasure as described by Freud, and echoed by Marcuse, can be further divided into two different elements: the force of *eros* and the death instinct. *Eros* refers to the positive desire for pleasurable things or experiences in life—especially sex. The

---

[340] For Freud, there are actually three principles, these two and the Nirvana principle. While Marcuse can similarly speak in a tripartite manner, he also recognizes that "it seems that there is a dichotomy hidden behind the tripartite division," in which "the Nirvana principle too would be a form of the pleasure principle." Marcuse, "Freedom and Freud's Theory of Instincts," in *The Essential Marcuse*, 165.

death instinct refers to the desire to negate the realities of pain, suffering, and displeasure that characterize life. The Nirvana principle identifies a desire for "regression into the painless condition before birth" inherent within the psyche.[341] This leads to these two contradictory elements of the mind: the life instinct (associated with *eros*) and the death instinct (associated with Nirvana). Or, put more simply, the instinct to seek pleasure and the instinct to mitigate displeasure. While in a sense these are two sides of the same coin, the self must balance the interplay between pleasure and avoidance of displeasure that characterizes the inner life, while also balancing the reality principle.

This construction of the psychological self set forth by Marcuse bridges theory and practice. It explains why proletarian revolutions did not come to pass as predicted, and it also provides a framework on which to build a program for future revolution. Applying Freud's work to the political, Marcuse contends that a psychological pacification has occurred in European societies, wherein the proletariat has been made to believe that their predicament, though negative, is not a dire one. The bourgeoisie, in this conception, have not *completely* divested the masses of their daily needs or desires. There is an element of pleasure that is still graspable by the masses. If the upper classes took absolutely everything from those who are marginalized in society, then the need for revolution would become obvious, and this would lead to the inevitable move toward socialism that Marx envisioned. As a means of suppressing these impulses of revolution, the bourgeoisie make sure that the most basic needs of the masses continue to be met in society, even while those individuals are being exploited in other ways. This results in the provision of *just enough*, which has blinded the proletariat to the seriousness of their situation and has thus resulted in pacification.[342]

---

[341] Marcuse, "Freedom and Freud's Theory of Instincts," in *The Essential Marcuse*, 165.
[342] This pacification also includes a suppression of critical thinking in society through the creation of false needs that culture provides solutions to. This leads to a

This pacification works because it plays on the intricate balance between the pleasure, nirvana, and reality principles. The pleasure principle is, to some degree, satisfied through being in a society where there is some sense of enjoyment or freedom, even if suppressed. Further, the possible consequences of revolution are viewed through the relation between pleasure and the avoidance of pain. While the results of a revolutionary fight might bring more pleasure to the masses if successful, the consequences of a failed revolution (or even one's own possible death in a successful one) are dire enough to dissuade people from getting involved in this type of activity. The death impulse, in which the human being is driven to take actions which mitigate pain or displeasure, moves people against these actions and movements due to the negative consequences that they might bring. In order to foment revolution, then, the masses must be convinced that their situation is bad enough that the consequences of revolution are worth risking.

In light of this pacification of the proletariat through minimal provision by the bourgeoisie, Marcuse affirms the need for some class of people to awaken the masses to the seriousness of their exploitation. Like both Lukács and Gramsci, Marcuse believes that the Marxist intellectual can, to some degree, fulfill this necessary societal role.[343] This once again demonstrates the prophetic role that Marxist intellectuals are perceived to play within society, illuminating people's ultimate problem (exploitation) and then pointing the masses toward the way of redemption from that dilemma (revolution). By assuming this role, intellectuals like Marcuse do not view themselves as the ultimate instruments of

---

one-dimensional society, devoid of serious intellectual engagement. This argument is made in Marcuse's book *One-Dimensional Man*.

[343] "[I]t is the task and duty of the intellectual to recall and preserve historical possibilities which seem to have become utopian possibilities—that it is his task to break the concreteness of oppression in order to open the mental space in which this society can be recognized as what it is and does." Marcuse, "Repressive Tolerance," in *The Essential Marcuse*, 33.

liberation; they expose societal structures of injustice, but lasting social impact must arise from within the masses themselves. The intellectual serves a transitional role in the move from late-stage capitalism to socialism. Regarding this transitional role of intellectuals, Edward Andrew writes,

> At times, [Marcuse] suggests an "educational dictatorship" by an intellectual elite as a transitional period until the masses become fully conscious and accept the ruling hierarchy structured by technological rationality.[344]

There is some difficulty in explaining Marcuse's views with precision here, as he is not always clear. He does not have a singular, consistent explanation in his writings of how the transition away from capitalism would occur, or of the precise role that distinct groups would play within that transition. This is further complicated by the fact that Marcuse often makes seemingly contradictory statements within a single essay, and that at times he speaks as if there is no hope of revolution at all—at least not in the present conditions of the West.

REVOLUTIONARY CONSCIOUSNESS

Throughout his writings, Marcuse uses the phrase *revolutionary consciousness* to describe the awakening among the masses that he hoped for. Later in his career, this became more than mere hope, as Marcuse believed that such a consciousness had made itself evident among the activist student groups that were formed in the 1960s counterculture of the hippies.[345] Marcuse contended that the revolutionary consciousness that was manifest in these cultural

---

[344] Andrew, "Work and Freedom in Marcuse and Marx," 253.

[345] "The student protests of the 1960s, the civil rights movement, the women's rights movement, the environmentalist movement, the hippies etc. were all examples of a revolt against repression, war, waste and oppression. These protests were proof that even in a repressive society and in a non-revolutionary time the instinctual structure of many human individuals cried out against this repression." Farr, "Herbert Marcuse," 158.

changes was not something novel but had existed among the masses for quite some time—though not clearly recognized. This class knowledge of exploitation is subconscious; it lies beneath the surface of one's self-awareness due to the psychological pacification imposed by the bourgeoisie.[346] It had, through these student groups, finally begun to move above the surface, as exploitation was now more clearly recognized. These countercultural movements would, Marcuse hoped, eventually lead to a socialist revolution.[347]

Marcuse's use of Freudian psychology helps him to explain why class consciousness is distinct from the consciously articulated beliefs and values of the individuals within that class (a distinction first clearly described by Lukács). As discussed in the previous chapter, Marxist intellectuals often promote ideas that are endorsed by the intelligentsia rather than by the working classes who they purport to represent. This leads to an elitism of the intellectual and a silencing of the voice of the working class—exactly the opposite of the Marxist mission. Using Freud, Marcuse is able to articulate exactly how it is that this disconnect between the working class and class consciousness arises.

Among Freud's most well-known concepts is his idea of repression. For Freud, the mind has both conscious and subconscious elements. The conscious mind consists in all the thoughts of an individual that are recognized by that individual, whereas the subconscious comprises those ideas, thoughts, or impulses which remain below the surface of conscious knowledge yet retain a significant effect upon the one who has them. These

---

[346] Marcuse uses Freud's notion of repression here.

[347] Marcuse's attitude toward student movements stands in stark contrast to that of Adorno. Aronowitz writes, "As Adorno and Horkheimer carefully distanced themselves from the student movement, suspecting it was little more than a return to barbarism in revolutionary garb, or worse, grist for strengthening the social machine, during the years of protest. Marcuse, already seventy years old, rarely refused an invitation to speak at a demonstration or lend his name to a petition or an appeal." Aronowitz, "The Unknown Herbert Marcuse," 148.

subconscious realities often lead to the individual to act in a way that is driven by fears, motivations, or feelings whose origin is unrecognized. One of the ways that ideas or events are placed into the realm of the subconscious is through repression. Traumatic events often lead the mind to forget such events as a defense mechanism, particularly when an event is so damaging to the individual that conscious awareness of it would significantly impact ordinary life, and thus one's survival. This process of repression is distinct from suppression in that the latter is a purposeful action, while the former is not a conscious one.

Repression is not only associated with trauma, however, as repression also occurs when an individual's inner instincts or desires are deemed inappropriate or harmful during the process of development. This occurs based on the pleasure and reality principles. When an individual's urges (often sexual) come into conflict with the reality principle, these desires are repressed for the sake of preservation. For Freud, this principle of repression is not corporate or social but individual. Each person has their own unique desires in the process of development (though they come through the same general stages of fixation), and their individual repression arises from the particular circumstances in which the person is raised and experiences that person has. This concept of repression is used in psychotherapy with the belief that uncovering hidden trauma, hurt, or feelings can help one to receive needed care and find psychological healing.

In Marcuse's conception of Freud's idea, repression helps to explain the nature of class consciousness. Rather than the individual repression that occurs in one's process of personal development, Marcuse contends for consciousness and repression within classes as part of historical development. Marcuse's conception of consciousness is a combination of Freud's psychoanalysis and Hegel's historicism. This means that Marcuse can speak of class consciousness in such a way that reconciles the disconnect between the conscious beliefs of the working class and their underlying class consciousness. While the conscious mind of the working class might be opposed to revolution, they still retain their subconscious revolutionary orientation. In speaking about this class repression, Marcuse speaks about *surplus repression* that can serve as a tool of political mobilization and can also be eliminated through social progress.[348]

For Marcuse, this surplus repression is not destined to remain within the masses in perpetuity. Hope for class awakening was found among students in the 1960s, as this consciousness was making itself known by moving from the unconscious to the conscious self. In his later career, Marcuse references several examples of the emergence of this revolutionary consciousness, such as the civil rights movement, feminism, protests against the Vietnam War, and various other fights for social change in the mid-twentieth century. As these movements were largely led by the young, Marcuse came to believe that it was the youth who would be the most central carriers of radical ideas; they are often the people who are most receptive to—and actively engaged in advocating for—transformative social change. With this reinvigorated, engaged youth, Marcuse has created a mechanism for revolution that relies upon the two groups most receptive to these ideas: intellectuals and college students. If intellectuals like Marcuse were able to construct various radical conceptions of politics, ethics, and culture, they could then spread these ideas to students—thus making students into social activists who were mobilized to achieve the socialist vision laid out by leftist intellectuals. In this way, theory and practice come together to fundamentally reorder civilization.

---

[348] Bernstein observes that "with the quasi-Marxist category of 'surplus repression' Marcuse argued for the possibility of moving beyond Freud's understanding of the 'reality principle' to a form of society where, while we might not eliminate all repression, we would eliminate all the 'surplus-repression' and guilt that is the source of so much human unhappiness." Bernstein, "Herbert Marcuse: An Immanent Critique," 103.

REDEFINING THE PROLETARIAT

One of the most significant developments that Marcuse makes within Marxist thought is his redefinition of the identity of the proletariat. When Marx wrote against exploitation in the nineteenth century, the term *proletariat* referred primarily to individuals who were involved in material production in the context of early industrialization. They often had to endure deplorable working conditions characterized by long hours, a lack of breaks, the absence of safety precautions, child labor, widespread abuse, and meager wages. One need not be a Marxist to recognize the real need to change these circumstances for the working class. Conditions were, in some measure, exploitative. Marcuse contends that in a twentieth-century context, the proletariat must be re-identified because the mechanisms and structure of capitalism had changed significantly.[349] This group is not to be identified only with those who produce objects materially or who work for low wages. He also includes those who would now be considered white-collar workers. It is not only the lower class that are victims of exploitation, but also the middle class.

According to Marcuse's characterization, the average middle-class person, who owns a home, affords an ample selection of food, dines out regularly, subscribes to streaming services, and enjoys internet access, is part of the proletariat. This leads to an expansion of the power dynamic at work within Marxist thought such that those who have economic stability are still actively engaged in the class struggle in a way that was not represented in classical Marxism. While Marcuse reframes the proletariat/bourgeoisie dynamic, the core meaning of that dynamic remains unchanged. As in classical Marxism, the proletariat are still defined by lack of control over the means of production. The bourgeoisie, in turn, retain their position of power and influence in society by controlling the means of production. The key differentiation here is that in Marcuse's

---

[349] Marcuse, *Marxism, Revolution, and Utopia*, 392.

conception, this production occurs, not only in the realm of material goods, but with regard to any service in society. Producing without controlling production identifies one as a member of the proletarian class, regardless of the field in which one works.

For Marcuse, even if someone holds a white-collar job, earns a decent income, and possesses educational qualifications, they can still find themselves trapped as a mere machine, lacking true self-determination. These people do not live for themselves but for the corporations in which they work. Like the factory workers abused in the nineteenth century, much of the twentieth-century middle class had been treated as products rather than persons through the processes of reification and commodification. This middle-class segment of society, which Marcuse argues is now part of the proletariat, exhibits what he terms *surplus consciousness*. Surplus consciousness refers to the mental energy that belongs to the middle class beyond that which is used to engage in labor or mass media consumption. In other words, even though the bourgeoisie have control over much of the mental life of proletarian workers, there remains a significant element of consciousness within middle-class workers that could be awakened and directed to revolutionary activities. The significance of surplus consciousness for Marcuse lies in this potential use of it by revolutionaries. Activists like Marcuse could tap into this surplus consciousness and convince these individuals to actively participate in various forms of revolutionary work.

Against Tolerance

While Marcuse spends a significant amount of time identifying what he perceives to be the cause of the lack of awakening to revolutionary change in Western society, he does occasionally address possible solutions to this dilemma, or at least pieces of a solution. He contends that social change must happen through various institutions that make up society, such as the academy and the state. The emphasis on the university in Marcuse's program is due to the strong tie between intellectuals and the invigorated youth that he experienced in his own later academic career.

Marcuse believes that social institutions should not be viewed as ideologically neutral, committed solely to free inquiry or engagement with differing ideas. In his view, all institutions are driven by ideology of one sort or another. If it is true that ideology is so deeply entrenched institutionally, then harmful ideologies must be rooted out of those institutions if social consciousness is to change. In pursuit of this developing social consciousness, Marcuse argues against the often-praised liberal value of tolerance in what is likely his most controversial writing—an essay from 1965 titled "Repressive Tolerance." For Marcuse, the allowance of freedom of speech, in an absolute sense, is in some way allowing for the prevalence and promulgation of bourgeois ideals. Systems of government, education, or other cultural institutions which rely on tolerance often lead to the presumption of the ideals of the reigning ideology in a society, which is usually that of the upper class. In an oft-cited passage in this essay, in opposition to this tolerance toward bourgeois ideals, Marcuse appears to allow for violence against established authorities in these spheres who do promote these ideals. He writes:

> Law and order are always and everywhere the law and order which protect the established hierarchy; it is nonsensical to invoke the absolute authority of this law and this order against those who suffer from it and struggle against it—not for personal advantages and revenge, but for their share of humanity. There is no judge over them than the constituted authorities, the police, and their own conscience. If they use violence, they do not start a new chain of violence but try to break an established one. Since they will be punished, they know the risk, and when they are willing to take it, no third person, and least of all the educator and intellectual, has the right to preach them abstention.[350]

---

[350] Marcuse, "Repressive Tolerance," 55.

By identifying law and order itself as inherently tied to the ruling hierarchy, and in identifying the ruling class as oppressive, Marcuse identifies law and order as inherently oppressive (at least in capitalist societies). The question here is what exactly defines the boundaries within which student action can be taken or restrained, if they cannot be constrained by law. In Marcuse's argument, even acts of violence are justified, because when violence is enacted against an oppressive group, it is the oppressive group that is at fault rather than the young agitator. One could imagine such an excuse being used for all manner of evil acts against any individual or group who is deemed oppressive. Further, Marcuse demonstrates here that the academic or intellectual must not interfere with violent acts or student pushback against authority structures. This is a manifestation of a recurring theme in Marcuse's thought, the deep tie between intellectuals and students needed to foment revolution.

Another important element of this essay—which has rightly been challenged—is Marcuse's denial of free speech when that speech is deemed to be "propaganda," which is harmful to society. He argues that

> tolerance cannot be indiscriminate and equal with respect to the contents of expression, neither in word or in deed; it cannot protect false words and wrong deeds which demonstrate that they contradict and counteract the possibilities of liberation.[351]

Tolerance is only to be applied to ideas which promote liberation, which means that whatever is determined to hinder these possibilities must be suppressed. As much as Marcuse writes boldly against authoritarianism, one wonders how such a perspective does not itself lead to authoritarianism of a different sort.

---

[351] Marcuse, "Repressive Tolerance," 37.

When challenged about this article in a 1978 interview, Marcuse acknowledged that he was purposefully provocative and that his article had been interpreted in a broader scope than was his intended point of critique. Marcuse confessed that his article is specifically speaking to fascistic society—particularly the Nazis or neo-Nazi movements. It was not his intention to critique fair-minded academics with more conservative perspectives than his own. This qualification is not new in this interview; it is present in the original article, as Marcuse both stands boldly against tolerance of conservative ideas and also confesses that this tolerance is "justified in harmless debates," including religious and academic discourse.[352] As the interviewer rightly recognizes, this distinction is hardly clear, as there are no strong lines drawn as to what makes something harmless intellectual debate versus public propaganda. The interviewer presses him on a specific scenario. In this scenario, New York City is running a deficit and is considering eliminating some social programs out of economic necessity. Should a conservative economics professor be able to speak freely about his support of the defunding of such programs? Responding to this, Marcuse makes a distinction between speaking on the issue in an "academic statement," which should be tolerated, and speaking to it as "propaganda against social welfare," which should not be tolerated.[353] After the interviewer continues to press him about what this distinction means and how it is precisely to be made, Marcuse is unable to articulate a coherent answer and reverts to a condemnation of fascism, diverting the conversation.

One notable thing to arise in this exchange is that, in the midst of this discussion of tolerance, Marcuse affirms that intolerance must be practiced for a time in order to move into a socialist system. After this system has come into place, tolerance can be reinstated, as no one will have a need to defend fascism any longer.

---

[352] Marcuse, "Repressive Tolerance," 37.

[353] Marcuse, interview by Malinovich, "Herbert Marcuse in 1978," 380.

For a thinker who is so deeply concerned with authoritarianism, this is an embarrassingly naïve argument to make. It is precisely with promises of temporary measures for the sake of protection that authoritarian regimes remove freedoms from a populace, with assurances that these restrictions are made in emergency scenarios to be rescinded at some later date. As much as Marcuse critiques Soviet communism, he remains nearly entirely blind to the dangers of left-leaning authoritarianism, building the entire edifice of his system as a reaction against Nazism.

It has often been noted that Marcuse's influence on the student movements of the 1960s was largely through a misreading of Marcuse's work. His writing has been used to justify things that Marcuse himself may not have actually promoted. I do not think the issue here is the misreading of Marcuse, however; the problem is Marcuse's own lack of clarity or consistency. He has a tendency in his writing to make provocative statements that would point one toward a severe radicalism beyond that of his colleagues. At other points, he seems to soften these harsh statements in one way or another. When one reads interviews with Marcuse (and there are several), it becomes abundantly clear that he was simply not a consistent or systematic thinker. His works are often obscure, not only because of the nature of his prose, but because of his ideology itself. This is perhaps due to Marcuse's desire to construct a purely negative philosophy, which only really purports to critique, rather than to positively affirm much of anything at all.[354] This is evident in that, despite arguing against capitalism consistently throughout his career, Marcuse never really attempts a thorough, clear, positive construction of the means, goal, and structure of a movement toward his desired socialist end.

---

[354] It must be acknowledged that interpretations of Marcuse are not uniform, and some have argued that Marcuse's system is a positive one, which distinguishes him from Adorno and Horkheimer. The only sense in which I can see how such a claim makes sense is if one defines his views as "positive" in that he foresees a future hope for utopian socialism. What I do not find is a significant or consistent plan to achieve such a thing.

The Radical Transformation of Western Civilization

As has been demonstrated repeatedly throughout this study of influential thinkers, the entirety of a person's ideological system is impacted by a subject central to these pages—human nature. Ethics, metaphysics, political life, and other facets of human existence can only be comprehended if one can identify what a human *is*. More than Marx or Gramsci, Marcuse has a significant amount to say on the topic.

Marcuse is among those Marxists who privilege the Hegelian underpinnings of early Marx over the less metaphysical and more strictly economic later Marx. It might even be said that Hegel was more of an influence over Marcuse's thought that Marx himself, even if Marcuse's interpretation of Hegel may be a questionable one. One of the things that Marcuse highlights in Hegel's work is the negative nature of the dialectic. Throughout his career, Marcuse is continually critical of those philosophies that are positive in orientation, that are unwilling to reckon with the contradictory nature of reality (whether socially or metaphysically). For him, there is a sense in which things are defined by what they are not, so that negation and affirmation necessitate one another: Negation is essential to identity. This means that identity is not constituted by a self-subsistent and self-identical nature.

What this means for human beings is that they are not determined by a universal or unchanging essence. Instead, humanity can only be understood by means of the relations into which individuals are placed.[355] This means that relations—whether with one another, with institutions, or with objects—are essential to one's nature rather than accidental. Human beings are only to be grasped

---

[355] As Held summarizes, "The particular exists only in and through the totality of relations of which it is a part. To grasp its nature is, therefore, to grasp the complete set of its relations or the universal that makes it what it is. Human beings ... are constituted as such only in the context of groups, classes and institutions. It is not as isolated particulars, but by virtue of their relations (such as being a father, worker, citizen), that they are what they are." Held, *Introduction to Critical Theory*, 225.

in their totality within the social relations through which they are constituted. In this formulation, Marcuse is strongly anti-individualistic, believing that the particular and the universal can only be grasped in relation to one another. He does not intend this in a realist sense, such that each individual is an instantiation of the universal idea or form of "human." Instead, the essence of "human" is historically conditioned as an outgrowth of historical development. It is also subject to change, just as history continues to transform.

Following this view, Marcuse's perception of humanity is that of a changing identity and constitution. A clear summary of Marcuse's position is found in that 1978 interview cited earlier. He says the following:

> There is no such thing as an immutable human nature. You can make with human beings whatever you want to, and unfortunately in history we have seen that. There is a natural sphere of human existence, certainly. I mean human beings are also animals, but that does not mean that this is unchangeable. It only means that the development of human beings is inexorably linked with the development of nature and of the natural sphere. The human being is also nature, but nature can be changed.[356]

While Marcuse does not posit freedom to change nature in an absolute sense (historical conditions limit the direction and scope of personal subjectivity), his view holds that human nature can be fundamentally altered by means of social change as part of the process of historical development. If human beings are constituted by their social relations, then change to the social situations can alter human nature.

Exactly what Marcuse means by this non-objective approach to human nature is explained through his previously mentioned idea

---

[356] Marcuse, "Herbert Marcuse in 1978," 367.

of the reality principle. Though humans have the innate desire for gratification (the pleasure principle), this is hindered by the harsh realities of the external world. The gratification-hindering reality into which one is placed includes nature but is also social. Societies have standards of right behavior, encourage shame toward people who engage in certain acts that are deemed improper or sinful, and enact criminal punishment on those behaviors that are determined to be harmful to society. This means that reason, which arises in order to live in accord with the reality principle, is socially constructed, just as the self is. In other words, if reason is that which creates the subject, and reason is socially determined, that means that the subject is ultimately the product of society.

In a much-cited article on this subject, Douglas Kellner argues that Marcuse's idea of radical subjectivity parallels the social-subjectivity present in the post-structuralist system of Foucault and Derrida.[357] In Kellner's reading of the Critical Theorists, the "entire tradition of critical theory – which draws on Hegel, Marx, Nietzsche, Freud, and Weber – posits the historical and social construction of the individual."[358] Through his view of humanity as a social construct, Marcuse argues for a redefinition of humanity through a complete overthrow of the foundational values upon which Western civilization is built. This may sound like an exaggeration, but Marcuse states it rather clearly when he calls for a "radical transformation of all basic values of Western civilization."[359] Such extreme statements flow from Marcuse's conception of society as a totality, following Lukács. Politics is not one isolated sphere in which the human is placed, but rather the political constitutes nature. Because of the thorough integration of the political within the rest of social life, a political change must be a complete cultural, and anthropological, one. If everything, including values, norms, and

---

[357] Kellner, "Marcuse and the Quest for Radical Subjectivity."
[358] Kellner, "Marcuse and the Quest for Radical Subjectivity," 81.
[359] Quoted from the *Routledge Handbook of Marxism and Post-Marxism*, 160

social structures, is part of a unified oppressive system, then all must be open to revolutionary change.[360] It is to this end that the dormant class consciousness within society must be awakened and mobilized to actively dismantle the existing order, paving the way for a new and more just society to emerge.

CONCLUSION

One thing which should be apparent by now is that the Critical Theorists are far from unified. Adorno's and Marcuse's approaches to culture, revolution, and counterculture differ significantly from one another. While Adorno would certainly not appreciate being labeled as such, his aesthetic preferences and temperament are often conservative. He opposes the use of media as political propaganda, favoring art as an escape from the monotony of ordinary life in modern society. He favors traditional art forms, as well as the avant-garde, which are both the preferences of the "elite" rather than the common citizen. When he sees revolutionary movements arising in his own career, rather than supporting them, he accuses them of barbarism and writes in opposition to achieving synthesis. Marcuse, in contrast, is radically supportive of political activism, seeking union between theory and practice. He supported nearly every activist movement that he encountered during the rise of student movements in the 1960s, seeking to mobilize both students and academics to strive for progressive emancipation from the restraints of capitalism. This led Marcuse to justify violence as a tool of revolution and protest and to argue for the suppression of ideas which he deemed to be propagandistic.

---

[360] As Kellner summarizes Marcuse's view, "A liberated Eros, Marcuse claims, would release energies that would not only seek sexual gratification, but would flow over into expanded human relations and more abundant creativity. The released Eros would desire, he suggests, a pleasurable aesthetic-erotic environment requiring a total restructuring of human life and the material conditions of existence." Kellner, "Marcuse and the Quest for Radical Subjectivity," 8.

While these thinkers diverge, there are also common points of contact and mutual influence on later political and postmodern thought. As a summary, four points are defined here that retain significance in the academy in the present day. First, the Critical Theorists reject Enlightenment rationalism, moving away from a view of academic work in which it is the goal of the intellectual to arrive at a series of disinterested, rationally conceived, objective propositional truths. They recognize that what is often deemed rationally provable is mere prejudice or personal interest. In this way, the Critical Theorists are precursors of postmodernity. Second, they continue the Lukácsian trend of viewing reality as a totality and of viewing the political as all-encompassing. Third, the Critical Theorists are part of another trend in the academy of defining disciplines as tools of critique rather than positive disciplines guided toward a *telos*. There is no cohesive, transcendent good to be found. Fourth, they deny the existence of a given human nature, conceiving of humanity's essence as constructed rather than inherent. As has been my contention throughout this study, it is this final point which often drives the others. Without a coherent conception of nature, there can be no clear guidance toward a common good to which nature points.

CULTURE AND LANGUAGE: THE STRUCTURALISM
OF SAUSSURE AND LÉVI-STRAUSS

While Marxist movements moved into the realm of cultural critique in the twentieth century, other significant philosophical developments were emerging at that same time—some of which also continue to shape contemporary social and political discourse. Among these was the rise of the linguistic philosophy of structuralism. One of many developments in the field of linguistics, structuralism was part of a broader shift in philosophical discourse in the early twentieth century that is often referred to as the "linguistic turn." Early modern philosophy experienced a similar move as thinkers like Descartes led philosophical discourse away from metaphysics toward epistemology, seeing earlier formulations of knowledge received from the ancient Greeks as inadequate. This move away from metaphysics toward the study of knowledge eventually led some philosophers to examine the structures that the human mind uses in order to classify the things that it perceives—namely, language.[361] As a result of this new interest in language, the twentieth century experienced the emergence of a variety of philosophies centered on language—including the systems of Wittgenstein, the emergence of speech-act theory through J. L. Austin, and several varieties of structuralism and post-structuralism.[362] This chapter addresses the emergence of the structuralist movement.

---

[361] For a brief overview of this linguistic turn through Wittgenstein's philosophy, see Scruton, *Short History of Modern Philosophy*, 281-294.

[362] On speech-act theory, see Austin, *How to Do Things with Words* and Searle, *Speech Acts*.

The first part of this chapter focuses on two figures who are widely considered the fathers of structuralism: Ferdinand de Saussure and Claude Lévi-Strauss. Most of the attention here is given to Ferdinand de Saussure, who pioneered the structuralist movement with the publication of his posthumous book *A Course in General Linguistics*. Since the focus of the present discussion is specifically on the linguistic elements of structuralism, the majority of the first part of this chapter is an exploration of the ideas present in that (his only) work. This chapter briefly touches upon the other father of structuralism, Claude Lévi-Strauss, whose contributions in the field of anthropology furthered the structuralist movement by expanding its ideas beyond linguistics and into other fields of research. Following this overview of the primary ideas of these two figures, the discussion shifts to the individual who initially moves the structuralist movement toward *post*-structuralism: Roland Barthes. With thinkers like Lévi-Strauss and Barthes (along with Lacan) the structuralist movement progressed beyond the narrowly linguistic concerns of Saussure through the incorporation of elements of various other disciplines and philosophies such as Freudian psychology, Marxism, and social anthropology. As a result of this, structuralism became a more comprehensive framework for understanding the world. For Saussure, however, the questions to be answered with structuralism are almost exclusively linguistic.

INFLUENCES ON STRUCTURALISM

The rise of structuralism must be understood, in part, as an attempt to resolve some of the problems posed by Immanuel Kant's philosophical system. Kant's so-called Copernican revolution brought about new questions regarding the nature of human knowledge and the relationship between the world as it is experienced by the subject and the world as it is in-itself. As discussed in the first chapter, Kant argued that there are knowable *a priori* truths (those that are not derived from experience) that are unchanging and universal. Kant sought to expand upon these universal, transcendental *a priori* truths in various fields of study, such as in ethics, aesthetics, and metaphysics. Our experiences of the world, for Kant, do not grant direct access to these universal truths. Instead, human experience brings the subject in contact with phenomena. These are various sensations which one experiences by means of the senses in our interactions with the external world. By an encounter with an object outside of the self, one gains knowledge about things like the look, smell, or sounds given by that object. Yet, this information does not relay anything about what the actual object is as it exists apart from human experience. The *noumena* is the realm of the thing-in-itself (or things as they actually are apart from human experiences of them), as is contrasted with the *phenomena*, which refers to how the noumena is experienced by a subject.

Kant's system sought to maintain a kind of objectivity within the external world, while also acknowledging the limits of human experience in delivering truth about the nature of this external reality. Philosophers after Kant recognized the difficulties created by Kant's affirmation of the existence of the noumena. The question was asked: If the subject only has access to the phenomena, rather than the noumena that stands behind it, then what reason does the subject have to affirm the existence of the noumena at all? On what ground does one affirm the existence of the totally inaccessible? There are some philosophers who are willing to deny the existence of the noumena altogether, while others adopt Hegel's solution of unifying subject and object, so that the subject is not the detached observer of an external world that Kant envisions. Still others believed that it was more fruitful to explore the categories through which we do understand the world (that which we use to interpret phenomena), rather than attempt to resolve the difficult metaphysical dilemma posed by Kant.

While Kant formulated some of these preconditions of experience, such as space and time, it was later thinkers who would expand these into the categories of language. As philosophers wrestled with the nature of human understanding, linguistic categories came to prominence as language serves as a fundamental framework that shapes human thinking. One does not have perceptions of the world that remain uninterpreted, but as one sees, hears, reads, listens, or smells things in the world, those sensations are unconsciously interpreted by the subject by means of their own psychological and cultural context. Linguists began to contend that this context includes linguistic categories. In other words, humans think about and perceive the world around them through the words and concepts present in their language.

Among many linguists, language ceased to be seen as a mere reflection or imitation of the real world. This is a move away from the dominant view of classical Greek thought, in which language points to the forms or essences—a perspective referred to as a *memetic* view of language.[363] For both structuralists and post-structuralists, language came to be seen not as a reflection of another greater reality outside of itself, but as the very structure of reality—at least as perceived by human subjects. Among these thinkers, language is to be understood primarily as a system of signs and symbols that forms the structure of human thought, on both an individual and a societal level. This central role of language in shaping perception explains many of the differences between cultural values and beliefs around the world, as distinct linguistic systems create distinct forms of thought. For some scholars, language was now seen as the most fruitful field of academic inquiry in determining answers to the great questions of philosophy. Language, in this view, is the primary medium of human understanding—both of the external world and of the processes of the mind. To summarize this shift in linguistics as concisely as possible, this newer perspective challenges the notion that concepts are merely reflected in language. It posits, instead, that language actively creates the conceptual framework through which we interpret and make sense of the world around us.

---

[363] On mimesis and poiesis, see Trueman, *Rise and Triumph of the Modern Self*, 39-42.

The significance of this move toward structuralism and post-structuralism is evident in several contemporary social debates and discussions. Current progressive views on pronoun use and the nature of gender and personal identity rely to a significant degree on the framework of structuralist and post-structuralist thought. Rather than assume that language reflects reality (the memetic view), these perspectives suggest that language actually creates reality. Those post-structuralists who are also activists believe that these linguistic categories and forms can be changed purposefully in order to transform society and, consequently, nature itself.

This is all a later development of structuralist thought. Saussure's writing is not political, even if some of his ideas would later be used in that context. Further, Saussure never argued that language should intentionally be changed, as its construction was a historical and organic process into which one is placed, rather than an absolutely mutable set of phrases to be altered at one's whims. Saussure's system is one of examination and understanding rather than praxis; it examines the nature of human interaction, the way that society becomes unified in its modes of speaking and thinking, and how language systems are formed and passed on. These linguistic studies address the fundamental theological and philosophical questions which drive many of the thinkers discussed in this work: What exactly is a human being, and What forms human beings? While Karl Marx viewed humanity through the lens of economic activity, Saussure and other linguists began to think of human persons as, at least in part, creations of locutionary acts. This linguistic perception of humanity remains an important one today, as in much of the academy these linguistic considerations are more central than economic ones.

Alongside this move toward the view that humans are creations of their social contexts stands an alternate move toward an internalized perception of the subject. This occurs among the existentialist philosophers. As a movement, existentialism is broad.[364] It is often thought to include Christian thinkers like Kierkegaard and Marcel along with atheists like Sartre and Camus. Though he denied the label, the German philosopher Martin Heidegger is also often included in this group. The most well-known definition of existentialism comes from Jean-Paul Sartre, who defines the philosophy by the belief that "existence precedes essence."[365] What this means is that humans have a determinative power over their own being, rather than simply having some fundamental nature that is given to them. For the Sartrean view, human nature is defined neither by an eternal soul nor by external cultural or linguistic forces. Instead, human beings are fundamentally self-created. Within each individual remains the power and the freedom to determine one's own life and destiny. These twin movements of existentialism and structuralism led to diverse conceptions of the self which remain in tension in the current era. For the former, identity is to be found internally, within the inner being of each individual, and the final determination of that identity is solely dependent upon the free actions of that man or woman. For the latter, human identities are formed by social categories and structures into which every person is placed, and there is no real internal "self" at all.[366]

One of the factors that differentiates the structuralist approach from the existential one is that the structuralists, like many of the thinkers discussed thus far, are reliant upon Hegel's notion of

---

[364] For an overview of existentialism, see the often-recommended volume *An Introduction to Existentialism* by Robert Olson. Another useful introduction is Barrett, *Irrational Man.*

[365] Sartre first uses this phrase in his lecture (published as a short book) *Existentialism is a Humanism.*

[366] Despite these areas of difference, there are similarities between the two conceptions. For both, human nature is not a given essence but is created through situations in which the individual is engaged. For those of a more Hegelian strain, these situations are social, whereas for the existentialist, they are personal and individual. The lines are not always clear to draw between these ideas, as is evident, for example, in Sartre's praise of Marcuse's writing.

totality (Kierkegaard, the father of existentialism, was a notorious critic of Hegel). The Hegelian shift away from perceiving reality as a collection of isolated and fragmented objects (a process referred to as atomization) led toward the examination of whole systems and the interrelation between parts of those systems. The structuralists extended this understanding of interconnectedness to language. Saussure argues that language must be viewed as an entire system, rather than as a compilation of individual words and rules of grammar. Language is a holistic arrangement of signs. To truly comprehend language, for the structuralists, one must grasp the totality of this system, recognizing that its elements are not separate entities but are rather mutually constituted.

One final area of influence on the structuralists, familiar from the previous discussion of Critical Theory, is the development of Freudian psychology. Due to the influence of Sigmund Freud, people began to think about the nature of the unconscious mind, which refers to those ideas and perceptions that exist within the psyche that one is not aware of. This idea of the unconscious opened up the possibility of exploring unrecognized elements of one's psychological life. These unconscious biases shape the way in which one thinks about the world around them. Freud's most well-known student, Carl Jung, expanded this idea with the concept of the *collective unconscious*, which refers to universal ideas that are inherited through culture and precede individual experience. Like the unconscious mind in Freud's theory, this collective unconscious shapes the way that people interpret their experiences. The exploration of language is part of this same quest found in both Freud and Jung to find unconscious factors that shape human perception.

FERDINAND DE SAUSSURE

Ferdinand de Saussure was born in 1857 in Geneva, Switzerland—a city that has been home to many influential thinkers, including John

Calvin and Jean-Jacques Rousseau.[367] Saussure pursued his education at the University of Geneva, where he was introduced to a variety of ancient languages.[368] After what he later referred to as a wasted year at that university, Saussure pursued further graduate studies at the University of Leipzig. Here, he encountered linguistic philosophy but did not pursue it as his own chosen field. Instead, he specialized in the ancient languages he had begun to learn in Geneva. In the culmination of these early studies, Saussure wrote his dissertation on Indo-European vowel systems. The work was published when Saussure was 21. He would not publish much else in his own lifetime, other than a few articles on Sanskrit, Lithuanian phonetics, and some other highly specialized subjects.

Saussure began his teaching career at the University of Paris, where he lectured almost exclusively on ancient languages. His expertise was in Sanskrit, Old High German, and Gothic. In these early years of his teaching career, Saussure did not venture into philosophy or general linguistics. After a decade teaching in Paris, Saussure was offered a teaching position in his hometown of Geneva in 1892. Initially, Saussure continued to teach the same subjects he had lectured on in Paris, but he would eventually shift his focus to that of general linguistics. In 1907, Saussure first taught his now-renowned course on general linguistics. It was in his preparation for this course that he developed and solidified the principles that later became known as structuralism. His ideas were only taught in the classroom—he taught this course only three times—rather than in writing. At one point, Saussure began writing a book but ultimately abandoned it due to his dissatisfaction with the work (this

---

[367] While it's unclear if Saussure was directly influenced by Calvin, there are some intriguing parallels between Saussure's views on signs and Calvin's perspective on sacraments. Calvin distinguished between the visible elements of the sacraments as "signs" and that which they represented as "signified." Saussure places both the signifier and signified within the category of sign.

[368] The biographical information here is taken from Wade Baskin's extensive introduction to Saussure, *Course in General Linguistics*, xv-li.

unfinished book was released in 2002, many decades after his death). Tragically, Saussure died at a young age in 1913, only six years after he had begun lecturing on his new philosophy of language.

Despite his own hesitancy to publish his ideas, Saussure's students recognized their importance and thus sought to preserve and promulgate the ideas of their beloved professor. A group of these former students took it upon themselves to compile and construct the book that they believed Saussure should have written. It was out of this effort that the work known as *Course in General Linguistics* was created. This book is largely a compilation of transcripts of lectures that were recorded by several of Saussure's students throughout his three times teaching the course. These notes, alongside some things that Saussure had written himself (without any intention to publish), were thorough enough that they resulted in the writing of one of the seminal linguistic texts in the twentieth century. This work of research and compilation was done expeditiously, as the book was published in 1916, only three years after Saussure's passing. While fragments of Saussure's thoughts can be found scattered in other writings, such as his now-published but still-unfinished textbook, it is almost exclusively through *Course in General Linguistics* that students and academics of many generations have been introduced to Saussure's ideas.

COURSE IN GENERAL LINGUISTICS

In *Course in General Linguistics*, Saussure presents his system as a comprehensive theory of the nature and function of language. In his linguistic approach, human language grounds the diversities of human experience in a universal phenomenon that shapes human perception of reality across cultures and times. Language is not a private enterprise.[369] While someone could theoretically construct their own private language without a social context in which it is

---

[369] "For language is not complete in any speaker; it exists perfectly only within collectivity." Saussure, *Course in General Linguistics*, 14.

used, such a thing would negate the essential purpose of language. Klingon and Elvish notwithstanding, language is not meant to be constructed and used by a single individual, since it is by its very nature public. It is the essence of language that it serves as the common means of communication and understanding among multiple people—either within or between cultural or social groups. As a public reality, rather than a private one, language ties individuals together through providing a shared system of symbols in which multiple parties participate. It is through these shared standards of public discourse by means of vocabulary and grammar that interpersonal understanding is possible. Language structures society. In his explanation of how exactly this public system of signs works, Saussure makes some important distinctions to clarify his approach.

THE DIACHRONIC AND SYNCHRONIC AXES

The first of these distinctions is the difference between the *diachronic* and the *synchronic* elements of linguistic study. These two elements of language are sometimes described as a vertical axis and a horizontal axis upon which any linguistic utterance could be examined. The diachronic element is the vertical axis, and the synchronic the horizontal. Diachronic analysis examines the historical development of a language system, and synchronic analysis examines the function of a language system as it presently exists.[370]

The diachronic study of language (sometimes referred to as *historical linguistics*) is chronological. In Saussure's time, this had become the predominant approach in linguistics. The move toward analysis of the historical development of language arose from the writing and influence of Charles Darwin's *On the Origin of Species*. As biologists began to set forth theories about mutations in species to

---

[370] "Everything that relates to the static side of our science is synchronic; everything that has to do with its evolution is diachronic." Saussure, *Course in General Linguistics*, 81.

find the process by which humans (among other animals) came to be in their present form, so did linguists attempt to reconstruct a possible story of how language similarly developed. This led to discussions about the nature and purpose of language as it developed among the ancestors of modern humans (as no other animal species uses language in the way *Homo sapiens* do), as well as examinations of how specific words and languages came to be. Some scholars, such as Max Müller, argued that language functioned much like a biological organism and that it should thereby be studied and examined in the same way as other biological entities.[371] In this view, linguistics is not to be categorized among the humanities but as a life science.

In contrast to this more popular Darwinian approach, the focus of Saussure's study was on the synchronic axis. This synchronic approach does not engage in questions of etymology or biological linguistic origins; instead it centers on the function of language as a system within a specific historical period. In other words, rather than tracing a language's historical trajectory from one age to another, the synchronic study halts at a given point in time and scrutinizes the language system as it exists in that specific culture and era. This specificity of culture differentiates Saussure not only from the historical linguists but also from the neo-grammarians in Leipzig, who contended that language could be understood by means of absolute and universal laws across culture and time. Using these supposed principles of universality, linguists like George Curtis (a teacher of Saussure) believed that they had the ability to reconstruct ancient languages based on very little data. Saussure believed that these principles were not nearly as clear and universal as Curtis believed them to be. There is a relative universality within a singular language system, but there are insufficient grounds to extend common patterns of language to all language systems in history. It is worth noting here that with the formulation of his synchronic

---

[371] Müller's work was extensive in scope and subject. For a work on his approach to linguistics, see his book *Three Lectures on the Science of Language*.

linguistic approach, Saussure does not downplay the necessity of the study of historic linguistic development, but he contends that the synchronic and diachronic aspects of language must be strongly distinguished if either is to be done well.

PAROLE AND LANGUE

Alongside this distinction between diachrony and synchrony lies another programmatic distinction in Saussure's writing: that between *parole* and *langue*—translated as "speech" and "language," respectively.[372] When Saussure refers to speech, he means the actual act of speaking, or the utterance of words. In essence, speech refers to the concrete, audible expression of language through vocalization.

Language, as Saussure defines it, is distinct from those instances of vocalization. Speech exists insofar as one is actively making noises, while language transcends such isolated acts.[373] Language identifies the underlying system that governs how words, grammar, syntax, and other linguistic elements interact with one another to form meaningful structures within a culture of shared signs. A study of language examines the rules that dictate how words combine to create coherent expressions of various kinds. Though Saussure is not a realist in the Platonic sense, the distinction between language and speech shares some similarities to the classical distinction between universals and particulars. For classical realist philosophers, universals are those ideas comprehended by the human intellect that identify essences. To revisit the example used in an earlier chapter, the category of "sheep" is universal. The idea of "sheep" *identifies* specific things, but it is not *dependent* upon specific things, as the essence of sheep is not contingent upon any one

---

[372] "But what is language? It is not to be confused with human speech, of which it is only a definite part, though certainly an essential one." Saussure, *Course in General Linguistics*, 9.

[373] "Language is not a function of the speaker; it is a product that is passively assimilated by the individual. ... Speaking, on the contrary, is an individual act." Saussure, *Course in General Linguistics*, 14.

instantiation of that essence within an animal. In the same way, language, for Saussure, is far more universal than specific instances of speaking. The universal stands behind, and gives meaning to, the particular.

To summarize the distinction, language, or *langue*, comprises the shared system of words, sounds, and grammar that allows individuals to communicate and understand one another. It extends beyond the confines of any single speaker. In contrast, speech, or *parole*, identifies the specific utterances that are produced by an individual within the framework of a given language. It is through the interplay between speech and language that communication is possible. The underlying language system (*langue*) provides the necessary structure for a person's speech to convey meaning, and when that structure—its rules, syntax, and grammar—is used by means of a speech act (*parole*), this meaning is conveyed.

LANGUAGE AS CHESS

A helpful analogy that Saussure employs to illustrate the relationship between language and speech is that of a game of chess.[374] In a game of chess, the player is both restricted and free when making decisions. Players possess the freedom to make a variety of moves when starting a game, with the ability to choose both which piece to use and how to use it. As free as the player is in taking such actions, they are also restricted, as the player must do so within the established rules of the game. A chess player is not free to move a knight straight forward or a rook diagonally. The pieces on the board cannot be placed arbitrarily without regard for the fundamental principles of the game. Language operates in a comparable manner. Like chess, language presents a set of rules and structures that provide the limits within which one must operate. Words, grammar, and syntax combine to create these rules so that meaningful communication is possible. Further, just as chess provides freedom

---

[374] Saussure, *Course in General Linguistics*, 88-90.

to the player to act within its rules, language offers a similar freedom to express thoughts and convey meaning using these structures. This freedom is not in tension with the confines of language; it is instead contingent upon established frameworks of the language systems. Without rules, mutual understanding would be an impossibility, and thus freedom to express one's ideas would be negated.

In this analogy, speech (*parole*) is likened to an individual making specific moves within the established rules of the chess game. Speech is not, for Saussure, some guarantor of absolute freedom, since it is constrained by the linguistic context in which it operates. This is not a problem for Saussure, as his approach to human nature does not elevate autonomy to a central position—in contrast to the existentialists. Saussure recognizes that humans are always subject to limitations in a variety of ways. To have any sense of social coherence within a society, there must be some mutual rules and standards within which individuals operate. Attempts to ignore these shared rules of language, or to go beyond the confines of one's linguistic context—such as assigning personal meanings to words that are totally different from their established definitions—would result in a complete breakdown of communication. This would render speech unintelligible and ineffective as a form of communication.

Saussure acknowledges that there are certain limitations with the chess analogy. Chess necessitates a conscious awareness of the rules of the game, while language often operates at a more unconscious level. People do not consciously and actively think about the rules of language during every act of communication. This unconscious nature of language is evident in childhood development. When children begin to adopt and work within linguistic systems through the uttering of their first words, they are not able to explain exactly how grammar works, or how it is that certain sounds relate to the ideas that they identify with those sounds. The rules of grammar are taught well after a person knows how to communicate in full sentences. Nonetheless, the analogy

Saussure uses here remains valuable in illustrating the relationship between speech and language as they function together to create coherent communication.

SEMIOTICS: SIGNIFIERS AND THE THING SIGNIFIED

Saussure's approach to the relationships between words within a coherent social system of comprehension led to the development of the field of study now known as semiotics, or semiology. This term can be literally defined as the "study of signs." For Saussure, these signs were specifically linguistic significations, while later thinkers would expand semiological study into other forms of ritual communication.[375]

In every human society, there exist a number of shared signs and symbols that serve to communicate ideas, relations, laws, or social status within various interpersonal contexts. These signs are instruments of communicative comprehension. For instance, in an English-speaking context, when one person greets another with the word "hello," this is understood as a general greeting or an acknowledgment of the presence of the other person. In an ordinary scenario, there is then a mutual signification in which the other individual reciprocates the action by offering a "hello" themselves. If such a sign is not reciprocated, this also serves as a means of communicating something, such as anger or offense toward the other person. Following the greeting of "hello," it is also common to ask the question, "How are you?" In such a scenario, there is both an appropriate response in terms of accepted social standards, and a response that is an actual literal answer to the question—which might *not* be socially appropriate. The expected response is a simple, "I am doing well. How are you?" while a literal response may be something like, "I am feeling like my bowels might explode after

---

[375] Saussure defines semiology as a "science that studies the life of signs within society." *Course in General Linguistics*, 16. He contends that such a study goes well beyond the linguistic, though that is his own focus.

eating that bean burrito." While the latter response may be technically true, it fails to understand the way in which linguistic signs relate within social contexts.

These shared signs extend beyond language, as they also include actions of non-verbal communication.[376] Consider, for example, the act of extending a hand for a handshake when meeting someone new. The holding out of one's hand is a friendly gesture, to be received as a greeting. In most scenarios, the other individual will also reach out their hand, and then the two parties grip each other's hands with a quick up-and-down motion and then let go. Similar to the reciprocation of a "hello," the gesture of the handshake is a sign that indicates greeting and welcome. In other contexts, such as where this sign is connected to the making of a deal in a business setting, a handshake can indicate something different. It is an acknowledgment of terms and a promise to fulfill one's obligations in a new commitment between parties. It is, thus, not the handshake *by itself* that communicates (or the handshake would mean the same thing in both scenarios), but the sign of the handshake as it relates other signs. Human beings exist in a complex web of signs and symbols that mutually reinforce and interpret one another. Semiotics investigates the various ways that people communicate, whether that is through language or through bodily expressions and non-verbal cues, as these signs explain structures and social dynamics of human societies.

Saussure distinguishes between two different parts of signs: the signifier and the signified. The signifier is the verbal utterance, the sound that is made when saying a word. The signified is that to which one is referring when using a given signifier. For example, if I were to hold up the mug in front of me and say "coffee," the word "coffee" acts as a signifier, while the liquid in my mug is that which is signified. The signifier serves as a communicative unifier between

---

[376] "Linguistics is only a part of the general science of semiology." Saussure, *Course in General Linguistics*, 16.

people who speak the same language. When you read that word in this paragraph, you (most likely) understood what beverage was being referenced. That is because there is a shared understanding between the writer and the reader that the letters in the word "coffee" when put together refer to a specific thing. There is a shared experience that all coffee drinkers have of what that drink tastes, smells, feels, and looks like, and when the word "coffee" is used, those associations arise within the mind. This shared understanding exists even when the reader has no idea about the specific coffee that I am drinking. I said nothing about the origin or roast, or whether I put cream or sugar in my coffee. And yet, the universal word and concept transcend such particularities.

For Saussure, words do not directly identify objects. When I use the word "coffee," I am not vocalizing some set of sounds that is inherently connected to the actual object that exists in front of me. This is evident, for Saussure, in that while my reader understands what I am talking about in using the words "coffee" or "mug," that same reader has no connection to the physical thing that is on my desk. You have never seen, smelled, or tasted this particular coffee. Further, by the time you are reading this book, this coffee will be long gone. And yet, despite your having no connection to this drink, there remains shared communication. This, for Saussure, is because the purpose in language is not so much in identifying the physical world itself as it is identifying concepts.[377] You understand me, not because you know anything about my cup of coffee, but because there is a shared idea that we both have of coffee.

What Saussure proposes here is similar in some ways to the earlier Platonic idea of the forms. Both thinkers contend that there is something universal among people within communities that establishes the possibility of interpersonal communication. For Plato, this common understanding of concepts among people arises

---

[377] "The linguistic sign unites, not a thing and a name, but a concept and a sound-image." Saussure, *Course in General Linguistics*, 66.

from a transcendent truth, that ideas are prior to language and to human communities. For Plato, the reason why there is a shared understanding of an essence, such as coffee, is that both the object and the intellect share in the same form. A cup of coffee is coffee in that it partakes in the form, or idea, of coffee. The human intellect comprehends what the coffee is because the mind also partakes in this same idea of coffee. Thus, the *idea* is what creates the unified experience of multiple minds that read the word "coffee" and understand the object that is being referenced by that term.

Despite the similarities between these two systems, however, Saussure diverges significantly from Plato on the issue of realism. For Saussure, rather than external universal ideas forming our linguistic constructs, language creates ideas. It is then language that is primary rather than immaterial concepts. This also means that concepts are not objective, for Saussure, in the way that Plato conceives of them.[378] They have a relative stability and unified societal understanding, but they are not transcendent. If ideas are all socially determined by means of language, then the basic commitments or values of a culture could be changed if the use of words changed (though it is to be remembered that such historical changes in language are not something that Saussure is particularly interested in).[379]

---

[378] Saussure criticizes the idea that "ready-made ideas exist before words" which prevails in the classical conception. *Course in General Linguistics*, 65.

[379] In contrast to some later post-structuralists, Saussure contends that linguistic signs are inherited, rather than created or changed by an intentional act of either an individual or social group. He writes that "the community itself cannot control so much as a single word; it is bound to the existing language." *Course in General Linguistics*, 71.

SIGNIFIERS ARE ARBITRARY

Central to Saussure's system is the idea that signifiers are arbitrary—something that would become key to the post-structuralist system.[380] This means that there is nothing inherently logical or necessitated in the connection between the signifier and the signified. This is why different cultures have terms that often sound completely different to refer to the same general ideas. For instance, the animal identified by the English word *dog* is referred to in Spanish as *perro*. These words do not sound similar at all. They share only one letter (which is pronounced differently in both words), have a different number of syllables, and necessitate the use of different parts of the tongue and mouth to pronounce. And yet they identify the same subject. When examining these words, it would be quite difficult to make a case that one of these words is more suited than the other to identify the object (What standards would one even use to arrive at a conclusion on that matter?). The significance in the words is not in their sounds, or in any inherent connection between them and the idea that they signify, but in the social agreement that exists within a given community as to the meaning of those words.

Another evidence of this arbitrariness is found in the fact that languages often use the same word for completely unrelated purposes. Though spelled differently, when spoken aloud there is no difference in sound between *meat* and *meet*. One identifies an object (usually in the context of its being eaten), while the other describes an action. There is no apparent connection between these two concepts to cause them to share a sound, and, like the prior example, it would be difficult to make the case that the sound is more suited to one of those things than the other. The identification of words with

---

[380] "The bond between the signifier and the signified is arbitrary. Since I mean by sign the whole that results from the associating of the signifier with the signified, I can simply say: *the linguistic sign is arbitrary*." Saussure, *Course in General Linguistics*, 67.

particular concepts is nothing more than social agreement and convention.

It is worth mentioning that despite this insistence on the arbitrary nature of language, Saussure does admit that there is a degree of non-arbitrariness when it comes to combined words.[381] When, for example, the words *apple* and *tree* are put together to form the phrase *apple tree*, the sounds that make up this object are a purposeful combination of other already identified signifiers. There is a logic to its composition that would not be present if society had instead chosen to call apple trees *orange plants* or *blabadoo*. Nevertheless, though the combination of signifiers is non-arbitrary, the individual signifiers, *apple* and *tree*, that create the compound identifier still lack any inherent connection to their respective references. Another exception to this arbitrariness in linguistic signifiers is onomatopoeia, in which the sound of the word is related to the sound a thing makes. For example, the sound that a dog makes is often referred to as a *bark*, which is an imitation of the sound made by a dog. Onomatopoeias, however, make up only a small number of verbal utterances. Despite the occasional exception, the arbitrariness of signifiers remains as a general rule for Saussure.

This arbitrariness that Saussure speaks of is in no way an attempt to make language meaningless. It is, instead, quite the opposite. Signifiers, when used by individuals within a shared linguistic context, become deeply meaningful, as they are the means by which individuals come to know one another and through which there is a common life lived within communities. Unlike Plato and other metaphysical realists, however, Saussure never moves beyond the meaning that is found within a language system toward something more fundamental or transcendent.

---

[381] Saussure, *Course in General Linguistics*, 68-70.

SIGNIFIERS AND SOCIAL CONTEXT

Saussure's conception of language is one that is holistic. Like many of the thinkers discussed in this volume who follow Hegel, Saussure views reality as a system of interconnected things, rather than as a series of isolated individualized essences. The problem in some older philosophical models of language, for Saussure, lies in the focus on the meanings of specific words by themselves and the identification of each of those words with one specific subject. Plato's portrayal of Socrates, for example, has him trying to find very specific meanings of concepts like "justice." For Saussure, words do not bear meaning within themselves but in how those words are used in relation to other words as part of a whole language system.

To illustrate this necessity of context and linguistic interplay in giving meaning to language, consider the distinction I just used between *meet* and *meat*. When written, the distinction between meanings is apparent in spelling differences, but when spoken, the audible utterance is identical. How exactly is one supposed to determine which meaning the word has in a given situation? My assumption is that you have most likely not run into much confusion about this when hearing the word spoken (if English is your primary language). But why does this confusion not occur more often? The answer, according to Saussure, is linguistic context. If I utter the phrase, "I am going to eat some meat," there is no need for clarification about what I mean by *meat*, because the words that are connected to that term give meaning to the utterance. It is the connection between *meat* and the earlier words *I am going to eat some* that creates meaning and understanding. Or, consider a sentence using the other meaning of the utterance: "I am going to meet my wife." In this instance, I am clearly not saying anything about food (directly, at least) but about a happening between me and my wife. The point is that a word has the meaning it does because of its connection to other words.

As meaning is found within these language systems, Saussure contends that the understanding of words is found not only in their positive relation to other words, but also in contrast. He contends that meaning can be derived by grasping what a word is *not* saying or how it is contrasted with other words or ideas.[382] *Darkness* and *light*, for example, can only really be understood in relation to the other. For Saussure, this contrast is essential to the understanding of multitudinous concepts—not just those that are obvious opposites. Linguistic meaning arises from negative differentiations of words from other words, along with relational connections to surrounding terms. There is something Hegelian about this concept, as Hegel believed that negation and contrast were essential elements of the self-development of the Geist. In a similar manner, Saussure contends that contrast and negation are fundamental elements of the whole of linguistic systems, so that contrast is not opposed to the unity of a system but a necessary element of it.

Paradigms and Syntagms

One final thing to be discussed in Saussure's system is his distinction between paradigms and syntagms.[383] These terms are tools for understanding the relationships between words within a given linguistic system. The syntagmatic structure focuses on the arrangement of words within a sentence, how individual words interact and connect with each other, such as in the examples *the old man cried* or *our king disappeared*. It is this approach that is taken when someone evaluates a particular piece of writing and does a grammatical analysis of each sentence or phrase.

---

[382] "Everything that has been said up to this point boils down to this: in language there are only differences. Even more important: a difference generally implies positive terms between which the difference is set up; but in language there are only differences *without positive terms*" (emphasis added). Saussure, *Course in General Linguistics*, 121.

[383] Saussure, *Course in General Linguistics*, 122-127.

The paradigmatic approach, on the other hand, explores how different parts of speech that share the same grammatical category relate to each other. For instance, one can examine the relationships between nouns, verbs, adjectives, and other parts of speech across different sentences. This is a more universal study in scope, as the paradigmatic approach to language analysis is not limited to any one specific sentence or phrase.

By employing both the syntagmatic and paradigmatic perspectives, Saussure offers a robust analysis of how words function within a language. The syntagmatic structure illuminates the relationships between words within a sentence, while the paradigmatic approach uncovers the connections between parts of speech across different sentences.

CLAUDE LÉVI-STRAUSS

While it is Saussure who formed structuralist thought, the popularization of this method of analysis is often attributed to the anthropologist Claude Lévi-Strauss. Widely read among French academics from a variety of disciplines, Lévi-Strauss's thought was formative for postmodernists like Derrida, Foucault, Lyotard, and Deleuze. Lévi-Strauss was born in 1908 to a French Jewish family in Belgium. He grew up in Paris with a father who worked as a painter until the outbreak of World War I, when Claude temporarily lived with his maternal grandfather who was a rabbi in Versailles (though Lévi-Strauss himself was a professed agnostic). Lévi-Strauss began studying philosophy at a young age, as well as studying leftist political thought. In 1926, Lévi-Strauss began his studies in law and philosophy at the renowned Sorbonne University in Paris. After the beginning of the Great Depression, Lévi-Strauss traveled to Brazil to teach sociology in Sao Paulo, where he would engage in ethnographic studies amid native populations.

The time spent with these natives helped form Lévi-Strauss's structuralist framework through which he worked for the rest of his career. His ideas were further developed through travels to various other parts of South America during his life, where he observed and analyzed patterns of action, thought, and language that appeared to share commonalities in distinct human communities with no shared history. This penchant for travel that Lévi-Strauss evidenced in these various cultural studies was also apparent in his teaching career, which extended to multiple countries including Brazil, France, and the United States. Lévi-Strauss published several influential books during his life and was engaged in the field until his death at 100 years old in 2009. His work caused a broader shift in structuralism beyond the purely linguistic element of semiotics toward a more comprehensive examination of cultural signs and their interrelationships, especially as such signs are observable across diverse cultures.

LÉVI-STRAUSS'S WORK

In his work, Lévi-Strauss applies Saussure's categories and ideas to cultural anthropology. He attempts to understand cultural signs and symbols by way of their systematic integration with one another, rather than solely through hypothetical accounts of historical development. Too many cultural anthropologists, in Lévi-Strauss's view, worked exclusively from the perspective of the diachronic axis, the historical development of social systems, taboos, and rituals. The making of such conclusions in non-literate cultures is difficult to do, with no written record and often scant archeological data. This leads to hypothetical constructions of historiography that cannot be verified. Saussure's structuralism provided a framework for understanding cultural signification that was not reliant on these hypothetical histories, as it allowed for a way to understand signs in their current symbiotic function in relation to other signs as a self-contained semiotic system.

Lévi-Strauss did not only examine individual linguistic systems as isolated from those of other cultures; he recognized several cultural concepts that appeared in multiple semiotic systems, interconnecting in ways that transcend historical or geographic boundaries. There are common taboos, rituals, or rites across cultures—think of ceremonies like weddings and worship practices—that make intercultural understanding possible. While the particulars of such rituals differ, there are apparent universal human ideas underneath them. Lévi-Strauss's work is, in some ways, a continuation of Kant's search for the universal preconditions of experience shared among humans that provide something that transcends the particulars of sense experience. Lévi-Strauss's semiotic structures are not, however, grounded in something so universal as the Platonic ideals or the Kantian transcendentals. Further, these semiotic structures are not so much inherent to consciousness (*à la* Plato and Kant) as they are merely the necessary results of language models with a shared logic between symbolic actions.

This thesis is explored in Lévi-Strauss's first influential work, *The Elementary Structures of Kinship*, published in 1949.[384] Lévi-Strauss argues that the concept of kinship can be studied using the same structuralist principles at work in phonological systems (particularly those used by Russian linguist Nikolai Trubetzkoy).[385] In order for a system to be suitable for semiotic analysis, it must have three necessary characteristics: It must be constituted by basic terms; the values within those terms must be identified in relation to one another; and this interrelation constitutes a self-functioning system.[386] Though a distinct type of system from phonetics, kinship retains each of these essential elements and is thereby capable of undergoing structural analysis.

In discussing the structural components of kinship, Lévi-Strauss draws on the work of French sociologist Marcel Mauss on the

---

[384] The English edition was translated in 1969.

[385] *Phonology* refers to the study of language systems as spoken, rather than as written. For Trubetzkoy's work, see Trubetzkoy, *Principles of Phonology*.

[386] Henaff, "Lévi-Strauss," in *A Companion to Continental Philosophy*, 508.

subject of gift-giving. There is, for Lévi-Strauss, a universal law of reciprocity that is constitutive of all human relations. This reciprocity is found in the relation between a gift and a counter-gift, which serve as binary corollaries to one another.[387] These gifts of exchange and reception foster mutual bonds and social cohesion both within and between social groups. The highest of these forms of gift giving is found in the granting of a wife from one group to a member of another group, which has historically been a tool of peace agreements and collaboration between parties. Lévi-Strauss uses this principle to identify why prohibitions on incest are so universal within human communities. The reason, he contends, for such a universal prohibition is that incestuous relations would retain women within a family, thereby denying the necessary social practice of giving the daughter to another man in order to form social bonds. This explanation allows Lévi-Strauss to comprehend the universal validity that some prohibitions seem to have among cultures without doing so in either a historical or moral framework. There is a kind of universality in cultural ritual and language, but this universality does not have moral importance. It arises instead from the consistent logic of social systems.

What is most important to understand about Lévi-Strauss for the current study is that his system locates social systems and rituals within the broader logical framework of conceptual signification or differentiation. Not only language, whether written or spoken, but also cultural ritual, institution, religion, and moral prohibition are self-contained reciprocal systems of signs. While Lévi-Strauss does not set forth a nihilistic rejection of systems of meaning in a Nietzschean sense, he does deny that there is meaning in social systems beyond the systems themselves. They are self-contained. This means that human culture is its own kind of game

---

[387] Though he does not use the concept in precisely the same way as Derrida, the two thinkers share a commonality in this idea of meaning by way of binary opposition.

that sets its own rules that are to be followed in order for it to work, but there is no transcendental ground of meaning that lies underneath. This move toward the analysis of social systems continues with Roland Barthes, who provides a more distinctly political direction for structural analysis.

ROLAND BARTHES

Roland Barthes is a transitional thinker, bridging the gap between structuralism and its child, post-structuralism. Barthes follows both Saussure and Lévi-Strauss in his focus on interconnected systems of signs and the necessity of those signs to provide an effective means of human communication. In significant ways, however, Barthes departs from these older thinkers in moving toward a more subjective conception of language—most popularly in relation to the reading of texts. With his idea of the "death of the author," Barthes seeks to remove the source of written works from the understanding of those texts, arguing that the reader is freed in interpreting a text when the intention of an author is no longer considered. This approach to reading has had a monumental impact upon the academy into the twenty-first century, especially in the humanities. Nearly every humanities student at a public university in the Western world has had some encounter with Barthes's ideas in one form or another.

THE LIFE OF BARTHES

Roland Barthes was born in Cherbourg, Normandy, France, in 1915.[388] Barthes's father passed away while serving in World War I when Roland was a young child. As a result, Barthes grew up without a father figure, primarily being raised by his mother, aunt, and grandmother. Barthes contracted tuberculosis during his youth and consequently stayed for a time in a sanatorium. These health issues in his youth persisted throughout Barthes's entire life, often

---

[388] For a biography, see Samoyault, *Barthes: A Biography*.

impacting his work and making teaching particularly difficult. At the age of nine, Barthes relocated to Paris, where he attended school and later pursued his studies at the influential Sorbonne (where Lévi-Strauss had also studied). After completing his studies at the Sorbonne, Barthes pursued and obtained a degree in literature from the University of Paris, where he wrote his thesis on Greek tragedy. Barthes initially focused his studies on classical literature but would soon move beyond this narrow focus on the classics after finishing his formal studies, exploring a wide range of subjects throughout his career, such as linguistics, philosophy, and media. Barthes spent different eras of his life focusing intently on a specific topic or set of topics, producing writings in that area, and then moving on to another area of thought for another years-long period of study and writing. His writings are diverse in subject, and within these various topics, Barthes displays an extensive knowledge of the academic and classical literature related to each.

One of these areas that Barthes explored was the study of grammar and philology. He grew an interest in examining the nature of words, the structure of sentences, and how language creates and delivers meaning. It was in the midst of this time of study that Barthes encountered the writings of the semiologists and began to create his own approach to the discipline. Due to his background in literature, Barthes had an interest in trying to synthesize linguistic semiological developments with the study of literature. It was through the creation of this semiological approach that Barthes began to move away from the accepted view of literary interpretation, in which the meaning of a text was to be extracted from the perceived intended authorial purpose of that piece of writing. Taking a semiological focus on relations between words as constituting a distinct system within itself, Barthes believed that consideration of the intentions of an author in putting those words together was unnecessary in order to extract meaning from a text. If language and grammar could be taken as a singular isolated system, then books could be interpreted without dependence upon any external source.

In 1948, Barthes began working full-time in academia, taking a series of short-term positions at various universities. In 1952, he received his first more permanent position at *Centre National de la Recherche Scientifique*, where he would spend the next seven years teaching and writing. During this period in the 1950s, Barthes's attention turned toward Western culture, which he examined through the lens of what he referred to as *mythology*. By mythology, Barthes did not mean those classical stories that he had studied in his earlier academic career in texts from the Greeks and Romans. Instead, the term mythology is used by Barthes to identify the core ideas, stories, and values of a culture, just as the classical myths displayed the general worldview of ancient cultures. Barthes did not only engage in analysis of what is generally deemed "high culture," but he also explored the mythology hidden within more popular and less sophisticated cultural products, such as in professional wrestling. Barthes' essays on myth and culture were compiled into *Mythologies*, published in 1957.

In the 1960s, Barthes turned his attention toward the study of literary theory. In a number of essays and full-length publications written during this period, he began to challenge older forms of textual examination through his new structuralist model. By the middle of that decade, Barthes had established himself as a leading academic in France, and his works were read widely. By the end of the 1960s, some of his most important works had been translated into English (such as his *Elements of Semiology* in 1968), and he had lectured in the United States, Japan, and several countries in Europe. His reputation had grown internationally. Barthes continued to write throughout the 1970s, when he focused on close textual examination, such as his in-depth analysis of Balzac's short story "Sarrasine," published under the simple title of *S/Z*. Barthes's life came to a sudden and unexpected end when he died from injuries four weeks after being hit by a laundry van while crossing a street in 1980.

BARTHES'S ANTI-REALISM

In the earlier part of his academic career, Barthes spent a significant portion of his time reading the works of the existentialists. Though interested in existentialism more broadly as a movement, he was particularly interested in the ideas of his fellow Frenchman Jean-Paul Sartre. At the heart of Sartre's philosophy was a perception of the human person as fundamentally free, as existence precedes one's essence. For the existentialist, there is no fixed nature or destiny by which an individual is bound. Human beings are self-creative. This Sartrean centering of freedom stands in contrast to Saussure's contention that human beings are bound to the semiological structures and categories that precede and transcend them. Drawing on both of these sources throughout his career, Barthes combines Sartre's commitment to unbounded freedom with a Saussurian prioritization of the linguistic.

Like most philosophers in the modern era, Barthes is a metaphysical nominalist, denying that the world is made up of concrete and unchangeable natures in which individual things participate. Such nominalism is an essential component of the existentialist paradigm, since Sartean self-creative framework cannot coexist with a realist commitment to the fixity of natures. With Sartre, Barthes purports that there is no essential and universal human nature in which all humans participate.[389] Human nature is, instead, a social construct arising from the signs and symbols used in human communities. Like Saussure, Barthes prioritizes linguistic categories, contending that they are constitutive of what humans wrongly perceive as consistent, changeless essences. Our perception of things as they are, or what we might deem common sense, is not to be taken for granted, as many of our most deeply held assumptions

---

[389] Barthes states rather bluntly that "the disease of thinking in essences ... is at the bottom of every bourgeois mythology of man." As cited in Graff, "Politics of Anti-Realism," 5.

are cultural creations.[390] Among his many rejections of commonly held mythologies, Barthes contends that there is no transcendent human nature or soul.[391] Barthes's critique of realism here is a denial not only of a fixed *human* nature, but of nature as such. For Barthes, there are no intrinsic essences or existences beyond perception and social construction.[392] To use Kantian distinctions, Barthes denies the existence or knowledge of the thing-in-itself, instead viewing reality solely as socially construed phenomena.

On the subject-object debate that pervades much post-Kantian philosophical discourse, Barthes departs from the strong Hegelian leanings of Marxist thought by rejecting the concept of a unifying synthesis. In opposition to the German idealist, Barthes's strong nominalism reduces everything to multiplicity, denying both the monism of Heraclitus's intellectual descendants and all forms of moderate realism. If reality is defined by language, as Barthes contends, then the only unifying element of thought and concept is the linguistic category into which a thing is placed. Barthes pushes beyond the nominalism of the medieval world here, as he eventually moves away from even linguistic concepts having universality or inherent meaning with his subjective approach to textuality.

Another distinction between Barthes and his medieval predecessors is that he does not write or think in metaphysical categories at all, but in political ones. Barthes's nominalism is an anti-essentialist type of pseudo-Marxism in which his opposition to

---

[390] As Jonathan Culler writes, "[T]he meanings that seem natural to us are cultural products, the result of conceptual frameworks that are so familiar as to pass unnoticed." Culler, *Barthes*, 23.

[391] Summarizing Barthes, Graff writes, "The revolt against realism and representation is closely tied to the revolt against a unitary psychology of the self." Graff, "Politics of Anti-Realism," 7.

[392] In his introductory text *Structuralism and Post-Structuralism for Beginners*, Palmer summarizes Barthes's view, stating: "Barthes goes beyond Sartre, who seemed to allow that objects other than human beings might have essences. But for Barthes, there are no essences at all. Essentialism is just a bourgeois ideology attempting to squeeze reality into its own mold and freeze-dry it there." 52.

metaphysical realism arises from political critique, rather than conceptual ontology.[393] Anyone well-versed in the writings of classical metaphysics is bound to be disappointed in Barthes's critiques, as they take the form of political protest rather than well-reasoned philosophical disputation.[394] Barthes's general argument is presented along the following lines: The bourgeoisie maintain their power through the absolutizing of truth claims that serve the interests of the ruling class.[395] This is done by perpetuating the idea that the bourgeoisie have privileged access to truths about the world and that all people within a given society must therefore give consent to them. If realism were correct, and the realities of the universe could actually be known, this would support the idea that the bourgeoisie are able to rightly reason toward these truths; as a consequence, bourgeoisie values and beliefs must be seriously considered and (if true) adopted by citizens. In order to tear down this pillar upon which the powerful have constructed their authority and privilege, the existence of universal or objective reality must be rejected—at least as accessible to human cognition. In his attack on the bourgeoisie, Barthes aims at nothing less than reality itself. It is through his rejection of realism, and his subsequent denial of the

---

[393] There has been significant criticism regarding the use of the term *postmodern neo-Marxism* by figures like Jordan Peterson. Critics argue that Marxism and postmodernity are fundamentally different and incompatible, and thus "postmodern neo-Marxism" is an oxymoronic concept. While it is true that these movements are significantly distinct, we can find some intersections and parallels between them when examining thinkers like Roland Barthes. Although Barthes is not typically categorized as a postmodernist, he shares several ideas with both postmodernity and neo-Marxism.

[394] Graff summarizes this non-rational approach to revolution that is prevalent in thinkers of this era, including Barthes, as a "revolt against the reality principle in the name of the pleasure principle, of the overcoming of oppressive reason by imagination." Graff, "Politics of Anti-Realism," 6.

[395] Barthes writes that the conservative bourgeois oppressor "is everything, his language is rich, multiform, supple, with all the possible degrees of dignity at its disposal: he has an exclusive right to meta-language." Barthes, "Myth Today," in *A Barthes Reader*, 139.

human intellect's ability to comprehend reality, that Barthes justifies revolution against the powerful.

This Barthesian methodology leads to a dismissal of truth claims by means of a professed power dynamic at work within those claims, rather than through serious engagement with contrary ideas. Such an approach is common in popular discourse today surrounding a variety of cultural and moral issues. For example, in discussions about gender, marriage, and sexuality, it is common for progressives to dismiss alternative positions as dependent upon the biased and arbitrary privileging of heteronormativity, or to dismiss arguments that favor a strong link between gender and biology as beholden to socially imposed binary thinking used as a tool of oppression, rather than to address the arguments as truth claims that can be verified or refuted by logical reasoning. The assumption lying behind this method of argument is that there is nothing more to these ideas than the imposition of bourgeois ideals masquerading as metaphysical claims. If truth claims are reducible to power, then their refutation must similarly be grounded in power, rather than in rigorous philosophical, scientific, or anthropological argumentation.

SIGNS AS TOOLS OF POWER

Barthes's system relies on his commitment that there are no objective and observable facts. There are, for him, *only* signs, which bear no underlying reality and have no objective referent toward which they point. Like Saussure, Barthes defines signs as composed of both a signifier and a thing signified. He also follows the earlier thinker in his contention that these signs make up linguistic systems that tie individuals together by means of a shared discursive life. Where Barthes differs from Saussure is in his bold denial of the existence of the thing-in-itself. For Saussure, linguistic systems bear meaning within themselves so that they do not need to have any underlying tie to reality beyond them as a prerequisite of comprehensibility. He does not, however, deny that there is a reality which preexists social interaction. Saussure's project was linguistic, rather than metaphysical, and he therefore made no strong claims about the essence of nature. Barthes does make such claims.

Another element of commonality and distinction between these two thinkers is in the arbitrary nature of the sign. Saussure contends that signs are arbitrary in that there is no inherent connection between the specific verbal utterance and the referent toward which the utterance points. Barthes agrees with the basic claim of Saussure here, but he extends the earlier author's perspective by politicizing it. For Barthes, signs are arbitrary in the sense that they do not have inherent meaning within themselves, but only that which is assigned to them (in agreement with Saussure). They are *not* arbitrary, however, in their creation and maintenance by a political class.[396] Social signs are enforced by the ruling class as instruments of control toward others, as they impose bourgeois values on the populace. For Barthes, myth, which is couched in signs, always has a motive, and it is the role of the social commentator to examine, critique, and deconstruct these signs for political purposes.

In order to get a better understanding of what Barthes is arguing here, let us use the example of clothing.[397] As Barthes moved beyond Saussure's narrow focus on verbal signification, he explored a wide range of social actions and behaviors that are involved in cultural systems. One of these common social signifiers is clothing, which differentiates classes from one another and signals how one perceives both oneself and others. Clothing is an example of both the arbitrary nature of social signifiers and of the way in which power is

---

[396] "We know that in a language, the sign is arbitrary: nothing compels the acoustic image tree 'naturally' to mean the concept of tree: the sign here is unmotivated. ... The mythical signification, on the other hand, is never arbitrary; it is always in part motivated, and unavoidably contains some analogy." Barthes, "Myth Today," 112.

[397] The example I give here does not come directly from Barthes himself (though he does discuss the mythological significance of clothing in other contexts) but is an example of how his theory might be applied. Barthes's own semiological analysis is found most popularly in his essays on various aspects of French culture compiled in his *Mythologies*. For a discussion of fashion in Barthes, see his book *The Fashion System*, which analyzes women's clothing.

exercised through them. Regarding arbitrariness, consider the types of attire worn by men at formal events throughout different eras. In the early twentieth century, it was standard that a man would wear a white-tie outfit, tailcoat and all, if he was invited to a formal event. Over time, the dress code has evolved, and the tuxedo (black-tie) became the most formal attire that most men would wear during their lifetime. As culture has become more casual, even the tuxedo has become something of a rarity, even for formal occasions, and men often wear a business suit to an event that would previously have necessitated a white-tie or black-tie dress code. This leads to the question: Who decided that these specific clothes should be worn at formal events? Why does society just suddenly change what is considered formalwear? Further, who decided that one cannot show up to a formal occasion wearing cowboy boots, a baseball cap, and jeans? For Barthes, these kinds of social decisions are arbitrary.

These arbitrarily chosen things not only signify formality and informality, but they are also used as a means of control in society. Whether clothing, ritual, music, or language, these signs serve to promote the hegemonic ideology of the bourgeoisie and to keep the masses in line. To continue using the example of clothing, the expectations that are set forth in society regarding appropriate attire serve to maintain class distinctions and reinforce the power of the bourgeoisie. For example, tuxedos are typically expensive to buy, such that hardly anyone owns one. They are therefore most often rented, but even that can be costly. Further, if several people are wearing tuxedos at a formal event, those who are wealthy and have purchased items of higher quality will be able to easily spot the cheap, stiff, polyester rented tuxedo in a crowd. This inaccessibility of more formal or higher-quality clothing keeps the lower classes at a disadvantage, and this fact perpetuates and reinforces the dominance of the upper class.

As another example of this dynamic, consider food. There are all sorts of luxury foods that are present only in higher-end restaurants, remaining financially inaccessible to those who are in a lower social stratum. Why, for example, is caviar considered a high-class item, while corn is not? One might point to the mass availability of corn as a reason for its low price and the relative rarity of roe as the reason for its far higher cost. While availability is certainly part of the equation here, it is not a comprehensive explanation for this difference. At one time, caviar was considered a lower-class dish—especially in Russia, where sturgeon are plentiful. It was eaten by Russian peasants in stew and was, at one point, often given away for free at bars in the United States. Though caviar briefly had status as a luxury item in the sixteenth century in Western Europe, its reputation today largely comes from its consumption by nineteenth-century Russian czars, who raised the social status of the dish. Through this association with royalty, caviar became a marker of status among influential people across the world, such as among the elite families in the United States during the Gilded Age. One could, then, attribute the popularization of caviar as a luxury item to the whims of un upper class who decided to use such a thing as a marker of status, which helped to perpetuate their own power while simultaneously disempowering the masses by making this item inaccessible.

Barthes's most famous example of this mythological examination of social signs is his examination of the phenomenon of professional wrestling.[398] In his essay on the subject, Barthes draws a comparison between professional wrestling—often considered to be the most low-brow form of entertainment—and activities that are traditionally regarded as refined art forms that are classically beautiful, such as opera and ancient theatre.[399] While Barthes acknowledges the obvious differences between the two art forms, he

---

[398] This essay is titled "The World of Wrestling" and was first published in Barthes's *Mythologies*. The page numbers cited here come from *A Barthes Reader*, 18-30.

[399] "The function of grandiloquence is indeed the same as that of ancient theater, whose principle, language and props (masks and buskins) concurred in the exaggeratedly visible explanation of a Necessity." Barthes, "The World of Wrestling," 20.

argues that there are several common themes between professional wrestling as a product of "low culture" and opera as a product of "high culture." Both portray stories that display the battle between good and evil is display. They both contain moral claims within their stories and have characters with their own inner struggles and outward obstacles to be faced.[400] Both art forms place characters on a stage where the audience watches the stories come to a (hopefully satisfying) conclusion. The moral claims made in these stories are unimportant here. Barthes's claim is simply that both art forms serve the same basic social function.

In engaging with semiological analysis of professional wrestling as one would with "higher" cultural products, Barthes questions the accepted hierarchy of art forms, whereby some forms of art are seen as more inherently valuable than others. If it is true that the themes between two art forms are the same and that they serve the same social function, differing only in the classes to which each form of art appeals, then there is only one factor that determines the hierarchical ordering of wrestling and opera: the particular tastes of the bourgeoisie. There is no inherent, objective property of beauty that a thing must have or align with that determines the value in an art form or in an individual piece of art.

Barthes uses this type of semiological analysis to unmask the power dynamics that function through various social signs that are enforced by the promulgation of bourgeois mythologies. The theme of power is essential for Barthes's system, as it becomes programmatic for all of his cultural analysis. This move toward centralizing power dynamics in social discursive analysis is by no means new in Barthes. Both Nietzsche and Marx moved academic conversation in this direction in the prior century. While he himself was neither a Nietzschean nor a Marxist (in the fullest sense at least), Barthes draws on both figures in his move toward examinations of

---

[400] "What is thus displayed for the public is the great spectacle of Suffering, Defeat, and Justice." Barthes, "The World of Wrestling," 23.

power. There are two things to keep in mind when examining how Barthes's approach toward cultural analysis works. First, for Barthes, there is always a power differential that is in play in cultural products, and there is always a motivation behind mythological construction. His examinations of culture are dependent upon a commitment to the ubiquity of power relations within all cultural signification. If this is the case, one does not approach an analysis of a story, artwork, or musical piece to discover whether there is a power differential at work within it, but instead one approaches these things with a commitment that such a dynamic *must* exist, and it therefore must be found and exposed. In other words, the methodology assumes its conclusion before it is even implemented. Second, Barthes's methodology assumes that power differentials are always problematic because they are always fueled by selfish drives for domination. Barthes does not allow for a simple recognition that authority by necessity must be delegated to some and not others due to a natural orientation toward organization and delegation of responsibilities within social groups.

ELEMENTS OF SEMIOLOGICAL SYSTEMS

Each of these examples—clothing, food, art—portrays a self-contained semiological system that consists of a series of signs that interact with one another to create a broader system of discursive meaning within a social group (or between distinct social groups). These semiological systems, for Barthes, contain three core elements: ordering, distinction, and classification.

The first of these, *ordering*, nearly always involves the creation of hierarchical structures of one kind or another. This ordering can be either more or less obvious depending upon the time, culture, or system that one examines. Consider, as one example, class differences as evident in distinct social signs.[401] The Victorian era in

---

[401] These hierarchical orderings are not only class ordering for Barthes, as hierarchies exist within the interrelation between signs in every area of life (and not always in a

England, pre-revolutionary France, and the early Industrial Age in the United States were times wherein behaviors and clothing differences were so pronounced that the upper and lower classes lived as if they were in two different worlds. The French had very particular rules of etiquette that were purposefully understood and known only to the nobility, so that upper class behaviors were inaccessible to others. In the United States, strong social barriers were created among the older upper-class families in order to keep out those who were of the rising wealthy industrial class categorized as "new money," such as the Rockefellers. Familial connections, neighborhoods, schools, churches, food, clothing, and etiquette have all been used as means of continuing these social hierarchical differentiations.

To some degree, the significance of these clear differentiations between classes has diminished in the twenty-first century. With regard to clothing, for example, fast-fashion brands have improved their ability to imitate the clothing of the wealthy, and the rise of T-shirt-wearing tech millionaires has blurred the lines between the clothing of ordinary people and that of those in the highest income bracket. This does not, however, mean that there is no differentiation at all anymore. Someone who knows about expensive clothing will never be fooled into thinking that the Gucci T-shirt is an actual sign of wealth or that a blazer from H&M might be made of a Super 110 wool from Loro Piana. While differences between social strata might be more subtle, these distinctions still remain.

Further, even apart from wealth disparities in hierarchical orderings, there remain other situations in which clothing is used as a social sign of hierarchical classification. Police continue to wear

---

negative way). For example, in his book on Barthes, Jonathan Culler speaks about the ordering of foods in relation to one another that is present in "food grammar." Distinctions are made between an appetizer, a main course, and a dessert. Within such language, there is both differentiation and also the hierarchical privileging of one course over the others (hence the name "main course"). Culler, *Barthes*, 68.

uniforms, and clergy wear white collars to mark themselves as distinct from their congregations. Doctors, judges, and pilots similarly have distinctive clothing that identifies their social function relative to their job. Individuals who wear these uniforms also remove them when not working, further denoting the symbolic association that each piece of clothing carries relative to specific situations. Each of these symbolic associations through clothing demonstrates the importance of ordering within a semiological system.

The second element of semiological systems outlined by Barthes is *distinction*. The identity of various elements within a collection of signs is dependent upon their differentiation from other signs.[402] To put it simply: things are often defined more by what they are not than by what they are. For example, when we divide society between those who are wealthy and those who are not, we only make the determination about what being wealthy is by comparison to those who are not considered wealthy. If all people in a society had significant amounts of money and resources, then the concept of "wealth" would cease to exist. Wealth is defined by its contrast to poverty. Since having wealth is a privileged status, and the maintaining of that status is a necessary part of the continued wielding of power, the wealthy have a vested interest in keeping others poor. This need for differentiation is why throughout history, when the lower classes have begun to imitate the fashion or manners of the upper class, the wealthy have continually sought new ways to differentiate themselves from others. In pre-revolutionary France, there were even laws enacted to disallow the poor from wearing certain fabrics and colors to keep such things the sole property of the upper class. If refined clothing was accessible to all, then it would no

---

[402] This is evident, as one example, in Barthes's *The Fashion System*, in which Barthes identifies the distinctions between social contexts and distinct types of clothing worn within them. A woman wears a certain kind of clothing to a ball that she will not wear when walking in the rain.

longer remain *refined*, as such an identity is defined by its opposition to those things which are *unrefined*.

The third element of semiological systems, as Barthes explains them, is *classification*. This is the aspect of language whereby linguistic categories are chosen to represent and group together a series of things or ideas. It is through classification that there is a common understanding by which distinct people can interact with one another. As a nominalist, Barthes is committed to the idea that the classifications made within systems of signs are not actually existent universals. The way in which various elements of the world are categorized or described is purely subjective. Further, this act of classification is decidedly political. The classifications that are made in a given society, whether through language or bodily acts, are often made in order to serve the interests of the ruling classes. If, for example, some type of behavior is declared to be "abnormal," that classification has the effect of marginalizing those people who engage in such behaviors and further reinforcing hegemonic ideology.

ORDERS OF SEMIOLOGICAL SYSTEMS

Another semiological distinction that Barthes makes is between the *first order* and *second order* of semiological systems. By speaking of a first-order system, Barthes refers to the kind of signification that is generally referenced when discussing semiotics. These are the systems in which there is a direct meaning given to the words or actions that comprise them. A handwave serves as a greeting, saying "thank you" is an expression of gratitude, and raising one's voice in an argument expresses anger. For Barthes, there is often more to signification than these direct signifier-signified connections. These first-order signs are often encapsulated and absorbed by larger ideological systems, which change the originally intended meaning of these signs in order to support an alternate agenda or mythology. Barthes's discussion of these second-order systems most often has capitalism in view. For Barthes, bourgeois capitalists take signs out of their original intended purpose in a first-order system and place them within a different mythological framework.[403] This, for Barthes, is another type of alienation that occurs in capitalist societies, wherein people are alienated from the true meaning of the signs and symbols that make up their culture through the commodification of these signs.

Barthes provides two often-discussed examples of this process of alienation through second-order semiological systems. In the first, Barthes explains the symbol of a rose or a bouquet of flowers.[404] Flowers are used in Western societies as expressions of love—especially romantic love. This gift is given when a man falls in love with a woman as an expression of the innermost feelings of passion within his heart. It is, when given with genuine intent, an expression of authentic desire and love. Flowers can serve other purposes as well, such as an attempt by a man to appease a woman that he previously offended, or the giving of flowers to a grieving family as a sign of compassion after a loss. Each of these things that are signified by the act of giving a flower has some direct purpose within person-to-person relationships and is thereby an element of a first-order semiological system. Capitalist systems, as second-order systems, take away these purposes by commodifying the flower, such as in the creation of Valentine's Day as an occasion when men are expected to buy women flowers (along with a variety of useless material products). Though such a thing appears to be connected to romantic attachment, the genuine love in the act has now been subsumed under corporations seeking profit. The flower is more

---

[403] "In myth, we find again the tri-dimensional pattern which I have just described: the signifier, the signified, and the sign. But myth is a peculiar system, in that it is constructed from a semiological chain which existed before it: it is a second-order semiological system. That which is a sign (namely the associative total of a concept and an image) in the first system, becomes a mere signifier in the second." Barthes, "Myth Today," 99.

[404] Barthes, "Myth Today," 97-98.

about buying and selling than it is about the meaning underneath the giving of the object in a romantic context.

The second example given by Barthes is more specific than the first.[405] He discusses an image that he had encountered, of a French soldier on the cover of a magazine. The man in this image is a young black male who is dressed in a typical French soldier's uniform. As a first-order sign, this image (the signifier) appears to represent a patriotic loyalty to France (the signified). It is rather common for nationalistic sentiments to display themselves through the artistic depiction of soldiers who are actively serving a given nation. National mythologies would provide enough evidence for a detailed analysis as is, but Barthes sees more within this image than just the display of national pride. Barthes notes the uniqueness of displaying a soldier of African descent in this image, rather than a Caucasian one. The skin tone of this man is not merely incidental, for Barthes, but is a purposeful inclusion that displays a message of solidarity between white Frenchmen and those of darker complexions. The African Frenchman ideal on display here shows a love of France from the African, rather than hostility. This, for Barthes, is an attempt to suppress knowledge of, or concern about, the colonial atrocities of the French in Algeria. This is an attempt to sanitize history and to pacify the minority population in France. In its direct first-order semiological meaning, this image is a simple display of patriotism. In this second-order system, it is an attempt to expand hegemonic power by pacifying the populace.[406]

MYTHS

This discussion of second-order systems is a significant element of Barthes's idea of myth. In using the term *myth*, Barthes identifies the form in which semiological systems are communicated. Myth is not

---

[405] Barthes, "Myth Today," 101-102.

[406] This mythological appropriation of signs in second order semiological systems, is both a distancing of the sign from it's intended meaning, and an emptying of the sign, making it "an empty parasitical form." Barthes, "Myth Today," 103.

to be identified with a specific type of story or with any particular set of ideas. To put it simply, "myth is a type of speech."[407] Because myth is identified as a particular kind of speech, "everything can be a myth" if it is in a mythical discursive mode.[408] Anything that is formulated as a second-order semiological system is mythical.

Myth is entrenched within social systems through a series of signs. It is present within the structure of various forms of interaction as often unrecognized underlying ideas and values. Myth permeates all aspects of human culture and communication, including storytelling, art, religion, education, media, clothing, ritual, speech, and far more. It is for this reason that Barthes engages so extensively in his semiological analysis of cultural products and rituals, as through this analysis, the theorist is able to understand the philosophical, moral, and theological values of a society (or at least of the powerful people within a society). There is then an unmasking that occurs through mythical analysis, in which the accepted narratives of a culture are exposed and their social constitution— rather than their supposed inherent, unchanging veracity—is revealed.

With his strong focus on oppressive power, it should come as no surprise that these myths, for Barthes, are almost always intertwined with political ideologies. In fact, it is difficult to find in Barthes any interpretations of mythology that aren't explicitly political. Barthes continues the trend of earlier Marxist thinkers like Lukács and Marcuse of totalizing the realm of politics, such that political dynamics are determinative of every element of human life. The political is all-encompassing. With this conviction driving his theorizing, Barthes seeks to find abusive power dynamics at play in even the most seemingly benign ideas or actions. More recent discussions concerning microaggressions are an outgrowth of this manner of thinking, in which nearly every word spoken or action

---

[407] Barthes, "Myth Today," 93.
[408] Barthes, "Myth Today," 93.

taken is viewed through the lens of hegemonic power and is thereby dissected in search of these dynamics. Myth, for Barthes, is never objective fact, nor is it the product of an ideology that is driven by transcendent truth (there is no such thing for Barthes). It is the imposition of bourgeois ideals that are propagated to defend those who are in positions of power. This is not just true of contemporary Western culture (though capitalism has made these things worse, for Barthes); the prominent myths of any society are similarly displays of the values of the upper classes.[409]

Barthes contends that every mythological system is inherently contradictory. Despite claims of universal principles or truths made by the leaders of various social systems, Barthes asserts not only that certain systems are wrong about their conclusions about truth, but that universal truths do not exist at all. Any attempt to find objective truth or transcendent values is futile, as mythological structures are only tools of systemic oppression and can never portray truths external to themselves. The contradictory nature of these false mythologies, for Barthes, is most clear in capitalism. Capitalist mythology contains within it the myths of equality and social/financial mobility. Capitalist economists contend that wealth in this system will naturally transfer from the bank accounts of the bourgeoisie to the hands of workers by means of the market. If the wealthy have money, they will spend that money. When that money is spent, it is then circulated in the market, and this increase in the amount of money in circulation helps the entire economy, creating the conditions whereby the entire populace can attain greater wealth. For Barthes this mythological perception stands in stark contrast to the economic realities of capitalist systems, in which the wealth of those in the highest financial bracket is often not put into the market but is hoarded such that the inequality between rich and poor grows, in contrast to the promise

---

[409] Barthes is also critical of those who are on the political left that are in positions of power if their ideas are not revolutionary.

of the diminishing of strict financial hierarchies. Promises of equality and the system of capitalism are, for Barthes, inherently contradictory, and this is evidence of the fact that such a system (as with all mythologies) is nothing more than a grasp for power under a mythological guise.

According to Barthes, most of what humans do falls somewhere within the realm of myth. He does, however, allow for one type of discourse that is not strictly mythological: the political.[410] Since, for Barthes, mythology is nearly always the veiling of some political ideology underneath, and most discourse is essentially mythological, then it is only openly political discourse that is honest about itself. Political discussion is thereby the most genuine, though it is important to note that Barthes does not include all political views or ideas underneath this non-mythological banner. By nature of the fact that it attempts to preserve the status quo, conservative political ideals are tools of the bourgeoisie to maintain power.[411] Since mythology is driven by the ruling classes with the goal of promoting hegemonic ideals, conservative political discourse is always, at its heart, mythological. It is only radical politics that is anything else.[412]

Barthes's methodological approach sets up progressive political discourse as the only valid means of academic inquiry and dismisses all critique offhand. For Barthes, there is no objective truth

---

[410] "If myth is depoliticized speech, there is at least one type of speech which is the opposite of myth: that which *remains* political." Barthes, "Myth Today," 134.

[411] He is clear that it is only revolutionary political discourse which is non-mythic. Barthes writes, "There is therefore one language which is not mythical, it is the language of man as a producer: wherever man speaks in order to transform reality and no longer to preserve it as an image, wherever he links his language to the making of things, metalanguage is referred to a language-object, and myth is impossible. This is why revolutionary language proper cannot be mythical." Barthes, "Myth Today," 135.

[412] In answering the question of whether there is also mythology on the political left, he answers that there is "inasmuch, precisely, as the left is not revolution." Barthes, "Myth Today," 135. Not only is conservative discourse mythological, but so is liberal discourse that is not radically revolutionary.

to be discovered, and there are no non-contradictory systems. Attempts to discover the essence of things or to logically set forth ideas of objective value or truth are dismissed as nothing more than a cover for bourgeois hegemony and an excuse for systemic oppression. The theorist who takes Barthes's perspective can simply dismiss all alternative views or critiques through the lens of this constructed ideology of ubiquitous power dynamics, without even attempting to engage in logical argumentation. This is then further cemented with the categorization of all non-revolutionary discourse as mythological, as Barthes approaches conservative ideas as mythological and thereby ingenuine. To clarify, Barthes does not dismiss all mythological language, as he acknowledges this to be an essential element of all human communication. Such a thing is, however, subservient to straightforward revolutionary discourse. This again reveals the consistent issue with Barthes's methodology. It appears to exist to justify itself and its own conclusions by assuming a certain set of dynamics, rather than arguing toward them. It is completely unfalsifiable, as it justifies dismissal of any and all opposition through the categorization of such ideas as hegemonic bourgeois mythology.

ÉCRIVANTS AND ÉCRIVAINS

In the construction of his theory of myth, especially in relation to writing, Barthes develops a distinction between two different types of individuals who write literature: écrivants and écrivains. In English, this has sometimes been translated as a distinction between writers and authors. In making this distinction, Barthes differentiates between those who are mythologically inclined within their works and those who are more straightforward in their texts. As much as Barthes rejects any attempt to formulate objective judgments, he certainly writes about this distinction with some rather authoritative declarations about the superiority of the latter over the former.

Écrivants, according to Barthes' definition, are those writers who engage heavily in myth. These people use their stories as a means to convey some other separate underlying set of ideas, such as truth claims about morality, politics, or religion. As is the case with all myth, Barthes believes that these writers conceal the true intentions of their writing beneath the surface of the narratives that they tell. Just as Aesop's fables are not stories for their own sake but instruments used to deliver moral claims to children, so are nearly all classic novels mere instruments that use language, not as an end, but as a means.[413] Barthes's viewpoint is radical; he includes nearly all of the most important figures in the history of Western literature in this category—William Shakespeare, Jane Austin, Miguel de Cervantes, and more. While Barthes does not completely dismiss these authors as valueless, they are inferior to experimental modernist authors, since these older writers use words as a means to deliver meaning. Political and religious ideas hide under the veil of mythology. Further, many of these older works are said to reinforce bourgeois ideals and are thereby anti-revolutionary. Barthes is part of a broader trend in literary studies throughout the twentieth century away from classic works, viewing these documents as products of oppressive regimes and ideas that have been influential upon Western civilization, not based primarily upon their literary merit, but based on the preferences of the ruling class.

Écrivains, in contrast to écrivants, are those who do not hide their political or religious views underneath mythology. Barthes speaks of these individuals as "authors of nobility." While one might assume here that Barthes is speaking about authors of political treatises, he isn't. Écrivains, instead, are those who are interested in words as words, rather than in using words as a mere means to express some underlying meaning beneath them which they might

---

[413] "The *writer*, on the other hand, is a 'transitive' man, he posits a goal (to give evidence, to explain, to instruct), of which language is merely a means; for him language supports a *praxis*, it does not constitute one." Barthes, "Authors and Writers," in *A Barthes Reader*, 189.

convey. They focus on the text itself, rather than on external things toward which the text points. For Barthes, these authors recognize that the value in a piece of writing should be intrinsic to the text rather than reliant on some extrinsic referent. There is, here, a valuation of the signifier over and against the signified. The words are more important than the meaning of those words. This semiological anti-realism that appears in Barthes is the ultimate end of the move toward arbitrariness in language that began with Saussure (though it departs quite radically from Saussure's own thought).

Barthes's radicalism on these points is furthered by a provocative claim he makes that truly good literature does not *bear* meaning (as nearly everyone has believed since the dawn of writing) but instead *critiques* meaning. This all-encompassing assertion questions the entire history of literature. It is not only a challenge to Western culture but to the manner in which writing has been understood globally across every literate civilization. This literary perspective found in Barthes is paralleled by the move from modern art toward postmodern art, which tends to be more of an instrument of critique than it is an attempt to portray beauty in a constructive manner. The 1960s saw the rise of *conceptual art,* in which artists began to present art pieces that presented challenges to the art world about exactly what art is and what its purpose in society is. In contrast to much earlier modern art—which was very often constructive in its purpose and intent—such works were more attempts at deconstruction, or questioning, than they were positive projects. Such is a lingering problem in much modern thought; it provides no clear path to move from deconstruction to construction, nor does it even deliver a clear picture of what such a construction should be. Pure critique devoid of teleology is critique for its own sake.

Regarding those authors who Barthes praises for their focus on words in themselves, he cites widely read modernist author James Joyce as a prime example of the écrivain. Barthes especially praises

Joyce's notoriously difficult *Ulysses*. This text claims to repristinate the basic narrative structure of Homer's *The Odyssey* through a single day in the life of a man in Dublin. The book is not a coherent linear narrative, nor is it an attempt at creating an epic poem in the form of the Homeric works. It, instead, is a combination of various writing styles without consistency from chapter to chapter. Often, chapters will present a number of shifts to distinct narrative approaches from one page to the next. It is generally written as a stream-of-consciousness series of ramblings (stream-of-consciousness literature was quite common among modernist authors) and does not always abide by the standard rules of grammar. Sometimes a sentence will continue through what would generally be broken up into multiple paragraphs, and at other points no grammar is used at all. In its most experimental sections, Ulysses devolves into incoherent babbling with no real words present on a page. Since Barthes seeks to divorce external meaning from texts, the use of language found in Joyce's work is praiseworthy to him.

Barthes's view of literary works is a novel one when examining his approach in light of the history of literature, but it is not unique among twentieth-century thinkers. There are significant parallels here between Barthes and Derrida (who is explored in the next chapter), though Derridian deconstruction is not identical with Barthes's method. What the two do share is a common commitment to the criticism of meaning rather than to the construction of meaning by means of texts. This approach, for both figures, leads to the inevitable question: If texts do not bear meaning, then what is the point of these literary critics' own writing? Barthes's writings themselves follow a rather standard structure in that he sets forth various claims and defends them. He is not an écrivain, in the sense that he praises here. Is Barthes himself exempt because he is clear about his revolutionary intentions?

THE DEATH OF THE AUTHOR

Finally, we turn to one of Barthes's most influential ideas: the death of the author. This concept, which first appears in an essay of that title from 1967, questions whether the intention of an author in writing a text is determinative in the interpretation of that text. This idea is part of Barthes's greater move away from ideas contained in texts toward texts as they exist in themselves, as is apparent in the exaltation of the écrivain.[414]

That an author's intent matters in one's interpretation of a text seems self-evident to most. When, for example, a student reads Shakespeare's *Romeo and Juliet* and comes across the phrase "I bite my thumb at you," they might initially be a bit confused about what all of this finger-biting is about. If they want to understand the text, that student will most likely seek some kind of historical explanation of the significance of that gesture in Shakespeare's time. If the teacher is asked about the meaning of the phrase, that teacher will most likely explain that biting one's thumb was an excessively rude gesture in sixteenth-century England and that Shakespeare intended to use this as an illustration of the animosity that existed between the Capulets and the Montagues. What if the student did not do this historical research and simply decided that Samson decided to bite his thumb because he thought that it tasted good after he had gotten some chocolate on his fingers, and that Abraham and Gregory are offended because they think that sticking a thumb into your mouth is gross? Which interpretation is correct? Or is any interpretation correct?

For Barthes, the answer to this question is not as clear as we might assume. If it is true, as structuralists contend, that all signs are

---

[414] Barthes argues that "the modern writer (scriptor) is born simultaneously with his text; he is in no way supplied with a being which precedes or transcends his writing, he is in no way the subject of which his book is the predicate; there is no other time than that of the utterance, and every text is eternally written here and now. ... [U]tterance has no other content than the act by which it is uttered." Barthes, "The Death of the Author."

arbitrary, in that there is no inherent connection between the signifier and that which is signified, then why is the author's intent not also arbitrary? Would a commitment to authorial intent not make meaning now depend upon something outside of the text? The prioritization of authorial intent decentralizes the text itself, moving the focus toward the individual who put those words together. Barthes does not deny, of course, that texts arise from authors. Clearly, there are a conglomeration of intentions at work in the construction of a story, article, or book that exist in the mind of an author or group of authors. The creation of the text, however, does not mean control over the text for Barthes. A text stands on its own and should thus be evaluated by its own merit, rather than that of an author.[415] Therefore, in order for a text to be truly examined in itself, there must be a "death of the author" in one's reading of it.

Along with this death of the author is a subsequent "birth of the reader."[416] Once an author's intentions in producing the text are cast aside as non-authoritative, the reader then becomes just as important (if not more so) than the author him- or herself. Through this birth of the reader, multitudinous interpretations of a given text are now possible, and none is authoritative.[417] With this being the case, the student who had the interpretation of biting thumbs that is totally disconnected from Shakespeare's intentions is in fact correct—not in the sense that they interpreted Shakespeare properly but in that they have a valid reading of the text that Shakespeare produced. It is out of this freeing of texts from their authors that a

---

[415] "We know that a text does not consist of a line of words, releasing a single 'theological' meaning (the 'message' of the Author-God), but is a space of many dimensions, in which are wedded and contested various kinds of writing." Barthes, "The Death of the Author."

[416] "[W]e know that to restore to writing its future, we must reverse its myth: the birth of the reader must be ransomed by the death of the Author." Barthes, "The Death of the Author."

[417] "The critic's job, Barthes argues, is not to discover the secret meaning of a work—a truth of the past—but to construct intelligibility for our own time." Culler, *Barthes*, 23.

number of disciplines arose in literary theory that are centered on specific lenses through which texts can be interpreted, with no concern for whether or not those interpretive frameworks make sense of the time period, life, or context of the author of that text. These disciplines encourage the reading of texts with questions of sexual or racial dynamics in view, for example, even if such things were beyond the concerns of the author. Such interpretive approaches are also valuable, for Barthes, in that they expose and challenge the mythologies that underlie texts.[418]

Barthes's approach shifts the meaning of words away from authors and historical contexts and toward one's experience with the text. This view of textual meaning (found in a stronger form in reader-response critics) finds meaning more in the reader's impressions and responses when encountering the text than in the text as an objectively existent and objectively purposive thing. Reading is a kind of performance where a back-and-forth interaction from text to reader creates interpretive meaning through the signs that the text contains. Many critics of Barthes have argued that this approach leads to pure subjectivism in textuality, such that a text could really mean absolutely anything depending on the reader. Is Barthes himself really convinced that his own texts bear no inherent meaning based on his own intention in writing them? He certainly does not write as if his words do not have meaning. He has a clear intention in his own essays and books to persuade others of the veracity of his view of the world. If someone read one of Barthes's volumes of essays and claimed that the text was a defense of capitalism and a critique of progressivism, would that constitute a valid reading of the text? If the experience of the reader is the only

---

[418] This, like everything else Barthes writes, has a political end. He argues that in refusing to read texts as having "an ultimate meaning" the reader "liberates an activity which we might call counter-theological, properly revolutionary, for to refuse to arrest meaning is finally to refuse God and his hypostases, reason, science, and the law." Barthes, "The Death of the Author."

element that matters, it would have to be. If that is the case, then why bother writing texts in the first place?

In response to such questions, it must be acknowledged that Barthes's essay is a bit more nuanced than simply allowing hermeneutical anarchy. For Barthes, the systems of signs and symbols that constitute a text precede the author and thus bear some meaning within a given sociolinguistic context. In his own interpretative writings (such as his *S/Z*) Barthes examines the relations between words, the social significations inherent within words, and his own encounter with the text. Through the interplay among these realities, the text has multitudinous interpretations that are all similarly valid but not purely arbitrary. Barthes's writing is, however, a significant factor in the move away from objectivity in a text toward an approach that identifies meaning as the imposition of a reader upon a written work. This arises is its most consistent form in reader-response criticism.

CONCLUSION

Structuralism, as a movement, attempted to address a variety of philosophical questions that had arisen since Kant by providing a linguistic conception of human understanding. In this view, words and actions are pieces of broader systems of signs that bear meaning in connection to one another. These semiotic systems, for most of the structuralists, are not connected to extrinsic essences but are instead self-referential. They make sense within systems but do not have any participatory connection with transcendent ideas. This is because signs are arbitrary and thus do not have any inherent tie to those ideas that they reference. Nonetheless, Saussure's purpose in his work is not the making of broad metaphysical claims but the analysis of how semiotic systems function and establish human communication. It is with Barthes that this changes.

Barthes's structuralism differs significantly from that of Saussure. Though Barthes is interested in the interrelation of words in order to create meaning (especially earlier in his writing), he increasingly moves toward the dissolution of meaning through semiotics. In Barthes, the structuralist approach serves to take apart accepted ideas and values in the Western world by exposing their mythological context. These mythologies are tools of the bourgeoisie as instruments of marginalization. They are nearly always driven by power. Barthes's system is adamantly anti-essentialist, as he denies that there are objective realities that human minds have access to. If anyone claims to have such privileged knowledge of truth, they are doing so as a grasp for power rather than out of sincere intellectual commitment. For Barthes, reason itself is to be doubted, as is the authority of an author over their own works. What matters is the subjectivity of the experience between a reader and a text, as well as the power dynamics that lie underneath nearly all action. These two themes—subjectivity in textual analysis and the ubiquity of power—are also prominent in the post-structuralists, toward which the discussion now turns.

THE POST-STRUCTURALISM OF DERRIDA AND FOUCAULT

Much ink has been spilled explaining the move from modernism to postmodernism in the mid-twentieth century. As has been evident in the last few chapters in this book, in the beginning of the twentieth century, the leading thinkers of the Western world began to move gradually away from reliance on pure reason as a definitive tool in human endeavors and a guarantor of moral progress and toward an increased pessimism about human rational capacity. The praising of unreason from Adorno, the popularization of the stream-of-consciousness literature discussed by Barthes, and the development of semiotics are all evidence of this move against reason. The line between later modernity and postmodernity is not always an easy one to draw, as the shifts away from Enlightenment ideals began prior to the era of postmodernity in a proper sense. In art, for example, the impressionist painters of the late nineteenth century had begun to move away from the standard artistic rules of the academy (which were largely rationally determined) toward an emphasis on personal expression.[419] The outbreak of World War I solidified this move away from reason. Technological developments were not leading to the moral progress

---

[419] The connection between art and ideology is one that is debated heavily in art theory. A popular work arguing for strong ties between art and philosophy is H. R. Rookmaaker's *Modern Art and the Death of a Culture*. In this work, Rookmaaker makes an argument for Western decline as evidenced by experimental movements in the early twentieth century. A less pessimistic interpretation of the connection between modern art and intellectual trends can be found in Herbert Reed's *The Philosophy of Modern Art*. Many artists themselves have resisted attempts to tie their work into philosophical trends. Picasso, for example, was consistently critical of attempts to define an ideology of cubism.

many hoped for but to the destruction of human lives on a mass scale. By the 1960s, the modernist paradigm no longer reigned, and other approaches to life, ethics, philosophy, theology, literature, and the arts dominated. This broad range of ideas and movements is characterized as postmodernism.

Postmodernism is more of a general label identifying tendencies by which various movements, thinkers, and ideas can be categorized than it is a specific ideology.[420] While there are elements that are shared by postmodern thinkers, such as the critique of metanarratives (the view that there are large cohesive stories in which history fits), the rejection of epistemic foundationalism (the idea that there is certainty in human knowledge which grounds our thinking), and a move toward subjectivity in interpretation, these things alone do not create a coherent ideological system.[421] This chapter is not, then, an overview of all of the major postmodern thinkers. As diverse as they are, it would be nearly impossible to address them all in a single chapter without either oversimplifying or conflating the ideas of a multitude of individuals with distinct views. This chapter instead focuses on the two most influential French intellectuals who are broadly identified with the postmodern label: Michel Foucault and Jacques Derrida.

Foucault and Derrida are often recognized as postmodern thinkers, but they are also both post-structuralists. Though post-structuralism is distinguished from postmodernism, its ideas and methods are essential to the postmodern project. Post-structuralism might in some sense be categorized as one of many movements within the broader category of postmodernity. Like Barthes, both Foucault and Derrida are influenced by the ideas of Saussure, believing that intellectuals should move away from attempts to understand the world as a collection of rational laws and objective

---

[420] For an overview, see Butler, *Postmodernism: A Very Short Introduction*; Powell, *Postmodernism for Beginners*; Hart, *Postmodernism: A Beginner's Guide*.

[421] Of course, the postmodernists don't actually want to create an ideological system, as such things are the subject of their critiques.

essences and toward an examination of the systems that make up human communication and interaction. Derrida and Foucault do not do this in the same way as Barthes, or as one another. Foucault explores the power dynamics that are at work within social systems; Derrida focuses on textuality, analyzing writing through the process of deconstruction. Despite the distinctions between them both in emphasis and in their actual claims, both French thinkers have, together, shaped humanities departments in modern universities. This chapter overviews some of the most important ideas from each of these public intellectuals.

MICHEL FOUCAULT

Any thorough discussion about intellectuals in the modern academy will inevitably include the name of Michel Foucault.[422] While his formal area of study was philosophy, Foucault's writing spans a variety of disciplines, including history, literature, and psychology. The breadth of his impact is expansive, as he has shaped nearly every academic discipline that he wrote on (and his own areas of interest in writing were multitudinous). It is not only in the academy, however, that Foucault's impact is apparent. As a public intellectual who made significant media appearances in France, Foucault also influenced the popular consciousness of Western radicals, especially within the student protest movements of the 1960s. Further, the development of disciplines like gender theory, critical race theory, and intersectionality are due in part to the categories and ideas created by Foucault. Most of what is given the (rather ambiguous and generally unhelpful) label of "woke" in popular discourse is at its heart Foucaultian. What is presented here is only a portion of Foucault's system, but it should give the reader a general conception of the primary ideas of the French intellectual that have helped shape the modern academy.

---

[422] For an overview of Foucault, see Gutting, *Foucault: A Very Short Introduction*; Taylor, *Michel Foucault*; Fillingham, *Foucault for Beginners*.

FOUCAULT'S LIFE

Michel Foucault was born in Poitiers, France, in 1926 to Catholic parents.[423] Like many of the radical thinkers discussed thus far, Foucault was raised in an upper-middle-class household with somewhat conservative leanings. While biographical information about his childhood is scant, it appears that his upbringing drove his rebelliousness against traditional cultural norms. While this book does not pretend to be a psychoanalysis text, much has been made of the fact that Foucault had a difficult relationship with his father, whom he seldom spoke of publicly. Regarding his parents' faith, the details that appear in Foucault's writings where his childhood is mentioned do not indicate a deep piety or consistent engagement in the Roman Catholic Church beyond attendance at Mass. Nonetheless, Foucault was surrounded by more devout members of the Roman Catholic Church at various points during his childhood, such as at the Jesuit school he attended. While these biographical details are not prevalent in Foucault's public speaking or writing, it is clear that his encounters with the Roman Church, and with conservative ideas more generally, were not positive ones.

Despite the difficulties he apparently faced in his home life, Foucault performed well in school, and his academic giftings were apparent at a young age. When departing from his childhood home, Foucault's educational journey took him to the prestigious Lycée Henri-IV in Paris, where he pursued a degree in philosophy. Once again Foucault's superior academic abilities were evident; both his professors and fellow students seemed to recognize that Foucault was destined for a successful career in academia. Foucault was initially interested in the philosophy of Hegel—much like Marx, Lukács, and Adorno before him. This interest in German idealism led to Foucault's thesis on the conception of the transcendental in Hegel's *Phenomenology of Spirit*. As with other thinkers discussed in this book, Foucault rejected conservative interpretations of Hegel,

---

[423] For Foucault's biography, see Macy, *The Lives of Michel Foucault*.

instead relying on the appropriation of Hegelian historicism by Marxist thinkers. Despite the topic of his dissertation, Foucault was not a metaphysician in a traditional sense; he was instead a cultural critic who used broader philosophical discussion for pragmatic and revolutionary ends.

In addition to the left-Hegelians, Foucault read multitudinous philosophers across centuries and disciplines. Like many academics in his day, Foucault was interested in existentialism—the most popular intellectual trend in France at the time. Though an academic movement, existentialism was also prominent in the broader public consciousness. Foucault's fellow Frenchman, Jean-Paul Sartre, was widely known throughout Europe, just as Foucault himself later would be. Among the existentialists, Foucault was interested not only in Sartre but also in the German philosopher Martin Heidegger (whose label as an existentialist is questionable). Beyond these contemporary thinkers, Foucault also read early modern writers like Immanuel Kant and other Enlightenment philosophers, along with the phenomenological works of Edmund Husserl. The thinker who perhaps had the most significant influence on Foucault was Friedrich Nietzsche. Such a connection might seem surprising, as Nietzsche's ideas are often associated with right-wing ideology, whereas Foucault is often deemed a radical leftist. It was Nietzsche who first spoke of the will to power and the Übermensch that would both be used to defend the Nazi regime in Germany, while Foucault was an ardent anti-Fascist. Of course, the connection between Nietzsche's ideas and fascism is often challenged, as the National Socialist party used sources of all sorts as propagandistic tools, ignoring historical context or nuance within such writings. Nonetheless, interpretation of Nietzsche's work is beyond the scope of the present discussion. Regardless of such connections, Foucault is certainly not dogmatically beholden to Nietzsche's ideas (or to any thinker) but draws primarily from one common theme in his writing—power. What Foucault appropriated from Nietzsche was the perception that all human action and all social institutions are driven by, and often constituted by, relations of power. With all these influences, from Hegel to existentialism to Kant to Nietzsche, Foucault displays an impressive ability to read and synthesize vastly different texts, ideas, and thinkers in the construction of his own philosophical project.

While biographical information does not determine the veracity of one's truth claims, and the motivations at work within someone's inner psyche when constructing an ideological system are ultimately hidden from the interpreter, some mention must be made of Foucault's own personal struggles here. It is quite evident that Foucault's biography and his philosophy are deeply interconnected. As Foucault himself contended, ideas are not acontextual and ahistorical propositions to be divorced from the person and social situation from which they arise. It is precisely the issues with which Foucault wrestled in his internal life that he wrote on, challenging inherited cultural norms.

During his time in college, Foucault had the reputation of being a mentally disturbed individual. He seemed to delight in dark subjects, decorating his room with imagery of death and destruction. This fascination with the macabre was also evident in his chosen conversation topics with other students, which included suicide, death, and sex. These interests remained with Foucault throughout the entirety of his career. These interests were more than theoretical; Foucault had several failed suicide attempts and engaged in regular forms of self-harm. He struggled with depression along with a variety of other mental issues. Foucault also engaged in orgiastic homosexual escapades, which is reflected in his writing. Psychologists of the time had claimed that Foucault's homosexuality was at the root of his disturbed psyche. These negative encounters with psychologists likely played a role in the development of Foucault's thoughts on sexual normalcy, power, and medical institutions. It must be clarified that Foucault's lifestyle was not merely one of subverting heteronormativity through homosexual relationships but was one of excessive promiscuity. Having many sexual partners, he engaged in violent BDSM practices and other fetishes. Most disturbing about Foucault's promiscuous lifestyle is the barrage of accusations of childhood sexual abuse at his hands in Tunisia. Foucault's sexual proclivities formed the ideas of one of his most influential works—a multi-volume study of the history of sexuality. In this book, Foucault challenges many established norms of sexual propriety in the Christian West, arguing that those in power attempted to suppress others through the control of bodies. As Foucault attempted to dismantle what he viewed as bourgeois oppressive ideals of heterosexual monogamy, it is hard not to see this through the lens of his own lifestyle and experiences. The fight to dismantle traditional power dynamics—particularly through the control of bodies—is not some theoretical or intellectual enterprise for Foucault. It is, instead, a validation of his own person and behaviors.

The penchant for the dangerous within Foucault's life was not only evident in his sexual behaviors and his series of failed suicide attempts; it is also displayed in his consistent use of harmful substances. As his popularity among the youth rose in the 1960s, Foucault adopted the lifestyle of many political radicals of that time. He engaged in heavy drug use, experimenting with a variety of hallucinogenics, delighting in the thrill of possible danger or death as a consequence. Each of these elements of Foucault's biography is important as background for the themes that appear throughout his career. They demonstrate that Foucault is deeply committed to his subject matter beyond the realm of theory.

Foucault's Relationship to Marxism

In some recent talks from a contemporary public intellectual, Jordan Peterson, Michel Foucault has been labeled as a proponent of postmodern neo-Marxism. This identification between Foucault and Marxism has led to various publications releasing articles refuting the supposed connection between the two intellectual schools.[424] It is argued that Peterson conflates two diametrically distinct ideologies when identifying postmodernity and Marxism.[425] While there may be overlap at points between them, they have fundamentally divergent foundations and goals. While Peterson's account of the relationship between Foucault and Marxism might overstate their points of convergence, it is not quite so simple to totally divorce the two as some critics of Peterson want to do. While it is true that Foucault himself repeatedly rejected the Marxist label, there remain parallels in both argumentation and points of concern between Foucault and Western Marxism. Further, it is undoubtedly true that the French thinker is influenced to some degree by the writings of Marx, especially as the two began their philosophical projects initially through a similar left-leaning examination of Hegel.

Foucault did briefly identify as a socialist when he was in college, but this association did not last. Adoption of the Marxist label was, at the time, a trend among many French intellectuals, such as among the Marxist-leaning existentialists who influenced Foucault. Foucault came to disagree with some of the central tenets of Marxist theory and thereafter diverged from it. After this departure from Marxism, Foucault labeled himself an anarchist, but this identification was also discarded rather quickly. Labels of any type

---

[424] See, for example, Savage, "Jordan Peterson's 'Postmodern Neomarxism' is Pure Hokum."

[425] Another point of critique is found in Peterson's universalizing claims about the influence of this ideology in the modern academy. In an article evaluating Peterson's argument, Panu Raatikainnen draws on surveys of philosophy professors to determine how prevalent postmodern ideology is in the academy and draws the conclusion that the majority of philosophers reject subjectivist views of reality. What these surveys fail to show, however, is the ideology inherent within the humanities as a whole—not just philosophy. Postmodernity (and Marxism) is most prevalent in literature, art, and the seemingly endless new fields of social critique (gender studies, queer studies, etc.) rather than in philosophy in a proper sense. Raatikainnen, Panu, "Jordan Peterson on Postmodernism, Truth, and Science," in *Jordan Peterson: Critical Responses*, edited by Sandra Woien.

never fit precisely on Foucault as he tended to prize independence in his own thinking, drawing from multitudinous sources rather than narrowing in on any one set of aligned thinkers. Nevertheless, despite his own hesitancy to adopt Marxism as a system, Foucault maintained significant connections to Marxists throughout his life. For example, when Foucault held a tenured professorship at Vincennes he was tasked with recruiting faculty. In doing so he almost exclusively hired Marxist professors. At the very least, he trusted the academic work of those in the Marxist tradition more than that of those who stood totally outside of it. Despite their differences, both Foucauldian postmodernism and Marxism hold many general principles and commitments in common. Both are radical ideologies based on their conceptions of a needed revolution to overthrow oppressive ideological hegemonic forces.

The tie between Marxism and Foucault is most clearly made, not in Foucault himself, but in later activist writing that amalgamates various leftist ideologies. Many activists draw from Marx's dichotomous approach to society as divided between the powerful bourgeoisie and a helpless proletariat, his progressive view of history, and his view of economic exploitation. Activists similarly draw from many of Foucault's views, such as the ubiquitous nature of power dynamics in human interactions and institutions, the conflation of human identity with social roles, the comprehensive nature of resistance, and the belief that resistance to oppression is largely a bodily act that is often sexual. For some activists on the social, cultural, and political left, this amalgamation of post-structuralist and Marxist ideas might be accurately described as "postmodern neo-Marxism," even if the term is not an appropriate identifier for Foucault himself.

SIMILARITIES BETWEEN MARX AND FOUCAULT

The closest point of contact between Foucault and Marx is their mutual interest in power relations. Neither figure is unique in this regard, as the nineteenth and twentieth centuries experienced a general move toward evaluations of power and its role in both the inner human drive and in social systems. Marx's concern regarding power is nearly exclusively economic. For him the powerful are those who hoard wealth and exploit the masses in order to both attain and maintain their control. When Marx discusses power in areas of society other than the market, he continues to see those relations through an economic lens, as both the root and motivation of exploitative social structures. Rather than Marx, it is Nietzsche who most comprehensively speaks about power in a psychological sense, positing that there is a "will to power" that guides and motivates human action.[426] Foucault draws from both thinkers as he contends that power defines all human interaction, both in the inner psyche and in social structures.[427] For Foucault, dynamics of power and oppression underlie nearly everything in society. If one is to understand society, one must use a critical framework of power to evaluate it, thus uncovering the inherent structures of power underlying any given institution.

The Marxists and Foucault also share a common target of critique: traditional Western Christian culture. For both schools of thought, bourgeois interests have determined which behaviors and systems are to be considered "normal" (and thereby privileged) and which are not. It is argued that the interests of the ruling class have

---

[426] There is quite a bit of debate about what Nietzsche meant by the will to power, as he never defines the idea precisely. It is clear that he is drawing on Arthur Schopenhauer's idea of *will* as the will to live, which is a universal force underlying all things (somewhat akin to Hegel's *Geist*).

[427] There is some disagreement in Foucault scholarship on whether the Nietzschean or Marxian strain is more prominent in Foucault's thought. Thiele, for example, argues that Marx had a stronger impact on Foucault's thought than Nietzsche, even though Nietzsche is cited directly more often. Johnson draws from an interview wherein Foucault himself defends his consistency with Marx, claiming that even though he does not cite Marx very often, Marx's ideas stand behind Foucault's historical method. Foucault even says at one point, "One might even wonder what difference there could ultimately be between being a historian and being a Marxist." Johnson, "Reading Nietzsche and Foucault: A Hermeneutics of Suspicion?" 582.

been artificially objectivized, viewed as universal inherent truths about nature, in order to retain the present hegemony. In this view, there are no transcendent truths; the values of Western culture are historically determined, mere tools used by the powerful to maintain their own interests. The Foucaultian and the Marxist share an inherent distrust of inherited institutions and ideals, since such things are most often a pretense for the maintenance of bourgeois hegemony. The institutions that conservatives often prize the most highly, such as the family and the church, are viewed with suspicion for their maintenance of the status quo and their anti-revolutionary nature.

Another commonality between Foucault and the Marxists is an anti-transcendental element within both systems. Their rejection of the objective truth claims taught by those in power is not due to their belief in another set of objective, competing truth claims. Instead, both Marxism and Foucault reject attempts to arrive at eternalized universal truths altogether. This anti-realism is also tied to their mutual rejection of the existence of a self-identical persistent subject, or a soul. Marx defines human nature, not as a given essence, but as a totality of social relations.[428] Along with Lukács, the Critical Theorists, and Barthes, Foucault rejects the givenness of human nature. Through the all-encompassing notion of power, Foucault contends that power dynamics not only arise *within* human relations but actually *create* human beings. This view of nature as socially constituted departs from both the Enlightenment belief in a transcendental subject and the Christian doctrine of the soul.

One final point of similarity that unites these two thinkers is the belief in a superstructure that lies beneath the visible, external occurrences in the world. For both Marx and Foucault, the world can be best understood through the unmasking of power dynamics at play within social structures and world history. Since power plays

---

[428] As discussed in the earlier chapter on Marx, this idea is explained in Marx's *Theses on Feuerbach*.

this central role as the seemingly only unifying element of experience and nature, power almost takes on the role of a Kantian transcendental for Foucault, as a necessary preconception to understand anything. Marx similarly engages in social critique through the unmasking of injustices within inherited institutions, though that injustice is strictly economic. The family is a means of hoarding wealth; the church is a means of promoting ideology that pacifies an oppressed populace; and so on. For Foucault, these underlying dynamics can be economic, but they are most often deeper than that, arising from an inner psychological need to exercise domination over others.

DIFFERENCES BETWEEN MARX AND FOUCAULT

Despite these areas of alignment between Foucault and Marx, there are also significant differences. The clearest of these is their divergent teleological perspectives. As a result of the Hegelianism underlying his project, Marx believes in the inevitability of historical progress and the eventual overcoming of exploitation over the working class. Society is like a biological organism that has determined stages of growth that will eventually lead to a just society under a socialist state. In other words, Marx is a progressive in the truest sense: He is committed to societal progress that decreases injustice out of historical necessity. Progress is not only possible, but inevitable. In contrast to this, Foucault rejects such optimistic teleological thinking.[429] While Foucault was an activist, he was not

---

[429] Hunt contends that "the major conflict between Foucault and Marx is about the possibility of causal explanations." Hunt, "Getting Marx and Foucault into Bed Together!" 604. Marx is concerned with the "why" questions in historically developed institutions, while causal explanations are rejected by Foucault because causal explanations are fitted within a teleologically driven metanarrative wherein each element of the historical process has some necessary role or purpose.

convinced that there was a grand end to political activism that he was part of moving toward.[430]

One of the hallmarks of postmodernity is the rejection of metanarratives, or grand universal stories into which all individual lives and historical events fit. For Foucault, Marxist views of history are essentially theological. Like religion, they posit a purpose within historical development and make claims about universal goods to be achieved and purposes in individual human life. All metanarratives that human beings adopt, whether religious or political, are the result of feeble human attempts to make sense of a world that is nonsensical. They are mere frameworks people use to approach history and do not reveal things as they truly are. This rejection of Marxism as a metanarrative does not mean that Foucault rejects all actions, values, or goals within Marxism. They align rather strongly with his resistance to received ideologies and systems. Nonetheless, Marxism cannot provide a true teleological vision of nature beyond that of mere hope or possibility.

Foucault is not alone here in his opposition to a belief in the historical inevitability of progress. As discussed above, many theorists in the Frankfurt School moved away from a belief in a grand synthesis within world history following the devastation of the Second World War. This denial of synthesis is evident in Adorno's idea of negative dialectics, in which tensions should be left to stand without resolution rather than absorbed into some grander unity. Even the more optimistic Marxists, such as Marcuse, did not speak so strongly of inevitability but of possibility. This once again raises the issue of precisely what it is that defines Marxism as an ideology, since hardly anyone adopts the entirety of the *Communist Manifesto* in all of its particulars. Historical development since Marx's lifetime hardly allows for any thinking person to hold an unwavering

---

[430] While the theme appears in some other works, Foucault's opposition to teleological narratives is most apparent in *Madness and Civilization*, wherein he opposes the narrative of a "progress of reason" that defines history.

affirmation of the ideas and writings of Marx and Engels. Twentieth-century Western Marxists like Lukács, Gramsci, Adorno, and Marcuse all diverge significantly from classical Marxism, while still being given that label. Foucault is simply a step farther from Marx in a continuing trajectory away from a belief in inevitable progressive synthesis.

This difference between Marx and Foucault regarding progress reveals an underlying philosophical distinction. While both thinkers began their academic careers as students of Hegelian philosophy, they both moved away from Hegel's commitments in different directions. Marx did so through his commitment to materialism, which was incorporated into his own unique blend of historicism and anti-idealism. Where Foucault departed most significantly from Hegel is in his rejection of historicism. Hegel's teleological orientation was the underlying principle of his entire system, as Geist is defined by development and progress. Foucault retained Hegel's historiographic method in other ways, however. In his historical genealogical writings, Foucault adopts Hegel's approach to historical epochs, studying periods of time as defined in unique eras bearing their own notions of truth, ethics, and value. These epochs are not, for Foucault, a series of organically connected parts of one historically developing reality. They are simply different relations of power. Rather than Hegel, it is Nietzsche who provides Foucault with a systematic ideological framework in which history is to be understood. In Nietzsche, Foucault finds the answer to Hegelian optimism through a non-teleological view of history that is centered on the all-encompassing impact of power in human relations. For both Nietzsche and Foucault, the exercise of power is an absolute inevitability. As an inner psychological drive, power and domination are simply the ways that humans—and subsequently the societies they create—interact.

This underlying difference between Marx and Foucault on the nature of power and history has significant implications for the examination of societal power dynamics. Marx's view of power is binary. Society is neatly divided into two distinct groups: the proletariat and the bourgeoisie. The former group is oppressed, or exploited, and the latter group is oppressive, or exploitative. In the Marxian approach, exploitation is easy to identify in relation to both those who enact it and those who are its victims. The simplicity of this bifurcation also leads to a clear solution to such problems. Liberation can be accomplished by the straightforward act of overthrowing the oppressive class. Foucault recognizes that dynamics of power are far more complex than this. Rather than positing a clear dividing line between oppressive people and oppressed people, Foucault contends that there are overlapping power dynamics present in all interpersonal relationships, such that to some degree everyone exercises power over others. Dynamics of power are not reducible to class relations, as domination is exerted between individuals, not only between clearly distinct groups. Power and oppression are pervasive realities, for Foucault, encompassing every human interaction and institution.[431] Power is not inherently tied to wealth, as coercion and domination are exercised in various parts of social life.[432] In some way, power itself creates social life. This Foucaultian move away from Marx's neat bifurcation of two distinct classes in which exploitation is found lays the groundwork upon which intersectionality later builds.

---

[431] "To understand subjection as well as resistance and change, we must examine power at a micro-level: relations between boss and worker, therapist and client, teacher and pupil, husband and wife." McWhorter, "Foucault," in *A Companion to the Philosophers*, 251.

[432] As Turkel writes, "[W]hile his studies use Marxian categories of class, ideology, capital accumulation, and the labour process, he was not only scornful of the official Marxism that was congealed in the French Communist Party, but he also faulted Marx's political economy for its continuity with liberalism and its tendencies to view liberation in economistic terms." Turkel, "Michel Foucault: Law, Power, and Knowledge," 171.

FOUCAULT ON POWER

In order to explain how Foucault's perception of power functions within his philosophical system, it is important to distinguish his view, not only from Marx, but from earlier treatments of power in Western philosophy. While it is not the case that *no one* discusses power in a non-political sense in early modernity, most philosophical discourse surrounding power in the post-Enlightenment West has surrounded the role of the state and the duties of citizens. Thomas Hobbes, for example, perceives the state as a great Leviathan, which must of necessity exercise power in order to stop members of a commonwealth from killing one another. In a Hobbesian framework, power is a good when exercised properly, as without it a functional society cannot exist. Later thinkers in the liberal tradition then speak about limitations on state power, viewing an excessive use of force and coercion as a threat to the good of liberty. In this view, power is generally perceived more as a danger than as a good. Through both these positive and negatives of power as expressed in the Hobbesian and Lockean traditions, political philosophers debate the relationship between power and freedom, coercion and rights, and other topics of the state and its duties. It is with Nietzsche that these discussions move significantly beyond the political into the psychological and social life more generally. While Foucault certainly does discuss power in an explicitly and narrowly political sense, he is more concerned with these broader dynamics of power relations that are found in Nietzsche. While drawing from Nietzsche as a groundwork, Foucault then extends these ideas into unique areas.[433]

One of the areas in which the Nietzschean influence on Foucault is most apparent is in the inseparability of power and knowledge. Though there is not an exact identification between

---

[433] As Foucault says, it "was Nietzsche who specified the power relation as the general focus, shall we say, of philosophical discourse—whereas for Marx it was the production relation." As cited in Turkel, "Michel Foucault: Law, Power, and Knowledge."

knowledge and power, these two things share a reciprocal relationship to one another.[434] For Foucault, an increase in knowledge coincides with a related increase in power. Similarly, if one gains power, that power will then be strengthened by and demonstrated in the growth and control of knowledge. It is this latter point, of power controlling knowledge, that leads Foucault toward a skepticism of received truths. Rather than accept the Enlightenment ideal of the disinterested observer, Foucault contends that received knowledge is often constructed by the powerful as a means of maintaining power. Knowledge is a tool, rather than an end in itself, meaning that things that are purported to be objective facts are often subjective biases that just so happen to serve the interests of the powerful.

Since Foucault is often concerned with issues of sexuality, an apt example here is the traditional family structure.[435] The Western Christian world has perceived a specific view of the family structure as normative for society, while alternative approaches are marginalized. In the received Western view, marriage is a heterosexual institution in which a man and woman make a lifelong commitment to one another with the expectation of childbirth and childrearing (excepting cases of infertility). Foucault argues that though the family has been claimed to exist only in such a way by religious, political, or educational authorities, this narrow definition of family is not inherent to the thing itself. There is no objective standard that has proven the superiority of this conceived familial structure. It has been declared such because it is in the vested interest of the ruling parties to do so. Familial power in government, for example, is maintained through genealogical lineage. Inheritance keeps wealth within families, and expectations of monogamous marriages are then used to ensure that the powerful only marry other

---

[434] For an overview of Foucault's view of power and knowledge as drawn from, and contrasted with, Nietzsche, see Gutting, *Foucault*, 72-75.

[435] This argument is found in the first volume of Foucault's *The History of Sexuality*.

individuals within similarly powerful families, securing further inheritance for children and preserving the power and wealth of these families. Motivated by this maintenance of power, leaders in various areas of society push their own way of life as normative for the populace and consequently marginalize other lifestyles, declaring them to be abnormal or deviant.[436]

This bourgeois domination through the imposition of their ideals is perpetuated in a number of different ways. It is done politically through the exertion of power by means of laws that disallow the freedom of action when it is not in accord with the interests of the ruling class. This domination also occurs within educational institutions, wherein the ideals of the powerful are the lens through which each subject is studied so that the hegemonic ideology is assumed and supported by academics. This continuation of power also occurs through various cultural mediums that include moral messages that support the ideals of the ruling class. In summary, Foucault contends that bourgeois norms are perpetuated by historical institutions, education, media, and the broader normalization of certain behaviors and views within interpersonal relationships. All of these ideas are present in earlier thinkers discussed here, such as in Adorno's notion of cultural hegemony. Foucault offers something new, namely the specifics of how these power dynamics function—such as in biopower.

BIOPOWER

One of the central themes of Foucault's ideas of power is what he refers to as *biopower*. Biopower is a specific element of many oppressive exercises of power—control over bodies.[437] Not content only to control ideas or wealth, powerful classes seek to maintain

---

[436] Foucault refers to these coercive means to reinforce monogamous heterosexual relations as a "technology of sex."

[437] Foucault speaks of modernity as the "era of 'bio-power,'" which arose in the seventeenth century and was further cemented through industrialization. Foucault, "Right of Death and Power over Life," in *Foucault Reader*, 262.

their power through the control of biology through the creation and maintenance of mechanisms that determine and enforce standards regarding what is or is not acceptable to do with one's body. The state exercises this type of control over individuals' bodies through laws and regulations that dictate what is deemed acceptable or unacceptable behavior with legal ramifications for disobedience. This power over bodies is not, however, solely coercive in the sense of legal enforcement; it also operates coercively through the privileging of certain ideas over others in social discourse within diverse institutions.[438] Schools, for instance, play a role in dictating societal norms and shaping individuals' perceptions of what is and is not permissible regarding the use of one's body. Religious institutions ground these rules about bodies in a transcendent order, thus declaring them to be immutable truths rather than mere social prejudice (which is what Foucault believes them to be).

Foucault's emphasis on biopower is connected to his rejection of the transcendental notion of the soul and his affirmation of the body as the foundational (and, really, the only) element of human identity. This perspective is epitomized in Foucault's inversion of the Platonic idea that "the body is the prison of the soul," where he asserts instead that "the soul is the prison of the body."[439] By identifying the body as the primary locus of human identity, Foucault argues that the worst forms of oppression are often those that hinder bodily freedom. Consequently, since the body is often the focus of oppression, the body is also identified as the central site of resistance, suggesting that acts of defiance against oppressive power are most effective when they include bodily disobedience.

---

[438] Of these institutions exerting biopower in nineteenth-century capitalism, Foucault mentions "the family and the army, schools and the police, individual medicine and the administration of collective bodies." Foucault, "Right of Death and Power over Life," 263.

[439] This is part of his discussion of juridical punishment in nineteenth-century France in the first chapter of Foucault, *Discipline and Punish*, 3-31.

To illustrate the impact of power on bodies, consider an example from the end of the twentieth century—the D.A.R.E. programs in public schools in the United States.[440] As part of the broader war on drugs that occurred throughout the 1990s, this government-funded program sent police officers into schools to teach children about the dangers of using illegal recreational drugs. It was believed that through this education, fewer children would choose to use these substances in high school and beyond. While the state did far more in this war on drugs than educate students (legal punishments for drug offenses were significantly increased at that time), government leaders recognized that the law cannot be the sole means by which behavior is changed. People are similarly influenced by education and media. Recognizing this, the educational institutions of the United States became part of this broader effort to stop recreational drug use through the imposition of the D.A.R.E. program. In addition to education and legal repercussions, media was used as a third component of this war on drugs. Television commercials were run on a regular basis to dissuade viewers from using recreational drugs—such as commercials showing someone cracking an egg and then declaring, "This is your brain on drugs." Further, anti-drug messaging was placed into children's programming through public service announcements at the end of cartoons. In using each of these mediums to convey a message about acceptable and unacceptable bodily behavior, those in power exercised coercion over the populace by defining what is normative and what is deviant, ultimately disallowing bodily autonomy.

This Foucauldian method of reasoning is evident today in a number of spheres. The argument is made that dynamics of power target bodily autonomy and that the legality or moral permissibility of bodily acts are dependent upon relations of power. In such argumentation, assumptions are made that one who differs from a

---

[440] To be clear, this is my own example. Foucault did not live long enough to have made such a reference.

standard progressive view of gender, sexuality, or abortion does so as a means of domination. As a prominent example, consider the issue of abortion. From a rationalist framework, one might conceive of these debates centering on the definition of personhood and then applying this concept to a preborn child, or perhaps examining the specifics of the developmental process throughout gestation. These approaches depend on a method of argumentation in which there is an objective moral claim that can be examined, evaluated, and affirmed or refuted. Many discussions on this issue in the current milieu do not attempt to do this, focusing instead on things like the gender of the lawmakers who have written a given law—as if the veracity of a moral or legal claim is dependent upon the sex of the individual involved in its promulgation. Or, the argument is made that abortion restriction is a tool of patriarchal domination by a prejudiced male contingent in society. Such statements avoid dealing with the moral, philosophical, and legal claims being made in the abortion debate by sidelining such concerns in favor of uncovering a hidden power dynamic that lies underneath such disputes. It is assumed that if a man supports a law that in any way restricts a woman, this must be due to a power differential and nothing else.

To summarize the point here, Foucault views the hindering of bodily acts as the apex of oppression, especially within capitalist societies. When the state exercises coercive power over a populace to maintain hegemonic control, it often does so through the oppression of bodies. This bodily oppression is not the control of isolated individuals in society but is instead most often directed toward a specific societal group or set of actions. This control is mediated by means of various institutions, so there is a normalization of the ideology that underlies the power dynamic at work. As shown in the example of the war on drugs in the 1990s, these multitudinous institutions that contribute to the exercise of biopower include the state, health organizations, religious institutions, and educational establishments.

POWER AND THE SELF

It must be clarified here that Foucault does not have a solely negative view of power, in contradistinction to what might be assumed from the critiques of oppressive power addressed above. For Foucault, power is inescapable, since it is deeply embedded within the human psyche rather than just the result of class distinctions or financial inequalities. Power is the way in which humans relate to themselves, to others, and to their environment. As this essential element of existence, there is no hope of eradicating power relations within the social sphere. Rather than eradicating power, then, the activist should aim at recognizing and using positive and constructive forms of power. One example of this more positive perception of power that appears in Foucault is in his discussion of what he refers to as *disciplinary power*.[441] This, like other forms of power, consists in exertion from external forces. Unlike most forms of biopower, however, this does not refer to a mere relation of servitude but also of the development of self-discipline. At a military bootcamp, for example, there is coercion placed on the recruit that forces the individual to exercise, eat, and sleep in specific disciplined ways in order that one might be formed into an effective soldier.[442] The result of this is not merely that the individual is more obedient to their superiors but also that they gain mastery over themselves.

This disciplinary power, in Foucault's reckoning, only developed in the late seventeenth century through a combination of the Cartesian model of the subject's relation to the mechanical world, the need for increased production, and the move toward urban expansion. Disciplinary power is a kind of "invisible" power that makes individuals into productive subjects. Rather than simply exerting force in an external and visible way as a monarch might, this

---

[441] This idea is found in Foucault's *Discipline and Punish*.

[442] This is more of an obvious example, but for Foucault, disciplinary power is also exercised in simple and subtle ways, such as in the passing on and enforcement of table manners in the home.

kind of power strives to form someone's inner person. It creates a certain *type* of subject to be a certain kind of citizen. In creating this new productive and creative subject, disciplinary power also leads to a recognition of the uniqueness of the individual and thereby lays the groundwork for self-definition and resistance to power. In Foucault's conception, power is always accompanied by the possibility of resistance. Power both constitutes the subject through bringing about self-awareness and also creates the resisting individual who is able to exert critical acts of protest against the structures of coercive power.

This leads once again to the topic of the subject, or of what constitutes a human being. Foucault's view has been referred to as *social constructionism*, meaning that the subject does not precede social relations but is constituted by them. In a striking passage in *Discipline and Punish*, Foucault writes,

> The individual is no doubt the fictitious atom of an 'ideological' representation of society; but he is also a reality fabricated by this specific technology of power that I have called 'discipline'. ... [P]ower produces; it produces reality; it produces domains of objects and rituals of truth The individual and the knowledge that may be gained of him belong to this production.[443]

For Foucault, individuals are not only impacted by, but are constituted by relationships of power and oppression.[444] Since power

---

[443] As cited in Hass, "Discipline and the Constituted Subject: Foucault's Social History," 66.

[444] As Hass states, "[A]s the builder constructs a house out of raw materials imposing her design upon them—so too, Foucault claims, does society shape the raw material that we are: its systems of language and representation 'inscribe' and 'differentiate' our bodies; its practices of knowledge and power 'infiltrate' them, are 'incorporated' by them; norms and ab-norms are 'implanted beneath modes of conduct.'" Hass, "Discipline and the Constituted Subject," 67. As bodies themselves do not constitute subjectivity for Foucault, and there is no eternal soul transcending the body, it is the social context that determines and brings about subjectivity, and thus the individual.

lies behind all human communication, all human society must consist in dynamics of power and domination. This means that society is formed by power, though the shape that power takes depends on social systems, meaning that society and power have a relation of reciprocity and mutual constitution. Society imposes power upon individuals, and in doing so it constitutes the individual. Social norms and discourse categorize, define, and subjugate human beings, who are through these means also given the ability to assert their individuality and resist oppressive forces.[445]

These linguistic and societal discourses that lead to subjectification are often centered on the categorization of certain behaviors as normative and others as disordered.[446] The powerful in society determine which people, actions, and institutions are deemed "normal" and consequently impose such norms on others. These imposed definitions of normalcy are often received by citizens as absolute truth, rather than as the arbitrary social bias that they actually are. This leads to the marginalization of those who are not aligned with these arbitrary determinations about superiority either ontologically or ethically. This Foucauldian discursive anthropology stands in opposition to the classical view of the human person as a self-subsistent subject. While a traditional Christian or Greek anthropology acknowledges the formative elements of social institutions and relations, these are deemed accidental properties of the human person rather than its constitutive nature. In this classical view, there is transcendental value inherent to the human essence that precedes any single or set of social interactions. It is this givenness of human dignity that stands behind the condemnation of

---

[445] Rabinow refers to this process of becoming a self-aware subject as *subjectification* in his introduction to *Foucault Reader*, 11.

[446] As Gutting writes, "[N]orms define certain modes of behavior as 'abnormal,' which puts them beyond the pale of what is socially (or even humanly) acceptable, even if they are far from the blatant transgressions that called for the excessive violence of premodern power. The threat of being judged abnormal constrains us moderns at every turn." Gutting, *Foucault*, 101.

the objectification of individual subjects in acts that are truly oppressive. Without a strong metaphysical grounding, one wonders exactly what it is that makes oppressive domination and marginalization morally impermissible within the Foucauldian system, especially as such domination is the essence of the human subject in the first place rather than a foreign imposition upon the individual.

Foucault follows Roland Barthes in his denial of an authentic inner self that is to be discovered through a life of authenticity or through rational contemplation. He also rejects notions of the individual that prize self-creativity at the expense of social determination. Through his Saussurian influence, Foucault contends that the individual is to some degree bound to the discourses into which he or she has been assimilated. Even the kind of resistance in which one is involved is historically determined, though such resistance grants a degree of autonomy and individuality to the subject. In the continued conversation in the contemporary academy surrounding the relation between the individual and the universal, Foucault stands closer to Hegel than to Kierkegaard, viewing the subject as a product of social factors, rather than perceiving social reality as an imposition upon, or hindrance to, individuals. There is no real individual in the fullest sense for Foucault.

FOUCAULT ON SEXUALITY

It has already been mentioned that sexuality is a prominent topic in Foucault's historical writings. Though the theme appears throughout his corpus, it is discussed most extensively in his 1976-1984 multi-volume work, *The History of Sexuality*. This book series was not yet completed at the time of Foucault's death in June of 1984, and the final (unfinished) volume was published posthumously in 2018 (with the English edition released in 2021). Despite the work's lack of completion, this series of texts has been highly influential in the development and growth of gender and sexuality studies in the last half century.

The first volume of this work is a study of sexual repression as it developed in the early modern world. According to Foucault, in the seventeenth century an "age of repression" began in which bourgeois societies attempted to exert control over bodies through the imposition of strict sexual norms.[447] These restrictions were part of a broader "restrictive economy" that sought to control acceptable speech.[448] This led, according to his argument, to an expansion of sexual discourse, such as in the strict requirements surrounding sexual sins during private confession within the Roman Church after the Counter-Reformation. This resulted in "transforming sex into discourse," which brought sexuality into the public sphere in a more comprehensive way than it had been previously.[449] It was an eventual outgrowth of this that brought sexual resistance and experimentation into the forefront of Western discourse.

Foucault's goal in this work is not only to trace the roots of contemporary sexuality in the modern era. He also seeks to challenge the concept of a unitary and consistent standard of sexual normalcy and deviance. Foucault makes the case that, like other values that develop historically, sexual norms show a serious lack of consistency throughout the centuries. As part of this argument, he engages in a comparative analysis between sexual behaviors in the pre-Christian Greco-Roman world and the post-Constantinian Christian West. One example of discontinuity is found in views of pederasty, which was common in the classical world but condemned as a crime in the Christian world. Similarly, both cultures had divergent views regarding homosexuality. It was prominent in Greece but condemned in the Christian West. The differences are not only between the pre-Christian and Christian worlds, as within

---

[447] Foucault, "The Repressive Hypothesis," in *Foucault Reader*, 301.
[448] Foucault, "The Repressive Hypothesis," 302.
[449] Foucault, "The Repressive Hypothesis," 304.

Christendom norms have changed regarding divorce and the permissibility of certain sexual practices within a Christian marriage. An important element of Foucault's argument here is that declaring certain elements of sexuality (or other norms) to be "deviant," rather than having the effect of eradicating such behavior, has the opposite effect. By categorizing the behaviors, society now creates a discourse in which those behaviors have a distinct life.[450]

While Foucault does not argue for the recapturing of an ancient Greek ethic, he undoubtedly contends for the superiority of the Greek view over the later Christian one.[451] The reason for this is that the Greeks did not condemn specific sexual behaviors, such as homosexuality or pederasty, but the overindulgence in such pleasures. The Greek world prized moderation over abstention. The Christian view, in contrast, holds to a rigorous form of sexual denial, in which only the sexual actions that occur within a heterosexual monogamous marriage are licit, while any and all sexual activity outside of such restrictions is immoral. Foucault further sees this as a distinction between a more positive view of sex among the Greeks,

---

[450] Speaking to various fetishes and sexualities defined in the nineteenth century, Foucault writes, "The machinery of power that focused on this whole alien strain did not aim to suppress it, but rather to give it an analytical, visible, and permanent reality: it was implanted in bodies, slipped in beneath modes of conduct, made into a principle of classification and intelligibility, established as a *raison d'etre* and a natural order of disorder." Foucault, "The Repressive Hypothesis," 323. This is an example of how power creates social realities. As power exerts itself in defining the abnormalities it perceives in others, it creates the reality it tries to dominate by such labeling, thereby bringing it into discourse.

[451] In an interview where Foucault was asked about whether the Greek view provided a better alternative to the Christian one, Foucault answers that "I am not looking for an alternative; you can't find the solution of a problem in the solution of another problem raised at another moment by other people." Foucault, "On the Genealogy of Ethics," in *Foucault Reader*, 343.

in which self-mastery is the *telos* of one's actions, and the Christians, in which self-denial is the ultimate good.[452]

While Foucault's contrast in the first two volumes of his *History of Sexuality* focuses on the distinction between classical Greek and Christian views, one might expand these arguments beyond this, as there are distinct codes of sexual ethics at work in different cultures in different epochs. Prior to the birth of the Christian world, many historic societies have similar divergences on marriage and sexuality, such as divergent strains on the issue of monogamy and polygamy. In the context of the Old Testament, for example (the Ancient Near East), polygamy was a common practice. This is evident in the fact that Israelite kings and the Jewish patriarchs had multiple wives. This changed by the first century, when Second-Temple Judaism asserted the sole validity of monogamous marriage within the divine moral will. It is this view that was adopted by the early Christians. In view of these constantly changing standards of sexual ethics, one must ask how it is that one norm is deemed superior to another, or whether there is such a thing as ethical superiority or deviancy in sexuality. For Foucault, there is no moral reality underlying sexual lifestyles, as all is discursively determined through dynamics of power and domination rather than by any inherent moral law.

In the fifty years since Foucault began writing this work, much has changed in the realm of marriage and sexuality. Divorce has become increasingly common; children are born to unwed parents at far higher rates than in the recorded past; and homosexual marriage has been adopted by most Western countries. While Foucault was involved in the sexual revolution of the 1960s, there remained elements of the Christian prioritization of marriage in

---

[452] "The root of the differences, says Foucault, is the Christian claim that *ta aphrodisia* are intrinsically evil and so primarily objects of ethical denial. For the ancients, by contrast, sex was a natural good. It became an object of ethical problematization not because it was essentially forbidden but because some aspects of it could be dangerous." Gutting, *Foucault*, 121.

Western culture throughout the 1970s and 1980s. Citizens of most Western countries continued to hold a general belief in marriage as a permanent, monogamous union between a man and a woman in which children are conceived, born, and raised. A world that normalizes this Christian perception of marriage is also one that marginalizes those who engage in alternative lifestyles. Women who get pregnant before marriage, non-monogamous marriages, homosexuals, and others with alternative sexual arrangements experience marginalization as their lives are declared deviant and degenerate. There are two results of this marginalization. First, it reinforces the hegemonic ideology of the dominant class and thereby sets boundaries around sexual propriety through an exertion of biopower on sexual minorities. Second, it introduces divergent sexualities into public discourse and thereby grants them real existence and identity, consequently leading to their ability to enter into public discourse and resist dominant narratives. Bourgeois dominance can be overthrown through the exercise of bodily acts of resistance against attempts to control people through biopower.

Foucault's formulation of normativity in social discourse surrounding sexuality here is at the root of much language used today in the field of gender theory. It is common to encounter the term *heteronormativity*, for example, which is used to identify the prominence of a particular social mode of discourse in which heterosexual relationships are determined to be the norm. Underlying the use of this term is the conviction that heterosexuality is not truly some biologically or theologically determinate norm in which human beings are to live but is instead a social imposition on the populace as a tool of domination from an oppressive class. One might object, perhaps, that there must be something more than social prejudice at work here simply due to the biological reality of conception, which necessitates the coming together of both male sperm and a female egg, and that the social institution of heterosexual marriage arises perhaps out of mere biological pragmatism rather than intentional marginalization. Such an argument, however, relies on a view of science that is beholden to an Enlightenment conception of unaided reason, which is simply another false metanarrative. As is evident in Foucault's other work engaging with medical institutions, the sciences are not as objective as they may seem, as they too are systems of power and oppression.

In this discussion of sexuality, it must be noted that Foucault's work is not mere theory or academic curiosity. The framework that he proposes here sets forth a method of activism to fight against received sexual narratives and norms. Foucault himself writes as one whose life has been characterized by multitudinous deviant sexual practices that are marginalized in traditional Christian society. He thus has a vested interest in this subject of sexual normativity and in trying to change cultural attitudes about marriage and sexuality. He also has a clear means by which activism is to be engaged. If domination occurs primarily in the suppression of bodies (biopower), then resistance must similarly engage itself in bodily form. For Foucault, transgressive sexual acts are a means by which domination can be effectively resisted. In the promotion of such resistance, Foucault turns deviant sexual acts into instruments of political activism and a fight for justice. The often-noted connection between progressive activism and public sexual displays is not one of mere happenstance but of interconnectivity. For the Foucauldian, public displays of sexual deviancy are actions of demonstrable discursive resistance to received dominant cultural narratives surrounding sex and marriage. Public sexuality is a challenge to bourgeois hegemony.

HISTORICAL METHOD

Foucault's writing on the history of sexuality is only one part of his broader work of historical analysis. Throughout his historical writings, Foucault approaches divergent subjects and analyzes them according to various historical epochs. In these works, referred to as genealogical studies, Foucault catalogs institutions, beliefs, and values as they change from age to age, focusing on the development of one central concept. It is in these broad historical overviews that Foucault is most clearly influenced by Hegel. Just as Hegel examined history through a series of epochs with clearly delineated sets of ideas, values, and actions that then developed into future epochs, so does Foucault distinguish between the values and ideas within a distinct culture and age and those of the epochs that follow. This also means that Foucault is open to the same critique that historians have made of this mode of historical study, of being too simplistic (something that is hard to avoid when writing on such a large period at once). Though Foucault does believe, like Hegel, that ages build upon one another and that there is gradual development from one set of values to the next, he does not believe that these changes are inherently progressive, such that later epochs are necessarily "better" than preceding ones.

Foucault's historical method marks a transition away from viewing historical study as an analysis of wars, important ideas, or great figures and toward an examination of the power dynamics and biases that have shaped both history and our understanding of history. For Foucault, historical events are, like all else, essentially comprised of dynamics of power and oppression. The Foucauldian method of historical study identifies the ruling class in each age and then analyzes how that class maintained its power through oppressive ideas, institutions, or laws enacted toward marginalized groups. This type of methodology is prevalent in modern discourse about history, such as in portrayals of the history of the United States as a story of the constant oppression of minority groups by the white Protestant hegemony.[453] To be clear, one need not be a Foucauldian to see that power and oppression are significant elements of human history and that people have been mistreated in every single human society. These are certainly elements of any honest historical

---

[453] The popular 1669 Project is often used as an example of this type of historical approach, which relies heavily on dynamics of power and oppression rather than presenting an unbiased account of historical events.

analysis. The difference is that, for Foucault, power dynamics are not merely one *element* of history, but define it.

Foucault's approach to history is most comprehensively explained in his work "The Archaeology of Knowledge," published in 1969.[454] By this time, Foucault had already published a number of historical works that used the general method outlined here, so this work serves as an explanation of the historical methodology that he had already been using for some time, rather than an introduction of a methodology yet to be tested. Foucault's use of the word *archaeology* in the title of this text is meant to identify the way in which he perceives the study of history to be done. For Foucault, the examination of a previous generation's acquisition of, and exposition of, knowledge shares similarities with an archaeological dig. Historians, for Foucault, are not ideologues who examine history in order to test the veracity of an ethical system or to judge the philosophical or theological claims of a given culture. Epochs are relics of history that should be examined in the same way that one would study a pot or weapon found in an archeological expedition. For Foucault, there are no universal ideas to be examined apart from social context, and therefore, there is simply no standard by which the beliefs or practices of another culture can or should be judged. If one were to do so, that would be an imposition of the ideas of one epoch over those of another—neither of which leads to any truth outside of themselves. What the study of history *can* reveal is the power dynamics at work in historical epochs.

Foucault speaks of the conditions surrounding the knowledge of each epoch as an *episteme*. As power and knowledge are intimately linked, for Foucault, a study of the means of knowledge in

---

[454] Along with this, I reference Foucault's work "Nietzsche, Genealogy, and Logic" from 1971, which expands upon similar themes. This work is found in *The Foucault Reader*, 76-100.

an epoch is also a study of the nature of power in that time period.[455] The structures of power are a determinative factor in what things can actually be known at any given time. Structures of power create and rely upon particular paradigms in which the world is understood. By nature, paradigms are limiting, such that individuals do not often step outside of the paradigm in which they live to search for or expand knowledge beyond it. These paradigms include truth claims, values, ethical assumptions, notions about God and the world, and the nature of knowledge itself. When Foucault uses this term, he is not identifying specific ideas that are necessarily explicit and stated within an epoch. Oftentimes, the paradigms within which people live are assumed or unrecognized. They live in the subconscious. These paradigms are all-encompassing, so that they impact every institution and field of study. Because that is the case, Foucault argues, sciences or other disciplines that claim to be objective in their method and analysis are not. All fields of study in any epoch are governed by the episteme of that age–even when these preconceptions affect us unconsciously. This is part of Foucault's larger critique of metanarratives, which is a common thread among the postmodern philosophers. There is no grand story or idea that grants direct access to the world as it is, including science.[456] All is understood through subjectivity, culture, and bias.

With this rejection of metanarratives, Foucault shows his divergence from both Hegel and many earlier Marxists. Marxism is

---

[455] "In a sense, only a single drama is ever staged in this 'non-place,' the endlessly repeated play of dominations. The domination of certain men over others leads to the differentiation of values; class domination generates the idea of liberty; and the forceful appropriation of things necessary to survival and the imposition of a duration not intrinsic to them account for the origin of logic." Foucault, "Nietzsche, Genealogy, and Logic," 85.

[456] "Genealogy does not oppose itself to history as the lofty and profound gaze of the philosopher might compare to the molelike perspective of the scholar; on the contrary, it rejects the metahistorical development of ideal significations and indefinite teleologies. It opposes itself to the search for 'origins.'" Foucault, "Nietzsche, Genealogy, History," 77.

itself a metanarrative, a grand story about history that places each age within a world process that culminates in the existence of a just society devoid of exploitation. Foucault's epochal view does not claim superiority of one episteme over another.[457] It is simply a recognition that such epistemes exist and differ from one another, so that we see divergent beliefs and values as merely the product of subjective, historically-determinate factors rather than as differences to be resolved by means of some field of objective inquiry. This means that, in contrast to the methodology of Hegel, which depends on the idea that history is the process of the self-development of the World Spirit, for Foucault, the historical task is largely a destructive, rather than constructive, one.[458] For Foucault, the task of the historian is to analyze the power dynamics at work in history through various epochs and to then discover and expose the episteme of that age. The underlying assumption here is that the dynamics of power guide the entire process of history, such that there is nothing else to be examined.

Another important aspect of Foucault's historical analysis is his displacement of the subject. For Foucault, history has wrongly placed the human subject at the center of world events. This was often done for religious reasons, with a theological commitment to the existence of a personal God who imbues the universe with transcendent purpose and an inevitable *telos* through which historical ages are to be grasped. In the Christian view, an eternal, self-existent subject stands at the center of history, guiding and governing nature. With an anti-metaphysical method derived from Nietzsche, Foucault rejects such purposive overarching thinking as a

---

[457] "Humanity does not gradually progress from combat to combat until it arrives at universal reciprocity, where the rule of law finally replaces warfare; humanity installs each of its violences in a system of rules and thus proceeds from domination to domination." Foucault, "Nietzsche, Genealogy, History," 85.

[458] "What is found at the historical beginning of things is not the inviolable identity of their origin; it is the dissention of other things. It is disparity." Foucault, "Nietzsche, Genealogy, History," 79.

futile attempt to discover the origin or purpose of things. Foucault contends that history is composed, not of theology or metaphysical necessity, but of discourses of power expressed through language, institutions, and established social norms, which differ from one epoch to another.[459] Humans live within these dynamics, but they do not stand over and above them or the societies in which they live, as their very being is created by these discourses of power. It is here that Foucault is at his most Nietzschean, rejecting all teleological theorizing, contending instead that power stands above all else in the drive from one age to the next.

To understand Foucault's method, it is helpful to review some of the subjects he addresses with these historical methods in view. Most readers of Foucault derive their knowledge of his methodology from his historical studies rather than from the select few places where he explains his methodology directly. Foucault wrote a number of these historical studies throughout his career, with varied levels of success in broaching his subject matter. For brevity, I give only a brief overview of some of the works in which the historiographic method of "The Archeology of Knowledge" is applied. For the interested reader, the full works, while lengthy, are not written as dense, academic texts and are generally more readable than the writings of other postmodern authors.

Among Foucault's most discussed works of historical analysis is his 1961 book, *Madness and Civilization*.[460] In this book, Foucault discusses how various epochs have viewed and treated those who are considered "mad" or insane. For Foucault, the distinction between those who are sane and those who are mad is not always as clear as is assumed. This is apparent in cultural differences

---

[459] "Genealogy ... seeks to reestablish the various systems of subjection; not the anticipatory power of meaning, but the hazardous play of dominations." Foucault, "Nietzsche, Genealogy, History," 83.

[460] The original English edition (which is what I used in my research for this chapter) uses this title, but a newer, longer text is also available in English under the title *The History of Madness*.

surrounding the categorization of individuals into these designations. What is deemed madness in one culture might be viewed as insight in another. Foucault contends that in some ancient societies, those whose mental life would not be considered "normal" today might have been viewed as spiritually inspired. Foucault presents a narrative of the gradual exclusion of these individuals from ordinary social life, which culminated in the creation of the insane asylum. This institution is a tool of exclusion through which individuals are labeled "mentally disturbed" and are removed from public life, being hidden inside the walls of the asylum. In Foucault's reading of history, these institutions display an imbalance of power and domination over the mentally ill. The powerful categorize their own patterns of thought and action as "normal," while excluding others who differ from their own conception of normalcy. In this approach, the mental institution is an instrument of marginalization that serves the interests and desires of the bourgeoisie, furthering their hegemonic power and influence. In this work, Foucault challenges readers to question whether their own ideas of mental normalcy are based upon some objective, scientifically verifiable conception of normal brains, or whether these perceptions are due merely to the acceptance of an oppressive power structure determined by the current episteme.

An arguably less effective work, continuing on the subject of modern medicine, is Foucault's 1963 book, *The Birth of the Clinic: An Archaeology of Medical Perception*. As in the earlier text, Foucault contends that a modern medical institution—in this instance, the clinic—was formed out of a desire for domination rather than goodwill or disinterested scientific advancement. Since Foucault is deeply committed to the centrality of the body in relations of domination, he perceives any field or institution in which judgment is made upon bodies to be susceptible to oppression and marginalization. In the medical clinic, there is a significant power differential between the doctor and the patient. This differential is evident in that during the process of a medical examination, the medical professional is treated as the expert in all things medicinal, whose words are to be taken as definite truth when making a diagnosis or medical recommendation. In this way, the doctor portrays him or herself as the arbiter of biological reality over the patient. Foucault's materialism limits the human being to a biological organism with social relations. This means that if the doctor controls the body, the doctor has nearly absolute control over the individual.

Though this text has retained some influence, it has been heavily criticized since its initial publication by both historians and physicians. In his quest to find abusive power dynamics in every social institution, Foucault fails to explore the many complexities that led to the development of modern medicine and the medical profession. Notwithstanding a number of cases of sociopathic doctors who abuse the trust of their patients, there is undoubtedly far more to the development of our current medical system than an obsessive desire for control. Further, in order to make his argument work, Foucault seriously mischaracterizes the role of the patient in medical care, portraying the physician as some uncontested lord who will force medicine or surgery on a patient without any necessity of consent. This work, more clearly than his other studies, demonstrates the problems inherent to Foucault's method. While a historical investigation of the development of any human institution is destined to uncover abusive practices, the reduction of all institutional dynamics to power is unsustainable, as it strains the historical evidence by imposing a preconceived systemic approach onto the data, even when it does not fit. This leads to a presumption of motivations within historic institutions and the neglect of dynamics that do not align with Foucault's preconceptions of institutional domination.

Foucault aims his criticism not only at the medical profession but at the scientific disciplines as a whole. Foucault's sweeping critique of the scientific establishment and method is set forth in his 1966 book, *The Order of Things: An Archaeology of Human Sciences*. In this work, Foucault engages in his usual practice of dividing history into a series of distinct epochs, each with its own episteme. In this work, he speaks of three historical periods and their distinct approaches to the scientific method: the Classical, the Renaissance, and the Modern. For Foucault, the scientific disciplines are both directed and limited by the episteme of each period of time. These preconceived ideas determine which categories are to be used when engaging in the discipline and which questions can and cannot be asked. There is, in each age, a standard of acceptable discourse in which science, among other disciplines, must remain. The primary purpose of this text is to challenge the Enlightenment value of objectivity within the scientific method. While modernists believed that science was a move away from the subjectivity of things like religious experiences toward something certain, unchanging, and definitive, Foucault argues that science, like everything else, is driven by biases. It is not just biases in a general sense that Foucault is speaking about here (it should be uncontested that our biases affect how we view and interpret anything, including scientific conclusions), but biases based specifically on the maintenance of power and exertion of force over others.

The final of these genealogical studies published prior to Foucault's work on sexuality is his *Discipline and Punish: The Birth of the Prison*, released in 1975.[461] In this work, Foucault changes course, analyzing an institution that is not associated with the sciences: the prison system. And, just as he does in his other studies, Foucault argues that the legal system primarily exists as an instrument of oppression and the exertion of domination. As Foucault divides history, he distinguishes between two different approaches to the judicial system. Earlier Western systems were largely retributive. Every crime had a correlating punishment that was meant to match the severity of the crime. In the modern system, language has moved away from retribution toward restoration. The idea of restorative

---

[461] For a critique of this work from a legal scholar, see Garland, "Review of Foucault's 'Discipline and Punish'—An Exposition and Critique."

justice contends that when a crime is committed, someone can and should be reformed, rather than merely punished for whatever they have done. It is this reasoning that supposedly created the modern prison system. Foucault contends that this oft-repeated narrative about restorative justice does not reflect the reality of the prison system and is a mythological cover for the real underlying purpose of prisons. Rather than upholding an enlightened desire for restoration, Western societies actually created the prison system as an instrument of dehumanization. In prisons, criminals are locked away from society as a means to marginalize them, separating them from anyone else. This marginalization of criminals also has the corresponding effect of granting excessive power to those who are in charge of prisons, so that this power can be exerted toward prisoners who are treated as the "other." Like all other social institutions, prisons do not exist for the common good but for the maintenance of ruling-class hegemony.

Foucault's studies are far-reaching in their intended targets. Foucault criticizes scientific, medical, and judicial institutions through this genealogical method. As diverse as the topics of study might be, however, the conclusions drawn by Foucault are essentially the same regardless of the institution. For Foucault, every single institution of society—family, hospitals, schools, prisons, churches— is driven by a desire to exert force over others through marginalization and to perpetuate the power of a ruling class. Foucault does not arrive at these conclusions through a disinterested examination of the evidence but through his own methodological presuppositions. He arrives at these conclusions because his methodology necessitates them. The underlying belief in all of this is that power is the ultimate reality and that the role of the historian is to unmask whatever might appear to be the case to find the oppressive powers that are undoubtedly standing behind it. Foucault summarizes his view well in an interview in which he distances himself from the semiotic approach of Saussure. He says,

> I believe one's point of reference should not be to the great model of language (*langue*) and signs, but to that of war and battle. The history that bears and determines us has the form of war rather than that of language: relations of power, not relations of meaning. History has no "meaning," though this is not to say that it is absurd or incoherent. On the contrary, it is intelligible and should be susceptible to analysis down to the smallest detail—but this in accordance with the intelligibility of struggles, of strategies and tactics.[462]

Foucault's view of history (and of human nature) is a dim one. The past is nothing more than a series of battles of power and domination. History is not constructive; it is not *for* anything, as it has no *telos* or meaning. As history does bear meaning, all the historian can do is deconstruct the dynamics at work within it. The deconstruction of history into power relations parallels a similar move of our next thinker, Jacques Derrida, in the field of literature.

JACQUES DERRIDA

DERRIDA'S LIFE

Jacques Derrida was born on July 15, 1930, in El-Biar, Algeria, into a Jewish family with French citizenship.[463] The historical backdrop of Derrida's early life was one of upheaval and exclusion for Jewish families across Europe and its colonies.[464] Algeria, at the time a French territory, was no exception. The rise of anti-Jewish sentiments and policies during Derrida's formative years resulted in social ostracization for his family. These tensions between the Jewish community and other Europeans led to educational segregation, wherein Jewish students were sent to separate schools. These early

---

[462] Foucault, "Truth and Power," in *Foucault Reader*, 56.

[463] Despite this Jewish upbringing, Derrida would later distance himself from the theological and philosophical convictions of the Jewish scriptures.

[464] For an in-depth biography, see Peeters, *Derrida: A Biography*.

experiences introduced Derrida to the realities of discrimination and division among people, which played a role in his conception of systemic marginalization. It was during this period that Derrida began to study philosophy, seeking intellectual refuge within this turbulent environment.

Derrida's initial philosophical explorations were in the works of the existentialist writers who dominated much of French thought in the mid-twentieth century. Like Foucault, Derrida engaged heavily in the works of Friedrich Nietzsche (whose philosophy is often regarded as a precursor to existentialism). Nietzsche's pointed critiques of the Christian values of the West laid much of the groundwork for Derrida's own critical writing toward traditional moral, religious, and metaphysical systems. Along with his study of Nietzsche, Derrida also delved into the writings of Jean-Paul Sartre and Albert Camus—two of France's most prominent existentialist thinkers and authors. Each of these figures would play a role in the development of Derrida's system in which Derrida questioned not only inherited values and traditions, but ultimately meaning itself.

After completing his primary education in Jewish schools, Derrida chose to deepen his engagement with philosophy as his intellectual curiosity had continued to grow. This led Derrida to France where he would pursue his studies formally at the prestigious Lycée Louis-le-Grand in Paris. Here, Derrida was exposed to a broader set of thinkers, movements, and ideas. He was particularly indebted to Étienne Borne, a French Catholic philosopher who introduced Derrida to diverse philosophical traditions, pushing him beyond the existentialist texts that had initially spurred his interest in the discipline. Paris, a city rich with intellectual engagement, became an essential part of Derrida's philosophical development, as this environment not only introduced Derrida to diverse philosophical traditions but also provided academic training and personal connections that would encourage Derrida to construct his own system of thought.

Following his studies at the Lycée Louis-le-Grand, Derrida had a desire to continue his studies in the city of Paris at the École Normale Supérieure (ENS). He was initially rejected from the master's program at the school after failing his entrance exam, but after reapplying, he was accepted into the program in 1952. While studying at the university, Derrida made a number of connections to influential leftist intellectuals—including the prominent Marxist philosopher Louis Althusser, whose friendship would play a significant role in Derrida's intellectual development. While, like Foucault, Derrida was not a self-confessed Marxist, he was sympathetic to many Marxist concerns and engaged regularly with socialist professors at the university. Derrida's own intellectual interests were political to some extent, but not directly so. Derrida's dissertation, reflecting his primary area of interest at this time, was on the ideas of the Austrian-German phenomenologist Edmund Husserl. After completing his master's degree, Derrida crossed the Atlantic to pursue further studies at Harvard University in Cambridge, Massachusetts. Rather than study phenomenology, which was the focus of his prior academic work, Derrida turned his attention to literary modernism—particularly the writings of James Joyce. It is through the combination of Derrida's philosophical background and his interest in modernist literature that Derrida would form his post-structuralist system of thought.

ACADEMIC CAREER

Derrida's career began with sporadic tutoring, which eventually led to a formal teaching position at the illustrious Sorbonne in France. During his four years at the Sorbonne, Derrida became acquainted with the prominent philosopher Paul Ricoeur, who wrote on the topics of phenomenology (the subject of Derrida's dissertation) and hermeneutics. It was largely through Ricoeur's influence that Derrida began to focus on the nature of texts and on the reader's experience of them. At the end of his tenure at the Sorbonne, Derrida would return, through the influence of Althusser, to the place where his academic studies after primary school had begun—ENS. He had a lengthy tenure at ENS, teaching for two decades from 1964 until 1984. This period marked a pivotal phase in Derrida's career, as it was during these twenty years that Derrida solidified his position as one of the most influential (and controversial) academics in France. Derrida's prominence on the international stage grew during the transformative decade of the 1960s, as the Western landscape shifted significantly on both a popular and an intellectual level. With the rise of student protest movements across the Western world, many younger activists began to look to established radical intellectuals for guidance. As they did with Critical Theorists like Adorno, some began to look to the work of Jacques Derrida, who became a well-known public figure among leftist activists.

Rather than from political activism, Derrida's initial academic acclaim stemmed largely from his engagements with Saussure's structuralism. At the outset of his career, Derrida was widely categorized as a structuralist, though it was clear from the outset of Derrida's work that he sought a reexamination of structuralism rather than a mere reiteration or expansion of the ideas of Saussure or Lévi-Strauss. These early contributions would eventually form Derrida's developed system, which was given the label *post-structuralism*, aligning his ideas with those of Barthes and Foucault. This post-structuralist system remains Derrida's most significant academic contribution. In recognition for his broad impact in the Western academy, Derrida was awarded an honorary doctorate from Columbia University in 1980 (the same college that had hosted the Institute for Social Research). Subsequently, Derrida also received an earned doctoral degree from the University of Paris through a submission of several previously written publications. After this, Derrida received several other honorary doctorates from schools such as the New School for Social Research and the University of Athens. He was also appointed as an honorary member of the American Academy of Arts and Sciences in 1985—an honor bestowed to those outside of the United States only on special occasions.

Amidst these many honors that Derrida received during his career, the situation surrounding Derrida's reception of an honorary doctorate from the University of Cambridge in 1992 is particularly noteworthy. When the university made the announcement that such an honor would be bestowed upon Derrida, the action was met with significant controversy. Several prominent analytic philosophers such as W. V. O. Quine, Ruth Marcus, and David Armstrong voiced their dissent, asserting that Derrida's work was marked by sophistry, engaging in mere wordplay devoid of substantive value. In a letter addressed to the University, these authors contended that Derrida's writing "seems to be little more than semi-intelligible attacks upon the values of reason, truth, and scholarship" and thus requested that the University not give a doctorate to Derrida. Despite the protests from these scholars, Derrida ultimately did receive the honorary doctorate promised to him. This incident displays the divided reception of Derrida's work into the present day. While many university departments continue to promote Derrida's deconstruction as a valid way to engage with historical texts, others continue to view him in the same light as those who protested this honorary doctorate at Cambridge, viewing Derrida's writing not as scholarship but as an attack on scholarship.

Following his twenty-year tenure at ENS, Derrida took the position of full professor at the École des Hautes Études en Sciences Sociales in Paris in 1984, where he would teach for two years. He was then offered the position of full professor of humanities at the University of California, Irvine, which he accepted. He taught there from 1986 to 2004. During these almost twenty years in the United States, Derrida also engaged in a series of visiting lectureships at various institutions primarily clustered around New York, including Yale, NYU, Stony Brook, and the New School. The widespread engagement with Derrida's work at these and other institutions speaks to both the global impact and the transdisciplinary nature of

Derrida's career. Derrida's impact is still felt in several academic fields, including philosophy, linguistics, and literature. Derrida passed away in 2004 after losing a battle with pancreatic cancer.

DERRIDA'S THOUGHT

Among Derrida's most influential ideas are his consistent challenges to various types of "centrism," wherein Western culture categorizes dualities and then privileges one side of those binaries over the others. Some common examples of this are hierarchical prioritizations of man over woman, white over black, and heterosexual over homosexual. Derridian critiques in this form are found far beyond the field of literature today; they are evident in popular discourse that uses concepts like *phallocentrism* to speak of the prioritization of male over female, or *eurocentrism* as the centering of European values and marginalization of non-European ones. These binaries are all, for Derrida, artificially conceived and arbitrary; they aren't metaphysically necessary or logically derived axiomatic truths. Dichotomies, for Derrida, are not only categorizations of distinct people groups, such as the Marxian bourgeoisie/proletarian divide. Binaries are found in all modes of categorization, such as in the favoring of presence over absence, speech over writing, and reason over feeling. Throughout his exploration of these hierarchical binaries, Derrida engages in a thorough critique of inherited Western philosophy, from Socrates to Saussure, as he contends that many of the most treasured ideas of the Western world are dependent upon arbitrary dichotomies.

PHONOCENTRISM

Among the most prominent hierarchical binaries challenged by Derrida is that of audible and immediate speech over writing, which he identifies as *phonocentrism*. This critique is found in Derrida's 1967 work, *Of Grammatology*, in which he posits a new way forward for understanding texts through a sweeping denial of all metaphysical approaches. The work is not only a critique of classical and Christian philosophy (though it is that), but it is also a response to many of Derrida's own more recent influences such as Saussure and Heidegger. Regarding these two latter thinkers, Derrida contends that despite their critiques, neither thinker departed enough from traditional assumptions about signification. For Derrida, the Western tradition has historically operated from what is essentially a theological approach, placing linguistic concepts into a system of eternal thought and speech identified with a divine person. It is this privileging of speech, in Derrida's view, that stands behind Saussure's distinction between signifier and the signified. As Kamuf summarizes,

> Derrida insists that linguistics remains a metaphysics as long as it retains the distinction between signifier and signified within the concept of the sign. This distinction is always ultimately grounded in pure intelligibility tied to an absolute logos: the face of God. The concept of the sign, whose history is coextensive with the history of logocentrism, is essentially theological.[465]

In Derrida's view, the Western philosophical tradition has consistently elevated speech over writing due to its theological and metaphysical commitments. Saussure, for Derrida, rightly moves away from transcendental signification to historically and contextually rooted linguistic systems but continues to operate with a sharp distinction between sign and signified, which retains theological significance.[466]

Derrida's relation to Saussure is not only one of discontinuity and critique, as he works within the framework of semiology to some degree. As explored below, Derrida expands upon Saussure's idea of the arbitrary nature of signs, as well as his belief that concepts are

---

[465] Kamuf, *A Derrida Reader*, 32.

[466] "The formal essence of the signified is *presence*, and the privilege of its proximity to the logos as *phone* is the privilege of presence." Derrida, *Of Grammatology* in *A Derrida Reader*, 34.

largely understood by way of distinction from other signs.[467] Nonetheless, as Derrida contends, Saussure holds to a clear differentiation between speech and writing and is thus guilty of phonocentrism. In his *Course in General Linguistics*, Saussure suggests that writing's relationship to speech is one of reflection, thus prioritizing the present act of speech over the written word. As an example, take the prior illustration of the word *tree* in relation to its intended meaning. If I use the word *tree* to label an object while speaking to someone in their direct presence, this audible utterance identifies a shared concept between me and my conversation partner. The utterance is one degree removed from the concept that it identifies. If instead of vocalizing the sound *tree*, I write the word down in a text message to that same individual, this further removes my language from the concept it identifies. Written words, for Saussure, identify spoken words which identify concepts. In this way, written statements are a farther degree removed from the ideas they identify than speech is. This makes writing a less direct means of communication than spoken language. As Derrida understands Saussure, there is a kind of impurity within writing as a lesser form of communication that degrades the purity of spoken words.

Derrida's rejection of phonocentrism leads him to form one of his most important ideas—the dismissal of a "metaphysic of presence."[468] This phrase expresses the belief that there is a greater reality or encounter when someone is in the direct presence of a subject as they are speaking. Take the following example: It is a relatively common practice (though less than it was in previous decades) to send out Christmas cards in the holiday season that include a letter detailing various life updates from the prior year. Imagine that you receive such a letter from your aunt and uncle,

---

[467] "Derrida affirms something of the differential conception of signs proposed by structuralist linguistics, according to which 'identity can only determine or delimit itself through differential relations to other elements.'" Glendinning, *Derrida*, 65.

[468] Derrida defines Western metaphysics as "the limitation of the sense of being within the field of presence." Derrida, *Of Grammatology*, 40.

whom you would also see in person during the holidays. When you see them, you could get life updates directly from your aunt and uncle without having to read the letter at all. The question here is: Which of these ways to get information about your aunt's and uncle's life is superior? In person, or in the letter? Or does it matter at all? In Derrida's portrayal of much earlier Western thought, there would be an inherent superiority to the personal encounter with your aunt and uncle since the presence of their bodies would provide a more direct form of communication, while the written word is only a stand-in for this more personal communicative act. For Derrida, this privileging of presence over absence is mistaken, giving an illusory sense of hierarchical ordering that is not inherent to these forms of signification.

Derrida endeavors to dismantle this accepted division between writing and speech or between presence and absence through his contention that there is no more immediacy in the spoken than the written word.[469] This false perception of the inferiority of writing, for Derrida, is dependent upon a classical view of texts in which a written record of one kind or another is an intermediary document, serving to bridge the gap between presence and absence when the speaker is at a physical distance from the other party. Such a view seems to rely on a connection between the written document and a living writer of this document. This poses a problem for intelligibility, however, in the case of an author's death. Does a letter sent cease to bear meaning if its author dies before the text is delivered? This is evidently not the case, for Derrida, as the writing is comprehensible even apart from the life of the writer. Understanding in any social context is derived through linguistic systems of differentiation and contrast. If it is true (as Derrida claims) that languages are self-contained systems of meaning, grasped only

---

[469] Though this idea is present in *Of Grammatology*, it is more systematically explored in Derrida's essay "Limited Inc.," which is a response to a critique from John Searle (then known for his contributions to speech-act theory).

internally within semiotic structures, their comprehensibility is not dependent upon any author or transcendent reality external to the text itself.

Derrida's critique, though it is in its most direct sense a claim about texts, is also a claim about persons. Derrida questions not only the priority of the presence of the act of speaking, but the priority of subjects to whom words belong. Like Foucault, Derrida denies that there is any coherent self-identical human subject.[470] There is no objective human essence, and there is no soul. Derrida believes that the human person, like everything else, is a mere construct, born from linguistic systems and other social signs. It is precisely because there is no inherent human essence that there is no prioritizing of human presences in grasping meaningful expression. The path taken by Derrida here bears a striking resemblance to the ideas of Roland Barthes in *The Death of the Author*. Derrida's *Of Grammatology* was published in the same year (1967), and both texts seek to differentiate meaning in texts from their authors. Barthes does this by freeing the text from authorial intent, viewing texts as complete things within themselves, and Derrida does so by challenging the prioritization of personal presences in the understanding of words. Both thinkers contribute toward a move in literary studies away from the objective data within a text toward an examination of one's experience of a text.[471]

---

[470] "This deconstruction of presence accomplishes itself through the deconstruction of consciousness, and therefore through the irreducible notion of the trace (*Spur*), as it appears in both Nietzschean and Freudian discourse." Derrida, *Of Grammatology*, 42.

[471] As with Barthes, Derrida's view of textual interpretation is not pure subjectivism, as deconstruction provides a specific methodology through which texts are to be examined. It is not identical with reader-response criticism.

LOGOCENTRISM

The second of these "centrisms" criticized by Derrida is *logocentrism*.[472] The use of this term predates Derrida, though it is most associated with Derrida's work. It was first employed by the German philosopher and psychologist Ludwig Klages, who used the word to critique what he saw as a Western overemphasis on rationality and conceptual thought (especially within Enlightenment rationalism), which he associated with the dominance of logos (reason) over life, spirit, and intuition.[473] In Klages's view, this logocentric focus on abstract reasoning wrongly de-emphasizes the more instinctual dimensions of human existence. For Klages, this centering of reasoning is responsible for the alienation of humans from their deeper connections to the natural world. While Klages's writing on logocentrism predates post-structuralism by forty years, he anticipates later postmodern thought in significant ways. Like Derrida, Klages rejects the idea of transcendental reason as grounded in both the Jewish and Christian theological systems and seeks to move beyond the modernist emphasis on pure reason.

The term *logos* has a rich history in Western philosophical and theological thought. Its philosophical origins are found in the pre-Socratic philosophy of Heraclitus (c. 500 B.C.), who used the term to identify divine reason, through which the world is made intelligible.[474] It is by means of the logos that there is order in the world that human cognition can grasp. This concept appeared in various Platonic philosophers and was central to the Stoic school in the Roman world. The Jewish theologian Philo placed this concept of

---

[472] Speaking of his discipline of grammatology, Derrida writes that "Its fundamental condition is certainly the undoing [*sollicitation*] of logocentrism." Derrida, *Of Grammatology*, 46.

[473] For an overview of Klages's esoteric reactionary psychology, see his work *Of Cosmogonic Eros*. Klages anticipates postmodernism in his anti-Enlightenment stance and in his use of Nietzschean notions of power and will.

[474] I have an overview of the concept of the logos in early Western thought in Cooper, *In Defense of the True, the Good, and the Beautiful*, 8-36.

the logos into his doctrinal system in the first century, and the apostle John speaks of Jesus as the Logos through whom the world was made. It is through the Son of God that the world is ordered and minds are enlightened to grasp God's creation. The Christian religion is a logocentric one, and thereby Derrida's critique of the centering of logos is a rejection of the West's Christian assumptions.[475] The entire Western tradition is implicated in Derrida's critiques of logos, from the classical Greek philosophers to the Jewish Scriptures to orthodox Christian theology.

Derrida's critique of logocentrism identifies two foundations of classical thought that he rejects. The first is phonocentrism, already discussed. Second is a metaphysical notion of origin, or the imposition of meaning from any source outside of semiotic systems. As Fergus Kerr writes,

> Any system of meaning is a round of references from one thing to another and back again—a chain of differences in the sense that each element is defined by its relation to, and difference from, all the others. The 'origin' of the system has to be traced from the effect one element leaves upon another, but all the way round, endlessly, because the interaction is mutual. The origin of meaning is not some fixed point, some source, outside the system, but the 'trace' each element in the system shows of the effect upon it of the others.[476]

Derrida critiques theological approaches to meaning, in which there is a singular intentional beginning or *telos* of human experience.

---

[475] There have been several attempts to incorporate Derrida's thought into a Christian schema or to argue that Derrida had something of a "theological turn" when he moved toward an examination of the ethical in his late career. I am not compelled by arguments in favor of Derrida's usefulness for theology. Those parts of his writings that are most useful can be found in others without such an anti-metaphysical stance. See Bradley, "Derrida's God: A Genealogy of the Theological Turn."

[476] Kerr, "Derrida's Wake."

There is, in the Derridian method, no ultimate being or truth that provides a clear and comprehensive explanation of reality.[477] As Glendinning notes, Derrida's philosophical project is a "radical critique of traditional philosophy."[478] This system is a critique of logic, discoverable objective truth, and transcendent reality. For Derrida, there is no eternal order beyond the physical universe; there is no ultimate divine source of existence. Instead, there are only societal structures and semiotic systems. These systems bear meaning only within themselves as systems of classification and differentiation; they do not mediate any greater reality outside of them (such as in the doctrine of biblical revelation or in a Platonic notion of forms). Meaning is collapsed into mere signification.

Derrida identifies both Judaism and Hellenism as causally linked to the predominance of logocentric philosophical dominance. The Hebrew Scriptures identify a transcendent source that stands behind, and gives meaning to, the material world and its functioning. The world is ordered and sensible, and as such human beings have access to it by means of revelation.[479] The second cause, Hellenism, holds to both a transcendent, unchanging world (that of the forms) and a physical, ever-changing world (that of our sense experience).

---

[477] For Derrida, theological views of reality and the metaphysic of presence are inherently connected. He writes that "Only infinite being can reduce the difference in presence. In that sense, the name of God, at least as it is pronounced within classical rationalism, is the name of indifference itself. ... Infinitist theologies are always logocentrisms, whether they are creationisms or not." Derrida, *Of Grammatology*, 43.

[478] Glendinning, *Derrida*, 77.

[479] For Derrida, phonocentrism is connected to the theological claim of speech originating in the eternal, which is mediated by linguistic signs, thus subordinating these signs to the reality that lies beyond them in the eternal. He writes, "The *signatum* always referred, as to its referent, to a *res*, to an entity created or at any rate first thought and spoken, thinkable and speakable, in the eternal present of the divine logos and specifically in its breath. If it came to relate to the speech of a finite being ... through the *intermediary* of a *signans*, the *signatum* had an immediate relationship with the divine logos which thought it within presence and for which it was not a trace." Derrida, *Of Grammatology*, 45.

In the Greek view, reason is valued above the passions, as reason can discern the very nature of reality, including transcendent being, immaterial ideas, and definitive ethical norms. The dominance of Christianity led to a synthesis of Judaism and Hellenism that secured a logocentric view in the Western world for many centuries.

These logocentric systems, in Derrida's view, are dependent upon hierarchies. These hierarchies arise in various forms. They occur in differentiations between people, such as in hierarchical orderings of power dependent upon age, sex, or race. Alternatively, hierarchies also express themselves in the prioritizing of ideas or concepts over their proposed opposites, such as good over evil or reason over feeling. Hierarchies of some sort are a mere fact of life. Every human society or institution is hierarchical in one form or another. Children, for example, often play within a structural organization of leaders and followers that comes into being without any imposition from adults. One child might take the lead in playing a game and direct the others where to go or what to do. Certain rules and boundaries are established that determine the values or rules of that game. What is notable about Derrida's view of hierarchies is not that he recognizes their pervasiveness but that he views them as both violent and arbitrary. For Derrida, there is no givenness to the privileging of one person or idea over another. Logocentric systems impose transcendental claims upon hierarchies, presenting the hierarchies as if they were rooted in some universal, unchanging order and then using the tool of reason to defend this order. These hierarchical binaries are instruments of marginalization. They support biases, ostracize alternative lifestyles, and diminish non-Western cultural practices. Hierarchies create irrational determinations of the value of one type of person over another, such as man over woman, heterosexual over homosexual, or European over African. The deconstruction of these hierarchies is at the heart of Derrida's philosophical approach.[480]

DECONSTRUCTION

For many, the name Derrida is synonymous with *deconstruction*. The term has been used so often today that it has become unmoored from Derrida's own writing. It is important to understand that the way this word tends to be used in current popular discourse is not what Derrida himself means by it. Deconstruction is not synonymous with *destruction*, nor is it merely the questioning of one's biases or philosophical and theological precommitments.[481] While these are elements of, or effects of, Derrida's method, they do not define it. Deconstruction refers to a specific method by which ideas and systems are examined and critiqued that is based upon his notion of binary oppositions. The questioning of received narratives *without* this examination of oppositions is not deconstruction in the Derridian sense.[482]

Derrida contends that constructs of speech and thought arise from oppositions that humans make between divergent ideas. As an example, examine the identifier *tall*, which is used to refer to a person of significant height. What exactly makes someone tall? Is there a specific height that distinguishes someone as tall rather than short? If so, is that identification a universal standard? Such a claim

---

[480] As Derrida states, "To accede to this necessity is to recognize that in a classical philosophical opposition we are not dealing with the peaceful coexistence of a vis-a-vis, but with a violent hierarchy. One of the two terms controls the other (axiologically, logically, etc.), holds the superior position. To deconstruct the opposition is first, at a given moment, to overthrow the hierarchy." Derrida, "Interview: Jacques Derrida," 36.

[481] This is commonly done in religious contexts in which someone who is either questioning or leaving their inherited faith tradition is said to be in a process of "deconstruction."

[482] In some ways, though, it is quite appropriate that a term used by Derrida would take on a totally novel meaning, as this supports Derrida's claims regarding the arbitrary nature of language.

would be a difficult one to substantiate, especially since there are genetic differences among people groups that make relative heights in some countries higher or lower than others. What is tall in one place might be considered average in another. The concept of *tall* is a relative one, determined by factors outside of itself. *Tall* is only comprehensible as it is contrasted with its opposite, *short*. Similarly, that which is *short* is also relatively determined by what is considered *tall*. In other words, there is a dichotomous comprehensibility of these two concepts in mutual contrast to one another. This definition by difference can be found in many linguistic signifiers, such as: large and small, dark and light, good and bad, thin and wide, intelligent and ignorant, and others. For Derrida, all human concepts are formed in their relation to other concepts. Language systems are only complicated, interwoven systems of references and contrasts to one another.

Derrida draws from Saussure's concept of arbitrariness in his understanding of binaries. Saussure's conception of arbitrariness refers to the lack of inherent connection between signifiers and that which they signify. Derrida expands this concept so that not only are signifiers arbitrary, but so are the ways in which those signifiers relate to one another. The contrasts made between words and concepts are not inherent to those concepts themselves. Language makes distinctions in an arbitrary manner, and these artificial linguistic binaries then form the ways that people who function within that system think and speak. For example, a strict opposition is made between men and women as opposites in a binary relation. In a Derridian approach, it is not inherent to women that they are the opposite of men, but the linguistic identification of them as such makes this to be the case in a societal perspective. This strict binary, in which humans are understood to be divided into two sexes who stand in contrast to one another, is a human construct rather than a biological necessity. This artificial opposition disallows non-binary perspectives on the sexes, and it enforces a hierarchical imposition of man over woman. If one either reverses the binary or contrasts ideas with other ideas (that are not normally used as opposites), these concepts can both be revealed as arbitrary and be changed. This argument echoes the earlier argument of Nietzsche, who questions the Western opposition between good and evil, arguing that *good* can similarly be contrasted with *bad*, making an alternate model through which *good* is to be understood.[483]

It is important to clarify here that in pointing out the universality of binaries, Derrida is not dismissing the use of binaries any more than Foucault rejects discourses of power. For Derrida, binary oppositions are a necessary element of human communication and all social structures, just as power is for Foucault. Derrida also does not attempt to critique binaries from outside of a linguistic system that is solely composed of them. This would be an impossibility, as language used to critique binaries would necessarily also be composed of binaries. Derrida often plays with binaries in his own writing, making purposeful points about their use and arbitrary nature. What Derrida rejects then is not binaries as such, but the universalizing and eternalizing of oppositions when it is claimed that binaries are inherent rather than constructed. The absolutizing of these dichotomies leads to hierarchical abuses of power and marginalization of one part of the binary. Thus, in the practice of deconstruction Derrida does not dismantle the concept of duality but instead reveals the arbitrariness inherent within binary oppositions, thereby challenging the givenness of defined concepts.

One of the common binaries that Derrida challenges is the division between mind and body.[484] The mind-body dichotomy is inherent to Western philosophy, both in its classical forms and in early modern thought. In classical Western philosophy, both the Hebraic and Hellenic traditions believe in the distinction between body and soul. In early modern philosophy, Descartes contends that

---

[483] See Nietzsche, *Beyond Good and Evil.*
[484] Lyngdoh, "Derrida and the Flesh of Metaphorical Language."

each person has a mental substance (mind) and a physical substance (body) that are distinct in kind and function. This leads to the creation of the mind-body problem, which remains one of the fundamental questions addressed by contemporary philosophers. For those who make a strong body-soul or mind-body distinction, it is generally believed that there is an inherent superiority of the mental aspects of a person over the physical. For Derrida, oppositions like this one nearly always involve the privileging of one end of the binary over the other. In this case, the mind is not only distinct from the body but superior to it. Derrida, like Foucault, questions this inherent prioritization of mind over body, contending that, like other oppositions, this is an arbitrary differentiation that speaks only to the nature of language rather than to anything inherent to human nature (which is neither objective nor universal anyway for Derrida).

Among the many other binaries that Derrida explores (good vs. evil, civilized vs. uncivilized, marginal vs. normal, etc.), the one that has been explored most in recent discourse is the distinction between male and female.[485] Both queer theory and third- to fourth-wave feminism draw from the Derridian emphasis on binary oppositions and the subversion of them. Feminist theorists have long argued that society has tended to define the female, not as a positive thing in its own right, but as the opposite of male. This definition of female as "other" has also coincided with a series of expectations placed upon women about exactly how they are supposed to act, what their personalities should be, or how they are to dress.[486] All of these expectations are not actually inherent to women, but they are purported to be so by religious institutions, governments, or other institutions in society. Derrida's deconstruction provides a methodology by which feminists can explain this more thoroughly

---

[485] For an example of an earlier use of Derrida within a feminist framework (and a reworking of Derrida's concepts in light of feminism), see Poovey, "Feminism and Deconstruction."

[486] This argument takes its most expansive form in Simone de Beauvoir's *The Second Sex*, discussed in the next chapter.

and by which resistance to imposed social norms can be enacted. If Derrida is right that binaries are arbitrary, then so is the male and female distinction. This allows for the subversion of these non-essential binary categories through the creation and enactment of non-binary gender identities. Further, deconstruction provides the framework for feminists to explain exactly what is wrong with the privileging of male over female, as it is another example of the arbitrariness of these linguistic categories, and it then gives impetus to feminist literary theorists to subvert these dichotomous prioritizations in their reading of these texts by reversing the binary opposition of male over female.

It seems to be the case that there is more to these oppositions than pure arbitrary chance, however, in that these binaries often persist for centuries without being seriously challenged. Without any objective grounding, why are these binaries so long-lasting and pervasive? Derrida, like Foucault, finds the answer to this question in hierarchical power structures. Once hierarchies are in place, they persist through a mutually reinforcing use (and control) of power and knowledge by those who benefit from such hierarchical orderings. Those who are powerful in society determine the boundaries around normalcy and abnormality (another binary opposition) by enforcing binaries that privilege some ideas or people over others. These categorizations of some persons or behaviors as disordered rather than properly ordered (another binary) reinforces the beliefs, behaviors, and status of the powerful and marginalizes those who are viewed as a threat to this hegemonic ideology. Society then reinforces these binaries with the proposal that there is a transcendent, divine order (logos) that grounds these historical-cultural dichotomies. Narratives about these binaries and their transcendent grounding are taught to children at a young age and are then reinforced throughout life, continually giving the impression that such divisions are simply the way things are rather than historically conditioned, arbitrary distinctions.

Derrida's approach ultimately leads one to continually challenge every presupposition and instinct that one has about the world. Nearly every idea that is taken for granted or seen as common sense is reframed as arbitrary social bias.[487] For example, if someone encounters an individual who is clearly identifiable as having male biological features and is also wearing women's clothing, one might instinctually identify such a thing as abnormal. This categorization of abnormality might not be the result of any well-formed consideration about philosophical anthropology or of a conscious physical examination of the individual's facial structure in order to determine which sex the shape of the skull seems to match. Instead, people develop the capacity to recognize various patterns in early brain development, which includes an unconscious identification of certain features as male and others as female. The Derridian would challenge such inherent assumptions about perceptions of the world, questioning whether there really is some kind of biological determinism involved in such identifications or whether a binary differentiation between male and female biology based on a glance is nothing more than a societal imposition enforced by the bourgeoisie. Derrida's approach challenges not only traditional religious perspectives on the world but also post-Enlightenment scientific ones. Both the Christian and Darwinian views on history and human nature contend that there is a broader grand narrative into which humans can be placed, out of which much human behavior and social interaction can be understood and explained. For Derrida, both are attempts to control others through the reinforcement of arbitrary conceptions about the world.

Derrida's method of deconstruction has profound implications for social life, politics, religion, science, and literary

---

[487] A perusal of academic databases reveals Derridian challenges to nearly every element of received knowledge about the world. There are, for example, multiple articles challenging the distinction between humans and animals. See Katsumori, "Derridean Deconstruction and the Question of Nature"; Oliver, "Sexual Difference, Animal Difference: Derrida and Difference 'Worthy of Its Name.'"

theory. This method of critique is totalizing in its application. Derrida himself was far more concerned with literary applications of these ideas, though he did increasingly address political issues later in his career. The application of Derridian concepts to gender and other non-literary issues is largely the product of other theorists who have extended the approach beyond the use of its originator. Regarding Derrida's literary use of deconstruction, he formed an approach to textual theory in which a given text could be examined through finding and exposing the binary oppositions within the work. Derrida would often then reverse these binary oppositions and ask how a text might be understood if the ideas were reversed (man and woman, light and dark, normal and abnormal). If, for example, the deconstructionist reads a text in which the author portrays an individual as morally superior to another because that person acts on the basis of reason while the other behaves primarily out of emotional impulse, the interpreter would identify the opposition that underlies this judgment: the superiority of reason over feeling. This opposition is then reversed, and the hierarchy is subverted. The reader then interprets the text as if the opposite were the case and the irrational person was superior to the rational one.

The purpose of all of this is not merely to play with texts and imagine "what if" scenarios in literature. It might, for example, be an interesting thought experiment to read *Don Quixote* with the assumption that the main character of the book actually is the noble knight that he claims to be, and everyone else are the ones who are confused. This would certainly be an example of deconstruction, in that a binary between sanity and madness is found in the narrative, where the former is placed in a position of superiority to the latter, and this hierarchical ordering is reversed in the interpretation of the text. This alone, however, does not exhaust the deconstructive method, as the method is to be used as a tool for ideological unmasking and the challenging of value systems rather than just the exploration of themes through practicing diverse forms of reading. Deconstruction would ask whether there really is any superiority of sanity over madness, seeking to show that such divisions are arbitrary constructions that have no clear philosophical veracity. In this way, while deconstruction is in its most specific sense about the reading of texts, its impact goes far beyond literature, in that the method questions the very nature of reality and challenges the entirety of Western thought (Derrida's critiques would apply to much of Eastern thought as well). Ultimately, Derrida does not provide some positive alternative view of the real or ethical life that can be truly known but offers only endless questioning, arbitrariness, and subjectivity.[488]

DIFFÉRANCE

The final element of Derrida's philosophy discussed here is one which has been referenced already—différance. This idea is connected to many of the other concepts discussed thus far, such as the arbitrary nature of language and the binary manner in which words are understood. The term *différance* is a purposeful wordplay, referencing the terms *difference* and *deferral*. These types of wordplay are common in Derrida's writing, as for him they demonstrate the arbitrary nature of signs, since one signifier (or related signifier) can have diverse ideas signified. Regarding this particular wordplay, Derrida speaks about the understanding of words as a method of "difference" or differentiation from other words.[489] As in the example used earlier, the word *tall* is only defined with reference to what is considered *short*. Second, Derrida believes that words are understood also by way

---

[488] Derrida does write some about ethics in works like *Of Hospitality* (2000) and *The Gift of Death* (1992). While he expands upon some positive themes like responsibility, the need for sacrifice, and the necessity of acting for the other, much of his focus is on the paradoxical nature of ethical decisions and the lack of a fixed moral law. With this lack of clear ethical guidance, Derridians often make the practice of deconstruction itself a moral imperative, such that there is an ethical necessity to subvert the socially accepted binary distinctions of the traditional Western world.

[489] "In a language, in the system of language, there are only differences." Derrida, "Différance," in *Derrida Reader*, 64.

of "deferral," as words are used in such a way that their meaning is deferred through referencing other words that are similarly deferred.[490]

In order to understand what Derrida means by différance, I will use the word *table* as an example. The table is a human creation, rather than some biological entity, such that we cannot define a table by its genetic material or other clear biological factors. How exactly does one determine what is a table and what is not a table? One might say a table is something with a flat surface and four legs, but that description also fits the definition of many chairs. Further, there are things that are undoubtedly tables but do not have four legs. Derrida contends that we define things by negation, or by contrasting them with other things. In some sense, we identify what is a table with reference to what it is not. A table is not a chair, or a floor, or a door—though it shares characteristics with all of those things. There is a kind of apophatic method of understanding at work here, where humans do not know so much about what things are, but about what they are not.[491]

One might object that while negation might be part of how an object is known, such as differentiating an item made for eating on, as a table, from one made for sitting, as a chair, there are also plenty of positive things one might say to define it as well. One might, for example, include the *telos*, or purpose, of an object in its definition. A dining table is not only a flat, raised surface, but it is a flat, raised surface that exists to create an area on which dishes and food can be placed and to serve as a shared space for those who are dining. For Derrida, this is not a positive definition but is instead an example of deferral. If one uses this example of the dining table and

---

[490] "Essentially and lawfully, every concept is inscribed in a chain or in a system within which it refers to the other, to other concepts, by means of the systematic play of differences." Derrida, "Différance," 63.

[491] *Apophaticism* is a term used in theology to denote that knowledge of God arises by way of negation, as God is without limit, matter, time, and other things that define creatures. It is often associated with the writings of Pseudo-Dionysius.

the proposed definition here, the identification of a dining table remains unclear because it depends upon definitions of other words. If a table is defined as a being a flat surface, then one has to define the concepts of both *flat* and *surface*. Flat is a binary, only understood in contrast to that which is not flat (after all, we refer to all sorts of things as *flat* that are not perfectly level). Similarly, a *surface* is only understood by, and in contrast to, what is underneath it. Even if these examples were not so clearly binary oppositions to other concepts, one still runs into the problem that every definition of a word, by nature, is composed of other words. Those words are then each defined by other words and so on.

For Derrida, all language systems are self-referential and *only* self-referential. Words never connect someone outside of those words to a world of objects or concepts external to the words themselves. Words relate to words which relate to words. This stands in stark contrast to the Platonic view, in which words are expressions of timeless realities, such that there is an inherent connection between words and external ideas. For Plato, language is meaningful because it points to something external to it. For Derrida, there is nothing external to language, and words are therefore their own internal system of meaning. They do not need some kind of logos to stand behind them and impart meaning to them. Derrida's view also stands in contradistinction to theological notions of inspiration, in which it is believed that a written text contains divine truth and transcendent value within it that both arises from and leads back to an eternal source.

Some of Derrida's writing on this issue is a response to the phenomenology of Edmund Husserl, which was the topic of the French philosopher's dissertation. In his philosophical writings, Husserl attempted to discover the objective truths behind perception, memory, and human encounters with phenomena. Discerning the relationship between the subjectivity of perception and the objective reality that stands behind such phenomena has been one of the primary endeavors of philosophy, at least since the time of Kant. Derrida rejects Kant's attempt to resolve these issues with a philosophical system that proposes a division between universal logical truths and contingent phenomenological claims. For Derrida, the search for objectivity either within the mind or external to the mind is a fruitless one and should simply be abandoned. There is no constancy within the human mind, or in human language. Memory, for example, is notoriously unreliable, as it can change from moment to moment and recollection is often inaccurate. Further, perception differs from person to person, and there is no reason to assume that one individual's perception of reality corresponds directly to anything external to that act of perception.

As much as Derrida's followers often want to differentiate him from subjectivism, it is inevitably where his philosophy ends. All human understanding, for Derrida, is connected to textuality as a system of signs and symbols that mutually interpret one another. The question of metaphysics is really one of reading, or hermeneutics. In the understanding of texts, Derrida argues against the notion that there is one universal meaning found within.[492]

CONCLUSION

Derrida and Foucault both provide attempts to view the world through the structuralist framework in which all that can be known is social systems. There is no logos, or reason, that orders the world or through which the world can be understood as it actually is. There is no grand narrative in which human beings find themselves out of which meaning or purpose for individuals can or should be extracted. For Foucault, everything is, at its root, a series of dynamics of power. The desire for domination drives the human psyche, and thereby it is

---

[492] Derrida contends that his approach to texts is not a proper hermeneutics because "hermeneutics always proposes a convergent movement towards a unitary meaning ... the word of God; deconstruction discerns a dispersive perspective in which there is no (one) meaning." Bennington, "Derrida," in *A Companion to Continental Philosophy*, 552.

the motive for most human interaction, determines the direction of history, and forms societal institutions. It is the role of the academic or theorist to discover these dynamics, which means that academic disciplines should be aimed more at exposing biases and unmasking exploitation that at arriving at knowable truth (an impossibility for Foucault).

Derrida sees power as pervasive as well, but not in the same sense as Foucault. For Derrida, the binary is all-encompassing. Societies create hierarchical distinctions that privilege some people, institutions, or ideas over others, and then they use those binaries as tools of marginalization. It is through this lens that texts should be read and understood. The literary scholar does not engage with a textual source in order to extract meaning from the author's own historical context, motive, or intention (and certainly not to find any eternal value in texts) but instead to uncover the biases present within the text. Constructive work involves the reversing of oppositions, thus demonstrating the arbitrary nature of pervasive dichotomies.

At their roots, the ideologies expressed by Foucault and Derrida are destructive. They provide methods of questioning meaning and exposing systems or ideas as arbitrary or abusive, but these methods have no positive vision or teleology. There is no good toward which scholarship points; it can only expose evil. The post-structuralists fundamentally reorient the purpose of the academy. In a traditional understanding, the purpose of the academy includes the discovery of truth, the passing on of inherited knowledge, the preservation and development of culture, and the formation of virtuous character. For Foucault and Derrida, not one of these elements of the educational system remains. For both, there is no truth that is accessible, as all things are determined by social biases and dynamics of power. Rather than viewing past knowledge with reverence or as long-received wisdom to be cherished, the past is a burden to be overcome, nothing more than a story of marginalization. Culture, similarly, is viewed with disdain, as cultural institutions and mediums have historically reinforced oppressive power structures and were built to maintain hegemonic hierarchical ideology. Finally, there is no virtue, as virtue necessitates a standard of the good toward which the virtuous life points, as well as a series of universal norms that reflect that good. For the post-structuralists, this, again, is nothing more than the imposition of bourgeois ideology. If there is anything like a moral life, it is defined (like everything else) by opposition. The good life is the life in which binaries are subverted, power is resisted through deviant sexual acts that challenge the status quo, and the oppressive classes are overthrown.

PHILOSOPHY GETS GENDERED: THE FEMINISM OF DE BEAUVOIR AND BUTLER

I n the history of philosophy prior to the twentieth century, relatively little attention was paid to the differences between men and women. This is not to say that there were no explanations of sex differences and relations, but these subjects did not constitute a separate branch of the philosophical science (or of any other science). By the beginning of the twenty-first century, this had changed. Nearly every academic field began to explore the relationship between gender and society. Academics focused on biases within various disciplines, contending that phallocentric heteronormativity had presumptively affected the conclusions derived from previous intellectual movements and ideas. This effect has been the strongest on the humanities; often contemporary scholarship in the humanities centers more on the deconstructing of gender binaries or race differentials in classical Western works than it does on a positive construction of the use of beauty within an art form, whether literature, music, or the visual arts. This move arises, not exclusively but significantly, from the rise of feminism.

Feminism is a term often used but not always clearly understood. As a term used to capture a wide-ranging set of ideas, thinkers, and movements, it is difficult to wholly affirm or wholly reject feminism. A historical study of the movements placed underneath this label produces examples in which some of its chief proponents contradict one another from one age to the next. This friction is playing out in real time as some feminist and intersectional thought contends for a feminism beyond gender, which appears to other feminists to be in contradiction to the very foundations of feminist ideology. How can one protect the rights of women without clarity about the nature of women?

To properly understand how these seemingly contradictory approaches to gender could both be given the label *feminism*, this chapter undertakes a historical study of the development of the feminist movement alongside other intellectual shifts through the last few centuries. The various waves of feminism did not develop in a historical vacuum but arose from broader philosophical commitments that undergird them. The differences among feminists are really metaphysical differences about the nature of a human being and how one knows the world. First-wave feminists rely on the principles of early liberalism, in which people are seen as free, autonomous beings who are defined by a series of inherent rights that should be recognized by law. Second-wave feminists are more indebted to existential philosophy, which views human beings as self-creative, defined by their own authentic, free existence, unhindered by social norms and expectations. Third-wave feminists move toward a post-structuralist social understanding of reality, in which gender is a mere series of semiotic actions rather than something inherent to nature. Each of these movements should be read in light of all of the contemporaneous developments set forth in the rest of this text.

This chapter is only an overview, as it would merit a second volume of this book to explore the unique contributions of each of the major influences on feminist thought.[493] The overview here proceeds as follows: First, the beginnings of first-wave feminism are discussed, with its roots in the writings of Mary Wollstonecraft and John Stuart Mill. This also includes an overview of the Seneca Falls Convention, through which feminism was organized as a social movement. Second, the writings of Simone de Beauvoir are discussed, which set the ideological framing for feminism's second

---

[493] For an overview of feminism and its history, see Stansell, *The Feminist Promise: 1792 to the Present.*

wave. Third is an explanation of Judith Butler's post-gender approach to feminism as defended in her book *Gender Trouble*. Fourth and finally is an introduction to intersectionality, in which feminism is placed within a larger framework that understands individuals within their manifold relations of identities of domination and oppression.

FIRST-WAVE FEMINISM

MARY WOLLSTONECRAFT

The ideological beginning of feminism is often identified with the publication of Mary Wollstonecraft's influential book *A Vindication of the Rights of Women* in 1792. This work arose in response to the ideals of the French Revolution (discussed in the second chapter of this book), which argued for an equalization of human rights for all members of society. This ideology, which purported to maximize free action so long as this free action does not infringe upon the free actions of others, challenged the European status quo and the accepted hierarchical orderings in Western society. Such a perspective would lend itself to the challenging of hierarchical views of gender relations.[494] Wollstonecraft noted, however, that these principles of equality were not being consistently applied when it came to male and female relations. Despite the talk of revolutionaries

---

[494] Much of Wollstonecraft's argument stems from Rousseau. With Rousseau, she contends that reason is necessary for free action for both men and women, though natural, inherent reason is suppressed by social norms that are imposed upon citizens from a young age. These externally imposed ideas of right action or social propriety hinder the individual from using reason rightly as a guide to moral action. She writes that men and women "both acquire manners before morals, and a knowledge of life before they have, from reflection, any acquaintance with the grand ideal outline of human nature. The consequence is natural; satisfied with common nature, they become a prey to prejudices, and taking all their opinion on credit, they blindly submit to authority." Wollstonecraft, *Vindication of the Rights of Women*, 56.

about universal freedom and equality, women were still viewed as a lesser sex who did not have access to male political rights.

The primary issue discussed throughout Wollstonecraft's book is children's education in England. While young women did receive a form of education at this time, it differed significantly from that of male children. Male education focused on logic, ideas, and preparation for the work force, while women's education prepared them only for marriage and motherhood. According to Wollstonecraft, this arises from a biased conception of men as the rational sex and women as guided primarily by their emotional whims. The value of women, then, is not to be found in their individuality but in their subservience to their husbands.[495] This opinion of women is reinforced within social structures in numerous ways. In addition to (and due in part to) their modified education, women cannot work independently and are thus unable to provide for their own needs. This means that women are destined for marriage and motherhood out of economic necessity.

For Wollstonecraft, the rights and values of men are inherent to all human beings, since they pertain to nature rather than to sex. These natural realities, however, were not reflected in civic law for women as they were for men. In order to enact this equality in the civic order, Wollstonecraft argues for a system of public schooling in which men and women attend together, giving them exactly the same education. Wollstonecraft also contends for women's suffrage. If government is given its authority through a social contract (as she affirms with Hobbes), this contract includes women as much as it does men. Women, therefore, deserve representation in government. Wollstonecraft also argues that women's views and ideas should be present in the public square through speaking and publishing. Finally, Wollstonecraft argues for a reformulation of

---

[495] Wollstonecraft does also speak about sex differences, or even the superiority of the male sex in some regard. She writes, "[F]rom the constitution of their bodies, men seem to be designed by Providence to attain a greater degree of virtue." Wollstonecraft, *Vindication of the Rights of Women*, 59.

marriage laws. Rather than a mere contractual arrangement in which the husband is the head of the wife, she contends for marriages of friendship that are freely chosen and based on love. These marriages would be of equal give and take.[496]

General principles of Enlightenment rationalism stand behind Wollstonecraft's argument. Rather than the social relativism that underlies much contemporary discourse about gender, Wollstonecraft repeatedly appeals to universal principles in her writing. She argues for a universal essence of humanity that has a series of divinely given rights inherent to it. She further speaks at length of universal moral principles that are derived by reason. Wollstonecraft does argue against externally imposed views of femininity and the female's social role, but she clearly affirms that the female sex in and of itself is a biological and metaphysical reality rather than a construct.

THE SENECA FALLS CONVENTION AND THE BIRTH OF FEMINISM AS A SOCIAL MOVEMENT

While Wollstonecraft's book was relatively popular at the time of its publication, feminism would not grow into a cohesive social movement until the following century. This beginning is often associated with the Seneca Falls Convention on Women's Rights in 1848 in which the ideas of Wollstonecraft moved from theory to praxis.[497] This convention was organized for the purpose of public discussion surrounding a variety of topics related to the woman's

---

[496] It is likely that this view of marriage is connected to her own unhappy marriage, which was not entered into on the basis of love. She had at least two affairs while married, as was made known after her death.

[497] In her book *The Myth of Seneca Falls*, Lisa Tetrault argues that the narrative surrounding the Seneca Falls Convention grew to proportions that outweighed its actual significance at the time. In other words, though it was later viewed as the beginning of the feminist movement, it is not quite clear that the Seneca Falls Convention really was, at the time, a singular point through which a movement was formed.

place in society in the United States (though the influence of this convention extends beyond North America). The majority of the organizers of the convention were Quakers—a religious group who championed a more egalitarian societal philosophy and theology. The Quakers were among the first abolitionists in the Unites States, arguing that the institution of slavery stood in direct opposition to the principle of equality under the law and the proclaimed philosophy of freedom within liberal society.[498] These same arguments were echoed in the nineteenth century regarding women.

The Convention included a series of six talks and the presentation of a document titled the Declaration of Sentiments. After a significant amount of debate about the document, it was signed by one hundred attendees.[499] The text begins with a declaration of the basic principles of liberal political philosophy, including self-evident rights and the equality of man. It then applies these principles to the female sex. Assuming a social contract theory of government, this document makes an argument that a government that derives its authority from the governed is bound to change when those involved in the making of the social contract have objections to the way in which their authority is exercised. This, the Seneca Falls document argues, is an instance in which the social contract must be changed. The legal system had wrongly yet systematically subordinated women to men in many areas of public life. This argument is followed by a list of grievances to be resolved. Among these desired reforms are: the right to vote, property rights, legal recourse in cases of divorce, the ability to earn wealth, access to a career in medicine and law, and a shift in the public view of women as living in a separate social sphere than men.

The aims of first-wave feminism were not only political but also theological. The Declaration of Sentiments, for example,

---

[498] See, for example, my own family member David Cooper's 1783 pamphlet, *A Serious Address to the Rulers of America*.

[499] Elizabeth Cady Stanton's account of the convention can be found in Stanton, *Elizabeth Cady Stanton, As Revealed in Her Letters, Diary and Reminiscences*.

criticizes women's "exclusion from the ministry" as well as not allowing any woman to become "a teacher of theology." This is a departure from the traditional Christian view of a solely male ordained clergy based on St. Paul's admonition in 1 Timothy 2:12.[500] In a far more drastic departure from traditionalist Christian convictions, one of the organizers of the Seneca Falls Convention, Elizabeth Cady Stanton, believed that traditional forms of Christianity were largely at fault for the vast inequalities women faced in society. This argument is made in her controversial 1895 book, *The Woman's Bible.* This work challenges traditional translations and interpretations of passages throughout Scripture that explicate differences between men and women, ignore women, or place men in a superior position. Her work does not merely dispute translations, however; she reveals at the end of this work that she rejects the inspiration of the biblical text and hopes for a future religion of rationality that elevates women to a more prominent position. Another prominent leader of the women's suffrage movement, Matilda Joslyn Gage, criticized Christianity even more explicitly in her 1893 book, *Woman, Church, and State.* In this work, Gage contends that much of ancient society was matriarchal and that Christianity was detrimental to this previous age, imposing an oppressive patriarchal regime upon the Western world. Christianity is, therefore, the greatest contributor to female subjugation. Another example of the post-Christian influence on early feminism is found in the one who is likely its most famous proponent—Susan B. Anthony. Though a Quaker in her younger years, she moved gradually toward a non-dogmatic religiosity and supported the formation of churches where "no doctrines should be preached and all should be welcome." Anthony pushed for the building of such a

---

[500] Female involvement in the public ministry of the church is more consistent with the Quaker view of the church, which is committedly non-hierarchical. Traditional magisterial Protestants, such as Lutherans and (most) Calvinists, had a different view of the role of the clergy as a whole in which public preaching and sacramental administration is delegated exclusively to called and ordained qualified clergy.

church in Rochester, which she believed would aid the feminist cause.[501] By the end of her life, Anthony appears to have had no religious commitments whatsoever.

All of this is not to say that the entire feminist movement was opposed to Christian doctrine and practice. As mentioned above, its roots are found in liberal Quakerism, and some early feminists similarly draw upon their Methodist heritage. Further, a group of early feminists tried to make arguments for their social views from the text of Scripture. In a series of letters to Mary S. Parker published as *Letters on the Equality of the Sexes, and the Condition of Woman*, Quaker reformist Sarah Grimke takes a more favorable stand toward the Bible, contending that male domination over women is the result of sin rather than a reflection of the created order.[502] It must further be noted that as the movement toward women's suffrage grew on a popular level, much of the anti-religious rhetoric was dropped, and figures like Stanton were marginalized. The important theme here is that even within the earliest forms of feminist thought there was a strain that proceeded from a strong opposition between Christian society and female liberation.

JOHN STUART MILL

While most early feminist writers and activists were women, there were male thinkers whose ideas helped to popularize and spread women's liberation. One of the most significant of these was the British philosopher John Stuart Mill. There are two factors behind Mill's concern for this subject matter. First, Mill was a proponent of individualism, equality, and liberty within the civic order (as outlined in his widely read text "On Liberty"). Mill believed that a consistent adherence to these principles led to their application to women. Second, Mill began a love affair with the married Harriet Taylor (who Mill married after her husband's death). While Mill was an advocate

---

[501] Harper, *The Life and Work of Susan B. Anthony: Including Public Addresses, Her Own Letters, and Many from Her Contemporaries During Fifty Years*, 167.

[502] Grimke, *Letters on the Equality of the Sexes, and the Condition of Woman*, 10-11.

of women's rights to some degree prior to meeting Taylor, her activism had a significant impact on his thoughts on the relationship between the sexes. Her influence extended into other areas of Mill's thought as well, as the two lived in a relationship of reciprocity with mutual influence on one another's ideas. It was out of many of their intellectual discussions that Mill composed his ideas about women in his 1869 essay "The Subjection of Women."[503]

In the beginning of this work, Mill sets forth his thesis quite clearly:

> That the principle which regulated the existing social relations between the two sexes—the legal subordination of one sex to the other—is wrong in itself, and now one of the chief hindrances to human improvement; and that it ought to be replaced by a principle of perfect equality, admitting no power or privilege on the one side, nor disability on the other.[504]

In order to understand his methodology here, it is important to highlight that Mill was a proponent of Enlightenment rationalism and of the mythology contained therein. Like many Liberals of his time, Mill believed that human society was on a trajectory of progress toward greater liberty, equality, and rationality. This was thought to be true especially (or perhaps even exclusively) in Europe and North America, where liberal democracies provided fertile ground for the continued advancement of human civilization. Mill's conception of progress arises from his centralizing of rationality. If reason drives progress, then education must serve to advance reason for such progress to become a reality. Because intellectual engagement is a prerequisite for societal improvement, it is necessary for civilized nations to invest in the education of their citizens. Mill argues further that a more just civil society must prioritize women's

---

[503] The version of the essay used here is in Mill, *On Liberty and Other Writings*.
[504] Mill, "Subjection of Women," 119.

education along with that of men. Hindering half of the population from educational advancement unnecessarily hinders progress in civic life.

In order for Mill to justify this position, he must prove that education benefits women in an equal measure to men. In Mill's time, it was often taken for granted that women were intellectual inferiors to their male counterparts. Men are oriented toward logical thinking with disinterested objectivity, whereas women are more indebted to feeling and sentiment in their inner lives.[505] This led to a division in education in which the women were taught in a way that was consistent with their sentimental orientation and men with their logical one. Mill's thoughts on this matter are likely due to his own experience with Taylor, who was Mill's intellectual equal in every way. Further, if anyone in their partnership was driven by shifting, unstable emotional states, it was Mill, rather than Taylor. This, of course, was only Mill's experience rather than something universal. Others argued that, as a whole, the general prejudices surrounding the sexes seem to bear themselves out when looking at trends in the broader population. Mill responds to this seeming universality of female sentimentality by pointing to the fact that universalizing claims about sex cannot be made when women have not been given opportunities for equal education.[506] Perhaps if women had such opportunities, such prejudices could be shown to be mistaken.

The question at issue here is that of nature versus nurture, which is a central component of any discussion of feminist theory. Women are raised—nurtured—with certain expectations about their place in society, their behavior, and their emotional nature, Mill observed. This, in turn, shapes the way in which women view

---

[505] Mill, "Subjection of Women," 173-189.

[506] "The masters of women … turned the whole force of education to effect their purpose. All women are brought up from their earliest years in the belief that their ideal character is the very opposite to that of men; not self-will, and government by self-control, but submission and yielding to the control of others." Mill, "Subjection of Women," 132.

themselves throughout life, the values they have, and the life goals that they pursue. In pointing to these many societal expectations that shape the self-perception of females, Mill does not deny that there are also natural distinctions between men and women. Without equality in opportunity between the sexes, however, there is no clear manner in which nature and nurture can be distinguished, so the borders of the natural differences cannot be identified. Mill argues, therefore, that society should grant the same rights to both men and women and allow for competition in the spheres of public life. In this way, nature would simply be allowed to take its course without the artificially imposed restraints of social expectation. Mill's argument is one for an equality of opportunity for men and women, not equality of outcome. In other words, Mill does not argue that society should artificially impose equality between the sexes—such that, for example, exactly one half of political representatives must be of the female sex. Instead, women should be placed in the same spheres as men where both can present their individual gifts or skills in the market, allowing free action to determine results.[507]

Mill offers some specifics as to how to achieve this goal. First, he argues for women's suffrage. Since the state exists for the good of the populace, and in a democratic society, that good is largely determined by popular vote to elect representatives, there is no reason why half of the population should have no say in who their representatives are. Women should be able to use political influence to support their interests as men do.[508] Second, as already discussed,

---

[507] As an example of the kind of equality he commends, Mill writes that "nobody thinks it necessary to make a law that only a strong-armed man shall be a blacksmith. Freedom and competition suffice to make blacksmiths strong-armed men, because the weak-armed can earn more by engaging in occupations for which they are more fit." Mill, "Subjection of Women," 135. In other words, a woman should enter into the marketplace like anyone else and see whether or not she is fit for any particular occupation.

[508] "To have a choice in choosing those by whom one is governed, is a means of self-protection due to every one." Mill, "Subjection of Women," 168.

Mill argues for more educational opportunities for women. Third, along with Wollstonecraft, Mill argues for a legal reformulation of marriage. He contends that marriage arrangements in nineteenth-century England often functioned like a kind of domestic slavery; men could simply demand whatever they wanted of their wives, stripping women of free agency. In contrast to this, Mill proposes a contractual view of marriage wherein two consenting adults enter into a freely chosen arrangement of mutual love and support, much as a business contract might be made for the benefit of two parties. Mill argues that this freer form of marriage strengthens the institution of marriage, as it is determined by love rather than by convenience or social necessity. Further, this mutual covenant is one, for Mill, in which the subservient role of the wife is replaced with a co-equal partnership between a husband and wife.

Like the other first-wave feminists discussed here, Mill draws his approach to women's liberation from Enlightenment premises of freedom, individuality, limited government, and rationality. He views history as a process of development, from an early human civilization in which the strong were victors over the weak, toward one that protects the value of all citizens. Abolitionism, democracy, and political revolutions were all proof of a progress away from older, barbarous societies composed of artificially imposed hierarchies of power and toward one of freedom for all. This civilization has grown due to the continued use of reason. For Mill, social expectations are often a hindrance to individual liberty and have stopped women from achieving their inherent potential. The solution to these inequalities is to allow women to access the same opportunities, institutions, and jobs as men and to allow competition in the free market to determine who is more capable of what position on an individual basis rather than a uniformly gendered one.

SIMONE DE BEAUVOIR

While the beginning of second-wave feminism is generally dated to 1963 with the publication of Betty Friedan's book *The Feminine*

Mystique, it is an earlier thinker, Simone de Beauvoir, who provides the most detailed intellectual framework for its formulation. In her book *The Second Sex*, Beauvoir sets forth a lengthy and comprehensive account of the nature of women and of the role that society has played in subordinating women to men, making women the "second sex." First published in French in 1949 and translated into English in 1953, this work brought the French existential philosophy of Jean-Paul Sartre into the domain of sex, providing an academically rigorous case for gender equality in the Western world.

Simone de Beauvoir was born into a wealthy French family in January of 1908 in Paris.[509] Following the First World War, the family lost the majority of their wealth, and her father made the decision to send Simone and her sister to a convent school. Beauvoir spent a large portion of her youth in a devoutly religious context. Her mother was a committed traditional Roman Catholic, while her father was less conventional in his beliefs and somewhat loose in his moral convictions. At a young age, Simone wanted to become a nun, but after a period of questioning her religious beliefs she abandoned them altogether. By the time she reached adulthood, Beauvoir was a committed atheist—a position she was committed to throughout her life. Eventually, Beauvoir would develop a negative view of Christianity, seeing religion as a hindrance to female equality and a tool for patriarchal hegemony.

Beauvoir exhibited a strong, independent will, even from a young age, and was determined to live a life of intellectual pursuit without reliance on a husband or family. She began a career in teaching and simultaneously began to write—a skill that would eventually provide a significant income. While she refused marriage, Beauvoir entered into a committed romantic relationship with Jean-Paul Sartre that would last half a century until his death in 1980. Their partnership was sexual, but it was also intellectual, as the two mutually influenced one another's academic pursuits and

---

[509] For a biography, see Kirkpatrick, *Becoming Beauvoir: A Life.*

formulations. Despite their lifelong commitment to one another, Sartre and Beauvoir rejected monogamy, engaging in diverse sexual relationships throughout their time together. Beauvoir, who identified as bisexual, had both male and female lovers. Rejecting traditional sexual norms, Beauvoir engaged in physical encounters with her own underage female students. In at least three recorded cases, female students accused both Sartre and Beauvoir of grooming and sexual abuse. Both Beauvoir and Sartre argued for the legalization of pedophilia in cases where such an encounter was consented to by both parties.[510] While the veracity of one's ideas is not dependent upon one's moral discretion, these incidents are tied to Beauvoir's (and Sartre's) rejection of traditional sexual ethics.

THE SECOND SEX

The premise of Beauvoir's book is straightforward: Western society has considered men as primary and women as secondary. The male is the default standard through which humanity is viewed. This means that conceptions of the male essence, function, and purpose are positively formulated, while women are portrayed by means of their contrast to this default male nature. Women are the "other." The essence and value of women is dependent not upon their own nature but upon the ways in which they relate to men.[511] These definitions of women arise in a twofold form. First, women are defined by attributes that contrast with the male (their supposedly less objective mind, for example). Second, they are defined by the ways in which they support and aid men (such as in giving birth, cleaning the home, or making food for their husbands). Men are defined by all manner of positive attributes, including career, religion, ideas, or other distinguishing identifiers. The man is not,

---

[510] See Mar, "The Impact of Referencing Academics Who Have Defended and Exercised Pederasty."

[511] "Humanity is male, and man defines woman, not in herself, but in relation to himself; she is not considered an autonomous being." Beauvoir, *The Second Sex*, 5.

however, defined by his spousal relation, while the wife often is defined by her husband.

The dominance of patriarchal views is to blame for the suppression of women, though there is a biological component to women's secondary place as well. The process of reproduction creates a kind of bodily slavery whereby the mother is forced to carry a child in her womb, destined to remain in the vocation of motherhood throughout her life. This is further reinforced by social systems in which the woman must depend on her husband for both bodily protection and financial stability, as she is not able to work while taking care of her offspring. It is through woman's reproductive capacity, and those social systems that arise from this reality, that man has dominated her. Beauvoir elevates the value of expressive individual autonomy, viewing marital social bonds and motherhood as hindrances to free action.[512] For this reason, Beauvoir is an ardent defender of abortion as necessary for woman to retain her sexual autonomy and promiscuity while also avoiding the natural biological consequences of such actions. [513]

With this emphasis on individual self-determination, Beauvoir argues that the marriage relationship is harmful to both men and women. As an institution, marriage is inherently unequal.[514]

---

[512] "Since the cause of women's oppression is found in the resolve to perpetuate the family and keep the patrimony intact, if she escapes the family, she escapes this total dependence as well; if society rejects the family by denying private property, woman's condition improves considerably." Beauvoir, *The Second Sex*, 96.

[513] She contends that "abortion is the only way out today in France for women who do not want to bring into the world children condemned to death and misery. ... Birth control and legal abortion would allow women to control their pregnancies freely." Beauvoir, *The Second Sex*, 532-533.

[514] "Marriage has always been presented in radically different ways for men and for women. The two sexes are necessary for each other, but this necessity has never fostered reciprocity; women have never constituted a caste establishing exchanges and contracts on an equal footing with men. Man is a socially autonomous and complete individual ... the reproductive and domestic role to which woman is confined has not guaranteed her an equal dignity." Beauvoir, *The Second Sex*, 439-440.

Men control women in the marital relationship both financially, making the wife dependent upon his income in order to survive, and sexually, by disallowing her from carrying out her sexual desires for other men or women. In Beauvoir's view, sexual satisfaction from a single partner is an impossibility, and the expectation that such a thing will be satisfying—to men and women—will inevitably lead to a state of continual disappointment. In this way, by forcing monogamous sexual bonds, the institution of marriage is oppressive to *both* spouses. In making this argument, Beauvoir seems to assume a kind of hyper-sexuality in women, believing that husbands will nearly always fail to satisfy their wives, leading to pervasive adultery. Further, Beauvoir contends that homosexual tendencies are "latent in almost all women" and that they tend to arise most prominently during the time of menopause.[515] All of this creates tension within the woman who is bound to her husband (who, Beauvoir suggests, she has probably grown tired of) but has significant sexual desire outside of that relationship that cannot be satisfied in the constraints of the marital contract.

Among the many social factors that reinforce patriarchal domination, according to Beauvoir, is Christianity. While she grants that women in early Christian communities were "relatively respected," the beliefs of Christianity "played no little role in women's oppression."[516] Though the Gospel accounts are to be commended for valuing women and slaves, Beauvoir contends that St. Paul reiterates the most patriarchal strains of Jewish thought in his writing and thereby embeds antifeminist notions into Christian ideology.[517] In St. Paul's view, women are always secondary to men, needing to live in submission to male authority in all spheres of life. This domination of the male arises from the text of the Jewish Scriptures, which predate Christianity. The biblical God is portrayed as an absolute

---

[515] Beauvoir, *The Second Sex*, 622.

[516] Beauvoir, *The Second Sex*, 104.

[517] It is anachronistic to speak of St. Paul as being "antifeminist," but this is language that Beauvoir herself uses. Beauvoir, *The Second Sex*, 104.

male authority to whom all must give total submission to avoid his wrath. These biblical stories are told to girls at a young age to imprint this conception of male dominance deep within their psyche, so that they know to obey men throughout their lives. In this view, authority is in its essence male. This is further reinforced, according to Beauvoir, in the writings of the church fathers and medieval theologians—especially St. Thomas Aquinas.[518] The structure of the church, with all male clergy, similarly supports the perception that one must go through the male as a kind of mediator in order to access ultimate reality.

The most often cited part of *The Second Sex* appears at the beginning of the second book. Beauvoir writes that "one is not born, but rather becomes, a woman."[519] Despite what may be assumed in light of more recent feminist ideology, there is no indication in Beauvoir's text that this statement intends to deny the existence of a female nature. While she does, at other points in the text, argue that binary sex categories are not as easy to clearly define as they often have been, the cited passage is about social expectation, rather than any metaphysical claim.[520] What Beauvoir means by this phrase is that the social expectations of womanhood are not inherent within all those who share in the female sex. Left to their own inclinations, young girls would not necessarily decide to wear dresses, play with dolls, or engage in what is considered to be typical feminine behavior. In Beauvoir's view, the youngest children are not behaviorally differentiated on the basis of sex. Entering into the ongoing debate between nature and nurture, Beauvoir highlights the importance of the latter in connection to gendered behavior. What is defined as

---

[518] Aquinas is cited by Beauvoir for his perception of woman as an "incomplete man." Beauvoir, *The Second Sex*, 11.

[519] Beauvoir, *The Second Sex*, 283.

[520] "Males and females are two types of individuals who are differentiated within one species for the purpose of reproduction; they can be defined only correlatively. But it has to be pointed out first that the very meaning of *division* of the species into two sexes is not clear." Beauvoir, *The Second Sex*, 21.

"womanly" behavior does not arise from the female sex inherently but is instead a set of patriarchally determined standards of propriety. These behaviors associated with the female sex are not arbitrary but are imposed by and for the patriarchy as they purposefully subordinate the second sex.

This strong differentiation that Beauvoir makes between biological sex and enforced gendered behavior anticipates the strong divide between sex and gender that occurs later. Since the medieval period, *gender* and *sex* were used interchangeably when applied to people. They were both references to a binary distinction between men and women. The only difference between these terms is that gender was also used with reference to grammar, while sex was not. The now-pervasive sex/gender distinction has its roots in the writings of the sexologist and John Hopkins University professor John Money, who argued like Beauvoir that gendered behavior is learned rather than biological. For Money, the youngest boys and girls have no inherent knowledge of gender or sex differentiations. Their conceptions of gender arise within the first two years of a child's life as a product of the expectations and norms perpetuated by their environment. This thesis was tested in an experiment surrounding two male twins, one of whom lost his sexual organ as a result of a botched circumcision.[521] On Money's recommendation, this child was raised as a girl, while the other twin was raised as a boy. Money believed, in accord with his social theory of gender, that the child who had the botched circumcision would easily adapt to female gender norms if they were impressed upon him throughout childhood. Money's experiment not only included directions to the parents regarding the raising of these children, but he also offered his services to them throughout their youth. In his sessions with these two young boys, Money exposed them to pornography and had them engage in simulated sex acts with one another. Ultimately, the

---

[521] Gaetano, "David Reimer and John Money Gender Reassignment Controversy: The John/Joan Case."

child who was raised female never adapted to this imposed identity as a girl and eventually began to live as a male after discovering the truth about this experiment in which he had no say. This led to years of depression and eventual suicide. This tragic series of events demonstrates that sex differences are not solely attributable to divergent social standards. Distinctions between male and female brains, psychology, and modes of speech have been repeatedly demonstrated by studies since this time, even while Money's basic claim retains significant influence.

In the mid-twentieth century, many second-wave feminists believed that studies of male and female dynamics would eventually prove that many perceived sex differences promoted in popular culture were the result of prejudice or social conditioning rather than innate biology. Throughout the 1970s, a number of psychological and sociological studies were conducted that feminists believed would vindicate these claims and consequently lead to the recognition of absolute female equality.[522] These studies demonstrated precisely the opposite, revealing that men tend toward those traits and actions that are stereotypically "male," and women toward those that are "female," regardless of factors of age, experience, and environment. As with any study that examines trends in broad populations, there is significant variance within each of these groups; there are some men who portray more feminine qualities and some women who have more masculine ones. Nonetheless, the findings of these studies show many social prejudices regarding both sexes to be rooted in real differences.

These studies did not change the direction of the feminist movement after the time of Beauvoir and Friedan toward a greater appreciation for or understanding of sex differences. Instead, the feminist movement gradually moved away from a commitment to any fixity in gender (or sex) whatsoever, instead contending that the concept of *female* is, as a whole, a social construct. The reason for this

---

[522] See Rhoads, *Taking Sex Differences Seriously.*

shift is largely the changing philosophical landscape. No longer were the principles of Enlightenment liberalism that stood behind Wollstonecraft and Mill held as evident truths, nor was Sartre's existentialism that stood behind Beauvoir's work a popular fad any longer within the European academy. Instead, many in the humanities began to adopt the post-structuralist commitments of Foucault, Derrida, and Barthes. It is this influence that led to the most prominent theoretician in third-wave feminism—Judith Butler.

Judith Butler

Judith Butler is the most influential academic in the field of gender theory from the late twentieth century into the twenty-first. She has impacted conversation on gender identity and feminism in both popular and academic contexts. Her work has been frequently cited across disciplines and has also been subjected to significant critique. In her work, Butler integrates a variety of thinkers, from Foucault to Beauvoir to early Marx. This synthesis leads to an ideology that affirms the post-structuralist decentering of the human subject, adopts the Foucauldian commitment to the ubiquity of relations of domination and oppression, and finds its *telos* in political activism. Each element of this system is placed into the context of gender, which, for Butler, is not inherent or innate but constructed through a series of repeated ritual actions.

Judith Pamela Butler was born in Cleveland, Ohio, on February 24 of 1956. Butler is of Jewish ancestry, and her parents sent her to Jewish schools throughout her younger years. Though raised in an observant traditionally Jewish context, Butler herself would become an avid anti-Zionist, sometimes getting significant media attention for her support of the Palestinian cause and relentless criticism of Jewish occupation as a form of colonial oppression. Butler attended Yale University where she received her bachelor's through her doctoral degrees. While studying philosophy, she specialized in German idealism but also spent significant time with the writings of Karl Marx, the existentialists, the linguistic philosopher John Austin, and Michel Foucault. She has had a successful teaching career, lecturing at the University of California, Berkeley; Columbia; the University of Amsterdam; and Johns Hopkins. As of the writing of this book, she continues to appear in the occasional news story for her new writings or interviews on debated subjects, moving beyond the academy into popular discourse.

BUTLER'S ANTI-ESSENTIALISM

Though she has written a number of widely read books, it is her 1990 book *Gender Trouble: Feminism and the Subversion of Identity* that is cited most broadly. While there have been some developments and clarifications in her work since the release of this text, nearly all of the elements of her developed system of thought are present here. Butler's later writings on the subject of gender have mostly been expansions of, clarifications on, and defenses of this work. The summary here is primarily drawn from this text, though I have reviewed some of her later books, articles, and interviews in preparation for this chapter.

Butler's work is an expansion of Beauvoir's claim that "one is not made, but rather becomes, a woman." As discussed above, the context of Beauvoir's quote is social rather than metaphysical—a comment about the social pressures put upon young girls to behave in certain ways that befit womanhood. Butler argues, in opposition to Beauvoir, that such a claim *must* be ontological, as in her perspective, there is no reality outside of social relations. Butler writes that "it becomes impossible to separate out 'gender' from the political and cultural intersections in which it is invariably produced and maintained."[523] In this view, it is not only gendered roles and expectations that are social products, but gender itself. Within this separation from Beauvoir is also an argument that this social

---

[523] Butler, *Gender Trouble*, 4-5.

ontology is consistent with Beauvoir's general premise. Bodies are identified as situations, and for that reason the subject could theoretically choose to embody a gender within one's own situation that differs from that which is biologically assigned. For Butler, in opposition to common classifications, gender is not made up of a set of biologically determined constraints.[524]

Butler's rejection of the givenness of gender and her affirmation of a sociolinguistic construction of gender identity stands behind the common rejection of gender essentialism by gender theorists. These theorists use the phrase *gender essentialism* to describe understandings of the male and female binary that attribute to each gender a series of immutable traits by which they are constituted. In classical metaphysicians like Aristotle or St. Thomas Aquinas, gender is not a self-subsisting essence but an accidental property of a shared human essence. In other words, the general essence of humanness is shared by all people, while each individual instantiation of humanness exists within a specifically gendered body. The sex into which any individual fits is a fixed reality, without the possibility of change, as it is more inherent to the individual subject than incidental properties such as one's hair color or height. While certain social expectations or external manifestations might be changed, gender as an inherent property within a person cannot be.

For Butler, and for other theorists who hold to a socially constructed perception of gender, the classical view removes the freedom of self-definition, since one's being is tied to biological factors that are totally outside of the individual's control. Butler is quite explicit in her desire to divorce gender from biology. She claims, for example, that the core essence of feminism is the "divorce of biology from destiny." As Butler understands a traditional view of sex and gender, there are certain aspects of female life that are biologically determined—most centrally, childbirth. This act is tied

---

[524] Butler, *Gender Trouble*, 11.

to the female essence as only women, by nature of their biological constitution, are able to bear children. Butler follows Beauvoir's view that children restrain women, because they hinder women from exercising their own bodily autonomy, forcing them into a life of servitude within the home. This biological obstruction impacts women in both the home and the workforce. The reality of the situation is this: Regardless of one's values or approach to human subjectivity, biology is an inherently limiting force, constraining one to the possibilities of a particular physical body. For philosophies that view autonomous action as the ultimate good, human anatomy becomes a roadblock toward authentic free action and identity. In order to free the subject from such a constraint, then, personal identity must be strongly differentiated from biological makeup— hence the rise of the strong sex and gender distinction.

Butler critiques not only gender essentialism but realist metaphysics as a whole. In presenting her case, Butler relies upon Nietzsche's critique of a "metaphysic of substance," which is part of his broader rejection of the classical tradition.[525] Like many philosophers discussed in this book, Butler defends a strong nominalism, rejecting the idea that there are universal ideas in which things participate. Her concerns are narrow in scope, related to gender and human identity, but her formulation of these ideas is dependent upon this broader conviction about the nature of reality and the socially constructed way in which human knowledge derives and categorizes experience. Drawing from Foucault, Butler believes that the conception of a "human" is, like all else, a linguistic category, formed by social relations rather than an inherent essence or set of properties. Similarly, the category of "woman," into which some

---

[525] "What is the metaphysics of substance, and how does it inform thinking about the categories of sex? In the first instance, humanist conceptions of the subject tend to assume a substantive person who is the bearer of various essential and nonessential attributes." Butler, *Gender Trouble*, 14.

humans are placed, is purely sociolinguistic and has no independent existence outside of the semiotic system that forms it.

RADICAL RETHINKING OF THE SUBJECT

In setting forth this anti-metaphysical basis for her ideas, Judith Butler calls for a "radical rethinking" of philosophical models of the human subject.[526] Butler criticizes both the classical model of humanity and the Enlightenment one—especially in its Cartesian form. For the classical approach (whether in the Greeks or early Christianity), the human person has a distinct, inherent essence that persists over time. Each individual is composed of both body and soul. While the body changes and decays, the soul is stable and eternal. Cartesian rationalism similarly contends for a differentiation between mind and body, in which the mind is able to grasp the nature of things by means of reason. Both of these models provide clear frameworks in which the individual subject has a self-consistent stability of identity. There is a unifying "self," or "consciousness," that remains constant underneath the reality of continual change. Following in a line of thought from early Marx through the post-structuralists, Butler rejects the idea of a continuously existing subject who persists over time in favor of a view of the subject as composed of social relations.[527]

If human subjects do not truly exist in the traditionally conceived sense, why do human beings have such a coherent and seemingly innate sense of self? Butler argues that our notions of the self are "socially instituted and maintained norms of intelligibility."[528] In other words, the idea of the self, like everything

---

[526] Butler, *Gender Trouble*, 15.

[527] Butler cites Michel Haar on this point, who writes, "All psychological categories (the ego, the individual, the person) derive from the illusion of substantial identity. ... The subject, the self, the individual, are just so many false concepts, since they transform into substances fictitious unities having at the start only a linguistic reality." Butler, *Gender Trouble*, 29.

[528] Butler, *Gender Trouble*, 23.

else, arises out of the need to classify social relations in order to make them intelligible. Language forms human concepts, and it references only itself rather than externally existent norms or ideas. Butler refers to both subject and predicate as mere attempts to simplify, categorize, and order constructs in an artificial way.[529] This mode of argument shares similarities with some forms of empiricist thought, such as that of David Hume. For Hume, there is no compelling argument for the existence of the subject, as all that can be known is the existence of mental impressions. It is out of a need to categorize and understand such impressions that a coherent concept of self arises. Rather than an innately true idea, then, the self is a constructed form of intelligible categorization of the individual consciousness. Of course, unlike Hume, Butler prioritizes semiotic systems as categorizing forces, rather than consciousness connected with mental impressions.

Butler's thoughts on the self are not merely Humean but distinctly post-structuralist. For Butler, self is not a mental concept at all but a linguistic one. Perceptions of a unified self arise from broader social discourse as a way to identify how various elements of interactive words and actions are related to one another within a semiological system. For the purpose of social coherence, particular actions and words are identified with specific subjects in order to give those actions greater intelligibility. The self then arises from the collective. When this concept of self arises, it does so in a gendered manner as a result of societally enforced binaries of differentiated identity.[530] It is only within a linguistic community that individual identity arises, and it does so as a mode of self-understanding within the connective elements of community life. In her explanation of this linguistic identity, Butler uses Derrida's idea of différance, as she

---

[529] Butler, *Gender Trouble*, 28.

[530] Summarizing Lacan, Butler writes, "[S]exual difference is not a simple binary that retains the metaphysics of substance as its foundation. The masculine 'subject' is a fictive construction." Butler, *Gender Trouble*, 38.

believes that subjective identity arises through contrast and comparison with other selves, social contexts, and concepts. While this concept of identity by means of deferral is not limited to gender identities, that is the place in which it is primarily applied by Butler.[531] The self therefore does not have a positive identity but a negative one, created by way of contrasts. Out of this denial of the subject, and out of the socially constructed nature of identity, Butler constructs a performative concept of gender.

GENDER PERFORMATIVITY

If the human subject is linguistically and socially constituted, then so is gender. Butler writes that "abiding substance is a fictive construction through compulsory ordering of attributes into coherent gender sequences."[532] In other words, attributes that are not inherently connected to any objective essence, such as male and female, are placed into the categories of gender in order to create socially useful identifiers to make sense of those attributes in a linguistic context. Thus, gender does not actually exist outside of semiotic systems. In brief, gender is a sociolinguistic category rather than a metaphysical one. This is not identical with a nominalist view, in which objective attributes, ideas, or things are placed within linguistically determined categories that are external to them. For Butler, gender is sociolinguistic because *everything* is sociolinguistic, including individual subjectivity. In such a system, one must not distinguish between objective facts and subjective categorizations of these facts, because there is no objective/subjective divide. All reality is reducible to the sociolinguistic.

Along with her rejection of the subject/object binary, Butler also rejects the distinction between being and doing. In a classical realist metaphysic, a given thing's actions arise from its nature, or essence. An apple tree produces apples because it is the nature of that

---

[531] "Gender is a complexity whose totality is permanently deferred, never fully what it is at any given juncture in time." Butler, *Gender Trouble*, 22.

[532] Butler, *Gender Trouble*, 33.

tree to do so. In Aristotle's categories, an apple tree contains potentialities within it that can and will be actualized when the proper conditions are met. The growing of apples exists in potency within the apple tree even prior to its actually doing so, as particular potentialities exist within the distinct nature of each essence. When the tree does grow apples, this potency has become actuality. This tree is of such a nature that it *can* grow apples and out of that nature now *does* grow apples. In this understanding, a tree does not become an apple tree because it produces apples. It grows apples because that is the nature of the essence of an apple tree. In short, the nature of an object precedes what it does. When classical metaphysics are applied to gender, the female essence is one which is capable (in *potentia*) of childbirth. A woman does not *become* a woman when she gives birth; the action of giving birth is possible *because of* her female essence. To clarify a common point of misunderstanding, within this classical approach any given instantiation of an essence may not actualize all of its potentialities (an impossibility apart from God, who exists as pure act). There may be a particular tree that rightly retains its identification as an apple tree but for whatever reason is not individually capable of producing apples. This does not mean that it is not an apple tree. Similarly, classical metaphysical approaches to sex and gender do not define the female essence in an exclusive manner that would negate the womanhood of a barren woman. Instead, even the barren woman is of the essence of that sex that can bear children, even if some developmental or other barrier has prevented that potentiality from becoming actuality in a particular case.

Butler rejects any of these static notions of gender that differentiate a gender as a nature shared in by some members of a species and the actions that are generally performed by individuals of that gender. Gender is more about doing than it is about being, for Butler. This doing is disconnected from biological acts and is instead connected to social signs and behaviors. These actions do not merely reflect gender but constitute it. She writes that "gender ought not to be construed as a stable identity or locus of agency from which various acts follow; rather, gender is an identity tenuously constituted in time, instituted in an exterior space through a stylized repetition of acts."[533] In this view, gender does not arise out of biological, anatomic, or mental differences between men and women but out of social actions and roles. To be a woman is to perform those ritualized actions that are associated with womanhood in a given culture.[534] Butler clarifies in other writing that these actions are not singular words, behaviors, or pieces of clothing but repeated actions or patterns of speech and behavior. Wearing a dress and lipstick one morning does not constitute womanhood. If, however, one repeats those behaviors continually, then that individual fills the social role of "woman" and therefore is a woman. If all reality is subsumed into signs that identify nothing outside of themselves, then to identify someone as a woman makes that person a woman, since there is no reality behind linguistic identifiers.[535] The identifier is connected with a series of gendered behaviors that, when repeated, become inherent to one's actions. These behaviors often dwell in the realm of the subconscious, so that one is habituated (to use Aristotle's language for a very non-Aristotelian ideology) into the patterns of a given gender. Butler calls this view that contends that gender is a performance *gender performativity*.

---

[533] Butler, *Gender Trouble*, 191.

[534] Somewhat ironically, this approach leans into gender stereotypes rather strongly, so that what culture deems feminine is an essential part of womanhood. If the wearing of dresses, liking flowers, speaking in a high-pitched voice, playing with Barbie dolls, and loving the color pink are all rituals and signs that identify what a woman is, then one who performs such actions *is* a woman.

[535] "Because there is neither an 'essence' that gender expresses or externalizes nor an objective ideal to which gender aspires, and because gender is not a fact, the various acts of gender create the idea of gender, and without those acts, there would be no gender at all. Gender is, thus, a construction that regularly conceals its genesis; the tacit collective agreement to perform, produce, and sustain discrete and polar genders as cultural fictions is obscured by the credibility of those productions." Butler, *Gender Trouble*, 190.

While both Butler and Beauvoir are influential in contemporary gender ideology and related academic fields, there are significant differences in their approaches. Beauvoir argues from an existentialist perspective, differentiating between the inner self and imposed social expectation. Such a view, for Butler, continues to rely on a false dualism of mind and body. When an individual with gender dysphoria makes the claim that they have an inner authentic self that identifies with a gender that differs from their anatomical sex, this reflects the more existential approach to gender and subjectivity, in which a subjective perception about one's nature identifies some innate reality of one's inner being. Butler's view moves the subject of gender outside of subjective perception altogether, arguing that using language like "feeling like a woman" reinforces a false binary in which a gendered feeling is declared as the opposite of something else—neither of which truly exist.[536] For Butler, gender is only performative social actions and is not internal at all. There are tensions within contemporary discussions on the subject of gender dysphoria that manifest these contrasting approaches. An existential view contends for a strong dualism between the body and the inner self, contending that the two can be in complete disharmony, leading to the need to conform one's bodily life to one's inner identity. The performative view, in contrast, views the individual only through the lens of the body, with that body being capable of distinct social roles by means of repeated acts.

Speech-Act Theory

Among Butler's many influences is the influential linguistic philosopher John L. Austin. Austin is most well known for his concept of speech-act theory, which has been used in fields as varied as linguistics, theology, and sociology. These ideas were most famously presented in a series of lectures delivered at Harvard University in 1955. The manuscripts of these talks were released in a 1962 book

---

[536] Butler, *Gender Trouble*, 30.

under the title *How to Do Things with Words*. Austin, like Saussure, identifies the social role of language and the way in which words can create social realities. He does this through his idea of the performative speech act, which not only delivers information but brings about new social realities

Austin's work differentiates between two types of speech—the constative and the performative. The first is the way in which speech is most commonly understood. Constative speech delivers information. For example, a woman might tell a friend about her upcoming wedding with a statement of mere factuality, such as "I am getting married on May 4." While this might be followed by a question, such as "Would you like to come to my wedding?" or a request, like "I would like you to be my bridesmaid," the initial statement by itself does not make any request, demand, or promise. The function of this sentence is the mere delivery of a fact—in this case, the date of her wedding. The second type of speech is distinct from this informative constative mode. Someone can use their speech to command, request, insult, or promise. These speech acts are performative; they are meant to *do* something.

One type of performative speech that Austin discusses is promissory speech. These statements bind an individual to some type of social obligation or community. Returning to the illustration of a wedding, when the bride and groom say "I do" to one another in their marriage vows, these words are more than pieces of information. They bind each party to a covenant in which there are obligations imposed on each spouse. In making the vows, the bride and groom are actually doing the act of marrying each other. Further, the one who presides over the wedding makes declarations about the couple when he declares, "I pronounce you husband and wife." The pronouncement enacts the reality of which it speaks. A new social bond is created through the locution. This relation between speech acts and social reality is not limited to the making of promises. Consider the pronouncement of a judge in a courtroom. The declaration that one is "innocent" or "guilty" brings about a new legal status for the defendant.

Austin divides speech acts in a threefold manner. The first element of a speech act is the *locution*. This refers to the verbal utterance itself, or the sounds that one makes when speaking. The opening and closing of the mouth, the moving of the tongue, and the vibration of the vocal cords create a distinct sound that differentiates one set of words from another. The second element of a speech act is the *illocution*. This refers to the type of speech that one engages in when uttering a series of words. In the wedding, "I do" is categorized as promissory speech, for example. The third and final element of a speech act is the *perlocution*. This is the result of an utterance in view of its context. It is important to note that the effect of words is dependent upon a social context. Uttering the words "I do" does not alone constitute a marriage. One might engage in that locutionary act in a variety of circumstances that do not create a marriage. Meaning depends on the social context in which an utterance is made. The words "I do" within a wedding ceremony bring about a particular result—the marriage of the couple.

Austin focuses on audible vocal utterances rather than social signs and symbols in a broader context. As those working in the field of semiotics have recognized, communicative acts include not only audible words but also bodily actions of various sorts. Wearing a formal outfit communicates that an occasion is important; shaking a hand communicates a greeting; walking away from someone in the middle of a conversation communicates that one is both bored of the conversation and rude. Gendered actions, for Butler, serve as communicative acts in a similar way. Wearing masculine clothing or speaking in a low voice communicate that one is a male. For Butler, these gendered actions, when done on a regular basis, do not only display a social reality but create it. Habitual gendered acts performatively constitute gender, just as performative speech constitutes a marriage bond or a legal state of guilt.

PERFORMANCE AS RESISTANCE

If gender is nothing more than a social category into which individual subjects (who are themselves social constructs) place themselves, then there is nothing inherent to a limited, binary definition of gender as male and female. Butler follows Derrida here, contending that binaries are tools of human categorization and oppression rather than objective divisions within reality. The categories that binary thinking places experience into are tools both of understanding the world and of controlling it. Implicit within these binaries are hierarchical orderings in which one side of the binary is privileged over the other. In this case, the gender binary reinforces the superiority of the male over the female. Butler writes,

> The univocity of sex, the internal coherence of gender, and the binary framework for both sex and gender are considered throughout as regulatory fictions that consolidate and naturalize the convergent power regimes of masculine and heterosexist oppression.[537]

If binaries are socially constructed, and they are tools of oppressive power, then the breaking of the binary is both metaphysically possible and politically advantageous. If gender is divorced entirely from biology, then there is no limitation upon the number of gender expressions that might be created in a given society. Since gender is created by performed actions, new actions and rituals can be embodied in order to bring about new gendered realities.

This breaking of the gender binary is, for Butler, an act of resistance to oppressive powers. If binaries are themselves instances of hierarchical ordering and control (as Derrida argues), and if the primary way in which control is exerted is over bodies (as Foucault contends), then any strong differentiation between male and female is in itself a tool of hegemonic oppression. The most powerful way to

---

[537] Butler, *Gender Trouble*, 46.

resist these oppressive heteronormative standards, then, is to break the binary with ritualized actions and speech. This is done in the creation of new discursive identities by adopting patterns of behavior and language that identify fluid gender expressions without strict dichotomies between male and female. Adopting and affirming new gender identities is something of a moral imperative in a system where resistance to hegemonic power is an ethical obligation (and often seemingly the only guiding principle of ethics). In the context of gender, the hegemonic patriarchal Christian heritage of the West is the oppressive force that is to be subverted.

Like Foucault, Butler views subversive sexual actions as essentially moral goods due to their role in resisting dominant power structures. With no clear, positive ethical vision in either thinker, the rejection of phallocentric regimes and ideologies becomes an end in itself as the sole clear guiding light of ethical decision-making. Butler specifically identifies drag performances here as an important element of this anti-patriarchal resistance.[538] When a male body takes on itself those elements of appearance and behavior that are generally considered to be female, this performance reinforces the performative nature of gender. The drag show is a small demonstration of the larger social reality in which ritualized actions are gendered, and there is no inherent gendered essence underneath them.

CONCLUSION

Judith Butler's ideas have moved gender theory away from a realist view, which contends for the ontological categories of male and female, toward what she refers to as "feminism beyond gender." The movements from first- to second- to third-wave feminism are all dependent upon underlying philosophical moves. Wollstonecraft and Mill argue from the values of classical liberalism, believing that

---

[538] "In imitating gender, drag implicitly reveals the imitative structure of gender itself—as well as its contingency," Butler, *Gender Trouble*, 187.

there is such a thing as a universal human nature with innate rights and equality that should be recognized by law. Second-wave feminists move away from Enlightenment conceptions of nature toward one that elevates authentic living through acts of self-definition. This leads Beauvoir to view social expectations as a hindrance to authentic life and further to a view of womanhood that rejects clearly defined parameters surrounding the female role in society. Third-wave feminism denies realism and the distinction between the inner and outer self, contending that the human subject is a mere social construct, as is all nature. There is then no essence of either male or female, as both are encapsulated within performative ritual—which is the only reality. Butler's thought relies on a metaphysical skepticism that denies not only that there is any objectivity within gender definitions but that the human being has any real consistent existence at all. One must not only ask the Butlerian gender theorist *what is a woman?* but, more basically, *what is a human?*

INTERSECTIONALITY

The basic framework of Butler's performative gender theory remains dominant within current feminist theory. Many have spoken of a fourth wave of feminism since Butler, but the general philosophy that underlies this latest iteration of the feminist movement is not significantly distinct from Butler's. This so-called fourth wave is centered on issues of representation and activism through emerging technologies in the internet age.[539] Roughly dated to 2013, this shift in feminism beyond the third wave created what has been called *online feminism*. This move has not been defined so much by academics or by any specific book publications but by the mass appeal for women's rights, and the need for representation, through social media campaigns. Among these are the #metoo movement, the women's protests against Donald Trump, and the promotion of body

---

[539] See Biana, "bell hooks and Online Feminism."

positivity. Activists also focused on representation of women in movies, television, videogames, and other forms of media. With this has also come an emphasis on diversity in light of multitudinous oppressed or marginalized identities that often overlap with one another. This is what is often (usually negatively) labeled as *identity politics.*

As difficult as fourth-wave feminism is to define, and thus to treat in a philosophically oriented volume like this one, this last element of more recent feminism is tied to a particular academic ideology—intersectionality. Though the roots of this system precede her, the formulation of intersectionality as an ideology and term are credited to Kimberlé Crenshaw. In a 1989 essay in the *University of Chicago Legal Forum*, she argues against the separation of gender and race in discussions of antidiscrimination law, arguing that the experiences of black women are not to be strictly identified as either a category of female experiences or of black experiences.[540] Social systems relate differently to white women than to black women just as they do to black women as compared to black men. Categorizations of people groups that dismiss or ignore the interrelation between sex and gender are referred to by Crenshaw as a "single-axis framework."[541] In response to this single-axis framework, Crenshaw proposes a new framework that contends that

> the intersectional experience is greater than the sum of racism and sexism, any analysis that does not take intersectionality into account cannot sufficiently address the particular manner in which Black women are subordinated. Thus, for feminist theory and antiracist policy discourse to embrace the experiences and concerns of Black women, the entire framework that has been used as a basis for translating "women's experience" or "the Black

---

[540] Crenshaw, "Demarginalizing the Intersection Between Race and Sex."
[541] Crenshaw, "Demarginalizing the Intersection Between Race and Sex," 140.

experience" into concrete policy demands must be rethought and recast.[542]

In other words, for Crenshaw, individuals are not only marginalized to the degree in which they share in broader marginalized identities (in this case, those of race and sex), but marginalization occurs in unique and identifiable ways through the interplay between several discursive identities.

Crenshaw's work is in the field of law, rather than philosophy, which is a subject that is beyond the scope of the present book. Nonetheless, Crenshaw's move toward intersectional feminism has several philosophical and sociological implications along with legal ones. Among authors who have applied Crenshaw's intersectional theory to other fields is Patricia Hill Collins. Just one year after Crenshaw initially used the term, Collins expanded on this concept in her book *Black Feminist Thought: Knowledge, Consciousness, and the Politics of Empowerment*. Building on Crenshaw's idea of an overlapping intersection of identity within marginalized groups, Hill introduces a related concept called the "matrix of domination." This term refers to the ways in which power structures relate to one another in their domination of others. Domination is, like identity, multifaceted, such that there are structural injustices that negatively impact people of distinct identity groups related to categories such as race, sex, gender identity, religion, age, financial status, weight, health, and more.

Collins differentiates this approach from the Marxian distinction between an exploitative class and an oppressed class as two clearly identifiable groups without overlap.[543] In this Marxist view, dynamics of oppression come from one identity group toward another identity group (in Marx's case the proletariat and the

---

[542] Crenshaw, "Demarginalizing the Intersection Between Race and Sex," 140.
[543] The best overview of intersectionality I have encountered is Collins and Bilge, *Intersectionality: Key Concepts*.

bourgeoisie). Collins differentiates the intersectional view by drawing from Foucault's conception that power underlies all social structures and relations, not just economic relations. Oppression is ubiquitous, extending to differences between people according to several identity markers. Because of this complex web of power relations, people are nearly always in simultaneous positions of both privilege and oppression according to their many identities within the matrix of power. A black, straight male, for example, finds himself in a position of privilege regarding his sexuality and his gender, but of oppression according to his race. This man's identity is intersectional, meaning it is defined according to the interrelation among his various identity markers, and the way in which he relates to the structures of power is similarly an intersection, or a matrix of domination, in which he shares in certain structural forces of privilege while also being marginalized by others.

With the rise of intersectionality, progressive theorists have continued to move away from the more simplistic Marxist approach to exploitation with a clearly defined set of oppressors who stand opposed to an oppressed population. Identities and relations are complex, as individuals cannot be categorized as purely belonging to a single group. Because of this complexity, people cannot be classified as wholly oppressed (and thereby innocent) or as wholly oppressive (and thereby guilty). Most people are a mix of both. Because of this complexity, resistance to oppressive powers must similarly be multilayered, rather than one singular political revolution that overthrows a corrupt ruling class. Political resistance within this framework, then, includes recognizing the ways in which power is wielded against several identity groups, including in non-coercive ways. If power relations are so tied to identity and social life, the dynamics of oppressive power can be found even within the most seemingly innocent words, beliefs, or gestures. Activists are to discover these elements of aggression that dominate social life, as these aggressions are tied to the matrix of power. A significant element of this mode of activism is the recognition of one's own privilege within those intertwining systems of power, followed by the empowering of others in those places where one's own identity has granted privilege. This ideology stands behind the many contemporary conversations surrounding white privilege, thin privilege, male privilege, and other types of dominating power formed through hierarchically structured identities by means of social bias.

The influence of this ideology is so broad that Collins says in the beginning of one of her more recent books that "So much has happened since the 1990s that the case for intersectionality no longer has to be made."[544] Academics across disciplines now teach from an intersectional approach, pointing out disparities in social structures (almost exclusively those of the Western world) and encouraging students toward activism in tearing down unjust power structures that are embedded within the matrix of power. With that being said, Collins likely overstates her case at this point, as while intersectional ideas have certainly dominated departments like gender studies and literary theory, fields like aerospace engineering, analytic philosophy, and statistics are not universally taught through an intersectional lens. The Foucauldian takeover of the academy may have been successful, but it is not absolute.

I use the phrase Foucauldian here because intersectionality in its usual application is essentially Foucault's view of power applied to identities as they relate to social structures. This methodology proceeds on the basis of certain assumptions about personal relations and human institutions that Foucault most popularly set forth. Each institution is viewed through a critical lens in search of the ways in which power has been exerted over various marginalized identity groups, assuming that such oppression always lies within the roots of social organizations. Without a strong metaphysical foundation, oppressive power becomes the one constant of history, the basic form of reality in which all things participate. This ideology

---

[544] Collins, *Intersectionality as Critical Social Theory*, 1.

does not simply seek to correct abuses of power where they are found but instead seeks to find them so that they may be exposed.

To be clear, it is not my assertion that there are no abusive power structures, or that society does not engage in the marginalization of certain people groups. History is full of such examples in every culture we have a record of. Human institutions and abuses of power live in a continual reciprocity. Those who gain power often abuse power, and the institutions in which they serve then reinforce that power. Nonetheless, hardly any social relation or institution is entirely *reducible* to power. Those who engage in intersectional activism often assume the worst of people, decrying motives of domination or oppression where such things are not clearly in evidence, much like Foucault's portrayal of the medical clinic as some psychopathic creation born out of an obsessive desire to control the bodies of others. There is far more involved in human relations than power dynamics. Human societies and organizations are nearly all a mix of good and evil (and not all of that is related to power). Further, even while intersectionality (rightly) tries to move away from the simplistic friend-and-enemy dichotomy that characterizes some revolutionary movements and toward a perspective that recognizes distinctness in individuals as one shares in identities, it still essentially defines these identities by power. In texts of intersectional authors, it often comes across as if being white *only* means being oppressive, or being queer *only* means being oppressed, as if identities are so simplistically reducible to dynamics of power. While on one level intersectional theory recognizes more complexity than Marxian approaches due to its multi-definitional approach to people and structures, on another, it is significantly more simplistic, as it reduces nearly all elements of life to that one underlying relation of power and oppression.

CONCLUSION

This overview of feminist movements throughout four waves demonstrates an important reality that underlies the purpose of this present book—activist movements are often dependent upon, and change based on, philosophical developments. One who engages with feminist ideas is likely to simply interact with the stated goals or conclusions of activists without considering the metaphysical commitments lying underneath such goals. It is much easier to affirm that women should be treated fairly and equally than it is to confess that the human subject has no inherent existence or that all of reality is reducible to dynamics of power with no ultimate origin or end to which humanity is destined. Considerations of feminist or any other ideas must always include an examination of the philosophical presuppositions underlying any of these movements.

The different waves of feminism discussed here are often viewed as progressive developments of one another, a series of consistent moves from inequality toward equality of the female sex. As has been demonstrated in this overview, this is not the case, as feminist authors often proceed from diametrically opposed viewpoints about the nature of humanity, the role of the law, and the relation between the sexes. The first-wave feminists operated from a classical liberal framework. They valued reason, fought for women's suffrage on the basis of a belief in limited government and individual freedom, grounded women's rights on the grounds of an inherent value in human beings who are created with a series of unalienable rights, and strongly affirmed the reality of the female sex as both inherent and as distinct to some degree from the male. The goal of the first-wave feminists was an equality of opportunity between the sexes rather than an absolute equality of social outcomes. Second-wave feminists, following Simone de Beauvoir, depend upon existential commitments, viewing the human subject as self-creative and defining the good life by mere freedom to act, including engagement in sexual promiscuity, so that one might be defined by a self-chosen authentic existence. Judith Butler and other third-wave feminists reject the givenness of the female sex altogether and, instead of committing to an existentialist authentic inner-self, define all human categorization and subjective experience as a series of socially determined rituals with no reality outside of themselves. Fourth-wave feminists incorporate intersectional perspectives into feminism, operating on Foucault's framework of pervasive power relations of dominance and oppression, reducing all sense of identity into nothing more than power. What is left at the end of this development is a feminism that denies the existence of the feminine and that has no clear teleology, viewing human relations as a series of power plays determined by an indeterminate number of identifying oppressed or oppressive categories in which one participates.

CONCLUSION: WHERE DO WE GO FROM HERE?

This work has not attempted to provide thorough critiques or alternatives to each of the systems explored throughout its chapters. Its purpose instead was informative—or to use Austin's language, this text is an example of constative writing rather than performative speech. It is my hope that these pages have provided some clarity regarding the systems of thought that have driven much contemporary academic and social life, especially in those institutions and cultural products that are identified as belonging to the ideological left. The thinkers and ideas explained here have spanned centuries and continents, and they differ from one another in significant ways. The philosophies of Immanuel Kant and Jacques Derrida, for example, could not be more opposed to one another in their perceptions of reason or the human subject. Nonetheless, they are all part of the same story of philosophical development in the post-medieval West, which continues to wrestle with its earlier Christian heritage in light of continual developments in technology, science, and history. In view of this, there are some general threads that extend throughout these discussions that I want to highlight here.

Alfred North Whitehead's claim that the history of philosophy is nothing more than a series of footnotes to Plato is as accurate today as it ever was. Many of the basic questions driving the philosophers in this book are not significantly different from those raised, and answered, by Plato and Aristotle. Among these is the continued relevance of the nominalism vs. realism debates that occupied philosophers in the late medieval period. Critiques of a Platonic realist account of the world are prevalent in most of the thinkers addressed in this work in one form or another. David Hume, among other empiricists, holds a strong nominalism in his conflation of all knowledge into experience by means of the senses, through which there are only impressions rather than firm knowledge of an external real world of essences. Kant attempts to balance the realist desire for universal objectivity with the subjectivism of Humean empiricism through his divide between the realm of the noumena (the thing in itself) and the phenomena (the realm of experience), functionally leaving any conception of Platonic or Aristotelian essences in the realm of the unknowable. The commitment to metaphysical realism is challenged more explicitly, and in different ways than the older nominalists, by many of the more politically driven thinkers in this work. Theodor Adorno, Herbert Marcuse, Roland Barthes, Judith Butler, and the postmodernists all associate realist metaphysics with a kind of identitarian thinking that is a means of both control and the perpetuation of bourgeois hegemony. In this activist nominalism, classification is not only a *function* of language but an exertion of dominance over the world *by means of* language. To claim knowledge of essences is to exert power over the world and to force differences into an imposed unity by means of hierarchically determined systems. This rejection of realism is also prevalent in gender theory, in which it is argued that the male and female dichotomy has historically been proposed as simply the essence of things, but this essentialist position is really a linguistic and sociological tool used to make some the "other" and to dominate them.

Another classical philosophical problem that threads through these diverse thinkers is the relation between the subject and object, or the one and the many. Many of the pre-Socratics addressed this relation through proposals of some unifying element, or set of elements, that makes up the entirety of nature, positing monistic approaches to reality in which all things are one. These stand in contrast to the Platonic and Aristotelian approaches, which sought to affirm unity between objects through the forms and also the individuality of objects in their particular instantiations.

Cartesian rationalism promotes a distance between subject and object, making a strong differentiation between the rational mind and the external world, leading to the view of Enlightenment man who is capable of disinterested, rational contemplation of nature while set apart from that which is studied and observed. Kant's bifurcation between reason and the senses had the simultaneous effect of both divorcing man further from nature through reason, which only grasps rational universal principles (but not the essence of the natural world as it is in itself), and strongly uniting man with nature in his sense experience. Hegel moved toward the pre-Socratic view, arguing for the unity of both subject and object within the World Spirit. This unity was then appropriated by Marx into a materialist framework, wherein all things are united within the processes of history in social and economic development. This solidification of the unity of things in left-Hegelianism is evident in Lukács's view of the totality of all reality within the political and in the consequent fight for absolute revolution. This idea of totality was then adopted by the Critical Theorists, with Adorno coming to reject synthesis, instead arguing that subject and object exist within a reality of tensions in history, though without any real ontological distinction from one another. Embedded in this view is Adorno's perception that the subject is not a given entity but a mere perception created out of evolutionary survival needs. This interconnectedness between subject and object is further developed in Saussure's linguistic theory of interconnected signs and in the structuralism of Lévi-Strauss. Post-structuralist theories then contend that human knowledge consists exclusively in the interrelation between signs and that the human subject is similarly created. For Foucault, as for Butler, the universal underlying essence of these social relations is power.

A further common topic addressed by these thinkers is that of history. In the Christian medieval West, it was a given that history is teleologically driven. It has both a purposeful beginning and a *telos* toward which human events point. Enlightenment philosophers began a process of de-sacralizing history, moving away from perceptions of divine causality and providential guidance toward a metanarrative of human progress through the use of reason. Hegel reinvigorated a strongly metaphysical historicism, in which the World Spirit develops through a dialectical process that is moving toward synthesis. This historical progress was interpreted by Marx as the progress of societies toward socialism. Marx's materialist historicism was committed to historical necessity as an element of scientific socialism. This then moved, through later theorists, away from a commitment to absolute historical necessity into a form of Marxism in which subjectivity took a stronger role. If the subjective consciousness of an oppressed proletariat could be enflamed by activists, socialist revolutions could arise. The belief that history is defined by progress was challenged by Adorno and the postmodernists, who argued that there is no ultimate narrative into which all historical events can be placed. History is, instead, nothing more than a display of power with no knowable beginning or end.

Perhaps the most important topic addressed throughout this volume is that of human nature. Nearly everything that can be said about reality depends upon one's view of humanity. Classical views argue for the persistent existence of an individual subject who is composed of both body and soul and whose mind is able to grasp reality as it is. Descartes's system contends for the same, but he moves toward a stronger division between the internal mind, which is rational and free, and a material body, which is part of nature and mechanistically conceived, thus creating the mind/body problem. Hume denies the existence of the persistent subject, contending that the mind is nothing more than a bundle of sense impressions. Kant believes in the transcendental subject, characterized by liberty and rationality who is set apart from nature by these faculties. This emphasis on freedom and human nature is developed further among liberal political philosophers, who contend for freedom as central to human nature and see human organization as an imposition upon, rather than an element of, that nature. With Marx, the immaterial element of human nature is denied, and the human is a composite of social relations. This leads to the prominence of philosophical anthropologies of social construction, in which the individual does not have inherent existence but is the product of various societal factors. As different as they are in their views of the internal vs. external element of human nature, both the existentialists and the post-structuralists deny that there is a human essence, claiming that the human subject is created by non-natural or non-essential factors (either one's self-creative decision or social systems). This leads to malleability within nature, so that humanity is free from constraints of theology, historical determinism, or biological necessity.

There is nothing left of humanity at the end of this mode of thought. If there is no divine causality or teleology within history, then there is no real purpose in human life other than that which is self-chosen. Further, in the Foucauldian mode, in which everything is viewed as pure relations of power, the only meaning that can be found is a negative one: One engages in an evaluation of social systems and institutions to discover their unique forms of domination. Rather than having a positive, clear end, academic disciplines and art forms are mere tools of critique. They diagnose problems rather than offering solutions that are truly meaningful beyond personal subjectivity or involvement in some form of political activism. These systems never provide a clear vision for the ethical life. They reject transcendent law along with historically received norms (which are nothing more than bourgeois prejudice). If there is no clarity about what human nature is, or whether such a thing even exists, then there can be no standard by which ethics are constructed. The question *what is a nature to do?* can only be answered with some clarity about the question *what is nature?* Theoreticians of the academic left have largely abandoned the search for answers to either of these questions, subsuming all things under the all-consuming dynamic of power. This is nothing more than a nihilistic loss of meaning in the end, with the ethical life conflated with whatever form of political activism is popular at the present moment.

MOVING TOWARD A POSITIVE PHILOSOPHY

The modern world is facing an unprecedented growth in human dependence on technology. People spend nearly all of their waking hours in relation to one form of technology or another, being consumed by the endless scrolling and monotony of social media feeds. This has created a crisis of meaning, with rising depression rates and anxiety since the popularization of the smartphone in 2013. Many young men and women seek meaning within those platforms, isolated from the kinds of personal connection and community that human beings have relied on as long as we have existed as a species. The solidarity found on these platforms is often around political causes or subjects of protest through which shared anger is expressed regarding some cause that may not have any direct impact on the one protesting. Unity between people in such cases is most often not the result of genuine concern for the particular cause. They simply feel that human drive inherent in each of us to serve *something*, to have some broader purpose in which we have a shared life with other human beings. With no positive place to direct these impulses, they find human connection in some shared object of hatred rather than in a bond of love that is part of a greater reality.

These problems are further exacerbated by the rise of artificial intelligence. Proponents of AI offer promises of an easier life, yet their promises do not inspire a hopeful future. New technologies bring about new conveniences, but they continue to divorce us from our shared purposes, struggles, and growth in which we find our humanity. The proliferation of AI images and video, with rapid improvements in these technologies, is bringing questions about beauty, art, and intentionality to the forefront of our conversations. If authorial intent is not determinative of the meaning or beauty inherent within a piece of art, then is there any reason to prioritize art made by a human being rather than a machine? After all, since AI is using human products as the basis of its calculations, its "art" is a product of the same discourses and histories that an individual's piece of art is. And yet, many recognize that in these products, there is something missing, even if that is not clearly identifiable.

The point of this is to say that the world is in a moment of crisis, and negative philosophies that deny the givenness of nature and cannot provide any coherent answer to the most basic questions of existence are absolutely incapable of providing any real or lasting guidance to isolated, depressed people living under servitude to technology. What we need is a clear and positive philosophy of life. Not one that provides further tools of criticism or offers political visions based on utopian fantasies, but one that presents a clear, good end toward which history drives and in which human beings are a part. We need a philosophy that expresses that human beings matter and that there is an ontological foundation of their being that is not dependent upon the arbitrary systems of society or upon unbounded personal freedom. This vision cannot be merely political, nor even exclusively philosophical. Maybe what we need is a return to that same theological vision of life that the modern West has continually tried to run from. Its best thinkers of the last four centuries have constructed one failing system of meaning after another to fill a gap that such systems simply cannot fill. That vision, however, must be the subject of another book.

BIBLIOGRAPHY

Abromeit, John, and W. Mark Cobb, eds. *Herbert Marcuse: A Critical Reader*. Routledge, 2004.

Adorno, Theodor W. *The Adorno Reader*. Edited by Brian O'Connor. Blackwell, 2000.

———. "The Idea of Natural History." In *Critical Models: Interventions and Catchwords*, translated by Henry W. Pickford, 252–269. New York: Columbia University Press, 1998.

———. *Kierkegaard: Construction of the Aesthetic*. Translated by Robert Hullot-Kentor. University of Minnesota Press, 1989.

———. "Theses on the Language of the Philosopher." In *Adorno and the Need in Thinking: New Critical Essays*, edited by Donald Burke, Colin J. Campbell, Kathy Kiloh, Michael K. Palamarek, and Jonathan Short, 35-40. Toronto: University of Toronto Press, 2007.

Adorno, Theodor, Else Frenkel-Brunswik, et al. *The Authoritarian Personality*. Reprinted with a new introduction by Peter E. Gordon. Verso, 2019. First published 1950 by Harper & Brothers.

Allen, Diogenes. *Philosophy for Understanding Theology*. Westminster John Knox Press, 1985.

Allen, Robert C. *The Industrial Revolution: A Very Short Introduction*. Oxford University Press, 2017.

Anderson, Ryan. *When Harry Became Sally: Responding to the Transgender Moment.* Encounter Books, 2018.

Andrew, Edward. "Work and Freedom in Marcuse and Marx." *Canadian Journal of Political Science / Revue Canadienne de Science Politique* 3, no. 2 (1970): 241–56. http://www.jstor.org/stable/3231633.

Aquinas, Thomas. *Introduction to St. Thomas Aquinas: The Summa Theologica, The Summa Contra Gentiles.* Edited by A.C. Pegis. Random House, 1945.

———. *On Law, Morality, and Politics.* Translated by Richard J. Regan. Hackett, 2003.

Ariew, Roger, and Eric Watkins. *Modern Philosophy: An Anthology of Primary Sources.* 3rd ed. Hackett, 2019.

Aristotle. *The Metaphysics.* Translated by H. L. Tancred. Penguin, 1998.

———. *Nichomachean Ethics.* Translated by Terence Irwin. Hackett, 2019.

———. *Poetics: With the Coislinianus, Reconstruction of Poetics II, and Fragments of On Poets.* Translated by Richard Janko. Hackett, 1987.

Aronowitz, Stanley. "The Unknown Herbert Marcuse." *Social Text*, no. 58 (1999): 133–54.

Arrington, Robert L., ed. *A Companion to the Philosophers.* Blackwell Companions to Philosophy. Blackwell, 1999.

Augustine. *The Confessions.* Translated by Maria Boulding. Works of Saint Augustine. New City Press, 2002.

Aune, Bruce. *Rationalism, Empiricism, and Pragmatism: An Introduction.* McGraw-Hill, 1970.

Austin, J. L. *How to Do Things with Words.* Harvard University Press, 1975.

Baker, Robert C., and Roland Cap Ehlke, eds. *Natural Law: A Lutheran Reappraisal.* Concordia, 2011.

Barrett, William. *Irrational Man: A Study in Existential Philosophy.* Doubleday, 1962.

Barrett, William, and Henry D. Aiken, eds. *Philosophy in the Twentieth Century: An Anthology.* Random House, 1962.

Barthes, Roland. *A Barthes Reader.* Edited and with an introduction by Susan Sontag. Hill and Wang, 1982.

———. "The Death of the Author." In *Image – Music – Text,* translated by Stephen Heath, 142–148. New York: Hill and Wang, 1977.

———. *The Fashion System.* Translated by Matthew Ward and Richard Howard. Berkeley: University of California Press, 1983.

———. *Mythologies: The Complete Edition in a New Translation.* Translated by Richard Howard and Annette Lavers. Hill and Wang, 2013.

Bates, Thomas R. "Gramsci and the Theory of Hegemony." *Journal of the History of Ideas* 36, no. 2 (1975): 351–66. https://doi.org/10.2307/2708933.

Beardsley, Monroe, ed. *The European Philosophers from Descartes to Nietzsche.* Modern Library Classics. Modern Library, 2002.

Beeke, Joel R., and Mark Jones. *A Puritan Theology: Doctrine for Life.* Reformation Heritage, 2012.

Bennett, John G. "A Note on Locke's Theory of Tacit Consent." *The Philosophical Review* 88, no. 2 (1979): 224–34. https://doi.org/10.2307/2184507.

Bernstein, Richard T. "Herbert Marcuse: An Immanent Critique." *Social Theory and Practice* 1, no. 4 (1971): 97–111. http://www.jstor.org/stable/23556661.

Biana, Hazel T. (2023) "bell hooks and Online Feminism," *Journal of International Women's Studies* 25, no. 2 (2023): Article 10. https://vc.bridgew.edu/jiws/vol25/iss2/10.

Bowie, Andrew. *Theodor W. Adorno, A Very Short Introduction.* Oxford University Press, 2010.

———. *Schelling and Modern European Philosophy: An Introduction.* Routledge, 1993.

Boyers, Robert. "The Politics of Anti-Realism: A Preface." *Salmagundi,* no. 42 (1978): 3. http://www.jstor.org/stable/40547134.

Bradley, Arthur. "Derrida's God: A Genealogy of the Theological Turn." *Paragraph* 29, no. 3 (2006): 21–42.

Bradley, James E., and Dale K. Van Kley, eds. *Religion and Politics in Enlightenment Europe.* Notre Dame Press, 2001.

Brenkman, John. "Theses on Cultural Marxism." *Social Text*, no. 7 (1983): 19–33. https://doi.org/10.2307/466452.

Bohm-Bawerk, Eugen. *Capital and Interest: A Critical History of Economical Theory*. Translated by William Amart. Macmillan, 1890.

Breines, Paul. "Young Lukács, Old Lukács, New Lukács." *The Journal of Modern History* 51, no. 3 (1979): 533–46. http://www.jstor.org/stable/1876636.

Bronner, Stephen Eric. *Critical Theory: A Very Short Introduction*. Oxford University Press, 2017.

Brotton, Jerry. *The Renaissance: A Very Short Introduction*. Oxford University Press, 2006.

Brown, Callum G. *Postmodernism for Historians*. Routledge, 2016.

Brower, Jeffrey E., and Kevin Guilfoy. *The Cambridge Companion to Abelard*. Cambridge University Press, 2004.

Buell, Lawrence, ed. *The American Transcendentalists: Essential Writings*. Modern Library, 2006.

Edmund Burke, *Reflections on the Revolution in France* (London: J. Dodsley, 1790), Alex Catalogue of Electronic Texts, 1998, https://www.infomotions.com/alex2/authors/burke-edmund/burke-reflections-1790.

Butler, Christopher. *Postmodernism: A Very Short Introduction*. Oxford University Press, 2002.

Butler, Judith. *Gender Trouble*. Routledge, 2006.

Callinicos, Alex, Stathis Kouvelakis, and Lucia Pradella, eds. *Routledge Handbook of Marxism and Post-Marxism*. New York: Routledge, 2020.

Collins, Patricia Hill. *Black Feminist Thought: Knowledge, Consciousness, and the Politics of Empowerment*. 30th Anniversary Edition. Routledge, 2022.

———. *Intersectionality as Critical Social Theory*. Duke University Press, 2019.

Collins, Patricia Hill, and Sirma Bilge. *Intersectionality: Key Concepts*. 2nd ed. Polity, 2020.

Cook, Deborah, ed. *Theodor Adorno: Key Concepts*. Rawat Books, 2012.

Cooper, David. *A Serious Address to the Rulers of America, on the Inconsistency of Their Conduct Respecting Slavery: Forming a Contrast between the Encroachments of England on American Liberty, and American Injustice in Tolerating Slavery*. Philadelphia?, 1783. In *Evans Early American Imprint Collection*. University of Michigan Library Digital Collections. https://name.umdl.umich.edu/N14096.0001.001. Accessed May 1, 2025.

Cooper, Jordan B. *In Defense of the True, the Good, and the Beautiful: On the Loss of Transcendence and the Decline of the West*. Just & Sinner, 2021.

———. *Prolegomena: A Defense of the Scholastic Method*. Weidner Institute, 2020.

Copleston, Frederick. *Greece and Rome: From the Pre-Socratics to Plotinus*. A History of Philosophy. Doubleday, 1962.

————. *Medieval Philosophy: From Augustine to Duns Scotus.* A History of Philosophy. Doubleday, 1962.

Corrigan, Kevin. *Love, Friendship, Beauty, and the Good: Plato, Aristotle, and the Later Tradition.* Cascade, 2018.

Cottingham, John, ed. *The Philosophical Writings of Descartes.* 3 vols. Cambridge University Press, 1985-91.

Crenshaw, Kimberlé. "Demarginalizing the intersection of race and sex: a black feminist critique of antidiscrimination doctrine, feminist theory and antiracist politics." *University of Chicago Legal Forum* 1989, no. 1 (1989): 139–167.

————. "Mapping the Margins: Intersectionality, Identity Politics, and Violence against Women of Color." *Stanford Law Review* 43, no. 6 (July 1991): 1241–1299.

Crisp, Roger, and Michael Slote, eds. *Virtue Ethics.* Oxford University Press, 1997.

Critchley, Simon, and William R. Schroader, eds. *A Companion to Continental Philosophy.* Blackwell Companions to Philosophy. Blackwell, 1998.

Culler, Jonathan. *Barthes: A Very Short Introduction.* Oxford University Press, 2002.

Cuttica, Cesare. *Sir Robert Filmer (1588–1653) and the patriotic monarch: Patriarchalism in seventeenth-century political thought.* Manchester University Press, 2012.

Davies, Ioan. "British Cultural Marxism." *International Journal of Politics, Culture, and Society* 4, no. 3 (1991): 323–44. http://www.jstor.org/stable/20007001.

de Beauvoir, Simone. *The Second Sex.* Translated by Constance Borde and Sheila Malovany-Chevallier. New York: Alfred A. Knopf, 2010.
Deneen, Patrick J. *Why Liberalism Failed.* Yale University Press, 2019.

Derrida, Jacques. *A Derrida Reader: Between the Blinds.* Edited and with an introduction and notes by Peggy Kamuf. Columbia University Press, 1991.

———. *The Gift of Death.* 2nd ed. Translated by David Wills. University of Chicago Press, 2017.

———. *Of Grammatology.* Translated by Gayatri Chakravorty Spivak. Johns Hopkins University Press, 2016.

———. "Interview: Jacques Derrida." Interview by G. Scarpetta and J. L. Houdebine. *Diacritics* 2, no. 4 (1972): 35–43.

———. *Limited Inc.* Edited by Gerald Graff. Translated by Jeffrey Mehlman and Samuel Weber. Evanston, IL: Northwestern University Press, 1988.

Derrida, Jacques, and Anne Dufourmantelle. *Of Hospitality: Anne Dufourmantelle Invites Jacques Derrida to Respond.* Translated by Rachel Bowlby. Stanford University Press, 2000.

Descartes, René. *Key Philosophical Writings.* Edited by T. Griffith. Wordsworth Editions, 1997.

———. *The World and Man*. Translated by Roger Ariew. Hackett, 2023.

Devine, Donald. "John Locke: The Harmony of Liberty & Virtue." *The Imaginative Conservative*. August 28, 2023. https://theimaginativeconservative.org/2023/08/john-locke-harmony-liberty-virtue-donald-devine.html.

Dietzgen, Joseph. *Some of the Philosophical Essays of Joseph Dietzgen*. C. H. Kerr and Co., 1917.

Doolan, Gregory. *Aquinas on Divine Ideas as Exemplar Causes*. Catholic University of America Press, 2014.

Duke, George, and Robert George. *The Cambridge Companion to Natural Law and Jurisprudence*. Cambridge University Press, 2017.

Dworkin, Dennis. *Cultural Marxism in Postwar Britain: History, the New Left, and the Origin of Cultural Studies*. Duke University Press, 1997.

Eagleton, Terry. *Why Marx Was Right*. Yale University Press, 2012.

Emmanuel, Chapman. *St. Augustine's Philosophy of Beauty*. Sheed and Ward, 1939.

Engels, Friedrich. *The Origin of the Family, Private Property and the State*. Translated by Ernest Untermann. C. H. Kerr and Co., 1902.

———. *Socialism: Utopian and Scientific*. Translated by Edward Aveling. C. H. Kerr and Co., 1914.

Faubion, James D., ed. *Power*. The Essential Works of Foucault. New Press, 2001.

Felluga, Dino Franco. *Critical Theory: The Key Concepts*. Routledge, 2005.

Feser, Edward. *Aquinas: A Beginner's Guide*. Oneworld, 2009.

———. *The Last Superstition: A Refutation of the New Atheism*. St. Augustine's Press, 2008.

———. *Philosophy of Mind: A Beginner's Guide*. Oneworld, 2006.

Feuerbach, Ludwig. *The Essence of Christianity*. Translated by George Eliot. Delphi Classics. eBook edition. Hastings, UK: Delphi Classics, 2017. ISBN 9781788770125.

Fichte, J. G. *Foundation of the Wissenschaftlehre and Related Writings (1794-95)*. Translated and edited by Daniel Breazeale. Oxford University Press, 2022.

Fillingham, Lydia Alix. *Foucault for Beginners*. Writers and Readers, 2007.

Fiori, Giuseppe. *Antonio Gramsci: Life of a Revolutionary*. Translated by Tom Nairn. 2nd ed. Verso, 1990.

Forgacs, David, ed. *The Antonio Gramsci Reader*. Lawrence and Wishart, 2000.

Foucault, Michel. *The Archeology of Knowledge: And the Discourse on Language*. Translated by Alan Sheridan. Vintage Books, 1982.

———. *Discipline and Punish: The Birth of the Prison*. Translated by Alan Sheridan. Vintage Books, 2005.

—. *The Foucault Reader*. Edited by Paul Rabinow. Vintage Books, 2010.

—. *The History of Madness*. Translated by Jonathan Murphy and Jean Khalfa. Routledge, 2006.

—. Foucault, Michel. *The History of Sexuality*. Vol. 1, *An Introduction*. Translated by Robert Hurley. New York: Vintage Books, 1990.

—. *Madness and Civilization: A History of Madness in the Age of Reason*. Translated by Richard Howard. Vintage Books, 1988.

Freeman, Eugene, and David Appel. *The Great Ideas of Plato*. Lantern Press, 1952.

Fresu, Gianni. *Antonio Gramsci: An Intellectual Biography*. Palgrave Macmillan, 2022.

Fretigne, Jean-Yves. *To Live is to Resist: The Life of Antonio Gramsci*. Translated by Laura Marris. University of Chicago Press, 2021.

Frost, S. E., Jr. *Basic Teachings of the Great Philosophers*. rev. ed. Dolphin, 1962.

Fulton, John. "Religion and Politics in Gramsci: An Introduction." *Sociological Analysis* 48, no. 3 (1987): 197–216. http://www.jstor.org/stable/3711518.

Gaetano, Phil. "David Reimer and John Money Gender Reassignment Controversy: The John/Joan Case." *Embryo Project Encyclopedia* (November 15, 2017). ISSN: 1940-5030 https://hdl.handle.net/10776/13009.

Gage, Matilda Joslyn. *Woman, Church and State: A Historical Account of the Status of Woman through the Christian Ages, with Reminiscences of the Matriarchate.* Chicago: C. H. Kerr & Company, 1893.

Garland, David. "Foucault's Discipline and Punish: An Exposition and Critique." *American Bar Foundation Research Journal* 11, no. 4 (Autumn 1986): 847-880.

German Bundestag. "Revolution and the National Assembly in Frankfurt am Main 1848/1849." https://www.bundestag.de/en/parliament/history/parliamentarism/1848/1848-200350. Accessed August 10, 2024.

Gilson, Etienne. *Being and Some Philosophers.* Pontifical Institute, 1949.

Girgis, Sherif, Ryan T. Anderson, and Robert George. *What Is Marriage? Man and Woman: A Defense.* Encounter Books, 2012.

Glendinning, Simon. *Derrida: A Very Short Introduction.* Oxford University Press, 2011.

Graff, Gerald. "The Politics of Anti-Realism." *Salmagundi,* no. 42 (1978): 4–30. http://www.jstor.org/stable/40547135.

Grelle, Bruce. "Hegemony and the 'Universalization' of Moral Ideas: Gramsci's Importance for Comparative Religious Ethics." *Soundings: An Interdisciplinary Journal* 78, no. 3/4 (1995): 519–40. http://www.jstor.org/stable/41178720.

Grimke, Sarah Moore. *Letters on the Equality of the Sexes, and the Condition of Woman: Addressed to Mary S. Parker.* Isaac Knapp, 1838.

Gutting, Gary. *Foucault: A Very Short Introduction*. 2nd ed. Oxford University Press, 2005.

Haines, David. *Natural Law: A Brief Introduction and Biblical Defense*. Davenant Institute, 2017.

Harper, Ida Husted. *The Life and Work of Susan B. Anthony: Including Public Addresses, Her Own Letters, and Many from Her Contemporaries During Fifty Years*. Bowen-Merrill, 1899.

Hart, David Bentley. *Atheist Delusions: The Christian Revolution and Its Fashionable Enemies*. Yale University Press, 2009.

———. *The Experience of God: Being, Consciousness, Bliss*. Yale University Press, 2013.

Hart, Kevin. *Postmodernism: A Beginner's Guide*. Oneworld, 2004.

Hass, Lawrence. "Discipline and the Constituted Subject: Foucault's Social History." *Symplokē* 4, no. 1/2 (1996): 61–72.

Hegel, G. W. F. *Early Theological Writings*. Translated by T.M. Knox. University of Pennsylvania, 1971.

———. *Introduction to the Philosophy of History, with an Appendix from The Philosophy of Right*. Translated by Leo Rauch. Hackett, 1988.

———. *Introductory Lectures on Aesthetics*. Translated by Bernard Bosanquet. Penguin, 1993.

———. *Hegel: The Letters*. Translated by Clark Butler and Christiane Seilar. Indiana University Press, 1984.

————. *The Phenomenology of Spirit.* The Cambridge Hegel Translations. Translated by Terry Pinkard. Cambridge University Press, 2018.

Held, David. *An Introduction to Critical Theory: Horkheimer to Habermas.* Polity, 1990. Nook edition.

Hicks, Stephen R. C. *Explaining Postmodernism: Skepticism and Socialism from Rosseau to Foucalt.* Expanded ed. Ockham's Razor, 2013.

Hildebrand, Pierrick. *The Zurich Origins of Reformed Covenant Theology.* Oxford Studies in Historical Theology. Oxford University Press, 2024.

Hobbes, Thomas. *De Cive: Philosophical Rudiments Concerning Government and Society.* J. C. Royston, 1651.

————. *Leviathan, or the Matter, Forme, and Power of a Commonwealth Ecclesiastical and Civil.* Andrew Crooke, 1651.

Hohendahl, Peter Uwe. "Art Work and Modernity: The Legacy of Georg Lukács." In *Reappraisals: Shifting Alignments in Postwar Critical Theory.* Cornell University Press, 1991. http://www.jstor.org/stable/10.7591/j.ctt1g69xjd.6.

————. "The Scholar, the Intellectual, and the Essay: Weber, Lukács, Adorno, and Postwar Germany." *The German Quarterly* 70, no. 3 (Summer 1997): 217-232.

Holmes, Leslie. *Communism: A Very Short Introduction.* Oxford University Press, 2009.

Horkheimer, Max. *The Eclipse of Reason.* Bloomsbury, 2013.

Horkheimer, Max, and Theodor Adorno, *Dialectic of Enlightenment: Philosophical Fragments*. Edited by Gunzelin Schmid Noerr and translated by Edmund Jephcott. Stanford University, 2002.

Hume, David. *A Treatise of Human Nature*. Edited by D. G. C. MacNabb. Collins Sons, 1962.

Hunt, Alan. "Getting Marx and Foucault into Bed Together!" *Journal of Law and Society* 31, no. 4 (2004): 592–609.

Hyland, Drew A. *Plato and the Question of Beauty*. Studies in Continental Thought. Indiana University Press, 2008.

Im, Hyug Baeg. "Hegemony and Counter-Hegemony in Gramsci." *Asian Perspective* 15, no. 1 (1991): 123–56. http://www.jstor.org/stable/42705295.

Israel, Jonathan I. *Radical Enlightenment: Philosophy and the Making of Modernity 1650-1750*. Oxford University Press, 2002.

Jeffries, Stuart. *Grand Hotel Abyss: The Lives of the Frankfurt School*. Verso, 2016.

Johnson, J. Scott. "Reading Nietzsche and Foucault: A Hermeneutics of Suspicion?" *The American Political Science Review* 85, no. 2 (1991): 581–92.

Kadarkay, Arpad. *The Lukács Reader*. Blackwell, 1995.

Kane, R. "The Modal Ontological Argument." *Mind* 93, no. 371 (July 1984): 336–350. https://doi.org/10.1093/mind/XCIII.371.336.

Kant, Immanuel. *Critique of Judgment.* Translated by Werner S. Pluhar. Hackett, 2002.

———. *Critique of Practical Reason and Other Works on the Theory of Ethics.* Translated by Thomas Kingsmill Abbot. Longmans, Green and Co., 1909.

———. *Critique of Pure Reason.* Translated by Mieklejohn, JMD. Collier and Son, 1903.

———. *Grounding for the Metaphysics of Morals with On a Supposed Right to Lie because of Philanthropic Concerns.* Translated by James W. Ellington. Hackett, 1993.

———. *Lectures on Ethics.* Translated by Peter Heath. Cambridge University Press, 2001.

———. *Prolegomena to Any Future Metaphysics.* 2nd ed. Translated by James W. Ellington. Hackett, 2001.

Katsumori, Makoto. "Derridean Deconstruction and the Question of Nature." *Derrida Today* 3, no. 1 (2010): 56–74.

Kauffman, Walter, ed. *Basic Writings of Nietzsche.* Modern Library, 2000.

Kellner, Douglas. "Marcuse and the Quest for Radical Subjectivity." *Social Thought & Research* 22, no. 1/2 (1999): 1–24. http://www.jstor.org/stable/23250102.

Kengor, Paul. *The Devil and Karl Marx: Communism's Long March of Death, Deception, and Infiltration.* Tan Books, 2020.

Kerr, Fergus. "Derrida's Wake." *New Blackfriars* 55, no. 653 (1974): 449–60, 458.

King, Margaret Leah. "The Social Role of Intellectuals: Antonio Gramsci and the Italian Renaissance." *Soundings: An Interdisciplinary Journal* 61, no. 1 (1978): 23–46.

Kirkpatrick, Kate. *Becoming Beauvoir: A Life.* Bloomsbury, 2020.

Klages, Ludwig. *Of Cosmogonic Eros.* Translated by Mav Kuhn. Theion Publishing, 2018.

Kolozi, Peter. *Conservatives Against Capitalism: From the Industrial Revolution to Globalization.* Columbia University Press, 2017.

Lavazza, Andrea, and Howard Robinson. *Contemporary Dualism: A Defense.* Routledge Studies in Contemporary Philosophy. Routledge, 2013.

Leinsle, Ulrich G. *Introduction to Scholastic Theology.* Translated by M. J. Miller. Catholic University of America Press, 2010.

Leithart, Peter. "Hegel's Trinity." *Theopolis,* November 28, 2007. https://theopolisinstitute.com/leithart_post/hegels-trinity/.

Lesaffer, Randall, and Janne E. Nijman. *The Cambridge Companion to Hugo Grotius.* Cambridge University, 2021.

Levering, Matthew. *The Theology of Augustine: An Introductory Guide to His Most Important Works.* Baker, 2013.

Levin, Yuval. *The Great Debate: Edmund Burke, Thomas Paine, and the Birth of Right and Left.* Basic Books, 2013.

Lévi-Strauss, Claude. *The Elementary Structures of Kinship.* Translated by James Harle Bell and John Richard Von Sturmer. Beacon, 1969.

Livingston, James C. *Modern Christian Thought: From the Enlightenment to Vatican II.* MacMillan, 1971.

Locke, John. *Essay Concerning Toleration and Other Writings on Law and Politics 1667-1683.* Edited by J. R. Milton and Philip Milton. Oxford University Press, 2010.

———. *Two Treatises of Government and A Letter Concerning Toleration.* Yale University Press, 2003.

Lowith, Karl. *From Hegel to Nietzsche: The Revolution in Nineteenth-Century Thought.* Translated by David E. Green. Anchor, 1967.

Lowy, Michael. *Georg Lukács: From Romanticism to Bolshevism.* Verso, 2023.

Lukács, Georg. *The Lukács Reader.* Edited by Arpad Kadarkay. Blackwell, 1995.

———. *Record of a Life: An Autobiographical Sketch.* Translated by Rodney Livingstone. Verso, 1983.

Lyngdoh, S. "Derrida and the Flesh of Metaphorical Language." *Open Journal of Philosophy* 11, no. 4 (2021): 466-481. doi: 10.4236/ojpp.2021.114031.

MacCulloch, Diarmaid. *The Reformation: A History.* Penguin, 2005.

Maclear, J. F. "Restoration Puritanism and the Idea of Liberty: The Case of Edward Bagshaw." *The Journal of Religious History* 16, no. 1 (1990): 1-17.

Macy, David. *The Lives of Michel Foucault*. Doubleday, 1995.

Malcolm, Joyce Lee, ed. *The Struggle for Sovereignty: Seventeenth-Century English Political Tracts*. 2 vols. Liberty Fund, 1999.

Manuel, Frank E., and Fritzie P. Manuel. *Utopian Thought in the Western World*. Belknap Press, 1979.

Mar, Joanpere, "The Impact of Referencing Academics Who Have Defended and Exercised Pederasty," *Sexes* 5, no. 3 (2024): 275-284.

Marcuse, Herbert. *Eros and Civilization: A Philosophical Investigation of Freud*. Boston: Beacon, 1955.

———. *The Essential Marcuse: Selected Writings of Philosopher and Social Critic Herbert Marcuse*. Edited by Andrew Feenberg and William Leiss. Boston, Beacon 2007.

———. "Herbert Marcuse in 1978: An Interview." Interview by Myriam Miedzian Malinovich. *Social Research* 48, no. 2 (1981): 362–94. http://www.jstor.org/stable/40970824.

———. *Marxism, Revolution, and Utopia: Collected Papers of Herbert Marcuse, Volume 6*. Edited by Douglas Kellner and Clayton Pierce. London: Routledge, 2014.

———. *One-Dimensional Man: Studies in the Ideology of Advanced Industrial Society*. With an introduction by Douglas Kellner. Beacon, 2012.

Marenbon, John, ed. *Medieval Philosophy*. Vol. 3 of *Routledge History of Philosophy*. Routledge, 1998.

Martensen, Hans. *Personal Ethics*. Vol. 2 of *Christian Ethics*. T&T Clark, 1884.

Marx, Karl. *Capital: A Critique of Political Economy*. Edited by Frederick Engels and translated by Samuel Moore and Edward Aveling. Random House, 1906.

———. *Critique of Hegel's Philosophy of Right*. Translated by Annette Jolin and Joseph O'Malley. Cambridge University Press, 1970.

———. *Economic and Philosophic Manuscripts of 1844*. Translated by Martin Milligan. Dover, 2007.

Marx, Karl, and Friedrich Engels. *Communist Manifesto*. Translated by Samuel Moore. Penguin, 2002.

———. *Selected Works in Three Volumes*. Progress Publishers, 1969.

McLellan, David. *Karl Marx: A Biography*. 4th ed. Palgrave Macmillan, 2006.

Meilaender, Gilbert C. *The Theory and Practice of Virtue*. Notre Dame Press, 1984.

Miles, Margaret R. *Plotinus on Body and Beauty: Science, Philosophy, and Religion in Third-Century Rome*. Wiley-Blackwell, 1999.

Mill, J. S. *On Liberty and Other Writings*. Edited by Stefan Collini. Cambridge Texts in the History of Political Thought. Cambridge University Press, 1989.

———. *Utilitarianism and the 1868 Speech on Capital Punishment*. Edited by George Sher. Hackett, 2002.

Mises, Ludwig von. "What the Nazis Borrowed from Marx." Mises Institute. https://mises.org/mises-daily/what-nazis-borrowed-marx.

Moreland, J. P. *Body & Soul: Human Nature and the Crisis in Ethics*. IVP, 2000.

Müller, Max. *Three Lectures on the Science of Language, Delivered at the Royal Institution of Great Britain in 1861*. Longman, Green, Longman and Roberts, 1861.

Müller-Doohm, Stefan. *Adorno: A Biography*. Translated by Rodney Livingstone. Polity, 2009.

Nahm, Milton C. *Selections from Early Greek Philosophy*. 4th ed. Appleton-Century-Crofts, 1964.

Neto, Jose R. Maia. *Academic Skepticism in Seventeenth-Century French Philosophy: The Charronian Legacy 1601-1662*. Springer, 2014.

Nietzsche, Friedrich. *Beyond Good and Evil*. Translated by Helen Zimmern. Dover, 1997.

———. *Genealogy of Morals*. Translated by Walter Kaufmann. Random House, 1967.

———. *The Portable Nietzsche*. Edited and translated by Walter Kaufmann. Penguin, 1976.

———. *The Will to Power*. Edited by Walter Arnold Kaufmann and R. J. Hollingdale. Random House, 1967.

Oberman, Heiko A. *A Harvest of Medieval Theology*. Baker, 1963.

Ockham, William of. *Philosophical Writings*. Translated by Philotheus Boehner. Hackett, 1990.

Oliver, Kelly. "Sexual Difference, Animal Difference: Derrida and Difference 'Worthy of Its Name.'" *Hypatia* 24, no. 2 (2009): 54–76.

Olson, Robert G. *An Introduction to Existentialism*. Dover, 1962.

Packer, Barbara L. *The Transcendentalists*. University of Georgia Press, 2007.

Paine, Thomas. *Rights of Man*. Dover, 2012. Nook edition.

Palmer, Donald D. *Structuralism and Post-structuralism for Beginners*. Writers and Readers, 1997.

Patnaik, Nishad. "The Emergence of Class Consciousness: Lukács on 'Objective Possibility.'" *Social Scientist* 45, no. 11/12 (2017): 41–62. http://www.jstor.org/stable/26405281.

Paul, Ari. "Cultural Marxism: The Mainstreaming of a Nazi Trope." FAIR. https://fair.org/home/cultural-marxism-the-mainstreaming-of-a-nazi-trope/.

Peeters, Benoit. *Derrida: A Biography*. Polity, 2016.

Pinkard, Terry. *Hegel: A Biography*. Cambridge University Press, 2001.

Plato. *Selected Dialogues*. Translated by Benjamin Jowett. Franklin Library, 1983.

Plotinus. *The Six Enneads*. Translated by Stephen MacKenna and B. S. Page. William Benton, 1952.

Pluckrose, Helen, and James Lindsay. *Cynical Theories: How Activist Scholarship Made Everything about Race, Gender, and Identity—and Why This Harms Everybody*. Pitchstone, 2020.

Poovey, Mary. "Feminism and Deconstruction." *Feminist Studies* 14, no. 1 (1988): 51–65.

Powell, Jim. *Postmodernism for Beginners*. Writers and Readers, 1998.

Raines, John, ed. *Marx on Religion*. Temple University Press, 2002.

Reed, Herbert. *The Philosophy of Modern Art*. Meridian, 1955.

Rex, Richard. *Henry VIII and the English Reformation*. British History in Perspective. Red Globe, 2006.

Rhoads, Steven E. *Taking Sex Differences Seriously*. Encounter Books, 2004.

Robinson, Dave, and Judy Groves. *Introducing Plato*. Icon Books, 2000.

Rookmaaker, H. R. *Modern Art and the Death of a Culture*. Crossway, 1994.

Rosen, Z. *Bruno Bauer and Karl Marx: The Influence of Bruno Bauer on Karl Marx's Thought*. Martinus Nijhoff, 1977.

Rozemond, Marleen. *Descartes's Dualism*. Harvard University Press, 1998.

Rubin, D. C., ed. *Remembering Our Past: Studies in Autobiographical Memory*. Cambridge University Press, 1996.

Rush, Fred, ed. *The Cambridge Companion to Critical Theory*. Cambridge, 2004.

Samoyault, Tiphaine. *Barthes: A Biography*. Polity, 2017.

Sartre, Jean-Paul. *Existentialism Is a Humanism*. Translated by Carol Macomber. Yale University Press, 2007.

Saussure, Ferdinand de. *Course in General Linguistics*. Translated by Wade Baskin. Columbia, 1959.

Savage, Luke. "Jordan Peterson's 'Postmodern Neomarxism' is Pure Hokum." *The Jacobin*, March 16, 2022. https://jacobin.com/2022/03/jordan-peterson-postmodernism-marxism-philosophy-zizek.

Schaefer, David Lewis. *The Political Philosophy of Montaigne*. Cornell University Press, 1990.

Scruton, Roger. *Beauty: A Very Short Introduction*. Oxford University Press, 2011.

———. *Culture Counts: Faith and Feeling in a World Besieged*. Encounter Books, 2021.

———. *Fools, Frauds, and Firebrands: Thinkers of the New Left.* Bloomsbury, 2015.

———. *Kant: A Very Short Introduction.* Oxford University Press, 2001.

———. *Modern Culture.* Bloomsbury, 2019.

———. *Modern Philosophy: An Introduction and Survey.* Penguin, 1994.

———. *A Short History of Modern Philosophy: From Descartes to Wittgenstein.* 2nd ed. Routledge, 1995.

Searle, John R. *Speech Acts: An Essay in the Philosophy of Language.* Cambridge University Press, 1969.

Shaw, Brian J. "Capitalism and the Novel: Georg Lukács on Modern Realism." *History of Political Thought* 9, no. 3 (1988): 553–73. http://www.jstor.org/stable/26213800.

Singer, Peter. *Marx: A Very Short Introduction.* Oxford University Press, 2018.

Skirry, Justin. "Rene Descartes (1596-1650)." In *Internet Encyclopedia of Philosophy*, ISSN 2161-0002. Accessed August 3, 2024. https://iep.utm.edu/rene-descartes/.

Stansell, Christine. *The Feminist Promise: 1792 to the Present.* Random House, 2011.

Stanton, Elizabeth Cady. *Elizabeth Cady Stanton, As Revealed in Her Letters, Diary and Reminiscences.* Edited by Theodore Stanton and Harriet Stanton Blatch Harper, 1922.

Sullivan, Richard J. *An Introduction to Kant's Ethics.* Cambridge University Press, 1994.

Swinburne, Richard. *Mind, Brain, and Free Will.* Oxford University Press, 2013.

Tanner, Michael. *Nietzsche: A Very Short Introduction.* Oxford University Press, 2000.

Taylor, Charles. *A Secular Age.* Harvard University Press, 2007.

Taylor, Diana, ed. *Michel Foucault: Key Concepts.* Routledge, 2010.

Tetrault, Lisa. *The Myth of Seneca Falls: Memory and the Women's Suffrage Movement, 1848-1898.* University of North Carolina Press, 2014.

Tihanov, Galin. "Ethics and Revolution: Lukács's Responses to Dostoevsky." *The Modern Language Review* 94, no. 3 (1999): 609–25. https://doi.org/10.2307/3736988.

Trubetzkoy, N. S. *Principles of Phonology.* Translated by Christiane A. M. Baltaxe. University of California Press, 1969.

Trueman, Carl R. *The Rise and Triumph of the Modern Self: Cultural Amnesia, Expressive Individualism, and the Road to Sexual Revolution.* Crossway, 2020.

Turkel, Gerald. "Michel Foucault: Law, Power, and Knowledge." *Journal of Law and Society* 17, no. 2 (1990): 170–93.

Unger, Harlow Giles. *Thomas Paine and the Clarion Call for American Independence.* Da Capo, 2019.

Van Nieuwenhove, Rik. *An Introduction to Medieval Theology.* Cambridge University Press, 2012.

Watkin, Christopher. *Jacques Derrida.* Great Thinkers. P&R, 2017.

———. *Michel Foucault.* Great Thinkers. P&R, 2018.

Westerman, Richard. "The Reification of Consciousness: Husserl's Phenomenology in Lukács's Identical Subject-Object." *New German Critique,* no. 111 (2010): 97–130. http://www.jstor.org/stable/40926573.

Westphal, Merold. *History and Truth in Hegel's Phenomenology.* Highlands Press, 1979.

Whitehead, Alfred North. *Process and Reality.* Corr. ed. Edited by Donald W. Sherburne. Free Press, 1979.

Woien, Sandra, ed. *Jordan Peterson: Critical Responses.* Open Universe, 2022.

Wolfson, Harry Austryn. *The Philosophy of the Church Fathers: Faith, Trinity, Incarnation.* Harvard University Press, 1956.

Wollstonecraft, Mary. *Vindication of the Rights of Women with Structures on Political and Moral Subjects.* Scribner and Welford, 1890.

Woolcock, Joseph A. "Politics, Ideology and Hegemony in Gramsci's Theory." *Social and Economic Studies* 34, no. 3 (1985): 199–210.

Woolhouse, Roger. *Locke: A Biography.* Cambridge University Press, 2008.

www.ingramcontent.com/pod-product-compliance
Lightning Source LLC
Chambersburg PA
CBHW020814270326
41928CB00006B/366